FROMMER'S

COMPREHENSIVE TRAVEL GUIDE

TOKYO '94-'95

by Beth Reiber
with Janie Spencer

PRENTICE HALL TRAVEL

NEW YORK • LONDON • TORONTO • SYDNEY • TOKYO • SINGAPORE

Diane Vandegrift

FROMMER BOOKS

Published by Prentice Hall General Reference
15 Columbus Circle
New York, NY 10023

ISBN 0-671-86800-4
ISSN 1045-9340

Design by Robert Bull Design
Maps by Geografix Inc.

FROMMER'S EDITORIAL STAFF
Editorial Director: Marilyn Wood
Editorial Manager/Senior Editor: Alice Fellows
Senior Editors: Lisa Renaud, Sara Hinsey Raveret
Editors: Charlotte Allstrom, Thomas F. Hirsch, Peter Katucki, Theodore Stavrou
Assistant Editors: Margaret Bowen, Christopher Hollander, Alice Thompson, Ian Wilker
Editorial Assistants: Gretchen Henderson, Douglas Stallings
Managing Editor: Leanne Coupe

Manufactured in the United States of America

CONTENTS

LIST OF MAPS

INVITATION TO THE READER

In this guide to Tokyo, we have selected what we consider to be the best of the many wonderful establishments that we came across while conducting our research. You, too, in the course of your visit to Tokyo, may come across a hotel, restaurant, shop, or attraction that you feel should be included here; or you may find that a place we have selected has since changed for the worse. In either case, let us know of your discovery. Address your comments to:

Beth Reiber & Janie Spencer
Frommer's Tokyo '94–'95
c/o Prentice Hall Travel
15 Columbus Circle
New York, NY 10023

DISCLAIMERS

We have made every effort to ensure the accuracy of the prices as well as the other information contained in this guide. Yet we advise you to keep in mind not only that prices fluctuate over time but that some of the other information herein may also change as a result of the various volatile factors affecting the travel industry.

A major problem with regard to prices is the frequent fluctuation in the **exchange rate** between the Japanese yen and the U.S. dollar. The wise traveler will add 15% to 20% to the prices quoted throughout, particularly during the second year (1995) of the lifetime of this edition.

The authors and the publisher cannot be held responsible for the experiences of the reader while traveling.

SAFETY ADVISORY

Whenever you're traveling in an unfamiliar city or country, stay alert. Be aware of your immediate surroundings. Wear a money belt and keep a close eye on your possessions. Be especially careful with cameras, purses, and wallets—all favorite targets of thieves and pickpockets. Although Japan is comparatively safe, every society has its criminals. It's therefore your responsibility to exercise caution at all times.

JAPANESE SYMBOLS & NAMES

Many hotels, restaurants, and other establishments in Japan do not have signs showing their names in English letters. Appendix B, "A List of Japanese Symbols," lists the Japanese symbols for such places appearing in this guide. Each establishment name in Japanese symbols is numbered, and the same number appears in an oval in the text following the boldfaced establishment name. Example: **Suehiro** (7) means that the restaurant's name is number 7 in the Japanese list of symbols.

In this guide, Japanese personal names are given in the Japanese style—family name first, followed by the given name.

CHAPTER 1

INTRODUCING TOKYO

- **WHAT'S SPECIAL ABOUT TOKYO**
1. **GEOGRAPHY, HISTORY & CULTURE**
- **DATELINE**
2. **FOOD & DRINK**
3. **RECOMMENDED BOOKS & FILMS**

Describing Tokyo to someone who has never been here is a formidable task. After all, how do you describe a city that—as one foreign visitor put it—seems as if it's part of another planet?

To be sure, Tokyo is very different from Western capitals, but what really sets it apart is its people—about 12 million of them, crowded into Tokyo's 800 square miles. In fact, almost one-fourth of Japan's total population lives within commuting distance of Tokyo. This crush of humanity packs the subways, crowds the sidewalks, and fills the department stores beyond belief. In some parts of the city the streets are as crowded at 3am as they are at 3 in the afternoon. Tokyo makes even New York seem like a deserted city.

With Tokyo so densely packed, it comes as no shock to learn that land here is more valuable than gold and that buildings are built practically on top of each other, shaped like pieces in a jigsaw puzzle to fit the existing plots of land. More than perhaps any other city in the world, Japan's capital is a concrete jungle, with few parks or trees to break the monotony, and it stretches on and on as far as the eye can see. Fires, earthquakes, wars, the zeal for modernization, and the price of land have all taken their toll on the city, eradicating almost all evidence of previous centuries. It's as though Tokyo were born only this morning, with all the messy aftermath of a city conceived without plan and interested only in the future.

Thus it is that first-time visitors to Tokyo are almost invariably disappointed. They come expecting an exotic Oriental city, but instead they find a megalopolis Westernized to the point of drabness. Used to the grand edifices and monuments of Western cities, they look in vain for Tokyo's own monuments to its past—ancient temples perhaps, exquisite gardens, imperial palaces, or whatever else they've imagined. Instead they find what may be, quite arguably, one of the ugliest cities in the world.

And yet Tokyo is one of my favorite cities, but it's an appreciation that came only with time. When I first moved here, I was tormented with the unsettling feeling that I was somehow missing out on the "real" Tokyo. Even though I was living and working here, Tokyo seemed beyond my grasp, elusive, vague, and undefined. I felt that the meaning of the city was out there somewhere, if only I knew where to look.

With time I finally learned that I needn't look farther than my own front window. Tokyo has no center, but rather is made up of a series of small towns and neighborhoods, merged together, each with its own history, flavor, and atmosphere. There are narrow residential streets, mom-and-pop shops, fruit stands, and stores. There's the neighborhood tofu factory, the lunchbox stand, grocery shop, and

✓ WHAT'S SPECIAL ABOUT TOKYO

Museums
- ☐ Tokyo National Museum, the largest repository of Japanese art in the world.
- ☐ Dozens of art museums and countless galleries, with collections ranging from contemporary art to traditional woodblock prints.
- ☐ Specialized museums, centering on furniture, clocks from the Edo Period, traditional Japanese crafts, drums, Japanese paper, clothing, swords, sumo, and more.

Temples and Shrines
- ☐ Sensoji Temple, Tokyo's oldest and most important Buddhist temple, and one of the city's top attractions.
- ☐ Meiji Jingu Shrine, Tokyo's most venerable Shinto shrine and one of Japan's best known.

Parks and Gardens
- ☐ Ueno Park, Tokyo's first public park and home of Ueno Zoo and a number of fine museums, including the Tokyo National Museum.
- ☐ East Garden (Higashi Gyoen), a formal Japanese garden located beside the Imperial Palace.
- ☐ Hama Rikyu Garden, Tokyo's finest landscape garden.
- ☐ Shinjuku Gyoen, formerly the estate of a feudal lord, with various styles of gardens ranging from English to Japanese.

Shopping
- ☐ Dozens of first-rate department stores, so large they're like self-contained cities.
- ☐ Boutiques of Japan's most famous fashion designers.
- ☐ Shops specializing in traditional crafts, including crafts from other regions of Japan.
- ☐ Wholesale and retail shops specializing in a certain product clustered in certain neighborhoods, offering concentrated shopping for such goods as plastic food and kitchenware, dolls, or electronics.

After Dark
- ☐ Clubs open until dawn.
- ☐ A wide range of music clubs.
- ☐ Summer beer gardens.
- ☐ A variety of nightlife "neighborhoods," each with its own distinctive atmosphere and clientele.

Great Neighborhoods
- ☐ Asakusa, Tokyo's old downtown, with traditional shops selling everything from wooden combs to handmade tatami mats.
- ☐ Harajuku, a mecca for Tokyo's young generation, many of whom perform to large crowds on Sunday near Yoyogi Park.
- ☐ The Ginza, Japan's swankiest shopping district.
- ☐ Shinjuku, home of Tokyo's skyscrapers and one of the most fascinating nightlife districts in the world.

Offbeat Attractions
- ☐ Sumo, with tournaments held three times a year.
- ☐ Tsukiji Fish Market, Japan's largest.
- ☐ The Tokyo Stock Exchange, with free tours in English.
- ☐ Tokyo Disneyland.
- ☐ The Yamanote commuter line during rush hour.

the tiny police station, where the police know the residents by name and patrol the area by bicycle. There are carefully pruned bonsai trees gracing sidewalks, women in kimonos bowing and shuffling down streets, old wooden houses, neatness, and order. Walk in the old downtown neighborhoods of Asakusa or Ueno and you're worlds apart from the trendy quarters of Harajuku. It's the neighborhoods that make Tokyo lovable and livable.

What's more, once visitors get to know Tokyo better, they learn that you can't judge Tokyo by what it looks like on the outside, for Tokyo is a city of interiors. Even those concrete monsters may house interiors that are fascinating in design and innovation. In the basement of that drab building you're standing next to could well be a restaurant with wooden beams, mud walls, and thatched ceiling, imported intact from a farmhouse in the Japanese Alps.

In addition, beneath Tokyo's concrete shell is a thriving cultural life left very much intact. In fact, if you're interested in Japan's performing arts as well as such critically diverse activities as the tea ceremony or sumo, Tokyo is your best bet for offering the most at any one time. Tokyo is also rich in museums and claims the largest repository of Japanese art in the world.

As the financial nerve center of Japan and the nation's capital, Tokyo is where it's happening in Asia. In a nation of overachievers, Tokyo has more than its fair share of intelligentsia, academics, politicians, businesspeople, artists, and writers, and it's the country's showcase for technology, fashion, art, music, and advertising. People rush around here with such purpose, with such determination, it's hard not to feel that you're in the midst of something important, that you're witnessing history in the making. Tokyo has already plunged headfirst into the 21st century. And with the unparalleled strength of the yen, it has emerged as one of the most expensive and richest cities in the world. Not only is the richest man in the world today Japanese, but more than half of the world's 10 largest banks are now headquartered in Tokyo.

✪ With a population of about 12 million, Tokyo is the largest city in the world—and one of the most exciting.

As for innovation, Tokyo has long been recognized as a leader. Indeed, Japan, once dismissed as merely an imitator with no imagination of its own, has emerged as a forerunner in things technological, from computers and cars to audiovisual equipment and kitchen gadgetry. Walking through the stores of Akihabara, Tokyo's electronic center, provokes an uneasiness few visitors can shake, for it's here that the latest goods are sold long before they reach Western markets.

1. GEOGRAPHY, HISTORY & CULTURE

GEOGRAPHY & PEOPLE

GEOGRAPHY Japan stretches in a sliver of an arc about 1,860 miles long from tip to tip but only 250 miles wide at its broadest point. Four main islands—Hokkaido, Honshu, Shikoku, and

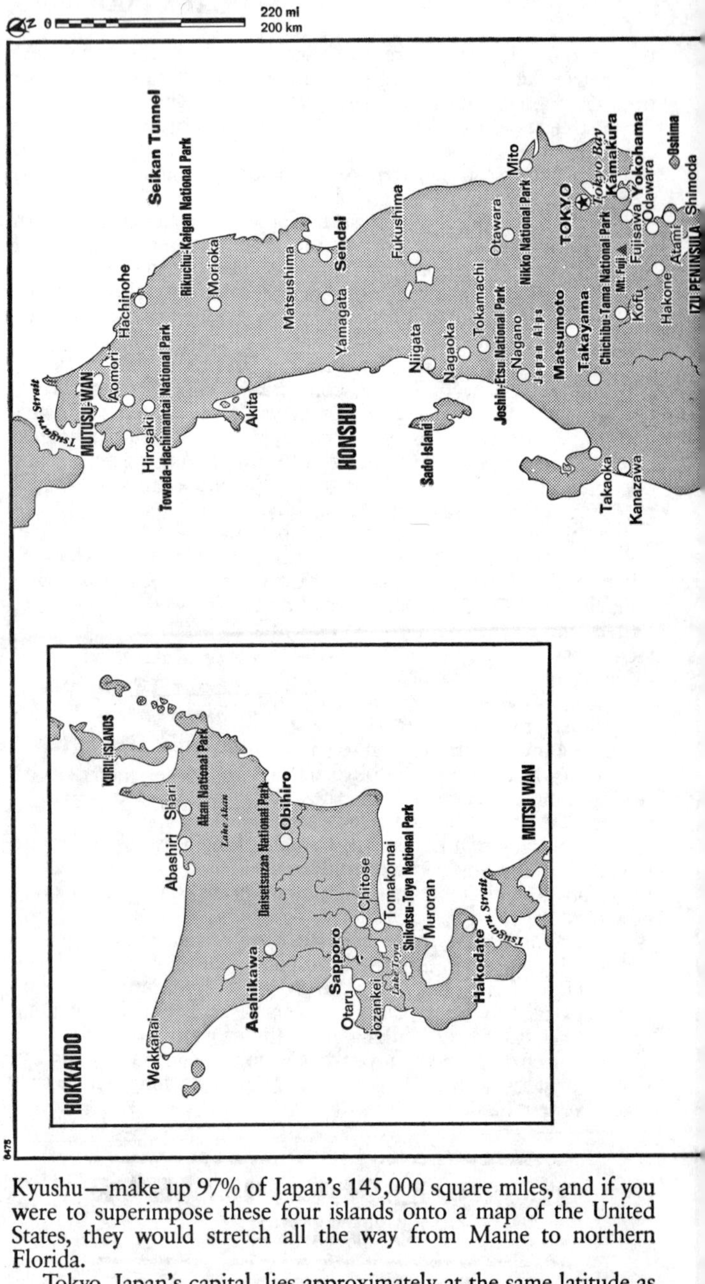

Kyushu—make up 97% of Japan's 145,000 square miles, and if you were to superimpose these four islands onto a map of the United States, they would stretch all the way from Maine to northern Florida.

Tokyo, Japan's capital, lies approximately at the same latitude as do Los Angeles, Athens, and Teheran and is located on the mideastern part of Honshu, Japan's largest and most historically important island. Sprawling westward onto the Kanto Plain (the largest plain in all Japan), the city faces Tokyo Bay, which in turn

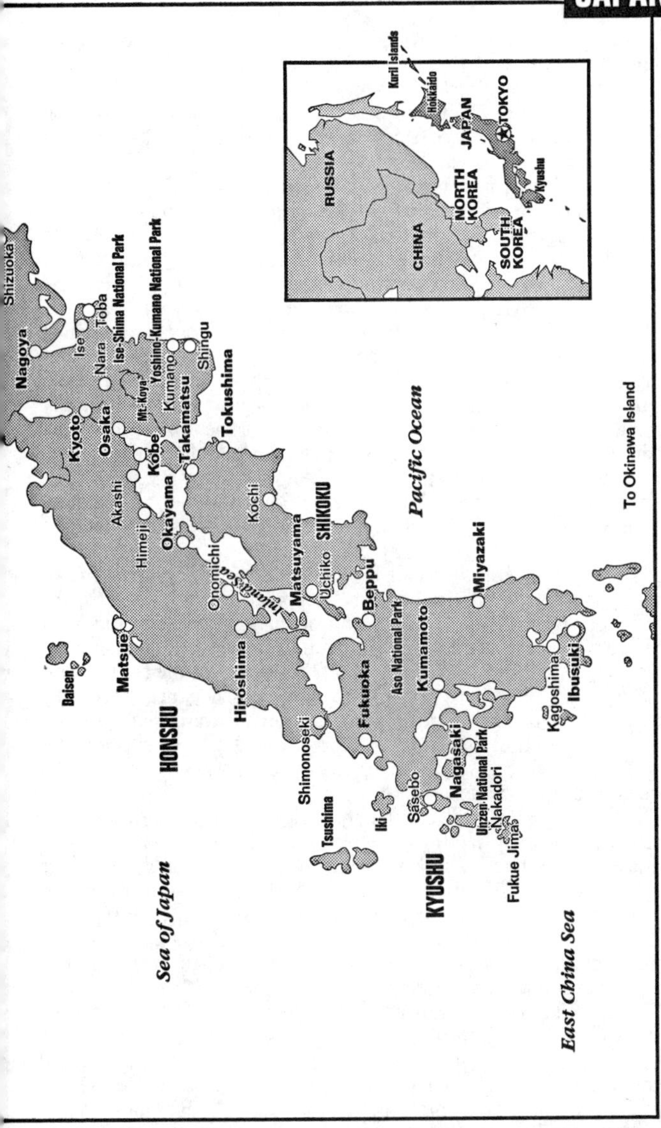

opens into the Pacific Ocean. For administrative purposes, Tokyo is broken down into 23 wards, known as *ku*. Its business districts of Marunouchi and Hibiya, for example, are in Chiyoda-ku, while Ginza is part of Chuo-ku. These two ku are the historic hearts of Tokyo, for it was here that the city had its humble beginnings. The central part of Tokyo is generally considered to be the section that is enclosed by a circular commuter railway line called the Yamanote Line. Within or near its oblong loop are most of Tokyo's major sights, hotels, and restaurants.

PEOPLE An island nation only slightly smaller in size than California, Japan nonetheless has about half the population of the United States. If you think that's crowded, consider this: Three-fourths of Japan is mountainous and therefore uninhabitable, which means that Japan's 124 million people are concentrated primarily on what amounts to 10% of the country's land mass, with the rest devoted to agriculture.

And yet, despite its limited space for harmonious living, Japan is a country with remarkably little crime or physical aggression. Even with its population of 12 million, Tokyo is one of the safest cities in the world. Hard-working, honest, helpful to strangers, and proud of performing a task well no matter how insignificant it might seem, the Japanese themselves are their country's greatest asset.

Because of its physical isolation and the fact that it was never successfully invaded before World War II, Japan is one of the most homogeneous nations in the world. Originally of Mongoloid stock, approximately 99% of Japan's population is Japanese, with hardly any influx of other genes into the country since the 8th century. The Japanese feel that they belong to one huge tribe different from any other people on earth. A Japanese will often preface a statement or opinion with the words "We Japanese," implying that all Japanese think alike and that all people in the world can be divided into two groups, Japanese and non-Japanese.

While in the West the recipe for a full and rewarding life seems to be in that elusive attainment of "happiness," in Japan it's the satisfactory performance of duty and obligation. While in the West individuality is encouraged and nurtured, in Japan individuality is equated with selfishness and a complete disregard for the feelings and consideration of others. From the moment they are born, the Japanese are instilled with a sense of duty toward the group—whether it be family, friends, co-workers, or Japanese society as a whole—so that consideration of the group always wins over the desires of the individual.

In a nation as crowded as Japan, such consideration of others is essential, especially in Tokyo where space is at a premium. The average Tokyo family lives in what Westerners would regard as intolerably tiny living quarters. It's not unusual for a family of four to share a two-room apartment, laying down futon mattresses each night when they go to sleep. If they are true Tokyoites rather than immigrants from the provinces, they may even share living quarters with parents and grandparents.

Because land and apartments in the center of Tokyo are so expensive, it's not unusual for commuters to spend two to three hours a day traveling to and from work on the city's trains and subways, which are often packed beyond belief. For the average white-collar company employee, known as a "salaryman," work hours are long, often until 7 or 8pm and sometimes followed by an evening out with his fellow workers, which he considers necessary for

---

IMPRESSIONS

In Japan the law of life is not as with us—that each one strives to expand his own individuality at the expense of his neighbor's.

—Lafcadio Hearn, 1891

promoting understanding and closeness. In fiscal 1992 the average Japanese worker spent 1,958 hours on the job.

Most likely the salaryman will work for the same company his entire life, taking only national holidays and one week's vacation a year. In return he is assured of lifetime employment (unless his company goes bankrupt, which is not uncommon), a pay raise according to his age, and promotion according to the number of years he has worked for the company. Although he may secretly complain of the long hours he has to work, he basically accepts it because everyone else is doing the same thing. What's more, his goal is the same as that of all his co-workers—to land one of the top positions in the company eventually. Only the most dedicated succeed.

For Japanese women, being a housewife and full-time mother is considered the most honored position. Many will go to college and then work for a few years, but the ultimate goal is to find a husband and have children, ideally before reaching the old age of 25. Those who fail to find mates can always find a match through arranged marriages, which still make up about 30% of the matches in Japan. Marriage ceremonies are elaborate and expensive—the average cost of a wedding and honeymoon is a whopping $40,000.

As ruler of the home front, the Japanese mother's job is to make sure her children study hard enough to pass the tough entrance exam to one of the country's best universities, from which graduates are recruited into the country's top companies. Thus, she will strive to get her children into the best kindergarten and thereafter into the best schools, and it's not unusual for students to attend evening or weekend cram schools in an attempt to get an edge over fellow students. Ironically, once in college, students are under little stress to study and the college years are basically viewed as four short years of freedom before a lifetime of servitude to the company or the home.

As for foreigners, even though treated with extreme kindness during a visit, they soon realize that they will never be totally accepted in Japanese society but rather will always be treated as outsiders. From 1986 to 1991 the number of foreigners working in Japan quadrupled, and many of them are in the nation's capital.

Meeting the Japanese If you've been invited to Japan by some organization or business, you will receive the royal treatment, and most likely be wined and dined so wonderfully and thoroughly that you'll never want to return home. If you've come to Tokyo on your own as an ordinary tourist, however, your experiences will depend largely on you. Although the Japanese will sometimes approach you to ask whether they might practice some English with you, for the most part you are left pretty much on your own unless you make the first move.

The best way to meet the Japanese is to participate in a super program launched by the Japan National Tourist Organization called the **Home Visit System,** which offers overseas visitors the chance to visit an English-speaking Japanese family in their home. It doesn't cost anything and the visit usually takes place for a few hours in the evening (dinner is *not* served). It's a good idea to bring a small gift, such as flowers, fruit, or something from your hometown. To apply, call Home Visit System in Tokyo (tel. 03/3502-1461) at least one day in advance of the intended visit.

Another good way to meet Japanese is to visit a so-called **English conversation lounge.** These are informal affairs, often attached to

IMPRESSIONS

The Japanese are in general intelligent and provident, free and unconstrained, obedient and courteous, curious and inquisitive, industrious and ingenious, frugal and sober, cleanly, good-natured and friendly, upright and just, trusty and honest, mistrustful, superstitious, proud, and haughty, unforgiving, brave, and invincible.

—CHARLES PETER THUNBERG, *TRAVELS IN EUROPE, AFRICA, AND ASIA*, 1795

English schools, to give Japanese the opportunity for unstructured conversations in English with anyone who drops in. Most are open in the evenings and offer the chance to play games or read magazines and drink coffee or beer. Usually foreigners are admitted free of charge; at some you must pay an entrance fee of ¥500 ($4.55) or so. The Japanese who come to these lounges often consider English their hobby, speak it perfectly, and will be delighted to talk to you. The *Tokyo Journal*, published monthly to describe what's going on in the capital city, lists conversation lounges.

And finally, another way to meet Japanese is to go where they play, namely Tokyo's countless bars and eateries. There you'll often encounter Japanese who will want to speak to you if they understand English, as well as slightly inebriated Japanese who will want to speak to you even if they don't. If you're open to it, such chance encounters may prove to be the highlight of your trip.

HISTORY & POLITICS

HISTORY

Archeological finds show that Japan was inhabited as early as 30,000 B.C., but it wasn't until the 6th century that Japan began spreading its cultural wings. Taking its cues from China, its great neighbor to the west, Japan adopted Buddhism, the character system of writing, art forms, and architecture, and molded them into a style of its own.

In A.D. 794 the Japanese imperial family established a new capital in Heiankyo (present-day Kyoto), where it remained for more than 1,000 years. The arts flourished, and extravagant temples and pavilions were erected. Noh drama, the tea ceremony, flower arranging, and landscape gardening developed. But even though Kyoto served as the cultural heart of the nation, it was often the nation's capital in name only. Preoccupied by their own luxurious lifestyle, the nobles and royal court of Kyoto were little match for rebellious military clans in the provinces.

The first important successful clan upris-

DATELINE

- **794** Kyoto becomes Japan's capital.
- **1192** Minamoto Yoritomo becomes shogun and establishes his shogunate government in Kamakura.
- **1333** The Kamakura Shogunate falls and the imperial system is restored.
- **1457** Edo Castle constructed in Tokyo (destroyed during World War II).
- **1603** Tokugawa Ieyasu becomes shogun and establishes his shogunate in Edo (present-day Tokyo), marking the beginning of a 264-

(continues)

ing took place at the end of the 12th century, when a young warrior named Minamoto Yoritomo won a bloody civil war that brought him supremacy over the land. Wishing to set up his rule far away from the imperial family in Kyoto, he made his capital in a remote and easily defendable fishing village called Kamakura, not far from today's Tokyo. He created a military government, a *shogunate,* ushering in a new era in Japan's history in which the power of the country passed from the aristocratic court into the hands of the warrior class. In becoming the nation's first *shogun,* or military dictator, Yoritomo laid the groundwork for military governments in Japan which lasted for another 700 years.

The Kamakura Period, from 1192 to 1333, is perhaps best known for the unrivaled ascendancy of the warrior caste, called *samurai.* Ruled by a rigid code of honor, the samurai were bound in loyalty to their feudal lord and would defend him to the death. If they failed in their duties, they could redeem their honor by committing ritualistic suicide, or *seppuku.* Spurning the soft life led by the noble court in Kyoto, the samurai embraced a harsher and simpler set of ideals and a spartan lifestyle, embodied in the tenets of Zen Buddhism's mental and physical disciplines.

The Kamakura Period was followed by 200 years of vicious civil wars and confusion as *daimyo* (feudal lords) staked out their fiefdoms throughout the land and strove for supremacy. Not unlike a baron in medieval Europe, a daimyo had absolute rule over the people who lived in his fiefdom and was aided in battles by his samurai retainers. In the second half of the 16th century, several brilliant military strategists rose to power, but none proved as shrewd as Tokugawa Ieyasu, a statesman so skillful in eliminating his enemies that his heirs would continue to rule Japan for the next 250 years. It was with him that Tokyo's history began.

For centuries present-day Tokyo was nothing more than a rather obscure village called Edo, which means simply "mouth of the estuary." Then, in 1603, after Tokugawa had seized power, he made the sleepy village the seat of his shogunate government, leaving the emperor intact but virtually powerless in Kyoto. He took over Edo Castle, originally built in 1457, and made it one of the most impressive castles in the land.

DATELINE

year rule by the Tokugawa clan.

- **1633** Japan closes its doors to foreign trade and subsequently forbids all foreigners from landing in Japan and all Japanese from leaving.
- **1787** The population of Tokyo reaches 1.3 million.
- **1853** Commodore Matthew C. Perry of the U.S. Navy succeeds in persuading the Japanese to sign a trade agreement with the U.S.
- **1867** Tokugawa regime is overthrown, bringing Japan's feudal era to a close.
- **1868** Emperor Meiji assumes power, moves his imperial capital from Kyoto to Tokyo, and begins the industrialization of Japan.
- **1923** Tokyo and Yokohama are devastated by a major earthquake in which almost 150,000 people lose their lives.
- **1937** Japan goes to war with China and conquers Nanking.
- **1940** Japan forms a military alliance with Germany and Italy.
- **1941** The Pacific War begins as Japan bombs Pearl Harbor.
- **1945** Hiroshima and Nagasaki suffer atomic bomb attacks; Japan agrees

(continues)

From then on Edo grew quickly, and by 1787 the population had reached 1.3 million, making Edo one of the largest cities in the world. However, it was a city few outsiders were ever permitted to see. Fearing the spread of Western influence and Christianity in Japan, the Tokugawa shogunate adopted a policy of complete isolation in 1633. The shogunate forbade foreigners to enter Japan and forbade the Japanese to leave. Those who defied the strict decrees paid with their lives. The only exception to this policy of isolation was a colony of tightly controlled Chinese merchants in Nagasaki, and a handful of Dutch, confined to a small trading post on a tiny island.

Known as the Edo Period (1603–1867), it was a remarkable time in Japanese history, during which Japan's doors were closed to the outside world for more than 200 years. It was a time of political stability, but the price was curtailment of personal freedom dictated by the shogunate government. Japanese society was divided into four distinct classes: the court nobles, the samurai, the farmers, and the merchants. Although the nobles occupied the most exalted social position, it was the samurai who wielded the real power, for they were the only ones allowed to carry weapons.

At the bottom of the social ladder were the merchants. But as peace reigned they began accumulating wealth, and new forms of entertainment arose to occupy their time. Kabuki drama and woodblock prints became the rage, while stone and porcelain ware, silk brocade for elaborate and gorgeous kimonos, and lacquerware improved in quality. Japan's most famous pleasure district was an area in northeast Edo called Yoshiwara, the "floating world of pleasure," where rich merchants spent fortunes to cavort with beautiful courtesans.

To ensure that no daimyo in the distant provinces could grow strong enough to usurp the shogun's power, the Tokugawa government ordered that every daimyo should reside in Edo for a period of four months every other year. Furthermore, the daimyo were required to leave their families in Edo as permanent residents, to serve as virtual hostages. There were as many as 260 daimyo in Japan in the 17th century, and each maintained several mansions in Edo for family members and retainers. In fact, almost half of Edo's population in the 17th century were samurai, acting as retainers to the various daimyo. By expending so much time and money traveling back and forth and maintaining residences in both the provinces and Edo, a daimyo would find it difficult to wage war.

By the mid-19th century it was clear that the feudal system was outdated. With economic power in the hands of the merchants, money rather than rice became the primary means of exchange.

DATELINE

to unconditional surrender.

- **1946** The emperor renounces his claim to divinity; Japan adopts a new, democratic constitution; women gain the right to vote.
- **1952** The Allied occupation of Japan ends; Japan regains its independence.
- **1956** Japan is admitted to the United Nations.
- **1964** The XVIII Summer Olympic Games are held in Tokyo.
- **1989** Emperor Hirohito dies after a 63-year reign.
- **1990** Hirohito's son, Akihito, formally ascends the throne and proclaims the new "Era of Peace" (Heisei).
- **1993** Crown Prince Naruhito weds Masako Owada, a Harvard-educated, one-time career woman.

Many samurai families found themselves on the brink of poverty, and discontent with the shogunate grew widespread.

In 1854, Commodore Matthew C. Perry of the U.S. Navy succeeded in forcing the shogun to sign an agreement granting America trading rights, thus ending two centuries of isolation. Then, in 1867, the Tokugawas were overthrown and the emperor was restored as ruler. The feudal era drew to an end.

Rather than remain in Kyoto, Emperor Meiji decided to take Edo for his own, and moved his imperial capital to its new home in 1868. Renaming Edo Tokyo, or "Eastern Capital," (to distinguish it from the "western" capital of Kyoto), the emperor was quick to welcome ideas and technology from the West. The ensuing years, known as the Meiji Restoration, were nothing short of amazing as Japan progressed rapidly from a feudal agricultural society of samurai and peasants to an industrial nation. The samurai were stripped of their power and were no longer permitted to carry swords; a prime minister and cabinet were appointed; a constitution was drafted; and a parliament, called the Diet, was elected. The railway, postal system, and even specialists and advisers were imported from the West. Between 1881 and 1898 as many as 6,177 British, 2,764 Americans, 913 Germans, and 619 French were retained by the Japanese government to help transform Japan into a modern society.

✪ Tokyo, or "Eastern Capital," became the seat of Japan's imperial government in 1868, replacing Kyoto, the capital since 794.

As the nation's capital, Tokyo was hardest hit in this craze for modernization. Ideas for fashion, architecture, food, and department stores were imported from the West—West was best, and things Japanese were forgotten or pushed aside. It didn't help that Tokyo was almost totally destroyed twice in the first half of this century. In 1923 a huge earthquake struck the city, followed by *tsunami* (tidal waves). Almost 150,000 people died and half of Tokyo was in ruins. Disaster struck again during World War II, when incendiary bombs laid most of the city to waste.

Japan's expansionist policies in Asia during the 1930s and early 1940s spread the flag of the rising sun over Hong Kong, China, Singapore, Burma, Malaysia, the Philippines, the Dutch East Indies, and Guam. However, World War II halted Japan's advance. Shortly after the United States dropped the world's first atomic bombs—over Hiroshima on August 6, 1945, and over Nagasaki three days later—surrender came, on August 14, 1945.

The end of the war brought American occupation forces to Japan, where they remained until 1952. It was the first time in Japan's history that the island nation had suffered defeat and occupation by a foreign power. The experience had a profound effect on the Japanese people. Emerging from their defeat, they began the long effort to rebuild their cities and economy. In 1946, under the guidance of the Allied military authority, headed by U.S. Gen. Douglas MacArthur, they adopted a new, democratic constitution that renounced war and divested the emperor of his claim to divinity. A parliamentary system of government was set up, and in 1947 the first general elections were held. The following year, the militarists and generals who had carried out the Pacific War were tried and many of them were convicted. To the younger generation of Japanese, the occupation was less a painful burden that had to be suffered than an opportunity to remake their country, with American encouragement, into a modern, peace-loving, and democratic state.

A special relationship developed between the Japanese and their American occupiers. In the early 1950s, as the cold war between the United States and the Communist world erupted in hostilities in Korea, that relationship grew into a firm alliance, strengthened by a security treaty between Tokyo and Washington. In 1952 the occupation ended, and Japan subsequently joined the United Nations as an independent country.

Avoiding involvement in foreign conflicts, the Japanese concentrated on economic recovery. Through a series of policies that favored domestic industries and shielded Japan against foreign competition, they achieved rapid economic growth. By the mid-1960s, they had transformed their nation into a major industrial power. In 1964, in recognition of Japan's increasing importance, the Summer Olympic Games were held in Tokyo.

As their economy continued to expand, the Japanese sought new markets abroad; by the early 1970s, they had attained a trade surplus, which they have consistently enjoyed ever since, as Japanese products—cars, electronic goods, computers—attract more and more foreign buyers. Tokyo's trade policies, however, have inevitably caused friction between Japan and the United States, its chief trading partner. In the 1980s especially, as Japanese automobile sales in the United States soared, while foreign sales in Japan continued to be restricted, disagreements between Tokyo and Washington over the issue of fair trade at times strained the alliance.

In the 1990s the demand by the United States—as well as the European Union, another major trading partner—that Tokyo liberalize its trade policies has been coupled with an appeal that the Japanese take a more active role in world affairs, consonant with their economic power.

POLITICS

Japan has both an emperor, who acts as head of state, and a prime minister, who is head of the government. The constitution, which was adopted in 1946, stipulates that the supreme power of the country resides with the people, who vote for members of the National Diet, the legislative body in Japan. There are six major political parties, dominated until 1993 by the right-of-center Liberal Democratic Party (LDP). The LDP held majority power for nearly 40 years, with prime ministers generally serving as its head before assuming the nation's top political position. A series of political scandals eroded public support and caused the resignation of several top LDP leaders and prime ministers, and eventually brought the government to its knees. Hoping to salvage their careers, LDP "rebels" formed the New Life Party, but the public and press remained skeptical. Morihito Hosokawa, head of the opposition Japan New Party, became prime minister, breaking the LDP's nearly four-decade-long hold on the country.

ART & CULTURAL LIFE

ART Similar to prehistoric cultures around the world, Japan's first artwork appeared in the form of clay and stone figures during the

Stone Age. After the spread of Buddhism to Japan in the 6th century, religious art found expression through architecture, sculptures, and paintings. Other art forms, including lacquerware, ceramics, and bronzes, were first brought to Japan from China. It wasn't until the 1600s that Japan began to develop its own styles and techniques for the arts, through *ikebana* (flower arrangement), the tea ceremony, Japanese gardens, bonsai, and such sport disciplines as judo and karate. During the Edo Period, traditional arts such as pottery and lacquerware received the patronage of feudal lords, which encouraged the spread of various techniques throughout the land. It was also during the Edo Period that *ukiyo-e* (woodblock prints) gained popularity among the masses both at home and abroad for their portraits of actors, beauties, and landscapes.

Today, the arts thrive in Japan, as various regions of the country produce distinct styles in pottery, lacquerware, and folkcrafts. In fact, the Japanese hold aesthetic beauty in such high esteem that the most skilled artists and craftsmen are recognized as "Living National Treasures." These Living National Treasures include carpenters, sculptors, swordsmiths, potters, weavers, and creators of Japanese paper and lacquerware, to name only a few.

✪ The Tokyo National Museum contains the greatest collection of Japanese art in the world.

The greatest repository of Japanese art in the world is in Tokyo—the Tokyo National Museum, which is Japan's largest museum, with a collection of more than 85,000 works. Other museums specialize in woodblock prints, folk art, kites, Japanese paper, and other traditional crafts. (For more information, see Chapter 6, "What to See and Do in Tokyo.")

CULTURAL LIFE Japan is known throughout the world for its appreciation of the aesthetic, whether it's in the presentation of food, a flower arrangement, or even the sleek simplicity of its furniture. Rich in cultural history, Japan has produced widely divergent forms of expression—the tea ceremony, sumo, Kabuki, Noh, and flower arranging, to name only a few.

Luckily for visitors to Tokyo, Japan's capital is the best place to see or participate in traditional cultural activities, since it offers the most at any one time. Several of the larger first-class hotels in Tokyo, for example, offer a few hours' instruction in English in the tea ceremony, and sumo matches and Kabuki performances are held several times during the year. For more information, see Chapter 6, "What to See and Do in Tokyo."

SOCIAL LIFE

JAPANESE ETIQUETTE & MANNERS When European merchants and missionaries began arriving in Japan almost 400 years ago, the Japanese took one look at them and immediately labeled them "barbarians." After all, these hairy and boisterous outsiders rarely bathed and didn't know the first thing about proper etiquette and behavior.

The Japanese, on the other hand, had a strict social hierarchy which dictated exactly how a person should speak, sit, bow, eat, walk, dress, and even live. Failure to comply with the rules could bring swift punishment and sometimes even death. More than one Japanese literally lost his head for committing a social blunder.

Of course, things have changed somewhat since then and the Japanese have even adopted some of the Western barbarians' customs. However, what hasn't changed is that the Japanese still attach much importance to proper behavior and etiquette, which developed to allow relationships to be as frictionless as possible—important in a country as crowded as Japan. The Japanese don't like confrontations, and although I'm told they do occur, I've never seen a fight in Japan.

Another aspect of Japanese behavior that sometimes causes difficulty for foreigners is that the Japanese find it very hard to say no. They're much more apt to say that your request is very difficult to fulfill or they'll simply beat around the bush without giving a definite answer. At this point you're expected to let the subject drop. Showing impatience, anger, or aggressiveness rarely gets you anywhere in Japan. Apologizing sometimes does. And if someone does give in to your request, you can't say thank you enough.

Bowing The main form of greeting in Japan is the bow rather than the handshake. Although at first glance it might seem simple enough, the bow and its implications are actually quite complicated—the depth of the bow, the number of seconds, and the total number of bows depend on who you are and to whom you're bowing. The Japanese also bow upon departing, and to express deep gratitude. The proper form for a bow is to bend from the waist with a straight back and to keep your arms at your sides, but as a foreigner you'll probably feel foolish and look pretty stupid if you try to imitate what the Japanese have spent years learning. A simple nod of the head is enough. Knowing that foreigners shake hands, a Japanese may extend his hand, though he probably won't be able to stop himself from giving a little bow as well. The Japanese will bow even when speaking to an invisible someone on the telephone.

Visiting Cards You're a nonentity in Japan if you don't have a business or visiting card, called a *meishi* in Japanese. Everyone from housewives to plumbers to secretaries to bank presidents carries meishi with them to give out upon introduction. If you're trying to conduct business in Japan, you'll be regarded suspiciously if you don't have business cards. As a tourist you don't have to have business cards, but it certainly doesn't hurt and the Japanese will be greatly impressed by your preparedness. The card should have your address and occupation on it. As a nice souvenir you might consider having your meishi made in Japan with the Japanese syllabic script (*katakana*) written on the reverse side.

There's a proper way, of course, to present a meishi that depends on the status of the two people involved. Generally, you should present your meishi with both hands, so that it's right side up and immediately readable to the person you're giving it to, bowing slightly as you do so. Meishi are exchanged simultaneously or presented first by the lower person on the totem pole.

Shoes Nothing is so distasteful to the Japanese as the bottoms of shoes, and therefore shoes are taken off before entering a home, a Japanese-style inn, a temple, and even some museums and restaurants. Usually there will be some plastic slippers at the entranceway for you to slip on, but whenever you encounter tatami you should take off even these slippers—only bare feet or socks are allowed to tread upon tatami.

Restrooms present a whole other set of slippers. If you're in a home or Japanese inn you'll notice another pair of slippers—again plastic or rubber—sitting right inside the restroom at the door. Step out of the hallway plastic shoes and into the bathroom slippers and wear these the whole time you're in the restroom. When you're finished, change back into the hallway slippers.

The Japanese Bath On my very first trip to Japan I was certain that I would never get into a Japanese bath. I was under the misconception that men and women bathed together and I couldn't imagine getting into a tub with a group of smiling and bowing Japanese men. I needn't have worried. The good news (or, I suppose, bad news for some of you) is that in almost all circumstances bathing is segregated for men and women in Japan. There are some exceptions, primarily outdoor hot-spring spas in the countryside, but the women who go to these are usually grandmothers who couldn't care less. Young Japanese women wouldn't dream of jumping into a tub with a group of male strangers.

Anyway, Japanese baths are delightful—and I, for one, am addicted to them. You find them at Japanese-style inns, at hot-spring spas, and at neighborhood baths (not everyone has his own bath in Japan). Sometimes they're elaborate affairs with many tubs, plants, and statues, and sometimes they're nothing more than a tiny tub. The procedure at all of them is the same. After completely disrobing in the changing room and putting your clothes in either a locker or a basket, hold your wash cloth in front of you so that it covers the vital parts and walk into the bath area. There you'll find plastic basins and stools (they used to be wood), and faucets along the wall. Sit on the stool in front of the faucet and repeatedly fill your basin with water, splashing it all over you. If there's no hot water from the faucet, it's acceptable to dip your plastic basin into the hot bath. Soap yourself down completely—and I mean *completely,* rinsing away all traces of soap. I have never seen a group of people wash themselves so thoroughly as the Japanese, from their ears to their toes. Only after you're squeaky clean are you ready to get into the bath.

Your first attempt at a Japanese bath may be painful—simply too scalding for comfort. It helps if you ease in gently and then sit perfectly still. You'll notice all tension and muscle stiffness ebbing away, a decidedly relaxing way to end the day. The Japanese are so fond of baths that many take them every night, especially in the winter, when a hot bath keeps one toasty warm for hours afterward.

Guest Etiquette If you are invited to a Japanese home, it is a rarity and an honor. Most Japanese consider their homes too small and humble for entertaining guests, which is why there are so many restaurants, coffee shops, and bars. If you are invited to a home, don't show up empty-handed. Bring a small gift, such as candy, fruit, or flowers. Alcohol is also appreciated.

Instead of being invited to a private home, you may be invited out to dinner and drinks, especially if you're in Japan on business, in which case your host will most likely have an expense account. In any case, it's nice to reciprocate by taking Japanese to your own territory, say, a French or other Western-style restaurant where you'll feel comfortable playing host.

If you're among friends, the general practice is to divide the check equally among everyone, no matter how much or little each consumed.

In any case, no matter what favor a Japanese has done for you—whether it was giving you a small gift, buying you a drink, or

IMPRESSIONS

Etiquette is the Kaiser of Japan.
—Douglas Sladen, *Queer Things About Japan*, 1903

even just making a telephone call for you—be sure to give your thanks profusely the next time you meet. The Japanese think it odd and rude not to be remembered and thanked upon the next meeting, even if a year has elapsed.

Miscellaneous Etiquette When the Japanese give back change, they hand it back to you in a lump sum rather than counting it out. Trust them. It's considered insulting for you to sit there and count it in front of them because it insinuates that you think they might be trying to cheat you. The Japanese are honest. It's one of the great pleasures of being in their country.

Don't blow your nose in public if you can help it, and never at the dinner table. It's considered disgusting. On the other hand, even though the Japanese are very hygienic, they are not at all averse to spitting on the sidewalk. And even more peculiar, the men urinate when and where they want, usually against a tree or a wall and most often after a night of carousing in the bars.

This being a man's society, men will walk in and out of doors and elevators before women, and in subways will often sit down while their wives stand. Some Japanese men, however, who have had contact with the Western world, and who know that in the West it's women before men, will make a gallant show of allowing a Western woman to step out of the elevator or door first.

LANGUAGE Without a doubt the hardest part of being in Tokyo is the language barrier. Suddenly you find yourself transported to a crowded city of 12 million people where you can neither speak nor read the language. To make matters worse, many Japanese cannot speak English, and many signs, menus, and shop names are often only in Japanese.

No one knows the exact origins of the Japanese language, but we do know that it existed only in spoken form until the 6th century. It was then that the Japanese borrowed the Chinese characters, called *kanji,* and used them to develop their own form of written language. Later, two additional phonetic alphabets, *hiragana* and *katakana,* were added to kanji to form the existing Japanese writing system. Thus, while Chinese and Japanese can recognize common pictographs in each other's written language, they cannot communicate verbally.

✪ Written Japanese uses three different character systems—*kanji, hiragana,* and *katakana.*

There are about 10,000 Japanese kanji, but the average adult knows only 2,500 or so, which is enough to read newspapers, most books, and novels. The Japanese written language, a combination of kanji, hiragana, and katakana, is probably one of the most difficult systems of written communication in the modern world. Even the spoken language has different levels of speech and forms of expression that relate to social status, age, and sex. Little wonder that Saint Francis Xavier, a Jesuit missionary who came to Japan in the 16th century, wrote that Japanese was an invention of the devil designed to thwart the spread of Christianity. And yet the most astounding thing is that literacy in Japan is estimated at 99%.

Realizing the difficulties foreigners have with the language barrier in Japan, the Japan National Tourist Organization (JNTO) has put out a nifty booklet called "The Tourist's Handbook" with sentences in English with Japanese equivalents for everything from asking directions to shopping to ordering in a restaurant to staying in a Japanese inn.

If you need to ask directions in Tokyo, your best bet is to ask younger people. If they don't understand what you say, write it down, since most of them can read English but may not understand the spoken word. If you still have problems communicating, you can always call the Travel-Phone, a toll-free nationwide helpline set up by JNTO to help foreigners in distress or in need of information (for information on Travel-Phone, see "Fast Facts: Tokyo," in Chapter 3). And if you're heading out for a particular restaurant or shop, it helps to have your destination written out in Japanese to show to taxi drivers or to passersby.

Though many hotels, restaurants, and sightseeing attractions in Tokyo have signs showing their names in English transliteration, many others do not. To help you find such places mentioned in this book, the Japanese symbols for their names are listed in the Appendix. When you see a number in an oval following the name of any restaurant, Japanese-style inn, or other establishment, turn to "Japanese Symbols" in the Appendix and look for the corresponding number to find the name of that establishment.

English words are quite fashionable in Japan and have penetrated the Japanese language to such an extent that they are now estimated to make up 20% of the words used by the Japanese, though the pronunciation and usage are usually so different from the English that they're often unrecognizable. Would you, for example, recognize *terebi* as television, *biiru* as beer, or *koohi* as coffee?

You'll see English on shop signs, billboards, posters, shopping bags, and T-shirts. However, words are often wonderfully misspelled or used in such unusual contexts that one can only guess at the original intent. My days have been brightened innumerable times with the discovery of some zany or unfathomable English. What, for example, could possibly be the meaning behind "Today birds, tomorrow men," which appeared under a picture of birds on a shopping bag? I have a treasured ashtray that reads "The young boy grasped her heart firmly." In Matsue a "Beauty Saloon" conjures up images of beauties chugging mugs of beer, and in Gifu one can only surmise at the pleasures to be had at the Hotel Joybox.

But the best one I saw was at Narita airport. At all the check-in

---

IMPRESSIONS

It has always seemed a grave reflection on the Japanese character that their language, with the exception of the word "fool"—and "countrified fool" is extremely strong—should contain no opportunities for invective.

—Peter Quennell, *A Superficial Journey Through Tokyo and Peking*, 1932 counters was a sign telling passengers they would be required to pay a service facility charge at "the time of check in for your fright." I explained the cause of my amusement to the person behind the counter, and when I came back two weeks later, all the signs had been corrected. That's Japanese efficiency.

RELIGION

The main religions in Japan are Shintoism and Buddhism. Ask a Japanese whether he is Buddhist, and he'll probably answer yes with strong conviction, even though he may visit a temple only once or twice a year. Ask him whether he subscribes to Shintoism, and he's also likely to answer in the affirmative. Although a Westerner may find it difficult to understand how a person could belong to two completely different religious faiths, the Japanese find nothing incongruous about adopting both Buddhism and Shintoism and incorporating them into their lifestyles. Most Japanese marry in a Shinto ceremony, but when they die their funeral will probably be Buddhist.

Unlike the West, where churches have religious services weekly, the Japanese generally visit a temple or shrine only for a specific purpose. On New Year's, for example, many Japanese throng to shrines to pray for good fortune in the coming year, while in mid-July or mid-August they go to pay respects to their ancestors. In addition, annual festivals are nearly always tied to religion, and every major shrine and temple has at least one annual festival, with events ranging from traditional dances to colorful processions in which portable shrines are carried through the streets by groups of Japanese in traditional costumes. During the Sanja Matsuri held every May in the Asakusa district of Tokyo, for example, more than 100 portable shrines are carried back and forth through the streets to bless the neighborhood.

SHINTOISM Of the two religions, Shintoism probably strikes closer to the national heartbeat of the Japanese, since it is the country's native religion, with roots that stretch back centuries before Buddhism's arrival. Shintoism is essentially the worship of ancestors and national heroes, as well as all natural things both animate and inanimate. These natural things are considered to embody gods, called *kami,* and can be anyone or anything: mountains, trees, the moon, stars, rivers, seas, fires, animals, a rock, and even vegetables. In this respect it resembles the beliefs of some Native Americans. Shintoism also embraces much of Confucianism, which entered Japan in the 5th century and stressed the importance of family and loyalty. There are no scriptures in Shintoism, and no set of morals or ethics.

✪ The Japanese people's reverence of nature is part of their native religion, Shintoism, which embraces the worship of all natural things.

The most important goddess in Shintoism is Amaterasu, the sun goddess, who is considered the progenitor of the Japanese imperial family. Central to the principles of Shintoism through the centuries, therefore, was the belief that the emperor was a living god. He held this revered position for more than 1,500 years, until the end of World War II. It was then that the emperor was made to renounce his claim to divinity and admit that he was a human being just like

IMPRESSIONS

Japan is essentially a country of paradoxes and anomalies, where all—even familiar things—put on new faces, and are curiously reversed. [The Japanese] write from top to bottom, from right to left . . . and their books begin where ours end, thus furnishing examples of the curious perfection this rule of contraries has attained.

—SIR RUTHERFORD ALCOCK, *THE CAPITAL OF THE TYCOON*, 1863

everyone else. At this time Shintoism also lost its official status as the national religion, a position it had held since the Meiji Restoration (1868). However, Shintoism has not lost its popularity and claims more than 80 million followers in Japan. As for the imperial family, they still occupy a special place in the hearts of the Japanese. The imperial family is the longest-reigning imperial family in the world.

The place of worship in Shintoism is called a shrine, *jinja* in Japanese. Every city, town, village, and hamlet has one or more shrines and to most inhabitants they embody the soul of their district. In Tokyo, the most famous shrine is Meiji Shrine, dedicated to Emperor Meiji.

The most obvious sign of a shrine is its *torii*, an entrance, usually of wood, that consists of two tall poles topped with one or two crossbeams. Sometimes there will be several of these torii spread out over the pathway leading to the shrine, reminding visitors that they are approaching a shrine and giving them time to achieve the proper frame of mind. Before reaching the shrine itself you'll pass a water trough with communal cups where the Japanese will rinse out their mouths and wash their hands. Purification and cleanliness are important in Shintoism because they show respect to the gods, aspects that have carried over even today in the Japanese custom of bathing and of removing shoes indoors.

At the shrine itself the worshipper will throw a few coins into a money box, clap his hands three times to get the attention of the gods, and then bow his head and pray. Sometimes there will be a rope attached to a gong that's even louder in calling the gods. And what do worshippers pray for? Good health, protection, safe delivery of a child, that sons get into good universities and daughters get good husbands. Some shrines are considered lucky for love; others are good against certain ailments. You can ask any favor of the gods. Shrines are also sites of many festivals and are visited on important occasions throughout one's life, including marriage and on certain birthdays.

BUDDHISM Buddhist places of worship are called temples (*otera* in Japanese). Instead of torii, temples will often have an entrance gate with a raised doorsill and heavy doors. Temples may also have a cemetery on their grounds, which Shinto shrines never have, and a pagoda. The most famous Buddhist temple in Tokyo is Sensoji Temple in Asakusa.

Founded in India in the 5th century A.D., Buddhism came to Japan in the 6th century via China and Korea, introducing the concept of eternal life. By the end of the 6th century, Buddhism had gained such popularity that Prince Shotoku, one of Japan's most remarkable historical figures, declared Buddhism the state religion and based many of his governmental policies on its tenets. Another important Buddhist leader was a priest called Kukai, known posthumously as Kobo Daishi. After studying Buddhism in China in the early 800s, he returned to Japan, where he founded the Shingon Sect of Buddhism and established his monastery atop Mt. Koya. The temples that he built throughout Japan, including the famous 88 temples on Shikoku island and those on Mt. Koya, continue to attract millions of pilgrims even today.

Probably the Buddhist sect best known in the West, however, is Zen Buddhism. Considered the most Japanese form of Buddhism, Zen is the practice of meditation in a strict, ascetic lifestyle with the object of overcoming desire so that one can achieve enlightenment. There are no rites in Zen Buddhism, nor are there dogmas nor a theological conception of divinity. Knowledge is not gained by rational analysis but rather through intuition. The strict and simple lifestyle of Zen had a strong appeal for Japan's samurai class, and many of Japan's arts, including the tea ceremony, arose from the practice of Zen.

2. FOOD & DRINK

FOOD

Tokyo is a treasure trove of culinary surprises—just as America has more to offer than hamburgers and steaks, Japan has more than sushi and tempura. Altogether there are more than a dozen different and distinct types of Japanese cuisine as well as countless regional specialties. Generally speaking, only one type of cuisine is served in a given restaurant—for example, only raw seafood is served in a sushi bar. There are some exceptions to this, especially in those restaurants where raw fish may be served as an appetizer. In addition, some of Japan's drinking establishments offer a wide range of foods, from soups and salads to sushi or skewered pieces of chicken.

In Japan's more expensive traditional restaurants, presentation of food is as important as the food itself, and dishes are designed to appeal to the eye as well as to the palate. In contrast to the American way of piling as much food as possible onto a single plate, the Japanese use lots of small plates, each arranged artfully with bite-size morsels of food. After you've seen what can be done with maple leaves, flowers, bits of bamboo, and even pebbles to enhance the

IMPRESSIONS

If the most celebrated cathedrals of Europe were situated in the Black Forest, and were all simple wooden structures resembling very large but plain log cabins, Christianity would approximate to Shinto in its aesthetic appeal.

—Alexander Campbell, *The Heart of Japan*, 1962, on the Ise Jingu Shrines appearance of food, your relationship with what you eat may be changed forever.

DINING CUSTOMS As soon as you're seated in a Japanese restaurant you'll be given a wet towel, which will be steaming hot in winter or pleasantly cool in summer. Called an *oshibori,* it's for wiping your hands. In all but the fancy restaurants men can get away with wiping their faces as well, but women are not supposed to.

The next thing you'll probably be confronted with are chopsticks. The proper way to use them is to place the first chopstick between the base of the thumb and the top of the ring finger (this chopstick remains stationary) and the second one between the top of the thumb and the middle and index fingers. This second chopstick is what you move to pick up food. The best way to learn is to have a Japanese show you how. It's not difficult to learn, but if you find it impossible some restaurants might have a fork.

As for etiquette involving chopsticks, if you're taking something from a communal bowl or tray you're supposed to turn your chopsticks upside down and use the part that hasn't been in your mouth. After transferring the food to your plate you turn the chopsticks back to their proper position. Never stick your chopsticks down vertically into your bowl of rice and leave them there—you do that only when a person has died. Similarly you're not supposed to pass anything between chopsticks since that's how cremated bones are passed in a Buddhist funeral. If you're eating soup, you won't use a spoon but will pick up the bowl and drink from it. It's considered in good taste to slurp with gusto, especially if you're eating noodles. Noodle shops in Japan are well orchestrated with slurps and smacks. And by the way, it's considered bad manners to walk down the street in Japan eating or drinking.

✪ To the Japanese, how a prepared dish looks is at least as important as how it tastes.

RICE There is no problem here, since everyone is familiar with rice. The difference, however, is that in Japan it is quite sticky, making it easier to pick up with chopsticks. It's also plain white rice (called *gohan*)—no salt, no butter, no soy sauce. Like other Asians, the Japanese have used rice as a staple in their diet for about 2,000 years, though not everyone in the old days could afford the expensive white kind. The peasants had to content themselves with a mixture of white and brown rice, millet, and greens. Today some Japanese still eat rice three times a day, though the younger ones are now just as likely to have bread and coffee for breakfast.

KAISEKI Kaiseki is the epitome of delicately and exquisitely

IMPRESSIONS

There is a saying that the Chinese eat with their stomachs and the Japanese with their eyes.

—BERNARD LEACH, *A POTTER IN JAPAN,* 1960

arranged food, the ultimate in aesthetic appeal. It's also among the most expensive, and meals can easily cost ¥20,000 ($182) per person. Some restaurants, however, do offer mini-kaiseki meals that are much more affordable. The reason kaiseki is expensive is that it's a complete meal consisting of many dishes, each requiring much time and skill to prepare. Even the plates are chosen with great care to enhance the color, texture, and shape of each piece of food. Kaiseki restaurants generally serve only complete, fixed-price meals, though some may offer à la carte side dishes and appetizers as well.

Kaiseki cuisine is based on the four seasons, with the selection of food and its presentation dependent on the time of the year. In fact, so strongly does a kaiseki meal convey the mood of a particular season that the kaiseki gourmet can tell what season it is just by looking at his meal. The roots of kaiseki go back to the development of the tea ceremony, when monks ate small morsels of food to protect the stomach against the effects of strong tea.

A kaiseki meal is usually a lengthy affair, with various dishes appearing in set order. First comes the appetizer, clear broth and one uncooked dish. That's followed by boiled, broiled, fried, steamed, heated, and vinegared dishes and finally by another soup, rice, pickled vegetables, and fruit. Since kaiseki is always a set meal there's no problem in ordering. Some restaurants offer a lunchtime mini-kaiseki.

SUSHI & SASHIMI The average Japanese eats an estimated 80 pounds of seafood a year, six times the amount of an American. Although this seafood may be served in any number of ways, a great deal of it is eaten raw. The idea of eating raw fish might seem a little strange to you at first, but if you'll just try it you'll probably like it.

Sashimi is simply raw seafood. A good choice to start out with if you've never eaten it is *maguro,* or tuna. Contrary to what you might think, it doesn't taste fishy at all and is so delicate in texture it almost melts in your mouth. The way to eat sashimi is to first mix wasabi, pungent green horseradish, into a small dish of soy sauce and then dip the raw fish into the sauce.

Sushi, also called *nigiri-zushi,* is raw fish, seafood, or vegetables placed on top of vinegared rice with just a touch of wasabi. It's also dipped into soy sauce. Use your chopsticks or your fingers to eat sushi; you're supposed to eat it in one bite, which is quite a mouthful but about the only way to keep it from falling apart. Another trick is to turn it upside down when you dip it into the sauce so that only the fish and not the rice touches the sauce.

Typical sushi includes flounder (*hirame*), sea bream (*tai*), squid (*ika*), octopus (*tako*), prawn (*ebi*) and omelet (*tamago*). Ordering is easy because you usually sit at the sushi bar, where you can see all the food in a refrigerated glass case in front of you. You also get to see all the action of the sushi chefs at work. The typical meal starts out with sashimi followed by sushi, but if you don't want to order separately there are always various set meals (often called *seto* in a sushi bar).

TEMPURA A well-known Japanese food, tempura was actually introduced by the Portuguese who came to Japan in the 16th century. Tempura is deep-fried food that has been coated in a mixture of egg, water, and wheat flour and is served piping hot. To eat it, dip it into a soy sauce that has been mixed with a fish-stock base and flavored with radish and grated ginger. Various tempura specialties may include eggplant, mushroom, green pepper, slices of lotus root, prawn, squid, and many kinds of fish. Again, the easiest thing to do is to order the daily special, the *teishoku*. If you're still hungry you can always order something extra à la carte.

SUKIYAKI Until about 100 years ago the Japanese could think of nothing so disgusting as eating the flesh of animals (fish was okay). Considered unclean by the Buddhists, meat consumption was banned by the emperor in the 7th century. It wasn't until Emperor Meiji himself made a public announcement a century ago that he was going to eat meat that the Japanese accepted the idea. Today the Japanese have become skilled in preparing a number of beef dishes. And according to a survey conducted a couple of years back by the Japan Fisheries Association, grilled meat, curry rice, and hamburger were the three top favorite dishes among senior high school boys living in Tokyo. The girls, by the way, still preferred sushi.

Sukiyaki is thinly sliced beef cooked, at the table, in a broth of soy sauce and sake along with scallions, spinach, mushrooms, tofu, bamboo shoots, and other vegetables. Diners serve themselves by taking what they want out of the simmering pot and then dipping it into their own bowl of raw egg. You can skip the raw egg if you want, but it adds to the taste and also cools the food down enough so that it doesn't burn your tongue.

SHABU-SHABU Similar to sukiyaki, shabu-shabu is also prepared at your table and consists of thinly sliced beef cooked in a broth with vegetables. The main difference between the two is the broth. Whereas in sukiyaki it consists of soy sauce and is slightly sweet, the broth of shabu-shabu is relatively clear and has little taste of its own. The pots used are also different.

Named for the swishing sound the beef supposedly makes when it's cooking, shabu-shabu is a meal in which you hold your own piece of meat in the watery broth with your chopsticks until it cooks, usually only a few seconds. Vegetables are left in longer to swim around until you fish them out. Sauces are either sesame with diced green onions or a more bitter sauce made from fish stock. Restaurants serving sukiyaki usually serve shabu-shabu as well.

TEPPANYAKI A teppanyaki restaurant is a Japanese steak house, in which the chef slices, dices, and cooks your meal of tenderloin or sirloin steak and vegetables on a hot smooth grill right in front of you. Because beef is relatively new in Japanese cooking, some people categorize teppanyaki restaurants as Western cuisine. However, I consider its style of cooking and presentation unique, and throughout this book I refer to such restaurants as Japanese.

ROBATAYAKI Robatayaki refers to restaurants in which seafood and vegetables are cooked over a robata grill. In the olden days, an open fireplace (*robata*) in the middle of an old Japanese house was the center of activity for cooking, eating, socializing, and simply keeping warm. Today's robatayaki restaurants, therefore, are like

IMPRESSIONS

Frequent outbreaks of fire constitute one of the greatest perils to life in Japan. In Tokyo, burning houses are given the poetic name of "the flowers of Edo."

—JAMES KIRKUP, *HEAVEN, HELL AND HARA-KIRI*, 1974

nostalgia trips back into Japan's past and are often decorated in rustic farmhouse style, with staff dressed in traditional clothing. Many robatayaki restaurants are open only in the evenings and are popular among office workers for both eating and drinking.

There's no special menu in a robatayaki restaurant—it includes just about everything eaten in Japan. The difference is that most of it will be grilled. Favorites of mine include gingko nuts, asparagus, green peppers, mushrooms, potatoes, and just about any kind of fish. You can also usually get skewers of beef or chicken as well as a stew of meat and potatoes (*nikujaga*), delicious in cold winter months. Since ordering is usually à la carte, you'll just have to look and point.

YAKITORI Yakitori is chunks of chicken or chicken parts basted in a sweet soy sauce and grilled over a charcoal fire on thin skewers. A place that serves yakitori, sometimes called a *yakitori-ya* and often identifiable by a red paper lantern outside its front door, is technically not a restaurant but rather a drinking establishment. It usually doesn't open until 5pm and is extremely popular with the working crowd as an inexpensive place to drink, eat, and be merry.

Although you can order a set dish of various yakitori (often called a *yakitori seto*), I usually refrain because it will frequently include various parts of the chicken like the skin, heart, and liver. You may like such exotica, but it's not for me. If you're ordering by the stick, you might want to try chicken meatballs (*tsukune*), green peppers (*piman*), chicken and leeks (*negima*), mushrooms (*shitake*), gingko nuts (*ginnan*), or chicken breast (*sasami*).

KUSHIAGE Kushiage foods (also called *kushikatsu*) are those that are deep-fried on skewers and include chicken, beef, seafood, and lots of seasonal vegetables. The result is delicious and I highly recommend that you try it. I can't understand why this style of cooking isn't better known—maybe someday it will be. Ordering the fixed-price menu is easiest, and what you get is often determined by both the chef and the season.

TONKATSU Tonkatsu is the Japanese word for "pork cutlet" and it's cooked by dredging pork in wheat flour, moistening it with egg and water, dipping it in bread crumbs, and deep-frying it in vegetable oil. Restaurants serving tonkatsu are generally inexpensive and therefore popular with office workers and families. The easiest order is the *teishoku,* which will offer either the pork filet (*hirekatsu*) or the pork loin (*rosukatsu*). In any case, your tonkatsu is served on a bed of lettuce and two different sauces will be at your table.

FUGU Known as the blowfish, puffer, or globefish in English, fugu is perhaps one of the most exotic foods in Japan, primarily because if not prepared properly it means almost instant death for the consumer. In the past decade or so as many as 200 people have died in Japan from fugu poisoning, usually because they tried preparing it at home. The ovaries and intestines of the fugu are deadly and must be entirely removed without puncturing them. So why eat fugu if it can kill you? Well, it's delicious for one thing, and for another, chefs are strictly licensed by the government and greatly skilled in preparing fugu dishes. You can eat fugu raw or in a stew (*fugu-chiri*) cooked with vegetables at your table. The season for fresh fugu is from October or November through March, but some restaurants serve it throughout the year.

UNAGI I'll bet that if you ate unagi without knowing what it was you'd find it very tasty. In fact you'd probably be very surprised to find out that you had just eaten eel. Popular as a health food because of its high vitamin A content, eel is considered especially helpful in fighting fatigue during the hot summer months but is eaten all year round. Broiled eel (*kabayaki*) is prepared by grilling filet strips over a charcoal fire along with repeated dips in a sweetened barbecue soy sauce. A favorite way to eat broiled eel is on top of rice, in which case it's called *unaju*.

NOODLES The Japanese love eating noodles, but I suspect that it stems at least partly from the way they eat them—they slurp and suck them in with a speed that defies gravity. If you ask me, "Gone in 60 Seconds" could describe the way a businessman attacks his lunchtime bowl of noodles. At any rate, you're *supposed* to slurp noodles; it's considered proper etiquette. Fearing that it would stick with me forever, however, slurping is a technique I never quite mastered.

There are all kinds of different noodles, eaten plain, in combination with other foods, hot or cold. *Soba* is made from buckwheat flour and is eaten hot or cold. *Udon* is a thick, white noodle originally from Osaka and is usually served hot. *Somen* is a fine, white noodle that is eaten cold in the summer and dunked in a cold sauce. Noodle shops are generally inexpensive, ranging from stand-up stalls seen around train stations to more traditional restaurants where guests sit at low tables on tatami.

OKONOMIYAKI Meaning literally "as you like it," okonomiyaki originated in Osaka and is a kind of Japanese pizza/pancake, to which meat or fish, shredded cabbage, and vegetables are added. Since it's a popular fare of street vendors, restaurants specializing in this type of cuisine are very reasonably priced. At some locales the cook makes it for you, but in others you're supposed to pour the batter and add the ingredients at your own tabletop grill, which can be quite fun if you're with a group.

OTHER TYPES OF CUISINE Other popular types of Japanese cuisine include *kamameshi*, a rice casserole with such toppings as seafood, meat, or vegetables, and *nabe*, a stew cooked in an earthenware pot at your table with ingredients that might include chicken, sliced beef, pork, or seafood, and vegetables. *Oden* is fishcakes, tofu, and vegetables steeped in broth.

Although technically Chinese fast-food restaurants, *ramen* shops are so much a part of dining in Japan that I feel compelled to include them here. Serving what I consider to be generic Chinese noodles, soups, and other dishes, ramen shops can be found everywhere in Japan, easily recognizable by their red signs, flashing lights, and quite often pictures of various dishes displayed right by the front door. In addition to ramen (noodle and vegetable soup), you can also get such things as *yakisoba* (fried noodles) or—my favorite—*gyoza*, which are fried pork dumplings. What these places lack in atmosphere is made up for in price: Most dishes average about ¥500 ($4.55).

DESSERTS If you think Japanese cuisine lacks variety because of the ubiquitous rice, seaweed, and beans (usually in the form of soy sauce), you won't be thrilled to find that traditional desserts are also made from these standbys. Each region has its own confections, but seasonings for the usually sticky rice or bean cakes include cinnamon and sesame. If you like the taste of molasses, you might try my favorite dessert, *anmitsu,* which is beans, molasses, sweet bean paste, and gelatin (probably made from seaweed). It's a national rather than a regional dessert and you can find it everywhere. *Kuremanmitsu* is the same thing with ice cream, while, a bit different, *oshiruko,* is a hot sweet bean porridge.

DRINK

If you're drinking in Japan, the main thing to remember is that you never pour your own glass. Bottles of beer are so huge that people often share one (or two, or three, or more, depending on how the evening goes). The rule is that everyone pours for everyone else; be sure to hold up your glass when someone is pouring for you. Only as the night progresses do the Japanese get sloppy about this rule.

All Japanese restaurants serve complimentary Japanese green tea with meals. If that's a little too weak, Japanese sake made from rice is an alcoholic beverage, served either hot or cold, that goes well with most forms of Japanese cuisine. Beer is also very popular, with the biggest sellers being Suntory, Kirin, and Sapporo. Budweiser is a big hit among young Japanese. Japanese businessmen are fond of whisky, which they usually drink with ice and water. Although cocktails are available in discos, hotel lounges, and fancier bars, most Japanese stick with beer, sake, or whisky. Popular also is *shochu,* an alcoholic beverage usually made from rice but sometimes from wheat or sweet potato. It used to be considered a drink of the lower classes, but its sales have increased so much that it's threatening the sake and whisky business. A clear liquid, it's often combined with soda water in a drink called *chu-hai,* but watch out—the stuff can be deadly.

3. RECOMMENDED BOOKS & FILMS

BOOKS

Japanese history, culture, life, society, and the arts are so rich and extensive that I have been able to give only a short overview in this book. Fortunately, there is a vast number of books in English covering every aspect of Japan, so you shouldn't have any problems reading up on specific subjects in more detail. Kodansha International, a Japanese publishing company, has published more books on Japan in English than probably any other company. Available at major bookstores in Japan, its books are distributed in the United States through HarperCollins, 10 E. 53rd St., New York, NY 10022. Another company that publishes numerous books on Japan is Charles E. Tuttle Company.

GENERAL For an introduction to Japan's history, a standard work is George B. Sansom's *Japan: A Short Cultural History* (Prentice Hall, 1962), which covers the country's history from antiquity to modern times. A former U.S. ambassador to Japan, Edwin O. Reischauer gives a detailed look at Japan's history in *Japan: The*

Story of a Nation (Knopf, 1974). If you're interested in Japan since World War II, *A History of Postwar Japan* by Masataka Kosaka (Kodansha, 1982) takes in the enormous changes that have occurred in Japan during the past few decades.

A general overview of Japanese history, politics, and society is provided in Reischauer's *The Japanese* (Harvard University Press, 1977). Delving deeper into the Japanese society and psychology are Kurt Singer's *Mirror, Sword and Jewel: The Geometry of Japanese Life* (Kodansha, 1981) and Chie Nakane's *Japanese Society* (University of California Press, 1970).

A classic describing the Japanese and their culture is the brilliantly written book by Ruth Benedict called *The Chrysanthemum and the Sword: Patterns of Japanese Culture* (New American Library, 1967), first published in the 1940s but republished many times since. A more contemporary book is *The Japanese Mind: The Goliath Explained* (Linden Press/Simon & Schuster, 1983), by Robert C. Christopher. I consider this book compulsory reading for anyone traveling to Japan because it describes so accurately the Japanese, the role history has played in developing the Japanese psyche, and problems facing the nation today.

In a more lighthearted vein, there's *Dave Barry Does Japan* (Random House, 1992). Trust in the inimitable Dave Barry to solve the mystery of the success of the Japanese car industry (they use steel!) and to offer invaluable travel advice, such as "I cannot overemphasize the importance, if you go there, of having Random House pay for everything" (page 74). A delightful account of the Japanese and their customs is given by the irrepressible George Mikes in *The Land of the Rising Yen* (Penguin, 1973). Because it was published nearly 20 years ago, I doubt you'll be able to find a copy in the United States; it is, however, in major bookstores in Japan and would make light and enjoyable reading during your trip.

Likewise, the Japan Travel Bureau puts out some nifty pocket-size booklets on things Japanese, including "Eating in Japan" and "Festivals of Japan." My favorite, however, is "Salaryman in Japan" (JTB, 1986), which describes the private and working lives of those guys in the look-alike business suits, Japan's army of white-collar workers who receive set salaries. The book is illustrated throughout and includes a picture of the typical salaryman, from his metal-framed, square-rimmed glasses down to his dark-red necktie with diagonal stripes and black leather shoes. The endearing thing about this work is that it was written in complete seriousness, with chapters devoted to life in the salaryman's company, the etiquette of business cards, company trips, the wife of a salaryman, and even the "salaryman blues." Easy to read, it is both entertaining and enlightening.

If you're interested in women's issues in Japan, read Alice Cook and Hiroko Hayashi's *Working Women in Japan: Discrimination, Resistance and Reform* (ILR Press, 1980). A book seemingly from

---

IMPRESSIONS

It is the man who drinks the first cup of sake,
then the second cup of sake drinks the first;
then it is the sake that drinks the man.
—Japanese Proverb

another era is *Geisha* (Kodansha, 1983), written by Liza C. Dalby; it describes her year living as a geisha in Kyoto as part of a research project.

For the religions in Japan, two beautifully illustrated books are *Shinto: Japan's Spiritual Roots* (Kodansha, 1980) and *Buddhism: Japan's Cultural Identity* (Kodansha, 1982), both by Stuart D. B. Picken with introductions by Edwin O. Reischauer.

If you find yourself becoming addicted to Japanese food, you might want to invest in a copy of *Japanese Cooking: A Simple Art* (Kodansha, 1980) by Shizuo Tsuji. Written by the proprietor of one of the largest cooking schools in Japan, this book contains more than 220 recipes, along with information on food history and table etiquette. The history and philosophy of the tea ceremony, beginning with its origins in the 12th century, is given in *The Tea Ceremony* by Sen'o Tanaka (Kodansha, 1983). Another lovely book is *Chanoyu: The Urasenke Tradition of Tea,* edited by Soshitsu Sen XV (John Weatherhill, 1989). It may well be the definitive book on tea and is lavishly illustrated.

THE ARTS An introduction to Japanese art is provided in Langdon Warner's *Enduring Art of Japan* (Grove Press, 1958). Kabuki and other stage arts are covered in Faubion Bowers's *Japanese Theater* (Greenwood Press, 1976).

FICTION Reading fiction is certainly one of the most relaxing and fun ways to learn about a country. Whenever I travel in Japan, I especially enjoy reading fictional accounts of the country because doing so puts me more in tune with my surroundings and increases my awareness and perception. The world's first major novel was written by a Japanese woman, Murasaki Shikibu, whose 11th-century classic *The Tale of Genji* (Knopf, 1978) describes the aristocratic life of Prince Genji. Lafcadio Hearn, a prolific writer about things Japanese in the late 1800s, describes life in Japan around the turn of the century in *Writings from Japan* (Penguin, 1985). An overview of classical literature is provided in *Anthology of Japanese Literature* (Grove Press, 1955), edited by Donald Keene. Soseki Natsume, one of Japan's most respected novelists of the Meiji era, writes of Tokyo and its tumultuous time of change in *And Then* (Putnam, 1982), translated by Norma Moore Field, and *Kokoro* (Regnery Gateway Co., 1985), translated by Edwin McClellan.

And finally, because it was also made into a television miniseries, most Westerners are familiar with James Clavell's *Shogun* (Dell, 1975), a fictional account based on the lives of Englishman William Adams and military leader Tokugawa Ieyasu around 1600. In addition, a vivid history of Japanese woodblock prints from the 17th to the 19th century comes alive in a first-person account written by James A. Michener in *The Floating World* (University of Hawaii Press, 1983). Nicholas Bouvier, the Swiss travel writer, mixes personal accounts and art with Japanese history that reads as easy as fiction in his vivid and sensual *The Japanese Chronicals* (Mercury House, 1992).

For more recent, personal accounts of what it's like for Westerners living in Japan, two entertaining novels are *Ransom,* by Jay McInerney (Vintage, 1985), and *Pictures from the Water Trade,* by John D. Morley (Harper & Row, 1986). Pico Iyer taps into the mysterious juxtaposition of the old Japan versus the new in *The Lady and the Monk: Four Seasons in Kyoto* (Alfred A. Knopf, 1991).

FILMS

Samurai flicks, like the American western, have never lost their appeal to the Japanese audience. The classic samurai film is probably Akira Kurosawa's *The Seven Samurai,* the Japanese original of *The Magnificent Seven,* about revenge and loyalty. Other Kurosawa films that deal with feudal Japan include *Kagemusha,* which was co-winner of the grand prize at the 1980 Cannes Film Festival, and *Ran,* an epic drama set in 16th-century Japan and based on Shakespeare's *King Lear.* Kurosawa, the grandfather of Japanese directors, is probably the best known and certainly one of the finest in his field. His films, from early ones like *Stray Dog,* a picture of Japan immediately after the war (it begins with a shot of a dog carrying a human hand in its mouth) to his more recent *Dreams,* said to be autobiographical, have never failed to interest an international audience.

For a look at the life of Japan's mountain people in the 1880s, nothing can beat Shohei Imamura's *The Ballad of Narayama* with its unsentimentalized portrait of an elderly woman who goes off into the snowy countryside to die, as was the custom of her people.

Another film providing insight into the psyche of the Japanese is Nagisa Oshima's *Merry Christmas Mr. Lawrence,* about a POW camp set in Java in 1942 and starring rock stars David Bowie and Ryuichi Sakamoto. Oshima created a stir in the film world with *In the Realm of the Senses,* a story of obsessive love between a prostitute and the master of the house. Considered too erotic, it was banned from its première at the New York Film Festival in 1976. Today accepted as "an erotic masterpiece," there's even a sequel, *Passion of the Senses.* These are obviously very adult fare.

Mishima, produced by Francis Ford Coppola and George Lucas and directed by Paul Schrader, relates the bizarre life and death of writer Mishima Yukio, one of Japan's most famous writers.

Juzo Itami, a well-known Japanese director, has recently done some very funny films, which though the finer points may be lost in the subtitles, have no trouble translating to an international audience. *Tampopo* is about a Japanese woman who strikes success with a noodle shop, while *The Funeral* is a comic look at death in Japan, including the surviving family's helplessness when it comes to arranging the complex rituals of the Buddhist ceremony. Itami's *A Taxing Woman,* about a gung-ho tax collector and her prey, a consumately devious tax evader, was so popular in Japan that he quickly came up with the sequel, *A Taxing Woman II.*

CHAPTER 2

PLANNING A TRIP TO TOKYO

Much of the anxiety associated with travel—especially when it's to the other side of the planet—comes from a fear of the unknown. Not knowing what to expect, or even what a place looks like, can give even seasoned travelers the butterflies. This chapter will help prepare you for your trip to Tokyo, but don't stop here. Reading through the other chapters before leaving home will also help you plan your travels.

1. INFORMATION, ENTRY REQUIREMENTS & MONEY

SOURCES OF INFORMATION

The **Japan National Tourist Organization (JNTO)** publishes a wealth of free, colorful brochures and maps covering Tokyo and other cities. Free brochures and maps dealing with Tokyo and its environs include: a Tourist Map of Tokyo; "Fuji-Hakone-Kamakura-Nikko," a color brochure with text and maps of popular destinations in the vicinity of Tokyo; "The Tourist's Handbook," a phrase booklet to help foreign visitors communicate with the Japanese; and "Your Traveling Companion," with money-saving advice on traveling, lodging, and dining.

If you'd like information and literature before leaving home, contact one of the following JNTO offices: Rockefeller Plaza, 630 Fifth Ave., New York, NY 10111 (tel. 212/757-5640); 401 N. Michigan Ave., Suite 770, Chicago, IL 60611 (tel. 312/222-0874); 2121 San Jacinto St., Suite 980, Dallas, TX 75201 (tel. 214/754-1820); 360 Post St., Suite 601, San Francisco, CA 94108 (tel. 415/989-7140); and 624 S. Grand Ave., Los Angeles, CA 90017 (tel. 213/623-1952).

Other offices are located at 165 University Ave., Toronto, ON M5H 3B8, Canada (tel. 416/366-7140); 167 Regent St., London,

W.1, England (tel. 071/734-9638); and 115 Pitt St., Sydney, N.S.W. 2000, Australia (tel. 02/232-4522).

ENTRY REQUIREMENTS

DOCUMENTS Americans traveling to Japan as tourists need only valid passports to enter Japan for stays up to three months. This is a change from several years back when Americans used to be required to obtain visas for entry to Japan. Now, however, during a trial period that allows for reciprocal visa exemption, American tourists do not need visas. Note that this exemption applies only to American tourists: those who visit Japan for sightseeing, sports activities, family visits, inspection tours, meetings, or short study courses. In other words, you cannot work in Japan or engage in any remunerative activity—including teaching English (though many young people ignore the law). No extensions of stay are granted, which means that American tourists *absolutely* must leave the country after three months.

For other nationals: Australian tourists must possess a passport and a three-month visa for entry; Canadians and New Zealanders do not need visas for stays up to 90 days, while citizens of the United Kingdom and Ireland can stay up to 180 days without a visa.

If you're coming to Japan on business you must obtain a commercial visa. The period of stay granted varies depending on the case of each applicant. In addition, if you're coming to study and plan on being in the country longer than three months, you will also need a visa. For more information, contact the Japanese embassy or consulate nearest you.

If, after your arrival in Japan, you have a question regarding visas or you've been admitted on a working visa that you wish to extend, contact the **Hakozaki Immigration Office** at the Tokyo City Air Terminal (TCAT), 42-1 Nihonbashihakozaki-cho, Chuo-ku (tel. 03/3665-7157). It is less crowded than the **Tokyo Regional Immigration Bureau,** 1-3-1 Otemachi, Chiyoda-ku (tel. 03/3213-8111). The nearest subway station is Otemachi. Both are open Monday through Friday from 9:30am to 5pm. If you remain in Japan longer than three months, you must also obtain an alien registration card from your local ward office to carry with you at all times. The registration card is free but you'll need two passport-size photos.

Once in Japan, foreigners are required to carry with them *at all times* their passport or alien registration card (issued to foreigners staying longer than three months). The police generally do not stop foreigners, but if you're caught without the proper identification you'll be taken to the local police headquarters. It happened to me once and, believe me, I can think of better ways to spend an hour and a half. I had to explain in detail who I was, what I was doing in Japan, where I lived, and what I planned on doing the rest of my life. I then had to write a statement explaining how it was that I rushed out that day without my passport, apologizing and promising never to do such a thoughtless thing again. The policemen at the station were very nice and polite—they were simply doing their duty.

Note that if you intend to drive in Japan (not recommended for Tokyo, which is too crowded and too expensive), you'll need either an international or a Japanese driver's license.

CUSTOMS You can bring duty free into Japan up to 400 cigarettes or 500 grams of tobacco or 100 cigars, three bottles (760cc each) of alcoholic beverages, and two ounces of perfume. In addition to the items above, you can also bring in gifts and souvenirs whose total market value is less than ¥200,000 ($1,818).

A Word of Caution: Do not bring any pornographic material with you, including *Playboy* or *Penthouse.* It's prohibited to show pubic hair in Japan and the Japanese equivalents of these magazines have had the offensive parts blackened out. As for drugs, don't even think about it. A number of musicians have been busted at the Narita airport and are prohibited from returning to Japan. Penalties for offenders are severe and strict, though it's far from the death penalty imposed by several other Asian nations.

Upon returning to the United States, you're allowed to bring back free of duty $400 worth of goods purchased abroad; the next $1,000 worth of goods is assessed at 10% duty. If you're shipping purchases home by mail, you're allowed to send up to $50 per package duty free.

MONEY

CASH/CURRENCY The basic unit of currency in Japan is the **yen,** symbolized by **¥.** Coins come in ¥1, ¥5, ¥10, ¥50, ¥100, and ¥500. Bills come in ¥1,000, ¥5,000, and ¥10,000 denominations. Although the conversion rate varies daily and has experienced wild swings in the past years, the prices in this book are based on ¥110 to $1 U.S. In your own rough calculations of what things cost, therefore, you can generally approximate the price of items by figuring $9 to every ¥1,000. If something costs ¥5,000, for example, you know it's around $45. Keep in mind, however, that the exchange rate varies. Be sure to check the exact dollar–yen rate at the time you make your plans and just before departure.

As you can see, Japan's highest bill of ¥10,000 is worth only about $91 (I think it's time they came out with a higher denomination). And yet many Japanese pay with cash. Because the country has such a low crime rate, you can feel safe walking around with lots of money. When I worked as editor of a travel magazine in Tokyo, I was paid in cash; I often left the office for a night on the town with a whole month's salary in my purse and never feared being mugged. I certainly wasn't the only one. Because the Japanese feel so safe in their own society, sadly, they're often easy targets when they travel abroad. The only time you should be alert to possible pickpockets is when you're riding a crowded subway during rush hour.

TRAVELER'S CHECKS Traveler's checks can be exchanged for yen at most banks and generally fetch a better exchange rate than cash. Personal checks, however, are virtually useless in Japan. Even if you have an account at a Japanese bank, it costs about $36 and takes a couple of weeks to process a personal check.

CREDIT & CHARGE CARDS As an example of how adaptable the Japanese are, just five years ago credit and charge cards were accepted only at the major hotels and you'd be hard-pressed to find a restaurant that would accept anything other than cash, even at expensive kaiseki restaurants where meals averaged more than $182.

Nowadays, virtually all hotels, department stores, tourist shops, and many restaurants generally accept such credit and charge cards as American Express, MasterCard, and Visa, as well as such Japanese credit cards as JCB. Shops and restaurants accepting credit and charge cards usually post which cards they accept at their front door. However, some establishments may be reluctant to accept cards for

THE JAPANESE YEN

For American Readers At this writing $1 = approximately ¥110 (or ¥10 = 9.1¢), and this was the rate of exchange used to calculate the dollar values given in this chapter.

For British Readers At this writing £1 = approximately ¥170 (or ¥10 = 5.8p), and this was the rate of exchange used to calculate the pound values in the table below.

Note The rates given here fluctuate from time to time and may not be the same when you travel to Japan. Therefore this table should be used only as a guide:

¥	U.S.$	U.K.£	¥	U.S.$	U.K.£
10	.09	.06	1,500	13.64	8.82
25	.23	.15	2,000	18.18	11.76
50	.45	.29	2,500	22.73	14.71
75	.68	.44	3,000	27.27	17.65
100	.91	.59	4,000	36.36	23.53
200	1.82	1.18	5,000	45.45	29.41
300	2.73	1.76	6,000	54.55	35.29
400	3.64	2.35	7,000	63.64	41.18
500	4.55	2.94	8,000	72.73	47.06
600	5.45	3.53	9,000	81.82	52.94
700	6.36	4.12	10,000	90.91	58.82
800	7.27	4.71	15,000	136.36	88.24
900	8.18	5.29	20,000	181.82	117.65
1,000	9.09	5.88	25,000	227.27	147.06

small purchases. In addition, note that the majority of Tokyo's smaller businesses, including noodle shops, fast-food joints, and ma-and-pa establishments, do not accept credit or charge cards.

WHAT WILL IT COST?

No doubt you've heard horror stories about how expensive Japan can be. The truth is, hardly anyone comes to Japan without suffering an initial shock, simply because almost everything is shockingly expensive. With the dramatic fall of the dollar against the yen, Tokyo has emerged as one of the most costly cities in the world if you're converting dollars, even though prices have remained fairly stable.

During your first few days in the capital city, money will seem to flow out of your pockets like water. Almost everyone panics initially (I've seen it happen repeatedly), but then slowly comes the realization that values are different here and that all it takes is a bit of readjustment in thinking and in habits.

The secret is to live and eat much as the Japanese do. This book will help you do exactly that, and by exercising a little caution of your own, you should be able to cut down needless expenses and learn more about Japan in the process.

And how much should you expect to spend every day for food and lodging in Tokyo? If you are willing to stay in budget accommodations and eat inexpensive Japanese food, you can live in Tokyo on

¥10,000 ($91) a day. It's best, however, if you can budget at least ¥15,000 ($136) a day, plus extra for occasional splurges, shopping, and emergencies. Just one evening out in Tokyo can easily cost ¥10,000 to ¥15,000 ($91 to $136) in eating and drinking alone.

Thus a lot depends on you. I've covered rock-bottom places, but I haven't neglected the finest and most expensive establishments—after all, even though you may flinch at spending $200 on a meal, many such restaurants do exist and you may be interested in reading about them.

Keep in mind that although every effort was made to be as accurate as possible, prices do change—which means that they go up. Always inquire about prices before checking into a hotel to avoid embarrassment when it comes time to pay the bill.

CUTTING EXPENSES If you're on a budget, avoid eating breakfast at your hotel. **Coffee shops** are plentiful in Tokyo and offer what is called "morning service" until about 10am, which generally consists of a cup of coffee, a small salad, a boiled egg, and the thickest slice of toast you'll ever see for about ¥450 ($4.10). That's a real bargain when you consider that just one cup of coffee usually costs ¥300 to ¥500 ($2.75 to $4.55) and sometimes as much as ¥1,500 ($13.65) in the best hotels.

Coffee is considered somewhat of a luxury, and most Japanese are astonished at the thought of drinking four or five cups a day. For the most part, the bottomless cup is not a concept in Japan. Thus, if you're addicted to the stuff, you can save money by purchasing instant coffee and drinking it in your hotel room. Most hotels and inns in Japan provide a Thermos of hot water or a heater for water in guest rooms. Jars of instant coffee are available at all grocery stores and convenience shops, but if you like powdered cream and sugar as well, you might want to purchase individual packets of coffee that combine cream and sugar.

By the way, though Japanese green tea is often provided in your room, black tea is not. So if you want your tea black, then you'd be wise to purchase black tea bags in convenience stores. Both teas and coffee (usually about ¥110/$1 per can) are available from ubiquitous vending machines, hot or cold, with sugar and cream or without, but unless you read katakana, you'll be hard-pressed to know what you're getting.

Eat your biggest meal at **lunch.** Many restaurants offer a daily fixed-price lunch, called a *teishoku,* at a fraction of what the fixed-price dinners might be. Usually ranging in price from ¥700 to ¥1,500 ($6.35 to $13.65), they're generally available from 11 or 11:30am to 2 or 3pm. A Japanese teishoku will often include the main course (such as tempura, grilled fish, or the specialty of the house), soup, pickled vegetables, rice, and tea, while the fixed-price menu in a Western-style restaurant usually consists of an entree, salad, bread, and coffee.

If you really want to save money, you can avoid restaurants altogether. Japan is one of the most accomplished countries in the world when it comes to prepared foods. The ***obento*** is a lunchbox with a complete meal, commonly sold on express trains, at train stations, and in neighborhood kiosks. Department stores also have food floors, usually in the basement, with counters of take-out foods. More information on inexpensive meals and suggestions are given in Chapter 5, "Tokyo Dining."

Other ways to save money include staying in simple, Japanese-style accommodations and using public transportation instead of taxis. And if you plan on doing much travel outside Tokyo, you'd be wise to purchase a **Japan Rail Pass.** Not only does it save you the hassle of buying a ticket each time you board a train, but it's also the most economical way to travel. The Japan Rail Pass is available only to foreigners visiting Japan as a tourist, and can be purchased only outside Japan. *You cannot buy the Japan Rail Pass once you're in Japan.* You can purchase the pass from an authorized travel agent or from Japan Airlines. Rates start at ¥27,800 ($253) for ordinary coach class for a 7-day pass, and passes for 14 days, 21 days, and for a first-class Green Car are also available.

WHAT THINGS COST IN TOKYO	U.S. $
Taxi from Narita airport to city center	181.80
Subway from Akasaka to Roppongi	1.25
Local telephone call	.09
Double room at the Imperial Hotel (deluxe)	354.50
Double room at the Gajoen Kanko Hotel (moderate)	200.00
Double room at the Ryokan Mikawaya Bekkan (budget)	95.50
Lunch for one at Gonin Byakusho (moderate)	9.10
Lunch for one at Genrokusushi (budget)	4.55
Dinner for one, without drinks, at Inakaya (deluxe)	100.00
Dinner for one, without drinks, at Seiyo Hiroba (moderate)	50.00
Dinner for one, without drinks, at Irohanihoheto (budget)	13.65
Glass of beer	4.55
Coca-Cola	3.65
Cup of coffee	4.55
Roll of ASA 100 Fujichrome film, 36 exposures	5.90
Admission to Tokyo National Museum	3.65
Movie ticket	15.55
Theater ticket to Kabuki	18.20

2. WHEN TO GO — CLIMATE, HOLIDAYS & EVENTS

Although Tokyo's busiest foreign-tourist season is in summer, the city lends itself to visiting year-round. In fact, when the rest of Japan is besieged with vacationing Japanese at the beginning of May and in August, Tokyo is usually blissfully empty, as Tokyoites pour out of the city to the countryside. Keep in mind, however, that popular tourist destinations outside Tokyo such as Nikko, Kamakura, and Hakone will be jam-packed on major holidays, especially the so-called Golden Week (April 29 to May 5).

THE CLIMATE

The Japanese are very proud of the fact that Japan has four distinct seasons and seem astonished to learn that there are other countries with the same.

Summer, which begins in June, is heralded by the rainy season, which usually lasts from about mid-June to mid-July in Tokyo. July has, on the average, 10 rainy days, but even though it doesn't rain every day umbrellas are imperative. When the rain finally stops, it gets unbearably hot and humid through August—you might want to head for Hakone for a bit of fresh air. The end of August and September is typhoon season, though most storms stay out at sea and vent their fury on land only as thunderstorms.

Autumn, which lasts from September through November, is one of the best times to visit Japan. The days are pleasant and slightly cool, the skies are a brilliant blue, and the maples turn scarlet.

Winter lasts from about December to March in Tokyo, with days that are generally clear and cold with extremely low humidity. Tokyo doesn't get much snow, but it can snow, so be prepared. I remember one winter when it snowed a sloshy mush through March. In any case, the temperature is usually above freezing.

Spring is ushered in with a magnificent fanfare of plum and cherry blossoms in March and April, an exquisite time of year when all of Japan is set ablaze in whites and pinks. The blossoms themselves last only a few days, symbolizing to the Japanese the fragile nature of beauty and life itself.

Tokyo's Average Daytime Temperatures & Rainfall

	Jan	Feb	Mar	Apr	May	June	July	Aug	Sept	Oct	Nov	Dec
Temp. (°F)	37	39	45	54	62	70	77	79	73	62	51	41
Temp. (°C)	3	4	7	13	17	21	25	26	23	17	11	5
Days of Rain	4.3	6.1	8.9	10	9.6	12.1	10	8.2	10.9	8.9	6.4	3.8

HOLIDAYS

National holidays in Japan are January 1 (*New Year's Day*), January 15 (*Adults' Day*), February 11 (*National Foundation Day*), March 20 or 21 (*Vernal Equinox Day*), April 29 (*Greenery Day*), May 3 (*Constitution Memorial Day*), May 5 (*Children's Day*), September 15 (*Respect-for-the-Aged Day*), September 23 or 24 (*Autumn Equinox Day*), October 10 (*Health and Sports Day*), November 3 (*Culture Day*), November 23 (*Labor Thanksgiving Day*), and

December 23 (*Emperor's Birthday*). When a national holiday falls on a Sunday, the following Monday becomes a holiday.

The most important holidays for the Japanese are at New Year's, Golden Week (April 29 to May 5), and the O'bon Festival time, in mid-July or mid-August. Since trains, airports, and accommodations are crowded at this time, try to avoid traveling during these peak times. Tokyo is a good place to be during the holidays, since many Tokyoites leave for their hometowns or vacations.

Although government offices and some businesses will be closed on public holidays, restaurants and most stores remain open. The exception is during the New Year's celebration from January 1 to 3, when almost all restaurants, public and private offices, and stores close up shop; during that time you'll have to dine in hotels.

Major museums remain open during public holidays. If a public holiday falls on a Monday (when most museums are closed), most museums will remain open, but will close instead the following day, on Tuesday. Note that privately owned museums, such as art museums or special-interest museums, generally close on public holidays. To avoid disappointment, call beforehand.

TOKYO CALENDAR OF EVENTS

Because Japan has two major religions, Shintoism and Buddhism, it celebrates festivals throughout the year. Every major shrine and temple in the land observes at least one annual festival, with events that might include traditional dances, archery, or colorful processions when portable shrines are carried through the streets by chanting groups dressed in traditional costumes.

Below are major festivals and events held in Tokyo and cities close by. However, in Tokyo alone there are so many small, neighborhood festivals that you could probably visit one almost every week of the year. For more information consult the *Tokyo Journal* or *Tokyo City Guide,* two publications that report on current happenings in the capital city.

JANUARY

- ☐ **New Year's Day,** nationwide. The "festival of the festivals," the most important national holiday in Japan. Like Christmas in the West, it's a time of family reunions and a time when friends gather to drink sake and eat special New Year's dishes. Streets and homes are decorated with straw ropes and pine or plum branches. Because the Japanese spend this holiday with their families, and almost all businesses, restaurants, and shops close down, it's not a particularly rewarding time of the year for foreigners to visit. January 1.
- ☐ **Dezomeshiki (New Year's Parade of Firemen),** on Harumi Chuo Dori in Tokyo. This annual event features agile firemen in traditional costumes who prove their worth with acrobatic stunts atop tall bamboo ladders. You'd certainly feel safe at the thought of being rescued by one of them. January 6.
- ☐ **Adults' Day,** nationwide. A national holiday in Japan that

honors young people who have reached the age of 20, when they are allowed to vote, drink alcohol, and assume other responsibilities. Young women wear kimonos. At Meiji Shrine, there's a traditional archery ceremony. January 15.

FEBRUARY

- ☐ **Setsubun (Bean-Throwing Festival),** held at leading temples throughout Japan. This festival celebrates the last day of winter according to the lunar calendar. People throng to temples to participate in the traditional ceremony of throwing beans to drive away imaginary devils. February 3 or 4.
- ☐ **Hari-kuyoo,** Awashimado, near Sensoji Temple in Asakusa. This unique event is considered an advantageous time for women to bring broken pins and needles to Awashimado, a custom since the Edo Period. February 8.
- ☐ **National Foundation Day.** A national holiday. February 11.

MARCH

- ☐ **Hinamatsuri (Doll Festival).** Observed throughout Japan in honor of young girls, to wish them a future of happiness. In homes where there are girls, dolls dressed in ancient costumes representing the emperor, empress, and dignitaries are set up on a tier of shelves along with miniature household articles. Many hotels also showcase doll displays. March 3.
- ☐ **Vernal Equinox Day.** A national holiday, it's celebrated throughout the week by Buddhist temples that hold ceremonies to pray for the departed. March 20 or 21.

APRIL

✪ ***CHERRY BLOSSOM SEASON*** *The bursting forth of cherry blossoms represents the birth of spring for Tokyoites. Popular cherry-viewing spots in Tokyo include Ueno Park, Yasukuni Shrine, Aoyama Bochi Cemetery, and the moat encircling the Imperial Palace. Japanese company employees gather en masse under the trees to drink sake, eat, and be merry. A good opportunity to observe the Japanese at play.*

Where: *Ueno Park is Tokyo's most popular cherry-viewing spot.* ***When:*** *Early to Mid-April.* ***How:*** *Go in early evening and stroll past businessmen celebrating spring by drinking and eating. Who knows, you may be asked to join in the merriment.*

- ☐ **Buddha's Birthday,** nationwide. Ceremonies are held at all Buddhist temples, where a small image of Buddha is displayed and doused with a sweet tea called amacha in an act of devotion. April 8.
- ☐ **Jibeta Matsuri,** Kanayama Shrine in Kawasaki. This festival extols the joys of sex and features a parade of giant phalluses. Needless to say, this is not your average festival, and you can get some unusual photographs here. Mid-April.
- ☐ **Kamakura Matsuri,** Tsurugaoka Hachimangu Shrine in Kamakura. Honors heroes from the past, including Yoritomo Minamoto, who made Kamakura his shogunate capital back in

1192. Highlights are horseback archery (truly spectacular to watch), a parade of portable shrines, and sacred dances. Second to third Sunday in April.

- ☐ **Yayoi Matsuri,** Futarasan Shrine in Nikko. This festival features a parade of gaily decorated floats. April 16 and 17.
- ☐ **Greenery Day.** A national holiday, marking the birthday of Japan's former emperor Hirohito, who died in January 1989 and was known for his love of nature. April 29.
- ☐ **Golden Week.** A major holiday period throughout Japan and one of the most popular times for family vacations. It's a crowded time to travel, making reservations a must. Because so many factories and businesses close during the week, this is said to be the best time of year for a clear view of the city and beyond from atop Tokyo Tower. April 29 to May 5.

MAY

- ☐ **Constitution Memorial Day.** A national holiday. May 3.
- ☐ **Children's Day.** A national holiday, this festival honors young boys. Throughout Japan colorful streamers of carp are flown from poles to symbolize perseverance and strength, considered desirable attributes for young boys. May 5.
- ☐ **Kanda Festival,** Kanda Myojin Shrine in Tokyo. Held every other year in odd-numbered years, it features dozens of portable shrines paraded through the district and a tea ceremony. Saturday and Sunday closest to May 15.
- ☐ **Grand Festival of Toshogu Shrine,** in Nikko. One of Nikko's biggest spectacles, it commemorates the day in 1617 when Ieyasu Tokugawa's remains were brought to his mausoleum in Nikko, accompanied by 1,000 people. This festival re-creates the drama with more than 1,000 armor-clad men escorting three palanquins through the streets. May 17 and 18.

✪ ***SANJA MATSURI*** *This is one of Tokyo's best-known festivals, and features a parade of 100 portable shrines carried through the streets of Asakusa on the shoulders of men and women dressed in traditional garb.*

Where: *Asakusa Shrine and Sensoji Temple, Asakusa.* ***When:*** *Third Saturday and Sunday in May.* ***How:*** *This festival can get quite crowded, but the best viewing spot for the parade is on Nakamise Dori.*

JUNE

- ☐ **Sanno Festival,** Hie Shrine in Tokyo. This festival first began in the Edo Period (1603–1867) and features the usual portable shrines transported through the busy streets of the Akasaka district. June 10 to 16.

JULY

- ☐ **Ueki Ichi (Potted Plant Fair),** on the streets around Fuji Sengen Shrine near Asakusa on the Ginza subway line. On display are different kinds of potted plants and bonsai (miniature dwarf trees), as well as a miniature Mt. Fuji symbolizing the opening of the official climbing season. July 1.
- ☐ **Tanabata (Star Festival).** Celebrated throughout Japan, it's

based on a myth of two stars named Vega and Altair, which represent a weaver and a shepherd who are allowed to meet only once a year on this day. If the sky is cloudy, however, the celestial lovers cannot meet but must wait until the next year. July 7.

- ☐ **Hozuki Ichi (Ground Cherry Pod Fair),** on the grounds of Asakusa's Sensoji Temple in Tokyo. It features hundreds of street stalls selling ground cherry pods and colorful wind bells. July 9 and 10.
- ☐ **Obon Festival,** nationwide. A festival in memory of dead ancestors, who, according to Buddhist belief, revisit the world during this period. Obon Odori folk dances are held in neighborhoods everywhere. Many Japanese return to their hometowns for the event, especially if a member of the family has died recently. As one Japanese, whose grandmother had died a few months before, told me, "I have to go back to my hometown—it's my grandmother's first Obon." Mid-July or mid-August.

✪ ***HANABI TAIKAI (FIREWORKS DISPLAY)*** *A huge fireworks display over the Sumida River in Asakusa, this is the capital city's largest, and is great fun.*

Where: *Along the Sumida River along the Sumida Koen Park, near the Kototoibashi and Komagatabashi bridges.* ***When:*** *Last Saturday of July or early August.* ***How:*** *Get there early, and spread a blanket along the banks of the Sumida River.*

AUGUST

- ☐ **Waraku Odori,** in Nikko. This is one of the most popular events for folk dances, with thousands of people dancing to the accompaniment of music. August 5 and 6.

SEPTEMBER

- ☐ **Respect-for-the-Aged Day.** A national holiday. September 15.
- ☐ **Yabusame (Horseback Archery),** Tsurugaoka Hachimangu Shrine in Kamakura. The archery performances by riders on horseback recall the days of the samurai. September 16.
- ☐ **Akibasho (Autumn Sumo Match),** at the Kokugikan. The last sumo match of the year. Mid-September.
- ☐ **Autumnal Equinox Day.** A national holiday. September 23 or 24.

OCTOBER

- ☐ **Health-Sports Day.** A national holiday. October 10.
- ☐ **Oeshiki Festival,** Hommonji Temple. This is the largest of Tokyo's commemorative services held for Nichiren (1222–82), a Buddhist leader. Followers march toward Hommonji Temple carrying large lanterns decorated with paper flowers. October 11 to 13.
- ☐ **Autumn Festival of Toshogu Shrine,** Toshogu Shrine in Nikko. Armor-clad parishioners escort a sacred portable shrine. October 17.

NOVEMBER

- ☐ **Culture Day.** A national holiday. November 3.
- ☐ **Daimyo Gyoretsu,** in Hakone. On this day the old Tokaido Highway that used to link Kyoto and Tokyo comes alive again with a long parade that is a faithful reproduction of a feudal lord's procession in the olden days. November 3.
- ☐ **Shichi-go-san (Seven-Five-Three).** An event held throughout Japan in honor of children who have reached the ages of 3, 5, and 7. On this day they are taken to shrines by their elders to express thanks and pray for their future; especially Meiji and Asakusa Shrines. November 15.
- ☐ **Tori-no-Ichi (Rake Fair),** Otori Shrine in Asakusa. This fair features stalls selling rakes lavishly decorated with paper and cloth that are thought to bring good luck and fortune. The date, based on the lunar calendar, changes each year. Mid-November.
- ☐ **Labor Thanksgiving Day.** A national holiday. November 23.

DECEMBER

- ☐ **Hagoita-Ichi (Battledore Fair).** Popular since Japan's feudal days, this fair features decorated paddles of all types and sizes. Most have designs of Kabuki actors, images made by pasting together wadded silk and brocade, and make great souvenirs and gifts. December 17 to 19.
- ☐ **Emperor's Birthday,** nationwide. The birthday of Akihito, Japan's 125th emperor, is a national holiday. December 23.
- ☐ **New Year's Eve,** nationwide. At midnight many temples ring huge bells 108 times to signal the end of the old year and the beginning of the new. Many families throng to the temples and shrines at midnight to usher in the coming year. In Tokyo, Meiji Shrine is the place to be for this popular family celebration. December 31.

3. HEALTH & INSURANCE

HEALTH PREPARATIONS You don't need any inoculations for entry to Japan. As for drug prescriptions, they can be filled at Japanese pharmacies, but it's always better to bring along extra supplies of special medications, especially if you prefer name brands from your own country.

Another consideration for visitors flying to Tokyo, especially on long flights from North America, is the effects of jet lag. For some reason, flying west has slightly less effect than flying east, which means that the hardest flight to overcome is the journey from Japan back to North America.

To minimize the adverse effects of jet lag—primarily fatigue and slow adjustment to your new time zone—refrain from smoking and consumption of alcohol and carbonated beverages during the flight. In addition, eat light meals high in vegetable and cereal content the day before, during, and after your flight. During the flight, exercise your body by walking around the cabin every so often and by flexing your arms, hands, legs, and feet. It also helps to set your watch (and your mental clock) to the time zone of your destination as soon as you board the plane.

Once you reach Tokyo, schedule your first day according to your new time zone. Put in a normal day, even if you're tired. Go for a walk in the sunlight, and once in your hotel, turn on the lights as brightly as you can until it's time to go to bed in the evening. If you follow these instructions, your body should be back to normal within two days.

INSURANCE Medical and hospital services are not free in Japan and can end up being quite expensive. Before leaving home, therefore, you'd be wise to check with your health-insurance company as to whether you are covered for a trip to Japan. If not, you may wish to take out a short-term traveler's medical policy that covers medical costs and emergencies.

You may also want to take extra precautions with your possessions. Is your camera or video equipment insured anywhere in the world through your home insurance? Is your home insured against theft or loss if you're gone longer than a month (some insurance companies will cover theft of an unoccuppied home only for a certain length of time)? If you're not adequately covered, you may wish to purchase an extra policy to cover losses.

4. WHAT TO PACK

I've racked my brain trying to come up with something the traveler might need that is unavailable in Japan, and have finally given up. It seems that virtually everything is available.

You should bring all prescription medicines with you. In addition, you will need a good pair of walking shoes (if your feet are bigger than tiny you may not find shoes that fit in Japan). Keep in mind, too, that because you have to remove your shoes to enter Japanese homes, shrines, inns, and sometimes even museums, you should pack a pair that's easy to slip on and off. And since you may be walking around in stocking feet, bring socks without holes so that you won't be embarrassed among the meticulously groomed Japanese.

Because the electricity in Tokyo—100 volts AC, 50 cycles—is close to that in the United States, you can use many American appliances, such as radios or hairdryers, in Japan. For sensitive equipment, either have it adjusted or use battery-run equipment.

Items you will need are readily available. A folding umbrella is a good idea, especially if you're coming in June or July. It's also a good idea to carry a supply of pocket tissues since most public restrooms don't have toilet paper. You can pick up pocket tissues at newspaper stands near and in train stations. In the summer when the weather is hot and humid, you'll see women walking around with wet cotton handkerchiefs that they use to wipe their faces. Try it—it helps keep you cooler.

Although most hotels and Japanese-style inns provide towels, soap, washcloths, toothbrushes, toothpaste, and a cotton yukata, some of the budget-priced inns do not. If you're traveling on a budget, you may need to supply these items yourself. Many hotels and inns also provide a Thermos of hot water or a water heater as well as green tea. Remember that coffee and black tea addicts can save money by buying instant coffee or tea bags and drinking a morning cup in their rooms.

Although it might seem superfluous to say this, pack lightly. Struggling through crowded train stations with big bags is no fun, and stations often consist of multitudes of stairways and overhead and underground passageways. If you're going on a weekend excursion outside Tokyo, it might be wise to leave your big suitcase at your Tokyo hotel and travel to your destination with only a light bag.

5. TIPS FOR THE DISABLED, SENIORS, SINGLES, FAMILIES & STUDENTS

FOR THE DISABLED Tokyo can be a nightmare for the disabled. Most subways are accessible only by stairs, and crowds on many city sidewalks can be so jam-packed that getting around on crutches or in a wheelchair is exceedingly difficult. Japan has a very advanced system when it comes to facilities for the blind. Throughout subway stations and on many major sidewalks throughout Tokyo and other cities, there are raised dots and lines on the ground to guide blind people at intersections and to subway platforms. In some cities, street lights chime a certain theme when the signal turns green. Even Japanese yen notes are identified by a slightly raised circle—the ¥1,000 note has one circle in a corner, while the ¥10,000 note has two. And finally, many elevators have floors indicated in braille.

FOR SENIORS Senior citizens do not receive discounts in Japan for admission fees to museums and other expenses.

FOR SINGLE TRAVELERS Traveling alone to Tokyo and the rest of Japan poses no difficulty, even for women. The main obstacle, however, is expense, since the price of accommodations is lower for couples and groups. Single travelers, therefore, should do what traveling businessmen do, which is to stay at so-called business hotels which cater almost exclusively to solo travelers with a large number of single rooms.

FOR FAMILIES The Japanese are very fond of children, so that traveling with them in Japan can be a wonderful experience. The usual reserve of the Japanese just seems to melt in the face of children (especially if yours happen to be blond or red-headed, obviously a novelty). When I traveled with my daughter we were often invited into the homes of complete strangers, which never happened when I was alone. Children may not be very fond of Japanese foods like sushi, but my daughter readily ate soba and udon noodles, which are close enough to spaghetti (and very inexpensive). Many restaurants in department stores have children's menus. Western foods, like McDonald's and Kentucky Fried Chicken, are everywhere.

Children 6 to 11 years old generally pay half price for transportation and admission fees. Children under 6 are generally free of charge. In fact, if your under-6-year-old sleeps with you (it is common practice for children to sleep with their mother in Japan—I had a friend who slept with her mother until the age of 12) and partakes of your meal, you probably won't be charged for him or her at a ryokan or minshuku. However, it's always prudent to ask in advance.

The safety of Japan make it so easy to travel with children. You don't need to worry about shootings, kidnappings, or a lot of weirdos. Still, you will need to plan your itinerary with care. To avoid crowds, visit tourist sights on weekdays. Never travel on city transportation during rush hour or on the trains during popular public holidays. Many of the major hotels provide babysitting services, although they are almost prohibitively expensive. Expect to fork over about $70 for two hours of sitting.

FOR STUDENTS Students sometimes receive discounts at museums, though occasionally discounts are available only to students enrolled in Japanese schools and discounted prices are often never displayed in English. Your best bet is to bring along an International Student Identity Card (ISIC; you can apply for one at your university), along with your university student ID. Show these at the ticket windows of museums to see whether there are student discounts.

6. GETTING THERE

BY PLANE

THE MAJOR AIRLINES In choosing which airline to fly, you will want to consider such factors as safety, ticket price, available destinations and departure points, in-flight service (there's nothing quite so frustrating as being stuck in a small space for 12 hours or more with inadequate service), and even mileage programs. Here is a partial list of carriers you may want to consider:

Northwest Airlines (tel. toll free 800/447-4747) is the largest American carrier into Japan, offering the traveler a wide choice of destinations as well as departure points. Ranked fourth worldwide in terms of overall passenger volume, Northwest boarded a million passengers at Tokyo's Narita airport alone in 1992. Northwest services Tokyo from Honolulu, Los Angeles, San Francisco, Seattle, Detroit, New York, and Chicago in North America. Japan-bound flights also depart from Sydney, Singapore, Manila, Bangkok, Taipei, Seoul, Beijing, Shanghai, Guam, Saipan, and Hong Kong. The fact that Northwest flies to so many destinations in Asia makes coordinating travel plans to go on to, say, Hong Kong or Beijing, simple, and the wide range of departure points makes it easy to get to Asia from wherever you start off.

As the longest-operating U.S. carrier in the Pacific (since 1947), Northwest has tailored its services to meet the specific needs of tourists and business travelers to Asian destinations. Flight attendants and on-board service to Japan are based on traditional Japanese cuisine and style, including starting out with oshibori, the Japanese hot steaming towels, with which to refresh yourself. Northwest's service has attracted even the hard-to-please Japanese; some 65% of its passengers out of Japan and 55% out of the United States are Japanese.

One of the benefits of flying Northwest—especially important to the business traveler—is the carrier's strong on-time record. Northwest has been the number one on-time airline in the United States since 1990 (according to the U.S. Department of Transportation).

You'll appreciate the extra on-board services, as flying time to Tokyo is about 12 hours from Los Angeles and 13½ hours from Chicago or New York. Service is important on these long hauls, especially if you're flying with children. Northwest provides bassinets (reserve in advance), warms baby bottles, and stocks baby food on all international flights at no extra charge.

Some people I know fly Northwest simply for its great mileage program, WorldPerks, which has one of the lowest requirements for free trips. There's no fee to enroll and with your first 20,000 miles you earn a free trip within the continental United States (if you fly from the States) or within Asia on Northwest's extensive route system. Round-trip mileage Los Angeles to Tokyo is 12,000 miles, while New York to Tokyo, at 18,000, miles is almost a free trip. If you fly executive or first class you are awarded bonuses of 25% and 50%, respectively. So with one first-class Los Angeles–Tokyo round-trip or one New York–Tokyo executive class round-trip you earn one free flight anywhere in the continental United States or Asia. You can also earn mileage by using MCI as your long-distance telephone service, staying at select hotels, renting cars, or using the WorldPerks Visa card. Northwest has a global alliance with KLM Royal Dutch Airlines, so you can earn mileage on both and use your WorldPerks awards on either carrier. The two airlines even earn offer an around-the-world ticket. Check with Northwest WorldPerks (tel. toll free 800/447-3757) for details.

All Nippon Airways (tel. toll free 800/235-3663) is Japan's largest domestic carrier flying more people annually (some 33 million) than any other Japanese airline. It's also the eighth-largest passenger carrier worldwide. ANA operates more than 400 flights a day on 72 domestic routes connecting around 30 major cities in Japan, making it *the* airline to fly within Japan. In 1986 Japan Airlines' monopoly on Japanese airlines' overseas routes was challenged when ANA began international flights. Although 40 years old, ANA was little known outside of Japan before 1986, so they've had to try harder to please—and they do. ANA now offers 78 round-trip flights a week to 20 cities in 14 countries. ANA has round-trip service from Japan to Washington, D.C., New York, Los Angeles, Honolulu, and Orlando in the United States.

American Airlines (tel. toll free 800/433-7300) has daily flights to Tokyo from Dallas, Seattle, or San Jose, Calif.

China Airlines (tel. toll free 800/227-5118) has one flight a day on Monday, Tuesday, Wednesday, Friday, and Saturday from Honolulu to Tokyo.

Continental Airlines (tel. toll free 800/231-0856) flies to Tokyo, Fukuoka, Sendai, Sapporo, and Nagoya in Japan. However, the only direct flight is from Honolulu to Tokyo. The other flights are routed through Guam, Continental's Asian hub, so to fly Los Angeles–Nagoya, for example, you fly to Honolulu, then to Guam, and finally to Nagoya.

Delta Airlines (tel. toll free 800/241-4141) services Tokyo with direct daily flights from Los Angeles and Portland, Ore.

Japan Airlines (tel. toll free 800/525-3663), Japan's flagship carrier, is noted for its excellent service. JAL flies to Tokyo from New York, Chicago, Los Angeles, San Francisco, Atlanta, Vancouver, Washington, D.C., and Honolulu in North America. JAL also operates JALTOURS, with 23 different tour packages to Japan. Contact JAL or your travel agent for more details.

Korean Air (tel. toll free 800/438-5000) has daily flights from

Los Angeles to Tokyo. Korean also flies from Los Angeles to Seoul and from Seoul to Osaka, Nagoya, Fukuoka, Okayama, and Oita. Though it's not convenient to fly to Seoul to reach Fukuoka, for example, you might want to continue your trip onward to Seoul from Fukuoka.

Singapore Airlines (tel. toll free 800/742-3333) is one of the Asian airlines which, together with Thai Airways International (see below), is noted for its smiling service and winsome cabin attendants. Singapore has daily flights departing from Los Angeles to Tokyo. The flight continues on to Singapore.

Thai Airways International (tel. toll free 800/426-5204) has one flight a day from Los Angeles to Tokyo on Monday, Wednesday, Thursday, and Saturday. The flight continues on to Bangkok.

United Airlines (tel. toll free 800/241-6522) flies nonstop from Chicago and New York to Tokyo daily. United also has a good mileage program called Mileage Plus, with which you can earn a U.S. ticket with 20,000 miles. Contact United for details.

REGULAR AIRFARES Regardless of how you buy your ticket, there are certain regulations you should know about airfare pricing. While first-class, business-class, and basic-economy fares (those with no restrictions) are the same all year round to Japan, most airlines charge different APEX (Advance Purchase Excursion) fares depending on the season. Peak season, usually during the summer months, is the most expensive; basic season, during the winter, offers the lowest fares; and shoulder seasons are in between—both price- and timewise. Regardless of the season, weekend APEX fares are slightly higher than for flights during the week.

Listed below are some of the fare options from New York, Chicago, and the West Coast as of the fall of 1993. Be sure to contact the airlines or your travel agent for an update on prices once you've decided on your exact travel plans.

First Class All airlines provide some luxuries to their first-class passengers. Northwest's royal treatment begins with special check-in and luggage handling and complimentary entrance to WorldClub lounges located in airports in 24 cities. WorldClub service representatives are on duty to provide boarding passes, seat assignments, flight information, and reservations. Amenities include complimentary beverages, cocktails, and snacks; business machines and conference rooms; flight monitors; and newspapers, magazines, television, and credit-card telephones. The comfortable seating here sure beats hanging around on airport benches. On board the plane you'll have a comfortable, electronically operated seat that inclines to a 60° angle, and you'll be offered slippers for in-flight wear. Some flights even have a personal six-inch video screen built into the seat armrest. In addition to complimentary champagne and other alcoholic beverages, travel kits, and the use of headphones, you will be offered a choice of five entrees of Western- or Japanese-style cuisine. Northwest's first-class round-trip fares to Tokyo are $6,432 from New York, $6,274 from Chicago, and $5,058 from Seattle, San Francisco, or Los Angeles.

Business Class Most carriers offer a separate business class. Northwest's business class offers complimentary entrance, including the easy check-in, to the WorldClub lounges described above. Other perks include seats that recline 40°; complimentary champagne, cocktails, and wine; free use of headphones; and a complimentary

FROMMER'S SMART TRAVELER: AIRFARES

1. Shop all the airlines that fly to your destination.
2. Keep calling the airlines, since the availability of cheap seats changes daily. As the departure nears, you might be able to obtain a seat at a discount, since an airline would rather sell a seat than have it empty.
3. Read the advertisements of newspaper travel sections—they often offer special deals and packages.
4. You can also save money by buying your ticket as early as possible, since the lowest fares, such as APEX (Advance Purchase Excursion), usually require 30 days' advance purchase.
5. Ask whether there's a difference in price if you fly on a weekday—weekday flights are sometimes cheaper than weekend flights.
6. Travel off-season if you're trying to save money, since APEX and economy seats often cost less during the off-season.

travel kit. Some flights also offer personal videos you can watch from your own seat. Meals feature Western and Japanese cuisine. For health-conscious passengers, there's a special low-calorie menu. Northwest's business-class round-trip fares to Tokyo are $3,522 from New York, $3,370 from Chicago, and $2,664 from Seattle, Los Angeles, or San Francisco.

Economy Class An example of economy-class round-trip fares to Tokyo are Northwest's tickets costing $2,788 from New York and Chicago, and $2,038 from Seattle, Los Angeles, or San Francisco.

APEX [Advance Purchase Excursion] Fares You can cut the cost of your flight to Japan by purchasing your ticket in advance and complying with certain restrictions. Reservations, ticketing, and payment for the APEX fare usually must be completed no later than 21 days before departure, but rules vary depending on the airline. There's a minimum time you can stay in Japan, usually one or two weeks; the maximum stay may be up to six months. Rates vary according to season, with peak-season rates in effect June through August. APEX round-trip fares to Tokyo range from as high as $2,880 for a flight out of New York on a weekend in the summer to as low as $1,000 from the West Coast on a weekday in the winter.

OTHER GOOD-VALUE CHOICES Certainly the best strategy for securing the lowest airfare is to shop around. Consult the travel sections of major newspapers, especially those on the West Coast, since they often carry advertisements for low fares.

There are also companies that provide discounted tickets—as much as 50% less than the regular economy fare and about 30% less than the APEX fare. Through them you can buy your ticket well in advance, or, if you're lucky, even at the last minute. Among firms that deal with Japan are **Japan Associates Travel,** 2000 17th St. NW, Washington, DC 20009 (tel. 202/939-8853); and **Japan Express Travel,** 1150 17th St. NW, Suite 408, Washington, DC 20036 (tel.

202/347-7730). In addition, consolidators like **C. L. Thomson Express International** in San Francisco and **CNH International** in Los Angeles also sell discounted tickets, but only through travel agents.

Finally, many airlines and tour operators also offer occasional promotional fares with tight restrictions as well as package tours, which might be the cheapest way to go since packages usually include hotels, transfers, some meals, and more. (See "Package Tours," below, for more information.)

A WARNING Remember that all fares, rules, and regulations are subject to change. Be sure to contact your travel agent or the airlines for current information.

BY TRAIN

If Tokyo is your destination, it's unlikely that you'll arrive elsewhere in Japan, especially since its main international airport is outside Tokyo. However, in the unlikely event that you do land at Osaka's international airport because of a conference or business trip, Tokyo is easily reached from Osaka by train. The Shinkansen bullet train connects Tokyo with Osaka in about three hours and costs ¥13,480 ($122.55) one-way. Once in Tokyo, you'll arrive at Tokyo Station in the heart of the city, where subway and commuter-train lines will take you to other parts of Tokyo.

BY SHIP

Yokohama, which is about 30 minutes from Tokyo by train, is a principal port of call for luxury cruises. Also, there's a ship that leaves Niigata, a three-hour train ride from Tokyo by Shinkansen train, for Vladivostok, which is the trans-Siberian terminus for the train from Moscow, on Tuesday from June to September. The two-day trip costs ¥32,600 ($296) one-way. For more information on travel to Russia, contact Japan-Soviet Travel Service, 5F Daihachi Tanaka Building, 5-1 Gobancho, Chiyoda-ku, Tokyo (tel. 3238-9101). It's located one minute from the JR Ichigaya Station and open Monday through Friday from 9am to 8pm and on Saturday until 5pm.

PACKAGE TOURS

If you're the kind of traveler who doesn't like leaving such arrangements as accommodations and transportation to chance, you may wish to contact tour operators for independent tour packages or escorted tours. Independent (unescorted) tour packages usually include five or six nights in a hotel and coach-class round-trip airfare for about $1,500 per person, based on double occupancy. However, prices vary according to the type of hotel, whether it's a weekend or weekday, the season of travel, and gate of departure in the States. Additional nights range from about $65 to $140, double occupancy.

Among the many tour operators offering both group and independent tours to Japan are **Journeys East,** 2443 Fillmore St., San Francisco, CA 94115 (tel. 415/601-1677); **Pacific Best Tours,** 228 Rivervale Rd., Rivervale, NJ 07675 (tel. 201/664-8778, or toll free 800/688-3288); **TBI Tours,** 787 Seventh Ave., Suite 1101, New York NY 10019 (tel. 212/489-1919, or toll free 800/223-0266); and **Visitours, Inc.,** Olympic Tower, 645 Fifth Ave., New York, NY 10022 (tel. 212/355-6077, or toll free 800/367-4368).

CHAPTER 3

GETTING TO KNOW TOKYO

This chapter will answer any questions you might have upon arrival in Tokyo and during your stay, from how to get from the airport to your hotel to what numbers to call during an emergency.

1. ORIENTATION

Tokyo may not be the easiest city in the world to get to know, but millions of foreign visitors before you have stayed here and navigated their way through the city with great success. Because Tokyo is so safe, and the people are so kind and helpful to strangers, much of the anxiety travelers have in other countries is eliminated.

ARRIVING

BY PLANE

NARITA AIRPORT Unless you're flying China Airlines, you'll probably arrive in Japan at the **New Tokyo International Airport** in Narita, about 40 miles from downtown Tokyo. There are now two terminals at Narita, Terminal 1 and Terminal 2. Whichever you arrive at, procedures and facilities are basically the same. After clearing Customs, but before you pass through the automatic doors to the arrivals lobby, you can change money at a **bureau de change** (there are also places to change money in the arrivals and departure lobbies). The arrivals lobbies in both terminals have counters for hotel reservations and limosine bus tickets, and both are connected to all ground transportation.

If you have purchased a Japan Rail Pass, you can turn in your voucher at one of the **Japan Railways (JR) Information and Ticket Offices** (tel. 0476/34-6008), located on the arrivals level of Terminal 1 and in the first basement of Terminal 2. Both are open from 7am to 9pm daily.

Tourist Information Centers (TIC), managed by the Japan National Tourist Organization, are located in both terminals. One, on the arrivals level of Terminal 1, is open Monday through Friday from 9am to 8pm and on Saturday from 9am to noon. The second, in the arrivals lobby of Terminal 2, is open daily from 9am to 8pm. The TIC offers free maps of Tokyo and sightseeing information, and its staff can direct you to your hotel or inn. If you do not yet have a hotel room and desire one at a modest price, you can make reservations here free of charge Monday through Friday from 9am to 7:30pm. Stopping off here can be a real time-saver, though there's another TIC in the center of Tokyo in Hibiya.

Other facilities include four **post offices,** two in Terminal 1 (one in the departure lobby, open daily from 9am to 8:30pm, and the second in the basement, open Monday through Friday from 9am to 5pm and on Saturday from 9am to 12:30pm) and two in Terminal 2 (one in the third-floor departure lobby, open daily from 9am to 8:30pm, and the second on the second-floor domestic departures level, open Monday through Friday from 9am to 5pm and on Saturday from 9am to 12:30pm).

There are also **Kokusai Denshin Denwa (KDD)** offices in both terminals where you can make an international telephone call or send a telegram. The office on the fourth floor of Terminal 1 is open daily from 9am to 8pm; the office in the third-floor departure lobby in Terminal 2 is open daily from 7am to 9:30pm.

Finally, if your **luggage** is too heavy to handle, you can have it delivered to your hotel in Tokyo by the next day through the abc Co., Kamataki Unyu Co., Airport Ground Service, or Sky Porter. All these companies have counters in the arrivals lobby, and rates start at ¥1,700 ($15.45) per piece of luggage up to 30 kilos (66 lb.).

GETTING FROM NARITA TO TOKYO Everyone grumbles about the Narita airport because it's so far away from Tokyo compared to the airports of other capital cities. In fact, Narita is a different town altogether, with miles of rice paddies in between. Of all the different modes of transportation listed below, the airport bus is the most convenient because it delivers passengers and their luggage to the doors of Tokyo's major hotels. The Keisei Skyliner train or the JR *Narita Express* are also convenient ways to reach the heart of Tokyo.

By Taxi Obviously, jumping into a taxi and driving straight to your hotel is the easiest way to get to Tokyo, but it's also prohibitively expensive—and may not even be the quickest method during rush hours. Expect to spend ¥22,000 to ¥24,000 ($200 to $218) for a taxi from the Narita airport for the one- to two-hour ride.

By Airport Bus The most popular way to get from Narita to Tokyo is via the **Airport Limousine Bus,** which deposits passengers at the Tokyo City Air Terminal (TCAT) as well as major hotels. Buses operate most frequently to TCAT, and the trip takes about 70 minutes; at TCAT there are usually taxis to take you to your hotel. And the subway is convenient since recent improvements in the central-city Hanzomon Line now connect its last stop, Suitengu-mae, directly to the TCAT with moving walkways and escalators (a blessing if you have luggage). Otherwise, buses go to both Tokyo and Shinjuku Stations as well as to more than a dozen of Tokyo's major hotels, including Keio Plaza, Century Hyatt, Shinjuku Washington Hotel, Hilton, Imperial, Okura, New Otani, Akasaka Tokyu, Akasaka Prince, ANA Hotel, Miyako Hotel, and Takanawa Prince Hotel. Check with the staff at the Airport Limousine Bus counter in the arrivals lobby for the bus most convenient to your hotel. Fares range from ¥2,700 to ¥3,800 ($24.55 to $34.55), depending on the distance; children 6 to 11 are charged from ¥1,350 ($12.25); children under 6 ride free.

Another company that operates buses to more than 20 hotels in Tokyo is the **Airport Shuttle Bus.** Fares for this service begin at ¥2,800 ($25.45), and the counter is in the arrivals lobbies of both terminals.

By Train You can also reach Tokyo by train, with several options available. Trains depart directly from the airport's two underground stations, called Narita Airport Station and Terminal 2 Station. The **JR *Narita Express* (NEX)** is the fastest way to reach Tokyo Station, Shinjuku, Ikebukuro, and Yokohama. The trip to Tokyo Station takes 53 minutes and costs ¥2,890 ($26.25) one-way, but if you have a validated JR rail pass, you can ride the NEX free. Note, however, that all seats are reserved, and you must first stop by the NEX counter near the train terminal for a seat assignment. Unfortunately, the NEX is so popular that seats are often sold out in advance. (If you want to reserve a seat for your return trip to the Narita airport, you can do so here at the NEX counter or at a travel agency.) If the NEX is sold out and you're still determined to use your rail pass, you can take the slower **JR Airport Liner** to Tokyo Station in 80 minutes. If you don't have a rail pass, this rapid train will cost you ¥1,090 ($9.90).

An alternative is the privately owned **Keisei Skyliner** train, which departs directly from the Narita Airport Station and reaches Ueno Station in Tokyo one hour later—it's the way I always travel to and from the Narita airport. There's a Keisei Skyliner counter in the arrivals lobbies of both terminals. The fare from the Narita airport to Ueno Station in Tokyo is ¥1,740 ($15.80) one-way. Trains depart approximately every 30 or 40 minutes between 6:03am (7:13am on Saturday and Sunday) and 9:59pm. If you're on a tight budget, you can take a slower **ordinary Keisei train** from Narita Airport Station to Ueno Station, with fares starting at ¥940 ($8.55). Used by commuters, the limited express takes 75 minutes to reach Ueno and the express takes 90 minutes, making many stops along the way.

At Ueno Station you can take either the subway or the JR Yamanote Line to other parts of Tokyo (see "Getting Around," later in this chapter). There are also plenty of taxis available.

By Subway If you're staying in the Ginza or the Asakusa area, you may wish to travel from Narita Airport Station via the **Toei Asakusa Line.** The trip to Higashi Ginza takes about 82 minutes and costs ¥1,030 ($9.35), or slightly less if you get off earlier at Asakusa Station.

RETURNING TO THE NARITA AIRPORT When you're returning to the Narita airport, if you're going by bus it's very convenient to travel via the TCAT if you're flying certain airlines like Northwest, because you can actually check your luggage in, get your boarding pass, and pay your airport departure tax directly at the TCAT. It's less crowded than Narita, and hassle-free.

To get there, take the subway's Hanzomon Line to the last stop, Suitengu-mae, and use Exit 1A or 1B at the front of the train. From Nagatcho Station, for example, the cost to Suitengu-mae is ¥140 ($1.25) and the journey takes 15 minutes.

HANEDA AIRPORT More than likely you'll only arrive at Haneda Airport if you've flown China Airlines or you've flown into Tokyo on a domestic flight. Older and closer to the heart of Tokyo than the Narita airport, Haneda Airport is linked to Tokyo's major hotels by **Airport Limousine Bus** (described above), which also shuttles passengers between the two airports. Rather than taking the Airport Limousine Bus, however, the locals are apt to board the **monorail** from Haneda Airport to Hamamatsucho Station, for which the fare is ¥300 ($2.75) for the 18-minute trip. From Hamamatsucho Station you can then transfer to the Yamanote Line or hail a taxi.

BY TRAIN

If you're traveling to Tokyo by train from other cities in Japan, you'll most likely end up at Tokyo Station, especially if you're on the Shinkansen bullet train. There are many commuter lines and subways that connect Tokyo Station to other parts of the city. For orientation purposes, you may wish to stop by the Information Bureau of Tokyo, located in Tokyo Station in a corner of the Travel Plaza at the Yaesu exit. Open Monday through Saturday from 9am to 6pm, it provides information on Tokyo and can answer questions on getting from the station to your hotel. If you need to exchange a JR Rail Pass voucher for the real thing, you can do so at the JR View Plaza (tel. 3213-1144), located by the Yaesu Central Exit and open from 6am to 10pm daily. You'll also find lockers at Tokyo Station, which cost ¥300 ($2.75) and ¥400 ($3.65) for 24 hours.

TOURIST INFORMATION

The **Japan National Tourist Organization (JNTO),** a branch of the government responsible for promoting tourism and the publication of brochures and other tourism information, maintains two tourist offices in the vicinity of Tokyo to handle inquiries from foreigners and the general public about Tokyo and the rest of Japan. The **Tourist Information Centers (TIC)** can answer questions about Tokyo and other destinations in Japan, and can provide free maps and sightseeing materials. In addition, there's a counter at the TIC where you can make reservations for inexpensive accommodations throughout Japan at no extra charge.

For foreigners arriving in Tokyo by plane, there are two TICs at the Narita airport. The one in Terminal 1 is open Monday through Friday from 9am to 8pm and on Saturday from 9am to noon, while the Terminal 2 TIC is open daily from 9am to 8pm.

Another TIC is in the heart of Tokyo at 1-6-6 Yurakucho, Chiyoda-ku (tel. 03/3502-1461). It's located close to both Hibiya and Yurakucho Stations (if you're arriving at Hibiya Station, take the A4 exit). It's also within a 10-minute walk from the Ginza or a 3-minute walk from the C1 exit of the Ginza subway station. It's open Monday through Friday from 9am to 5pm and on Saturday from 9am to noon. Although it doesn't make sense in a city as large as Tokyo, both TIC offices are closed on Sunday and national holidays.

The TIC, however, operates a telephone service from 9am to 5pm every day of the year, which it calls **Travel-Phone.** Call if you're having problems communicating with someone, are lost, or need information on Japan. If you're calling from inside Tokyo, the number is 3502-1461; if you're calling from outside Tokyo, you can call toll free by dialing 0088-22-2800 for questions pertaining to eastern Japan (Tokyo and vicinity, Hokkaido). If you have questions about western Japan (Nagoya, Kyoto, Shikoku, Kyushu, and other locales), the toll-free number is 0088-44-4800.

In addition to the TIC offices above, JNTO also operates the

Information Bureau of Tokyo, located at the JR Tokyo Station in a corner of the Travel Plaza at the Yaesu entrance. In contrast to the TIC, which handles questions concerning all of Japan, this bureau deals only with questions about Tokyo, including transportation throughout Tokyo, shopping, accommodations, and sightseeing. It's open Monday through Saturday from 9am to 6pm; closed Sunday and holidays.

Keep in mind that most cities, towns, and even villages maintain their own local tourist offices. For information on local tourist offices in the vicinity of Tokyo, consult Chapter 10.

If you want a quick rundown on what's happening in Tokyo, you can call 3503-2911 for a **taped recording in English** of what's going on in the city and the vicinity in the way of special exhibitions, performances, festivals, and other events.

Finally, another telephone service is sponsored by Nippon Telegraph Corp. (NTT) and Kokusai Denshin Denwa (KDD) that can answer questions in English on anything relating to Japan. Called the **Japan Hotline** (tel. 03/3586-0110), its staff advises callers on Japanese etiquette and customs, gives tips on daily life such as Japanese education and health services, and can answer questions ranging from the availability of instruction in flower arranging to obtaining tickets to Kabuki. Advisers are on duty Monday through Friday from 10am to 4pm; closed holidays.

TOURIST PUBLICATIONS The best publication for finding out what's going on in Tokyo in terms of contemporary and traditional music and theater, exhibitions in museums and galleries, films, and special events is the ***Tokyo Journal.*** Published monthly and available for ¥600 ($5.45) at foreign-language bookstores, restaurants, and bars, it also has articles of interest to foreigners in Japan. It even lists department-store sales, photography exhibitions, apartments for rent, schools for learning Japanese, and many other services.

Another English-language publication of interest to tourists is ***Tokyo Time Out,*** also published monthly and available for ¥500 ($4.55) at bookstores. It carries the same type of information as the *Tokyo Journal,* including what's happening in the theaters, music clubs, and art galleries in Tokyo. ***Tour Companion's Tokyo City Guide,*** a monthly distributed free to hotels, travel agencies, and the TIC, tells of upcoming events and festivals, as well as other information useful to the visitor. ***Weekender*** is also a free biweekly and is found in supermarkets, hotels, and other places where foreigners hang out. It's best known for its classified-ad section, but has articles and features as well. ***The Nippon View*** is a free monthly magazine with articles from restaurant reviews to health issues. English-language newspapers such as the *Japan Times* also carry information on the theater, films, and special events.

CITY LAYOUT

MAIN STREETS & ARTERIES One thing that makes finding your way around difficult is that most streets don't have names. Imagine what that means in Tokyo—12 million people milling around in a metropolis of nameless streets. Granted, major thoroughfares and some well-known streets in areas like Ginza or Shinjuku might have names that they received after World War II on the insistence of American occupation forces, but for the most part

Tokyo's address system is based on a complicated number scheme that must make the post office's job a nightmare. To make matters worse, most streets in Tokyo aren't straight but zigzag all over the place, a maze apparently left over from olden days when it was designed to confuse any enemies that might attack. Today the streets in Tokyo confuse not only foreign tourists but Tokyo residents themselves.

Among Tokyo's most important streets that do have names are Meiji Dori Avenue, which follows the loop of the Yamanote train line from Ebisu in the south through Shibuya, Harajuku, Shinjuku, and

TOKYO ORIENTATION

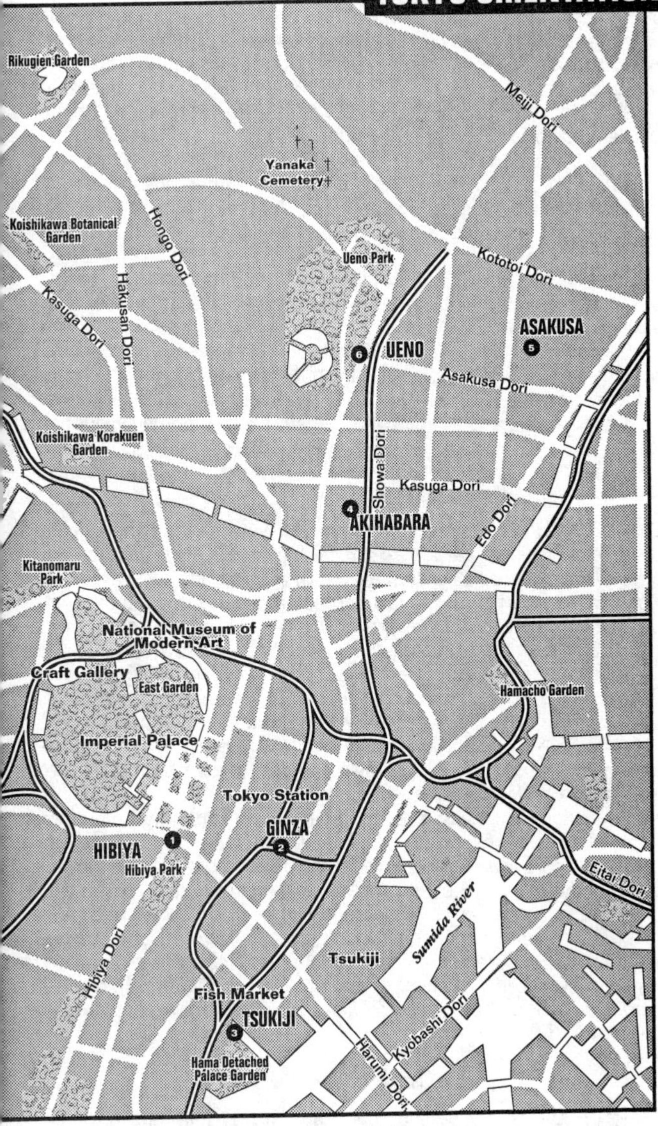

Ikebukuro in the north; Yasukuni Dori Avenue and Shinjuku Dori Avenue, which connect Shinjuku with Chiyoda-ku in the heart of the city; and Sotobori Dori Avenue, Harumi Dori Avenue, and Showa Dori Avenue, which pass through the Ginza.

FINDING AN ADDRESS Because streets did not have names when Japan's postal system was established, the country has a unique address system. A typical Tokyo address might read 7-8-4 Roppongi, Minato-ku, which is the address of the Inakaya restaurant. Minato-ku is the name of one of 23 wards that make up Tokyo (*ku* means "ward" in Japanese). Within Minato-ku are various districts; in this case the district is Roppongi. Roppongi is further broken down into *chome,* indicated by the first number in the series, in this case 7-chome. Number 8 refers to a smaller area within the chome, often an entire block, sometimes larger. Thus houses on one side of the street will often have a different middle number from houses on the other side. The last number, in this case 4, refers to the actual building. Although it seems reasonable to assume that next to a number 4 building will be a number 5, that's not always the case; buildings were assigned numbers as they were constructed, not according to location.

Addresses are usually, but not always, posted on buildings, beside front doors, and on telephone poles (the best place to look), but they are usually written only in kanji. In recent years, addresses have been added below stop lights at major intersections in some parts of the city. You will also notice maps throughout neighborhoods with a breakdown of the number system for the immediate area.

Another important source of information is the numerous police stations, called *koban,* spread throughout the city. The policemen staffing these tiny, neighborhood posts know their areas intimately, often have maps of the area, and are very helpful.

STREET MAPS Before setting out on your own, arm yourself with a few maps. Maps are so much a part of life in Tokyo that they're often included as part of a shop or restaurant's advertisement, brochures, business cards, and even on private party invitations. Even though I've spent several years in Tokyo, I rarely venture forth without a map. One I find particularly useful is issued free by the Tourist Information Center; it's called ***Tourist Map of Tokyo*** and includes smaller, detailed maps of several districts (such as Shinjuku) as well as subway and Greater Tokyo train maps. With this map you should be able to locate at least the general vicinity of every place mentioned in this book. Hotels also sometimes distribute their own maps. In short, never pass up a free map.

If you want a map with more detail, head to Kinokuniya, Maruzen or one of the other bookstores with an English-language section, where you'll find more than a dozen variations of city maps at various prices. Kodanshita's ***A Bilingual Map*** is a foldout map showing Tokyo's various areas and comes complete with an index to important buildings, museums, and other places of interest. Similarly, ***A Great Detailed Map,*** published by Nippon Kokuseisha Company, gives the postal addresses for neighborhoods throughout Tokyo and includes bus routes and a subway map. It's useful for finding specific addresses in Tokyo.

NEIGHBORHOODS IN BRIEF

Because Tokyo seems to sprawl on and on, it may appear rather formidable and unconquerable to the uninitiated. It's best, therefore, to think of Tokyo as nothing more than individual neighborhoods scrunched together, much like the pieces of a jigsaw puzzle. Holding the pieces together, so to speak, is the Yamanote Line, a commuter train that makes a loop around the central part of Tokyo, passing through such important neighborhood stations as Yurakucho, Tokyo, Ueno, Shinjuku, Harajuku, and Shibuya along the way.

Hibiya Although Tokyo does not have a clearly defined central district or downtown, the spiritual heart of the city probably lies near Hibiya. This is where you'll find the Imperial Palace, home of Japan's

125th emperor. It was also the site that the Tokugawa shogun chose for his castle and was thus the center of old Edo. Together with neighboring Marunouchi, Hibiya is the financial heart of the city, but most important for tourists, it's also where you'll find the Tourist Information Center. North of Hibiya and just one stop away on the Yamanote Line is Tokyo Station, where bullet trains depart for Kyoto and other major cities to the south of Tokyo. Hibiya is located in the Chiyoda-ku ward.

Ginza Within walking distance of Hibiya is the Ginza, the swankiest and most expensive shopping area of all Japan. When the country opened to foreign trade in the 1860s following two centuries of self-imposed seclusion, it was the Ginza that first displayed Western imports and adopted Western architecture. Today the Ginza is where you'll find a multitude of department stores, boutiques, exclusive restaurants, hostess clubs, and bars. It also has scores of art galleries. On the eastern edge of the Ginza is Kabukiza, famous for its grand productions of Kabuki.

Tsukiji Only two subway stops from Ginza, Tsukiji is famous for the Tsukiji Fish Market, Japan's largest wholesale fish market.

Shinjuku An upstart in Tokyo and a district that has been attracting businesses away from the more established Hibiya, Shinjuku is located on the western edge of the Yamanote Line loop. Shinjuku Station, the nation's busiest station, separates Shinjuku into an east and west side. The western part of Shinjuku boasts Tokyo's greatest concentration of skyscrapers and a number of hotels, as well as Tokyo's new City Hall. Eastern Shinjuku is known for its shopping and nightlife, especially Kabuki-cho, a thriving amusement and entertainment district.

Harajuku Just south of Shinjuku is Harajuku, mecca of Tokyo's younger generation in search of fashion and fun. Omotesando Dori is a fashionable, tree-lined avenue flanked by trendy shops, sidewalk cafés, and restaurants. Nearby is Takeshita Dori, a narrow pedestrian lane packed with teenagers looking for the latest in expensive clothing. On Sunday, Harajuku is the scene of street dancers and musicians, who perform near Yoyogi Park to large crowds. Harajuku is also the site of Meiji Shrine, dedicated to Emperor and Empress Meiji and considered the most important shrine in Tokyo. Not far from Omotesando Station is Koto Dori, or Antique Avenue. Once lined exclusively with antiques shops, these days Koto Dori is acquiring trendy restaurants and top-name fashion boutiques.

Asakusa Located in the northeastern part of central Tokyo, Asakusa served as the pleasure quarters for old Edo. Today it's known throughout Japan as the site of the famous Sensoji Temple, one of Tokyo's top attractions. It also has a wealth of tiny shops selling traditional Japanese crafts, most of them on Nakamise Dori. When Tokyoites talk about *shitamachi* (old downtown), they are referring to the traditional homes and tiny narrow streets of the Asakusa and Ueno areas. Asakusa is where you should go if you want to see what's left of old Tokyo.

Ueno Also located on the northern edge of Tokyo is Ueno, also part of the old downtown of Tokyo. Considered the playground of Tokyo families, Ueno boasts Ueno Park, a huge green space which also contains a zoo, a concert hall, and several acclaimed museums. Among them is the Tokyo National Museum, considered to have the largest collection of Japanese art in the world. North of Ueno is Nippori, a residential area of old traditional homes and temples.

Ikebukuro Located north of Shinjuku on the Yamanote Line loop, Ikebukuro is the working-man's Tokyo, less refined and a bit rougher around the edges. Crowded with commuters who live past Ikebukuro in less expensive areas of the metropolis, Ikebukuro is where you'll find Seibu and Tobu Plaza, two of the country's largest department stores, and the Sunshine City Building, one of Tokyo's tallest buildings and home of a huge indoor shopping center.

Akihabara This is Tokyo's center for electronic and electrical appliances, with more than 600 shops offering a look at the latest in gadgets and gizmos. It's a fascinating place for a stroll, even if you aren't interested in buying anything, since you'll see products here long before they hit the American market.

Shibuya Located on the southwestern edge of the Yamanote Line loop, Shibuya serves as an important nightlife and shopping area of Tokyo. There are as many as a dozen department stores in Shibuya, specializing in everything from designer clothing to housewares.

Daikanyama Shibuya's hipper southern neighbor, Daikanyama is at the cutting edge of fashion. Not only are fashion ateliers here, but their boutiques too. And it's one of the best used-clothes shopping areas—the only way some of us can ever hope to own clothes with labels like Romeo Gigli or Comme des Garçons. Trendy restaurants, interesting storefronts, and the Hillside Terrace area galleries make Daikanyama a nice place to stroll.

Roppongi Tokyo's best-known nightlife district for young Japanese and foreigners, Roppongi has more discos and bars than any other district in Tokyo, as well as a multitude of restaurants serving international cuisine. The action here continues until dawn.

Nishi-Azabu Once a residential neighborhood, over the years the overflow of Roppongi, just up the hill, has turned Nishi-Azabu into a restaurant and nightclub venue too.

Akasaka Another important nightlife district of Tokyo, this one caters more to businessmen. In addition to expensive hostess bars, Akasaka also has many restaurants, bars, and several large hotels.

2. GETTING AROUND

BY PUBLIC TRANSPORTATION

DISCOUNT PASSES & TRANSFERS If you think you're going to be using the subways a lot, you can purchase a **One-Day Free Ticket,** which, despite its name, is not free. It costs ¥650 ($5.90) for adults and ¥330 ($3) for children 6 to 11 (free for children under 6), and allows unlimited travel on the Ginza, Marunouchi, Hibiya, Tozai, Chiyoda, Yurakucho, Namboku, and Hanzomon Lines. These lines pass through more than 140 Tokyo stations, including Hibiya, Ginza, Shinjuku, Tsukiji, Ueno, Roppongi, Akihabara, Asakusa, Suitengu-mae, and major sightseeing destinations. However, these tickets are a savings only if you plan on using the subways more than five times in one day or for very long distances. If so, you can purchase this one-day ticket at more than a dozen subway stations, including Ginza, Shibuya, Ueno, and Akasaka-mitsuke. Contact the TIC for more information.

If you think you're going to be traveling extensively on JR

commuter trains in Tokyo, including the Yamanote Line loop, you may wish to buy the **JR 1-day pass** for ¥720 ($6.55) for adults and ¥360 ($3.25) for children 6 to 11 (free for children under 6), which allows unlimited travel on all JR trains except express trains. It's available at JR stations such as Shinjuku and JR travel centers. Ask for the **Tokunai Free Kippu.**

Transfers You can transfer between subway lines without buying another ticket, and you can also transfer between JR train lines on one ticket. However, your ticket does not allow a transfer between subway lines and JR train lines. You don't have to worry about this though, because if you exit through a wicket and have to give up your ticket, you'll know you have to buy another one.

In some transfers, however, you must pass through a ticket wicket (for example, when you transfer from the Yurakucho Line to the Hibiya Line at Hibiya Station). In this case, simply show your ticket when you go through the wicket. The general rule is that if your final destination and fare are posted on the map above the ticket vending machine, you can travel all the way to your destination on one ticket. If you make a miscalculation, the ticket collector will set you straight.

BY SUBWAY To get around Tokyo on your own, it's imperative to learn how to ride its subways. Fortunately, Tokyo's subway system is efficient, modern, clean, and easy to use, and all station names are written in English. Subway entrances are identified by a blue S logo. Altogether there are 12 subway lines crisscrossing underneath the city on more than 100 miles of track, some more than 100 feet below ground. Each line is color-coded, which makes transfers easy. The Ginza Line, for example, is orange, which means that all its coaches are orange. If you're transferring to the Ginza Line from another line, simply follow the orange signs and circles to the Ginza Line platform. There's a subway map on the *Tourist Map of Tokyo* distributed free by the TIC. Even more information is available in two free publications, "Tokyo Subway Map & Guide" and "How to Ride Tokyo Subways," both available free at the TIC.

The Ginza Line, so named because it runs underneath the Ginza, is Tokyo's oldest subway line, opened in 1927. It runs from Shibuya to Asakusa, stopping at Ginza, Ueno, and many other stations along the way. Hibiya is another important line, with stops at Roppongi, Ginza, Tsukiji (the fish market), Tokyo's stock-market district, the electronics center of Akihabara, and Ueno.

There are vending machines at all stations selling tickets, which begin at ¥140 ($1.25) for the shortest distance and increase according to how far you're traveling (children 6 to 12 travel for half price). Simply put money into the vending machine and then punch the price of the ticket you want to buy (adult tickets are on the upper rows; children's tickets are underneath a plastic flap). Vending machines give change and some even accept ¥1,000 notes. To determine fares, there's a large subway map above the vending machines with destinations and corresponding prices in numbers, but destinations are unfortunately in Japanese only. Major stations also post a small map listing fares in English, but you'll probably have to search for it. An alternative is to look at your TIC subway map—it lists stations in both Japanese and English. Once you learn how some Japanese characters look, you may be able to learn how to locate your station and the corresponding fare on the huge subway map above the vending machines.

If you still can't figure out the fare, simply buy the cheapest ticket for ¥140 ($1.25). When you exit at the other end, the ticket collector will tell you how much you owe. In any case, be sure to hang on to your ticket since you must give it up at the end of your journey. If you're confused about which exit to take from the station, ask the ticket collector. Taking the right exit can make a world of difference, especially at Shinjuku Station where there are more than 60 exits from the station.

Most subways run from about 5am to midnight, though the times of the first and last trains depend on the line, the station, and whether it's a weekday or weekend. There are schedules posted in the stations, and through most of the day trains run every three to five minutes. Avoid taking the subway during the rush hour, from 8 to 9am. The stories you've heard about commuters packed into trains like sardines are all true. There are even "platform pushers," men who push people into compartments so that the doors can close. If you want to witness Tokyo at its craziest, go to Shinjuku Station at 8:30am—but go by taxi unless you want to experience the crowding firsthand.

BY TRAIN In addition to subway lines, there are four electric commuter trains operated by Japan Railways (JR) that run above ground. These are also color-coded and fares begin at ¥120 ($1.10). Buy your ticket from the vending machines the same way you would for the subway. The **Yamanote Line** (green-colored coaches) is the best known and most convenient JR line. It makes a loop around the city, stopping at 29 stations along the way, including Shinjuku, Ueno, Tokyo, and Harajuku. In fact, to get a roundabout view of Tokyo, you may wish to stay on the Yamanote Line for its one-hour circuit around the city.

Another convenient JR line is the **Chuo Line,** whose coaches are orange. It cuts across the heart of Tokyo between Shinjuku and Tokyo Stations.

To estimate travel time on the train, consider that it takes approximately one hour to travel the entire loop of the Yamanote Line. Thus, if you're traveling from its northern end (say, Ueno) to a station on its opposite end (like Shibuya), you should count on a 30-minute ride.

BY BUS Buses are difficult to use in Tokyo because their destinations are often written only in Japanese and most drivers don't speak English. However, they can be useful for getting from Shibuya to Roppongi or from Roppongi to Shinjuku. If you're feeling adventurous, board the bus at the front and drop the exact fare into the box next to the driver. If you don't have the exact fare (usually ¥180/$1.65), there's a money machine beside the driver as well. Your change will come out below, minus the fare. To get off the bus, press one of the buttons on the railing near the door or seats.

BY TAXI

Hailing a taxi in Tokyo is just like in the movies: You step up to the curb, hold up your arm, and a taxi stops almost immediately. The only time you may have difficulty finding a taxi is when you need one the most—when it's raining and late at night on weekends after all the subways and trains have shut down for the night. Nightlife areas such as Shinjuku, Roppongi, Ginza, and Akasaka are especially bad, and I've waited as long as an hour in each of these places for a taxi after midnight. However, one important measure of the Japanese

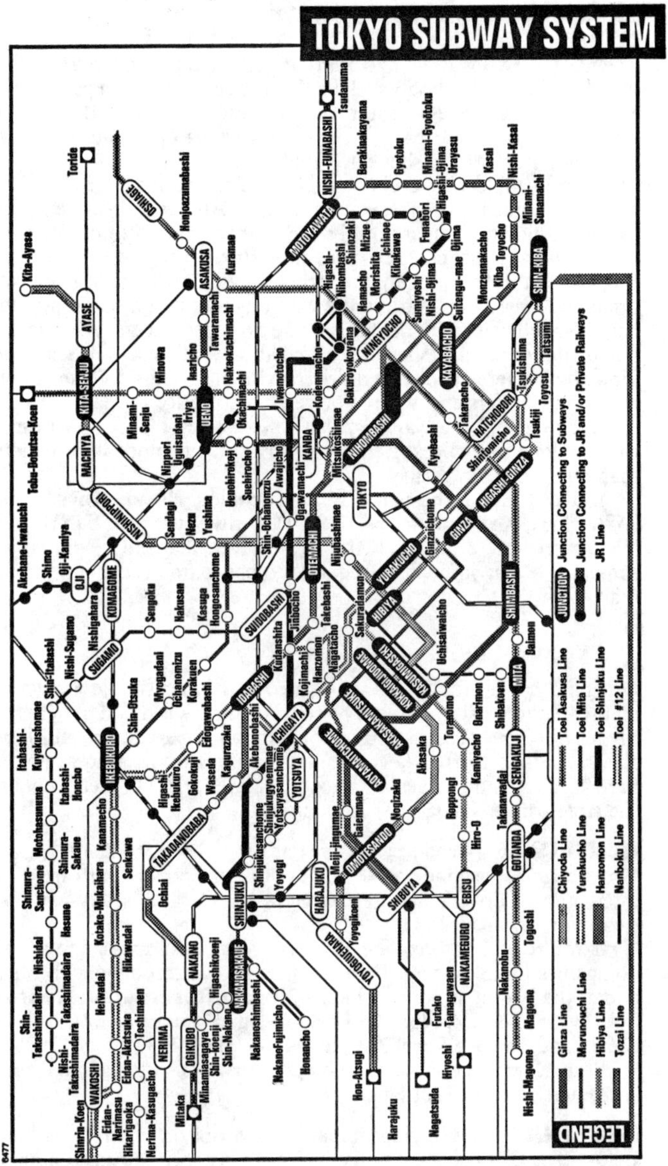

recession is the number of available taxis. One used to have to stay out until 2 or 3am to find a taxi, but not since companies are no longer paying for employees' expensive after-the-last-train taxi fares. (Some Tokyoites lament the passing of the good old days when no taxis to be found gave them an excuse to get home in the wee hours.)

Taxis are fairly expensive in Tokyo, starting at ¥600 ($5.45) for the first 1¼ miles (2km) and increasing by ¥90 (80¢) for each additional 1,128 feet (347m). From 11pm to 5am, a 30% surcharge is added to the fare.

You can hail a taxi from the street (except in the Ginza on

weekdays between 10pm and 1am) or go to a taxi stand. A red light will show above the dashboard if a taxi is free to pick up a passenger; a green light indicates that the taxi is already occupied. Be sure to stand clear of the left back door—it will swing open automatically and will automatically shut once you're in.

Keep in mind that traffic can become so snarled in Tokyo, it's sometimes much faster to take the subway. And unless you're going to a well-known landmark or hotel, it's best to have your destination written out in Japanese, because most taxi drivers do not speak English. But even that may not help. Tokyo is so complicated that often taxi drivers are not familiar with much of it, although they do have detailed maps with them. Don't be surprised if a taxi driver leaps out of the car and dashes into a neighborhood store—he's asking directions. There are also taxi drivers who may refuse to take you if they don't understand where you're going. Notice the taxi drivers' white gloves and the way they're always writing things down on a roster—Japanese taxi drivers must write down more information than any others on earth.

You can phone the major taxi companies: **Nihon Kotsu** (tel. 3586-2151), **Kokusai** (tel. 3491-6001), **Daiwa** (tel. 3563-5151), and **Hinomaru** (tel. 3814-1111). Note, however, that only Japanese is spoken and that you will be required to pay extra (usually not more than ¥550/$5).

BY CAR

Driving a car in Tokyo can make a roller-coaster ride at the local amusement park seem tame. The streets are crowded and unbelievably narrow, street signs are often only in Japanese, and driving is *on the left side of the road,* as in Great Britain. Parking spaces can be hard to find, and garages are expensive. Even parking meters along the street run ¥400 ($3.65) an hour.

RENTALS Car-rental prices start at around ¥6,500 ($59) for 24 hours, regular gasoline costs $3.50 per gallon, and you must have an international driver's license. Money-, time-, and safety-wise, it simply doesn't pay.

If you're still not convinced, there are a dozen major rental-car companies in Tokyo with branch offices spread throughout the city and at the Narita airport, including **Nissan Reservation Center** (tel. 03/3587-4123), **Nippon Rent-A-Car Service** (tel. 03/3485-7196), and **Toyota Rent-A-Car** (tel. 03/3264-2834).

Both **Hertz** and **Avis** can accept reservations for their affiliated car-rental companies in Japan.

PARKING Tokyo residents must have proof of off-street parking before they can buy a car, which in many instances means renting a space for as much as $200 a month. And yet finding a parking space is still a challenge in Tokyo. You'll pay about ¥400 ($3.65) an hour for the privilege of a metered parking space on the street, and about ¥600 ($5.45) per hour in a parking garage. Because space is at a premium, parking garages are usually tall and narrow, the cars transported heavenward by elevatorlike devices. In many garages, drivers drive onto a platform that can be rotated since there isn't even enough room to back up and turn around. Your best bet for parking is to choose a hotel with a garage (all the major hotels offer parking spaces) and then use public transportation to get around.

FAST FACTS TOKYO

Being in Japan can be frustrating because of the language barrier. In the beginning you won't be able to differentiate between a post office and a public bathhouse, much less read the hours they're open. Many of the larger first-class hotels, however, have guest-relations officers to answer any questions visitors may have. Another place to turn is the Japan National Tourist Organization, which has set up a tourist telephone helpline called **Travel-Phone** to help foreigners (see "Tourist Information" in "Orientation," earlier in this chapter). Similarly, another telephone service to help with questions about Tokyo and Japan is **Japan Hotline** (tel. 03/3586-0110).

American Express There are several American Express offices in Tokyo. The only one that handles client mail service and emergency card-replacement services is located in Yurakucho on the ground floor of the Yurakucho Denki Building, 1-7-1 Yurakucho, Chiyoda-ku (tel. 3/3214-0280). It's open Monday through Friday from 9am to 7pm and on Saturday and Sunday from 10am to 5pm. Another office is located in Toranomon in the Mitsui Building, 3-8-1 Kasumigaseki, Chiyoda-ku (tel. 3508-2400). It's open Monday through Friday from 9am to 5pm and on Saturday from 9am to 1pm; closed Sunday and public holidays. The closest subway station is Toranomon. A third office is in Shinjuku in the Shinjuku Gomeikan Building, 3-3-9 Shinjuku (tel. 3352-1555), open daily from 10am to 6pm. Note that all three offices have 24-hour access American Express cash machines.

Area Code If you're calling a number in Tokyo from elsewhere in Japan, the area code for Tokyo is 03. If you're calling Tokyo from most countries outside Japan, including from the United States, you should drop the "0" and dial only "3."

Babysitters Many upper-class hotels, like the Imperial, have professional child-care facilities, but expect to pay about $70 for two hours. Two baby-sitting services used to foreigners are Homeaid (tel. 3781-7536) and Tokyo Domestic Service (tel. 3584-4769). Both have been in business for years and both can provide bilingual sitters.

Bookstores There are several very good bookstores in Tokyo with a large selection of books about Japan, novels, and reference materials written in English. They are listed in Chapter 8.

Business Hours Government **offices** and private companies are generally open Monday through Friday from about 9am to 5pm. In reality, however, Japanese businessmen in the private sector tend to work long hours and it's not unusual to find someone in the office as late as 7, 8, or even 10pm. To be on the safe side, however, it's best to conduct business before 5pm.

Most **stores** in Tokyo don't open until 10am and they close about 8pm. Often they're closed one day a week, and it's not unusual for almost all the shops in a particular neighborhood to be closed on the same day. Some shops, especially those around major train stations and entertainment areas, stay open until 10pm. Some convenience stores are open 24 hours.

Department stores are open from 10am to 6 or 7pm. They close one day a week, but it's different for each store so you can always find several that are open, even on Sunday. In fact, Sundays are big shopping days in Japan.

Keep in mind that **museums** close their ticket windows and therefore require that you buy your ticket and enter at least 30 minutes before closing time. Similarly, **restaurants** take their last orders at least 30 minutes before the posted closing time, sometimes even earlier for kaiseki restaurants.

Car Rentals See "Getting Around," earlier in this chapter.

Climate See "When to Go," in Chapter 2.

Currency See "Information, Entry Requirements, and Money," in Chapter 2.

Currency Exchange Banks are open Monday through Friday from 9am to 3pm. You can exchange money in major banks throughout Tokyo, often indicated by a sign in English near the front door. The Bank of America is located in the Arc Mori Building, 1-12-32 Akasaka, Minato-ku (tel. 3587-3111), and the Chase Manhattan Bank is at 1-2-1 Marunouchi, Chiyoda-ku (tel. 3287-4000). Generally, banks give better rates of exchange for traveler's checks than for cash.

If you need to exchange money outside bank hours, inquire at one of the larger first-class hotels—some of them will cash traveler's checks or exchange money even if you're not their guest. If you're arriving at the Narita airport, you can exchange money from 9am until the arrival of the last flight.

Doctors and Dentists Your embassy can refer you to English-speaking doctors, specialists, and dentists. In addition, many first-class hotels offer medical facilities or an in-house doctor. A few clinics popular with foreigners living in Tokyo, where some of the staff speak English, are listed below. You can also make appointments to visit doctors in the hospitals listed under "Hospitals," below. You can also try the International Clinic, 1-5-9 Azabudai, Minato-ku (tel. 3582-2646), open Monday through Friday from 9am to noon and 2:30 to 5pm, and on Saturday from 9am to noon. They take walk-ins only. Station: Roppongi. The Ishikawa Clinic, Azabu Sakurada Heights, Room 201, 3-2-7 Nishi-Azabu, Minato-ku (tel. 3401-6340), is open Monday through Friday from 9am to 1pm and 3 to 7pm, and on Saturday from 9am to 1pm. Appointments are required. Station: Roppongi. Appointments are also necessary at the Tokyo Medical & Surgical Clinic, 32 Mori Building, 3-4-30 Shiba-koen, Minato-ku (tel. 3436-3028), open Monday through Friday from 9am to 1pm and 2 to 5:30pm, and on Saturday from 9 to 11am. Station: Kamiyacho, Onarimon, or Shiba-koen.

Documents Required See "Information, Entry Requirements, and Money," in Chapter 2.

Driving Rules See "Getting Around," earlier in this chapter.

Drugstores Drugstores are called *kusuri-ya* in Japanese and are readily found everywhere in Tokyo. However, there is no 24-hour drugstore in Tokyo, though there are convenience stores throughout the city that carry items such as aspirin. (If it's an emergency, I suggest going to one of the hospitals.) The **American Pharmacy,** Hibiya Park Building, 1-8-1 Yurakucho, Chiyoda-ku (tel. 3271-4034), is a good bet if you're looking for specific pharmaceuticals; it carries a number of the drugs, cosmetics, and health items you can find at home, many of them imported from the United States. It can also fill American prescriptions. Open Monday through Saturday from 9am to 7pm and on Sunday and holidays from 11am to 7pm. Station: Hibiya (located just a minute's walk from the Tourist Information Center).

Electricity The electricity throughout Japan is 100 volts AC, but there are two different cycles in use. In Tokyo and to the northeast it's 50 cycles, while in Nagoya, Osaka, Kyoto, and all points to the southwest it's 60 cycles. Leading hotels in Tokyo often have two outlets, one for 110 and one for 220 volts; many of them have hairdryers guests can use for free. Actually, you can use many American appliances such as radios or hairdryers in Japan. The American current of 110 volts and 60 cycles is so close that the only difference is that the appliance will run a bit more slowly; the prongs are the same.

Embassies and Consulates Tokyo is the location for most embassies and consulates, which are generally open Monday through Friday from 8:30 or 9am to about 4 or 5:30pm. Most close for an hour or so for lunch, and the visa or passport sections may be open only at certain times during the day. It's best to call in advance. The **American Embassy and Consulate,** located at 1-10-5 Akasaka, Minato-ku (tel. 3224-5000), is open Monday through Friday from 8:30am to noon and 2 to 5pm. Station: Toranomon; then an eight-minute walk. Contact the **British Embassy and Consulate** at 1 Ichibancho, Chiyoda-ku (tel. 3265-5511). It's open Monday through Friday from 9am to noon and 2 to 5:30pm. Station: Hanzomon; then a three-minute walk. The **Canadian Embassy,** at 7-3-38 Akasaka, Minato-ku (tel. 3408-2101), is open Monday through Friday from 9am to 12:30pm and 1:30 to 5:30pm. Station: Aoyama-Itchome; then a three-minute walk. The **Australian Embassy,** at 2-1-14 Mita, Minato-ku (tel. 5232-4111), is open from 9am to noon and 2 to 5pm. Station: Roppongi or Mita; and then by taxi. The **Embassy of Ireland,** 8-7 Sanbancho, Chiyoda-ku (tel. 3263-0695), is a 15-minute walk from either Ichigaya or Hanzomon Station and is open Monday through Friday from 9am to 4:30pm. The **New Zealand Embassy,** 20-40 Kamiyama-cho, Shibuya-ku (tel. 3467-2271), is open Monday through Friday from 9am to noon and 1:30 to 5pm, and is located a 15-minute walk from Shibuya Station.

Emergencies The national emergency numbers are 110 for **police** and 119 for both **ambulance and fire reports.** Be sure to speak slowly and precisely.

Etiquette See "Geography, History, and Culture," in Chapter 1.

Eyeglasses There are optical shops throughout Tokyo, so ask at your hotel which store is nearest you. Otherwise, try the Tokyo Optical Center, located in the Ginza at 6-4-8 Ginza (tel. 3571-7216). An English-speaking staff will assist you in replacing eyeglasses and contact lenses.

Hairdressers/Barbers Most first-class hotels have beauty salons and barbershops. In addition, check the advertisements and classified section of the *Tokyo Journal* for more listings of hairdressers used to dealing with foreigners. In any case, you will be pampered to death in a Japanese salon, making it a delightful experience.

Holidays See "When to Go," in Chapter 2.

Hospitals The following hospitals can be used for an emergency anytime, and they also have clinics staffed with doctors who will see patients at the times indicated below. For more information on doctors, see "Doctors and Dentists," above. The Seibo Byoin (International Catholic Hospital), 2-5-1 Naka-Ochiai, Shinjuku-ku (tel. 3951-1111), has a clinic open Monday through Saturday from 8:30 to 11am; appointments are necessary. Station: Meijiro. The Nihon Sekijujisha Iryo Center (Japan Red Cross Medical Center), 4-1-22 Hiroo, Shibuya-ku (tel. 3400-1311), accepts walk-ins at its clinic Monday through Friday from 8:30 to 11am and on the second and fourth Saturdays of each month from 8:30 to 10:30am. Station: Roppongi, Hiroo, or Shibuya; then take a taxi. The Seiroka Byoin (St. Luke's International Hospital), 1-10 Akashicho, Chuo-ku (tel. 3541-5151), has a clinic open Monday through Saturday from 8:30 to 11am. Station: Tsukiji.

Hotlines A number of services and hotlines offer help and counseling in Tokyo. Alcoholics Anonymous (tel. 3971-1471) has a program in Japan. The Tokyo English Life Line (tel. 5841-4347) is an English-speaking volunteer service providing free, confidential counseling over the phone. The Counseling Center of Tokyo (tel. 3953-2495) and the TELL Community Counseling Service (tel. 5481-4455) both offer professional face-to-face counseling, therapy sessions, and workshops; the latter works on a sliding-scale fee basis.

Japan Helpline does not offer counseling, but provides emergency services nationwide, like interpreting for a patient at a hospital and handling English-language inquiries to the police and fire departments.

Information The Japan Hotline (tel. 3586-0110) is open Monday through Friday from 10am to 4pm to give out general information (from ikebana instruction to obtaining Kabuki tickets) and to assist with daily-life problems you might encounter. Call the Japan National Tourist Organization's Travel-Phone (tel. 3503-4400) for sightseeing information; if you're calling from outside Tokyo, call 0088-22-2800 for information pertaining to eastern Japan (Tokyo, Yokohama, Hokkaido) and 0088-22-4800 for information regarding western Japan (Kyoto, Nagoya, Shikoku, Kyushu). Japan Helpline also offers general information related to travel and living. See also "Information, Entry Requirements, and Money," in Chapter 2, and "Tourist Information" in "Orientation," earlier in this chapter.

Language See Chapter 1 for further discussion. For assistance in frequently used phrases and other language translations, pick up a free booklet called *The Tourist's Handbook,* which has sentences in English with Japanese equivalents for everything from asking directions to ordering in a Japanese restaurant.

Laundry/Dry Cleaning All the upper-bracket hotels, and even some of the hotels for business travelers, offer laundry service and dry cleaning. Several of the Japanese-style accommodations in the budget category have coin-operated washers and dryers. Otherwise, launderettes are abundant, since not everyone in Japan has a machine. The cost is about ¥200 to ¥400 ($1.80 to $3.65) per load for the washer; dryers are about ¥100 (90¢) for 10 minutes.

Liquor Laws Don't drink even one alcoholic drink if you intend to drive in Japan. The legal drinking age is 20. You'll find vending machines dispensing beer and whisky in almost every neighborhood in Japan, but note that most close down at 11pm.

Lost Property If you've forgotten something on a subway, in a taxi, or even on a park bench, you need not assume that it's gone forever. In fact, if you left something, say, in a telephone booth or in a park, go back and look for it—more than likely it will still be there. Otherwise, if you've lost something along a street or outside, go to the nearest koban (local police office). Items found in the neighborhood will stay there for about three days. Afterward, contact the Central Lost and Found Office of the Metropolitan Police Board, 1-9-11 Koraku, Bunkyo-ku (tel. 3841-4151).

If you've lost something in a taxi or subway, you need to contact the appropriate office. For taxis it's the Taxi Kindaika Center, 7-3-3

Minamisuna, Koto-ku (tel. 3648-0300); for JR trains it's the Lost and Found Section at JR Tokyo Station (tel. 3231-1880) or at JR Ueno Station (tel. 3841-8069). For metropolitan buses, subways, and streetcars, contact the Lost and Found Section of the Tokyo Metropolitan Government, 2-8-1 Nishi-Shinjuku, Shinjuku-ku (tel. 5321-1111); another number for subways is the Lost and Found Center in Ueno Station (tel. 3834-5577). And finally, if you've lost something on one of the subways belonging to the Teito Rapid Transit Authority (such as the Ginza, Marunouchi, Yurakucho, Tozai, and Hanzoman Lines), call 03/3834-5577.

Luggage Storage/Lockers Because commuting distances are so great in Tokyo and many office workers and shoppers want to spend the entire day and evening in the city without being encumbered with bags and parcels, there are lockers at all major JR and subway stations in Tokyo, including Shinjuku, Shibuya, the Ginza, Roppongi, and countless others. Finding one that's empty, of course, is something else.

Mail If your hotel cannot mail letters for you, ask the concierge where the nearest post office is. All post offices are open Monday through Friday from 9am to 5pm, though international post offices are open much later, often until 7pm. There are international post offices throughout Tokyo. Tokyo's **Central Post Office** is located just southwest of Tokyo Station at 2-7-2 Marunouchi, Chiyoda-ku (tel. 3284-9527). It's open Monday through Friday from 9am to 7pm, on Saturday from 9am to 5pm, and on Sunday and public holidays from 9am to 12:30pm. If you need information on postage or mail, contact the Information Office of the **Tokyo International Post Office** at 2-3-3 Otemachi (tel. 3241-4891), located north of Tokyo Station.

Post offices are easily recognizable by the red logo of a capital T with a horizontal line above it. Mailboxes in Japan are painted a bright orange-red.

As for **postage,** airmail letters up to 10 grams cost ¥100 (90¢) to North America and ¥120 ($1.10) to Europe. Postcards are ¥70 (65¢) to both. Domestic letters up to 25 grams are ¥62 (55¢); postcards are ¥41 (35¢).

If you wish to mail a **package** abroad, keep in mind that only an international post office, or some of the larger neighborhood ones, can do so. They also sell cardboard boxes in three sizes that come with the necessary string and tape, which is certainly much easier than going out and buying all that stuff. Packages mailed abroad cannot weigh more than 20 kilograms (about 44 lb.). A package weighing 10kg (about 22 lb.) will cost ¥7,150 ($65) sent to North America via surface mail. As you can see, it's very expensive to ship packages abroad.

If you don't know where you'll be staying, you can have your mail sent to you c/o *Post Restante* to Tokyo's Central Post Office, the address for which is given above.

Maps See "City Layout" in "Orientation," earlier in this chapter.

Money See "Information, Entry Requirements, and Money," in Chapter 2.

Newspapers/Magazines Five English-language newspapers are published daily in Japan. They're the *Japan Times, Mainichi Daily News, Daily Yomiuri, Asahi Evening News,* and the *International Herald Tribune.* In addition, the international editions of both *Time* and *Newsweek* are also available. For city magazines that describe what's going on in Tokyo, pick up a copy of either the *Tokyo Journal* or *Tokyo Time Out*.

If you're interested in seeing the latest edition of your favorite magazine back home, check one of the bookstores listed in Chapter 8, under "Books," to see whether they carry it. Otherwise, your best bet is to drop in on the World Magazine Gallery, 3-13-10 Ginza (tel. 3545-7227). Located behind the Kabuki-za theater near Higashi-Ginza Station, it displays more than 1,200 magazines from 40 countries around the globe. Magazines are for reading here only and are not for sale. It's open Monday through Saturday from 11am to 7pm; closed Sunday and public holidays.

Photographic Needs See Chapter 8, "Shopping A to Z."

Police If you're lost or need assistance, your best bet is to find the nearest koban. These tiny neighborhood police stations are everywhere in Tokyo, recognizable by the red lights shining above their doors. In an emergency, call 110 for the police.

Post Office If your hotel cannot mail letters for you, ask the concierge for the location of the nearest post office. Post offices are easily recognizable by the red symbol of a capital T with a horizontal line above it. The Central Post Office is located just southwest of Tokyo Station. Also, see "Mail," above.

Radio The Far East Network (FEN, 810kHz) is the U.S. military station, with broadcasts of music, talk shows, U.S. sports broadcasts, and Tokyo sumo matches. Upper-bracket hotels in Tokyo also have KTYO, a cable radio station broadcasting music, news, and sports in English around the clock.

Restrooms If you're in need of a restroom, your best bet is at train and subway stations, big hotels, department stores, and fast-food chains like McDonald's. Many toilets in Japan, especially those at train stations, are Japanese style. They're holes in the ground over which you squat facing the end that has a raised hood. Men stand and aim for the hole. Although Japanese lavatories may seem uncomfortable at first, they're actually very sanitary because no part of your body touches anything.

Be sure to carry pocket-size tissue, since toilet paper is rarely provided. To find out if a stall is empty, knock on the door. If it's occupied someone will knock back. Similarly, if you're inside a stall and someone knocks, answer with a knock back or they'll just keep on knocking persistently. If you're staying in a Japanese-style inn or are in a place where you must remove your shoes to enter, you'll find special bathroom slippers to wear inside the restroom area.

Don't be surprised if you go into a restroom and find men's urinals and individual private stalls serving both sexes in the same room. Women are supposed to simply walk right past the urinals without noticing them.

Safety Japan is one of the safest countries in the world, much safer than the United States. You'll notice shortly after arrival that the country is safe and the people are honest. These are two of Japan's best attributes. Although crime is slowly on the increase, it's still negligible compared with crime in many other countries (guns are outlawed).

However, it doesn't hurt to exercise caution. You should stay alert whenever you're traveling in an unfamiliar city or country. Don't sling your camera or purse over your shoulder. It's your responsibility to be aware and alert in even the most heavily touristed areas. And be alert for possible pickpockets when riding a rush-hour subway.

Shoe Repairs All department stores have a shoe-repair

counter, usually a Mister Minit chain outlet. In addition, stations such as Yurakucho and Shibuya have streetside shoe repairers. Hotels also often offer such services.

Taxes In 1989 the Japanese government introduced a 3% consumption tax on goods and services, including hotel rates and restaurant meals. It has proved highly unpopular with the Japanese people and there has been talk of abolishing it, but as things stand now a 3% tax will be added to most goods you buy (though some of the smaller mom-and-pop shops and vendors are not required to levy the tax). Travelers from abroad are eligible for a refund of the tax on goods taken out of the country; however, only the larger department stores and specialty shops used to dealing with foreigners seem equipped or willing to follow the procedure. In any case, most department stores grant a refund only when the total amount of purchases exceeds ¥10,000 ($90.90). You can obtain a refund immediately by having the sales clerk fill out a list of your purchases and presenting the list to the tax-exemption counter of that department store. You will need to show your passport. Note that no refunds for the consumption tax are given for food, drinks, tobacco, cosmetics, film, or batteries. When you leave Japan at the Narita airport, you'll find a counter for the declaration of tax-free articles located just before Customs. Be sure to leave the receipt you received from the store here.

As for hotels and meals, a 3% consumption tax will be added to your bill if you stay overnight in lodgings that cost ¥15,000 ($136) or less per person. If your lodging costs more than ¥15,000 per person, both a 3% consumption tax and a 3% local tax will be added to your bill. Some hotels, particularly business hotels, include the tax in their tariff, while others do not. Be sure to ask, therefore, whether rates include tax. In restaurants, a 3% consumption tax is levied on meals costing ¥7,500 ($68) or less, while meals more than ¥7,500 are subject to both a 3% consumption tax and the 3% local tax.

In addition to tax, a 10% to 15% service charge will be added to your bill in lieu of tipping at most of the fancier restaurants and at many hotels. Thus, the 16% to 21% in tax and service charge can really add up. Note that most ryokan (Japanese-style inns) include service charge but not tax in their rates.

If you depart from the Narita airport outside Tokyo, you will be charged a ¥2,000 ($18.20) service facility fee (there is no departure tax at any of the other international airports in Japan); children 2 to 11 are charged ¥1,000 ($9.10). There are vending machines that sell departure-tax tickets just past the airline counters, before you descend downstairs to Customs.

Taxis See "Getting Around," earlier in this chapter.

Telephone, Telex, and Fax If you're staying in a medium- or upper-range hotel, most likely you can send Telexes or facsimiles from the hotel business center or front desk. You can also make local, domestic, and international calls from your room. Otherwise, there are number of different kinds of **public telephones** in Tokyo, all color-coded. You can find them virtually everywhere—phone booths on the sidewalk, stands outside little shops, on train-station platforms, in restaurants and coffee shops. There are even telephones in Japan's bullet trains. The red, pink, and blue phones take only ¥10 coins, while the yellow and green ones accept both ¥10 and ¥100 coins. A local call costs ¥10 (9¢) for the first 1½ minutes, after which a warning chime will ring to tell you to insert more coins or you'll be disconnected.

If you don't want to deal with coins, you can purchase a disposable **telephone credit card** that can be inserted into a slot on most of the green telephones. These can be bought at vending machines (located right beside many telephones), at many souvenir shops, telephone offices, and at some station kiosks for values of ¥500 and ¥1,000 ($4.55 and $9.10). Considered collectors' items in Japan, telephone cards are even sold at major attractions with photographs adorning the front.

If you need assistance with telephone **directory listings** in Tokyo, English-speaking operators can help you if you call 3277-1010. There are also several English-language telephone directories available that provide addresses and telephone numbers for many businesses, companies, shops, and restaurants in Tokyo. They're *CitySource,* the *English Telephone Directory,* the *Japan Times Directory,* and the *Japan Telephone Book Yellow Pages.* If your hotel does not have one of these and you're interested in buying one, check the bookstores listed in Chapter 8.

For **international calls** made from public phones, you can make a collect call or place a call through an operator anywhere in Japan by dialing 0051. An operator-assisted, station-to-station call to the United States costs ¥1,740 ($15.80) for the first three minutes. Cheaper, however, are calls made without the assistance of an operator, either through an international green public telephone or private telephones that offer direct-dial service (most medium- and upper-range hotels in Tokyo offer direct dial, but remember to ask about the surcharge). Note that not all green public telephones are equipped to handle international calls. If they do, there will be a sign with the phrase "International and Domestic Card/Coin Telephone." This is when those telephone cards come in handy.

Telephone rates for international calls have become more competitive as Japan's one-time monopoly Kokusai Denshin Denwa (KDD) has had to make room for competitors International Telecom Japan (ITJ) and International Digital Communications (IDC). In fact, at press time, KDD was considering lowering its rates since it has lost about 30% of the market to the two newcomers, which charge less. The direct-dial numbers are 011 for KDD, 0041 for ITJ, and 0061 for IDC. If you want to dial directly to the United States through ITJ, for example, dial 0041 + 1 + area code + phone number. Note that after dialing 0041, you must pause a few seconds until you hear a quick succession of beeps; then you can continue dialing. The cheapest time to call is between 11pm and 8am Japan time, when a three-minute call to the United States through ITJ (0041) costs ¥400 ($3.65).

If you wish to be connected with an operator in your home country, you can do so from green international telephones by dialing 0039 followed by the country code (for the United States, dial 0039-111). These calls can be used for collect calls or credit-card calls. Some hotels and other public places are equipped with special phones that will link you to your home operator with the simple push of one of several buttons, each labeled with a different country.

You can also place international telephone calls through the **Tokyo Telegraph & Telephone (KDD)** office at 1-8-1 Otemachi (tel. 03/3275-4343), located close to Tokyo Station. It's open Monday through Friday from 9am to 6pm, and on Saturday, Sunday, and holidays from 9am to 5pm. It can also handle facsimiles, phototelegrams, ISD calls, and Telex in addition to telegrams and telephone calls.

If you're calling a number in Tokyo from outside the city, the **area code** for Tokyo is 03. If you're calling Tokyo from the United States, drop the "0" from the area code; the country code is 81. To dial the Imperial Hotel from the United States, for example, you would dial 011-81-3-3504-1111.

Television If you enjoy watching television, you've come to the wrong country. Almost nothing is broadcast in English; even foreign films are dubbed in Japanese, and the only way to hear them in English is to have what's called a "bilingual television." Most of the best hotels in Tokyo do have bilingual televisions, though only a very few English-language movies are on the networks each week. The cable service available in Tokyo's better hotels has English-language programs throughout the day, including CNN broadcasts from America.

Incidentally, many hotels in Japan also offer in-house videos, including pornographic movies (with the offensive parts, of course, blacked out). If you have in-room video, you can be pretty sure it's an "adult" film. By the way, if you're traveling with children, you will want to be extremely careful about selecting your television programs. Many adult video pay channels I encountered appear with a simple push of the channel selector button—and they can even be difficult to get rid of.

Time Japan is 9 hours ahead of Greenwich mean time, 14 hours ahead of New York, 15 hours ahead of Chicago, and 17 hours ahead of Los Angeles. Since Japan does not go on daylight saving time, subtract 1 hour from the above times if you're calling the United States in the summer. Because Japan is on the other side of the International Date Line, you lose a day when traveling from the United States to Asia. Returning to North America, however, you gain a day, which means that you arrive on the day you left. In fact, it often happens that you arrive in the States at an earlier hour than you departed from Japan.

Tipping One of the delights of being in Japan is that there is *no tipping,* not even of waiters, taxi drivers, or bellhops. If you try to tip them they'll probably be confused or embarrassed. Instead of individual tips, a 10% to 15% service charge will be added to your bill at the higher-priced hotels and restaurants.

Water The water is safe to drink anywhere in Japan, though some people claim it's too highly chlorinated. Bottled water is also readily available.

Weather The *Japan Times* carries almost a full page of weather information daily, including forecasts for Tokyo and other major Japanese cities and a weekly outlook. In addition, local weather information for Tokyo can be obtained by dialing 177, though note that the information is only in Japanese.

CHAPTER 4

TOKYO ACCOMMODATIONS

Without a doubt, your biggest expense in Tokyo is going to be a place to sleep at night. Space is at a premium, so even a lot of money doesn't always buy a large room. In fact, rooms in Tokyo seem to come in only three sizes: adequate, small, and minuscule. On the other hand, your room will be spotlessly clean and the staff will be efficient and courteous. Indeed, the service at Tokyo's top hotels is nothing short of remarkable.

Unless otherwise stated, *prices given below are room rates only.* Remember that, in addition, a 3% consumption tax will be added to all rates that are less than ¥15,000 ($136) per person per night. For rates of ¥15,000 or more per person, both a 3% consumption tax and a 3% local tax will be added to the bill. And all expensive hotels and most moderately priced accommodations will add a 10% to 15% service charge. This is in lieu of individual tipping—in Japan, you never tip anyone who provides service in a hotel. Budget accommodations—those around ¥6,000 ($55) per person a night—do not levy service charges, since there's generally not much service rendered.

The majority of accommodations listed below are Western-style. Unfortunately, Tokyo does not have many *ryokan,* or Japanese-style inns. If you want to splurge, therefore, I suggest that you take a trip to one of the resort towns outside Tokyo such as Hakone, Izu, or Nikko (see Chapter 10 for accommodations outside Tokyo). As an alternative, most of the upper-bracket hotels offer at least a few Japanese-style rooms, with tatami mats, Japanese bathtubs (which are deeper and narrower than Western tubs), and futons. Although these rooms tend to be expensive (they're used mainly by wedding parties), they are usually large enough for four people.

On the other hand, if you're traveling on a budget, most of Tokyo's budget accommodations are Japanese style. They don't have the personalized service or grandeur of a true ryokan, but they do offer the chance to experience the Japanese style of living.

By the way, in case you don't know the difference between a double or twin room, a twin contains two separate beds, while a double contains one large full- or king-size bed. Some hotels charge more for a double; others, more for a twin.

For each accommodation, I've listed the nearest subway station and the walking time required to get from the station to the hotel. To further help in your orientation, hotels are arranged according to price and then further subdivided by location, beginning with the areas of Hibiya and the Ginza in the heart of the city and then fanning out to other locations such as Akasaka and Shinjuku.

Although Tokyo doesn't suffer from a lack of hotel rooms during peak holidays (most Japanese head for the hills and beaches during the holidays), there are times when rooms are in short supply because of conventions and other events. In addition, in summer when there are many foreign tourists in Japan, the cheaper accommodations are often the first to fill up. It's always best, therefore, to make your hotel reservation in advance, especially if you're arriving in Japan after a long transpacific flight and don't want the hassle of searching for a hotel room. Some of the hotels below belong to well-known groups such as the Hilton or Holiday Inn, for which you can easily reserve in advance by dialing the hotel's local representative or toll-free number. Reservations for the major hotels can also be made through travel agencies. And since most hotels have fax numbers, you can also reserve your room by facsimile. Once in Japan, call immediately to reconfirm your reservation.

Finally, word should be mentioned here about Tokyo's so-called love hotels. Usually found close to large entertainment districts and along major highways, such hotels do not provide sexual services themselves but, rather, offer rooms for rent by the hour to lovers or even married couples who have no privacy at home. Altogether there are an estimated 35,000 such love hotels in Japan, usually gaudy structures shaped like ocean liners or castles and offering such extras as rotating beds, video-recording equipment, or mirrored walls. Love hotels can be found in abundance in Shibuya, Shinjuku, and Asakusa.

PRICE CATEGORIES

VERY EXPENSIVE Tokyo has no old, grand hotel like Singapore's Raffles or Hong Kong's Peninsula. In fact, it doesn't have many old hotels, period. However, Tokyo's top hotels can rival upper-range hotels anywhere in the world.

Facilities at Tokyo's deluxe hotels are usually staggering. In addition to fine Japanese- and Western-style restaurants, they may also offer a travel agency, an executive business center with secretarial services, a guest relations officer to help with any problems you may have, a shopping arcade with designer boutiques, cocktail lounges with live music, and health club and swimming pool. Note, however, that an extra fee is almost always charged for use of a health club and swimming pool, often at exorbitant rates. Many hotels offer special "executive floors" with more guest amenities and such services as free continental breakfast and cocktails. Because they're accustomed to foreigners, most upper- and medium-range hotels employ an English-speaking staff. You can expect to pay ¥31,000 ($281) and more for two people in a "Very Expensive" hotel.

EXPENSIVE Many expensive hotels offer almost as much as Tokyo's very expensive hotels and would probably qualify as top accommodations anywhere else in the world. Others are expensive primarily because of location, especially those in the Ginza. Prices in

---

IMPRESSIONS

Japan, a country combining a feverish proficiency in many of the habits of advanced civilization with uncompromising relics of feudal crystallization.

—GEORGE CURZON, *TALES OF TRAVEL*, 1923

"Expensive" hotels, based on double occupancy, range from about ¥21,000 to ¥30,000 ($190 to $272).

MODERATE Moderately priced accommodations vary from tourist hotels to so-called business hotels, with business hotels making up the majority in this category. Catering primarily to traveling Japanese businessmen, a business hotel is a no-frills establishment with tiny, sparsely furnished rooms, most of them singles. There's no room service, and sometimes not even a lobby or coffee shop, although usually there are vending machines that dispense beer and soda. On the plus side, they're usually situated in convenient locations.

Hotels and business hotels in the "Moderate" range offer rooms for ¥12,000 to ¥20,000 ($109 to $182) for two people. Many include tax and service charge in their rates.

BUDGET It's difficult to find inexpensive lodgings in Tokyo the way you can in other big cities in Asia. The price of land is simply too prohibitive. You can, however, find rooms—tiny though they may be—for less than $60 a night for two people, which is pretty good considering that you're in one of the most expensive cities in the world. Budget accommodations include a bed, and usually a phone, television, heating, and air conditioning. Facilities are generally spotless, and prices often include tax and service charge, though the cheapest accommodations do not levy service charges because there is no service rendered. Inexpensive Japanese-style rooms make up the majority in this category, described in more detail below.

Other budget options include Western-style hotels, YMCAs and YWCAs, youth hostels, and capsule hotels. Even though they may never consider staying in a **youth hostel** in other countries, many foreigners find Japan so expensive that they end up becoming hostel regulars. There's no age limit, and although most require a youth hostel membership card from the International Youth Hostel Federation, they often let foreigners stay without one for an extra ¥700 ($6.35) or so per night.

If you plan on staying exclusively in youth hostels, however, you should apply for a youth hostel card (note that many youth hostels allow only a three-night maximum stay). If you fail to get one in your country, you can get one in Japan for ¥2,800 ($25). The **Japan Youth Hostel Association** is located in the Hoken Kaikan Honkan Building, 1-2 Sadohara-cho, Ichigaya, Shinjuku 162 (tel. 03/3269-5831). You can also buy a youth hostel card in Tokyo at YH information counters on the seventh floor of Keio Department Store in Shinjuku, the second basement of Sogo Department Store in front of Yurakucho Station, and on the eighth floor of Seibu Department Store in Ikebukuro.

It's advisable to make reservations beforehand, which you can do by writing directly to the youth hostel concerned, giving date and time of arrival, and number and sex of your party. Include two International Reply Coupons for the reply.

Although there are usually such restrictions as a 9 or 10pm curfew, meals at fixed times, an early-morning wake-up call, and rooms with many bunk beds or futons, they're certainly the cheapest places to stay in Japan.

So-called **capsule hotels** became popular in the early 1980s and are used primarily by Japanese businessmen who have spent an evening out drinking with fellow workers and missed their last train home—a capsule hotel is cheaper than a taxi ride home. At any rate, accommodation in one of these places is a small unit consisting of a bed and private color TV, alarm clock, and radio. These units are usually stacked two deep in rows down a corridor, and the only thing separating you from your probably inebriated neighbor is a curtain. Because of that, most capsule hotels do not accept women. A cotton kimono and locker are provided, and bath and toilets are communal. You may wish to stay at a capsule inn just for the novel experience. The two I recommend are in Akasaka.

JAPANESE-STYLE ACCOMMODATIONS

THE RYOKAN Although it can be very expensive, it's worth it to splurge at least once during your trip and spend the night in a traditional Japanese inn, called ryokan in Japanese. Nothing conveys the mood, simple beauty and atmosphere of old Japan better than these small enclaves of gleaming polished wood, tatami floors, rice-paper sliding doors, meticulously pruned Japanese gardens, and kimono-clad hostesses. Personalized service and exquisitely prepared meals are the trademarks of a ryokan, and staying in one of these is like taking a trip back in time.

Ideally made of wood with a tile roof, most ryokan are small, only one or two stories high, with about 10 to 30 rooms. The entrance is often through a gate and small garden, where you are met by a bowing woman in kimono. Remove your shoes, slide on the plastic slippers, and follow your hostess down long wooden corridors until you reach the sliding door of your room. After taking off your slippers, step into your tatami room, almost void of furniture—a low table in the middle of the room, floor cushions, an antique scroll hanging in an alcove, a simple flower arrangement, and best of all, a view past rice-paper sliding screens of a Japanese landscaped garden with bonsai, stone lanterns, and a meandering pond filled with carp. You notice that there's no bed in the room.

Almost immediately your hostess brings you a welcoming hot tea and a sweet, served at your low table so that you might sit there for a while and appreciate the view, the peace, and solitude. Next comes your hot bath, either in your own room if it has one, or in the communal bath. Be sure to follow the procedure on Japanese etiquette outlined in "Geography, History, and Culture," in Chapter 1, soaping and rinsing yourself before getting into the tub. After bathing and soaking away all tension, aches, and pains, change into your yukata, a cotton kimono provided by the ryokan.

When you return to your room you'll find the maid ready to lay out your dinner, which consists of locally grown vegetables, fish, and various regional specialties all spread out on many tiny plates. There is no menu in a ryokan, but rather one or more set meals determined by the chef. Admire how each dish is in itself a delicate piece of artwork, adorned with slices of ginger, a maple leaf, or a flower. It all looks too wonderful to eat, but finally hunger takes over. If you want, you can order sake or beer to accompany your meal.

After you've finished eating, your maid will return to clear away the dishes and to lay out your bed. Called a futon, it's a kind of mattress with quilts and is laid out on the tatami floor. The next morning the maid will wake you up, put away the futon, and serve a breakfast of fish, pickled vegetables, soup, dried seaweed, rice, and a raw egg to be mixed with the rice. Feeling rested, well fed, and pampered, you are then ready to pack your bags and pay your bill.

Your hostess sees you off at the front gate, smiling and bowing as you set off for the rest of your travels.

Such is life at a good ryokan. Sadly enough, however, the number of upper-class ryokan diminishes each year. Unable to compete with the more profitable high-rise hotels, many ryokan in Japan's large cities have had to close down, with the result that there are very few left in Tokyo. If you want to stay in a deluxe Japanese inn, therefore, it's best to do so at a resort or hot-spring spa, such as Nikko or Hakone (covered in Chapter 10). Alternatively, most of Tokyo's upper-class hotels offer Japanese-style rooms as well.

Although ideally a ryokan is a wooden structure at least 100 years old, many ryokan, especially those in hot-spring resort areas, are modern concrete affairs with as many as 100 rooms or more. What they lack in intimacy, however, is made up for in modern bathroom facilities and added attractions of perhaps a bar and outdoor recreational facilities. Most guest rooms are fitted with color television, phone, and a safe for locking valuables.

Unlike Western-style hotels, *rates in a ryokan are based on a per-person charge* rather than a straight room charge and include breakfast, dinner, and service charge. Although rates can vary from ¥8,000 to ¥150,000 ($73 to $1,364) per person, the average cost is generally between ¥10,000 and ¥20,000 ($91 to $182). Even within a single ryokan the rates can vary greatly depending on which room you take, which set dinner you select, and the number of people in your room. If you're paying the highest rate you can be assured of having the best view of the garden or perhaps even your own private garden, as well as a better meal than the lower-paying guests are getting. All the rates for ryokan in this book are based on double occupancy; if there are more than two of you in one room you can generally count on a slightly lower rate.

Although I heartily recommend that you try staying at least one night in a ryokan, there are a number of disadvantages that you should be aware of, though in my estimation the experience itself far outweighs the disadvantages. The most obvious one is that you may find it uncomfortable sitting on the floor. Second, because the futon is put away during the day, there's no place except the hard tatami on which to lie down for an afternoon nap or rest. And some of the older ryokan, though quaint, are bitterly cold in the winter and may have only Japanese-style toilets. As for breakfast, some foreigners might find it difficult to swallow raw egg, rice, and seaweed in the morning. Sometimes you can get a Western-style breakfast if you order it the night before, but more often than not the fried or scrambled eggs will arrive cold, leading you to suspect that they were cooked right after you ordered them (most ryokan do prepare breakfast the night before).

A ryokan is also quite rigid in its schedule. You're expected to arrive sometime after 4pm, take your bath, and then eat around 6 or 7pm. Breakfast is served early, usually by 8am, and check-out is by 10am. That means you can't sleep in late, and because the maid is continually coming in and out you have a lot less privacy than you would in a hotel.

The main drawback of the ryokan, however, is that the majority will not take you. They simply do not want to deal with the problems inherent in accepting a foreign guest, including the language barrier and differing customs. I saw a number of beautiful old ryokan that I would have liked to include in this book, but I was turned away at their doors. The ryokan in this guide, therefore, are willing to take in foreigners, but because management and policies can change, it's best to call beforehand.

The Japan National Tourist Organization offers a free publication called "The Tourist's Handbook," which describes the rules of etiquette for staying in a ryokan, along with handy translations for common situations that may arise.

JAPANESE INN GROUP If you want the experience of staying in a Japanese-style room but cannot afford the extravagance of a ryokan, you should consider staying in one of the participating members of the Japanese Inn Group. The Japanese Inn Group is a special organization of more than 60 Japanese-style inns throughout the country that offer inexpensive lodging and cater largely to foreigners. In fact, most of the budget accommodations covered in this book are members of this group. Although at first thought you may balk at the idea of staying at a place filled mainly with foreigners, you must remember that most of the cheap Japanese-style inns in Japan are not accustomed to guests from abroad and may be quite reluctant to take you in.

Although they call themselves ryokan, members of the Japanese Inn Group are not ryokan in the true sense of the word because they do not offer personalized service and many of them do not serve food. However, they do offer simple tatami rooms which generally come with a coin-operated TV and usually with an air conditioner as well. Some of them have towels and the cotton yukata kimono for your use. Facilities generally include a coin-operated washer and dryer and public bath. In many cases they are good places in which to exchange information with other travelers from all over the world and are popular with both young people and families.

This organization publishes a free pamphlet called "Japanese Inn Group," which lists the members and is available at the Tourist Information Center in Tokyo.

MINSHUKU Technically, a minshuku is inexpensive lodging in a private home, usually located in resort areas or smaller towns. The average per-person cost runs about ¥6,000 ($55) per night, including two meals. Because minshuku are family-run affairs, you are expected to lay out your own futon at night, supply your own towel and nightgown, and tidy up your room in the morning. Rooms do not have their own private bathrooms but there is a public bath. Meals are served in a communal dining room. Although, officially, the difference between a ryokan and a minshuku is that the ryokan is more expensive and provides more services, the difference is sometimes very slight. I've stayed in cheap ryokan that provided almost no service at all and in minshuku too large and modern to be considered a private home.

1. VERY EXPENSIVE

GINZA & HIBIYA

HOTEL SEIYO GINZA, 1-11-2 Ginza, Chuo-ku 104, Tokyo. Tel. 03/3535-1111. Fax 03/3535-1110. 80 rms and suites. A/C MINIBAR TV TEL **Station:** Ginza-Itchome (then a two-minute walk) or Ginza (then a five-minute walk).

$ Rates: ¥48,000–¥72,000 ($436–$655) single or double; ¥85,000–¥280,000 ($773–$2,545) suite. AE, CB, DC, JCB, MC, V.

One of Tokyo's most exclusive luxury hotels, this is also one of the smallest and most discreet. It caters to foreign executives or personalities who want to avoid publicity. The hotel is not open to the public—that is, you must either be a hotel guest or have a reservation at one of its exclusive restaurants to enter. But the main entrance is so subdued that you could easily walk right by without even knowing it's a hotel. A hush prevails throughout the premises, and instead of a front desk there's a comfortable reception room that resembles a living room. As one hotel employee explained, "The hardware is a Western-style hotel, but the software is traditional Japanese service." Indeed, with only 80 rooms and a staff numbering more than 200, service is superior.

Rooms, located on the 7th to 12th floors, are quite large for Japan and come with safes, humidity-control dials, videocassette players (the hotel's library stocks 200 video titles), and walk-in closets. Bathrooms are huge, with separate shower and tub units and even mini-TVs and music. With the busy executive in mind, telephones have two lines and there are computerized "Do Not Disturb" and "Maid Service" buttons linked to hotel personnel so that they can respond immediately to their guests. Each guest has a personal secretary, introduced on arrival, who will take dictation, order tickets, organize trips, buy gifts, or do whatever else is needed.

Dining/Entertainment: There are four restaurants serving French, Italian, and Japanese food, including the Pastorale, which specializes in French nouvelle cuisine and has one of Japan's largest and best wine cellars, with 300 vintages and 15,000 bottles. Attore serves specialties from northern Italy and is a good place for a business lunch.

Services: 24-hour room service; a personal secretary to organize business needs, travel arrangements, and other requests.

Facilities: Fitness room, two theaters.

IMPERIAL HOTEL, 1-1-1 Uchisaiwaicho, Chiyoda-ku 100, Tokyo. Tel. 03/3504-1111, or toll free 800/223-5652 in the U.S., 800/223-6800 in the U.S. and Canada. Fax 03/3581-9146. 1,068 rms and suites. A/C MINIBAR TV TEL **Station:** Hibiya (then a one-minute walk).

$ Rates: ¥30,000–¥56,000 ($272–$509) single; ¥35,000–¥61,000 ($318–$555) double or twin; from ¥60,000 ($545) suite. Extra person ¥3,300 ($30). AE, DC, JCB, MC, V.

This is one of Tokyo's best-known hotels. Located across from Hibiya Park within walking distance of Ginza, the Imperial's trademark is excellent and impeccable service. Here guests are treated like royalty and the atmosphere throughout is subdued and dignified. Although the present hotel dates from 1970 with a 31-story tower added in 1983, the Imperial's history goes back to 1922, when it opened as a small hotel made of brick and stone with intricate designs carved into its facade, designed by Frank Lloyd Wright. The Imperial won lasting fame when it survived almost intact the 1923 earthquake that destroyed much of the rest of the city. Alas, the structure did not survive Tokyo's building fever of the past few decades, and the original building was torn down in 1968 to make way for a larger building. Part of Wright's building, however, was moved to Meiji-Mura, an outdoor architectural museum outside Nagoya.

Rooms are located in both a main building and a newer tower. While those of the main building are quite large for Tokyo, tower rooms offer the advantage of floor-to-ceiling bay windows with fantastic views of either the Imperial Palace or Ginza and the harbor. In any case, all rooms are outfitted with everything you could possibly wish for, including practical writing tables, three telephones, remote-control television, cotton yukata, terry-cloth robes, safes, hairdryers. If you don't see what you need, simply ask.

Dining/Entertainment: There are 13 restaurants and four

FROMMER'S SMART TRAVELER: HOTELS

VALUE-CONSCIOUS TRAVELERS SHOULD TAKE ADVANTAGE OF THE FOLLOWING:

1. Smaller, cheaper rooms in large hotels, where guests can take advantage of facilities ranging from outdoor pools to a variety of restaurants.
2. Japanese-style rooms in Western-style hotels, which often sleep as many as four people and offer the opportunity to experience traditional Japanese living.
3. Japanese-style inns, which are often cheaper than business hotels and sometimes include breakfast and dinner in their price.
4. Inexpensive hotels outside the city center, which are much cheaper than those in the heart of Tokyo and still convenient to local transportation.
5. Rooms without private bathroom in the budget accommodations, which are much cheaper.
6. Youth hostels and the Ys, open throughout the year.

QUESTIONS TO ASK IF YOU'RE ON A BUDGET

1. Are service charge and tax included in the price? If not, what is the total charge per night?
2. Are prices different for a double- or twin-bedded room? Some hotels charge more for a twin; others, for a double.
3. Is there a cheaper room available than the price quoted? Many hotels have rooms in various price categories but may try to sell the more expensive room first, especially if they feel the cheapest rooms and beds are too small for foreigners.
4. Does your room have a window? Does it face an inner courtyard? Sometimes the difference between a windowless room and one that faces the street is only a few dollars.
5. How much is the surcharge on local and long-distance telephone calls?
6. Is there parking space at the hotel, and if so, what is the charge per day?

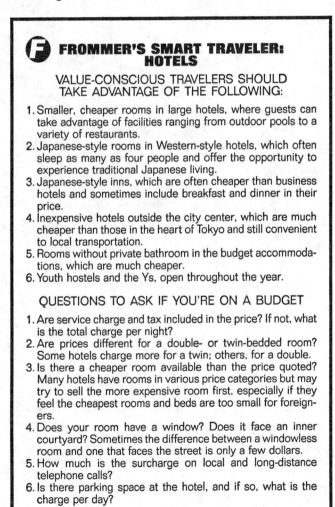

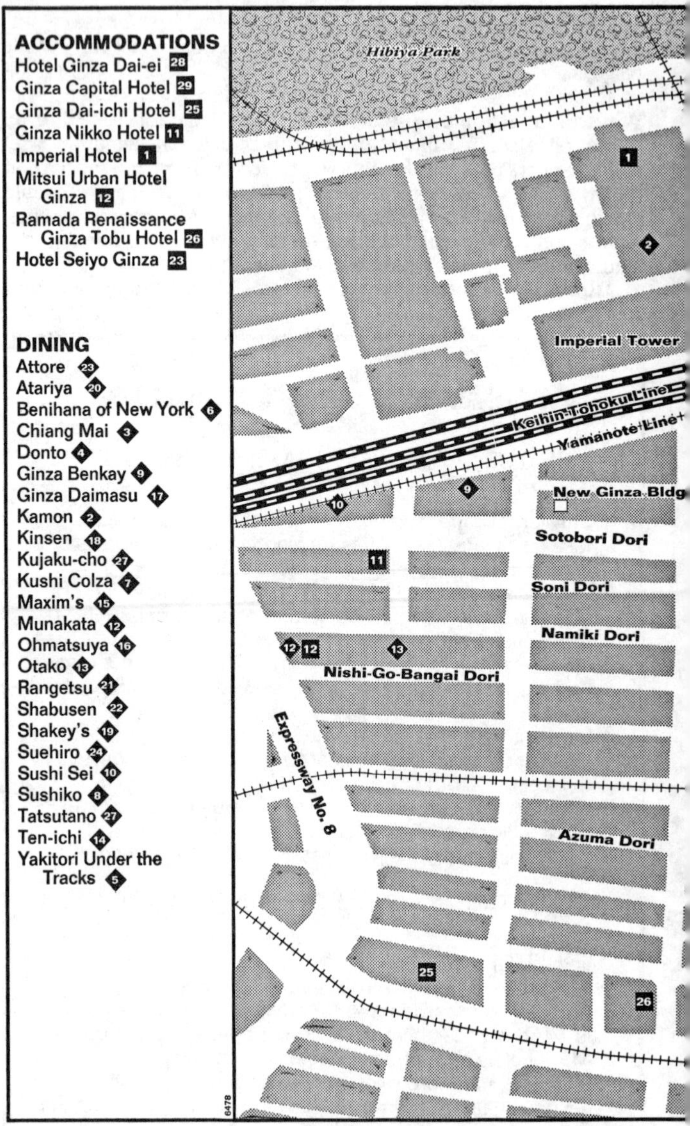

bars. Its top restaurant, the Fontainebleau, serves exquisitely prepared French cuisine, while the Prunier, founded in 1936, specializes in seafood, as does the more lighthearted and very popular Les Saisons. Other restaurants specialize in various types of Japanese food, including sushi, Kyoto-style cuisine, and sukiyaki, as well as Chinese and casual Western food, and the new Kamon serves teppanyaki in a sleekly modern Japanese interior.

Services: Babysitting, limousine and car-rental services, same-day laundry service, free newspaper, physician and dentist.

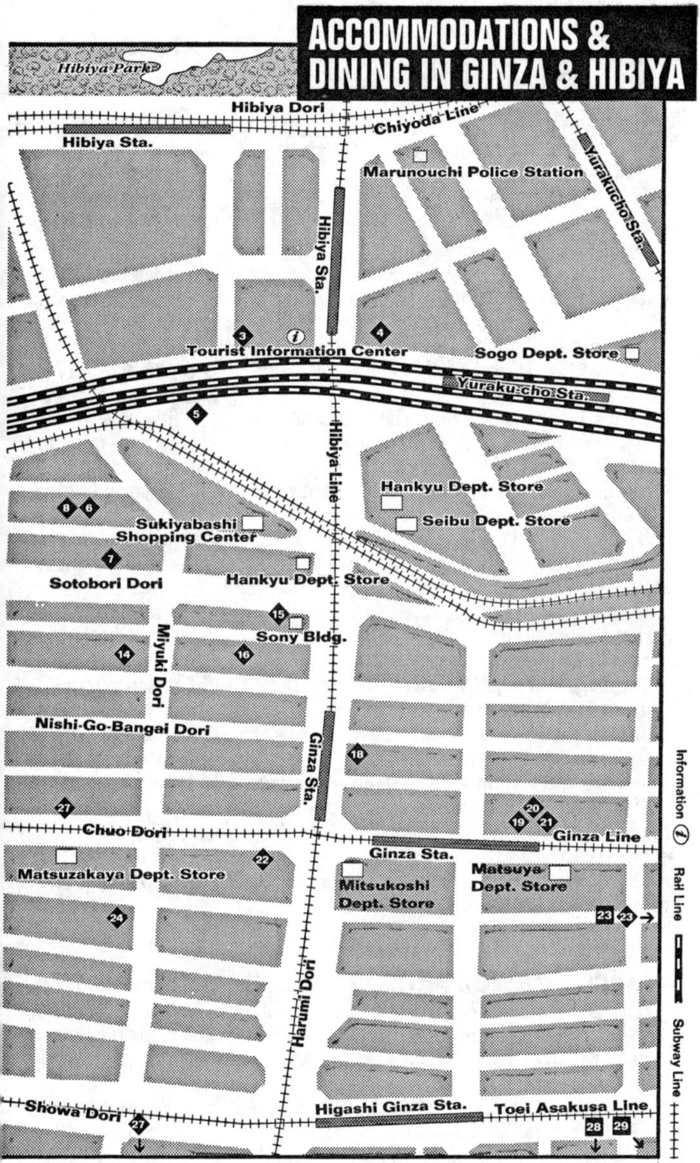

Facilities: An impressive shopping arcade, barbershop and beauty parlor, business center, post office, tea-ceremony room, sauna, and Tokyo's most dramatic swimming pool, located on the 20th floor with a breathtaking view of Tokyo Bay (fee: ¥1,000/$9.10).

TORANOMON

HOTEL OKURA, 2-10-4 Toranomon, Minato-ku 105, Tokyo. Tel. 03/3582-0111, or toll free 800/223-6800 in the U.S.,

800/341-8585 in Canada. Fax 03/3582-3707. 888 rms and suites. A/C MINIBAR TV TEL **Station:** Toranomon or Kamiyacho (then a 10-minute walk).

$ **Rates:** Western-style rooms, ¥32,000–¥66,000 ($290–$600) single; ¥40,000–¥60,000 ($363–$545) double or twin. Japanese-style rooms, ¥37,000–¥75,000 ($336–$682) single; ¥40,000–¥75,000 ($363–$682) double. From ¥90,000 ($818) suite. Extra bed ¥5,000 ($45). AE, CB, DC, JCB, MC, V. **Parking:** Free garage.

Built just before the 1964 Olympic Summer Games were held in Tokyo, the Okura is one of Tokyo's most venerable hotels. Located across the street from the American Embassy, it's the favorite of visiting U.S. dignitaries, as well as such celebrities as rock star David Bowie and the late pianist Vladimir Horowitz. Conservative and traditional in decor, the Okura combines Western comfort with Japanese design in the use of shoji screens, flower displays, and a beautifully sculptured garden. This is one of my favorite hotels in Tokyo. In a city where the newest means flashy and borderline pretentious, the Okura comes across as downright old-fashioned.

There are 11 different kinds of rooms, including a dozen Japanese-style rooms with tatami floors, shoji screens, and Japanese tubs. Western-style rooms on the fifth floor feature good-size balconies overlooking a small but meticulously groomed Japanese garden. Televisions receive English-language cable with CNN and offer in-house movies.

Dining/Entertainment: The Okura has eight restaurants and four bars, including La Belle Epoque French restaurant on the 12th floor with views of the city and the casual Terrace Restaurant which looks out onto the garden.

Services: Room service, laundry service, free newspaper.

Facilities: Indoor and outdoor swimming pools (fee: ¥1,200/$10.90), health club and gym (fee charged), a shopping arcade with 41 exclusive boutiques, barbershop, beauty parlor, massage, steam bath, business center, medical clinic, packing and shipping service.

AKASAKA

AKASAKA PRINCE HOTEL, 1-2 Kioicho, Chiyoda-ku 102, Tokyo. Tel. 03/3234-1111, or toll free 800/542-8686 or 800/637-7200 in the U.S. Fax 03/3262-5163. 761 rms and suites. A/C MINIBAR TV TEL **Station:** Akasaka-mitsuke (then a three-minute walk).

$ **Rates:** ¥24,000–¥38,000 ($218–$345) single; ¥32,000–¥41,000 ($290–$373) twin; ¥37,000–¥45,000 ($336–$409) double; from ¥95,000 ($864) suite. AE, DC, JCB, MC, V. **Parking:** Free.

When this hotel opened in 1983, it caused quite a stir, as some Tokyoites complained that it was too cold and sterile. In my opinion, however, this 40-story gleaming-white skyscraper was just ahead of its time. Japanese style, after all, has always called for simplicity, and this hotel's design projects that simplicity into the 21st century. Its lobby is intentionally spacious and empty, lined with almost 12,000 slabs of white marble. The hotel was designed by Kenzo Tange, who wanted to keep the decor uncomplicated so as not to compete with the brilliant Japanese kimono. Judging by the number of wedding receptions here, the design paid off. The bare, spacious look is now very much in vogue in Tokyo.

Each of the hotel's rooms is set at a 45° angle from the center axis of the core of the building, giving each one a corner view with expansive windows overlooking the city. If you request a room overlooking the Akasaka side, you'll be treated to a view of neon lights below and Tokyo Tower off in the distance. Room color schemes are a soothing powder-blue and white, bright with a lot of sunshine. The single rooms are among the nicest in Tokyo, with three windows forming a pleasant alcove around a sofa. Sinks and vanities are located separately from the toilet and bath area. There's even a no-smoking floor.

Dining/Entertainment: There are 12 international restaurants and bars. Le Trianon, the hotel's top Western restaurant, has all the grace, decor, and atmosphere of a fine French restaurant. Other restaurants serve Chinese, Japanese, and continental cuisine, including the Blue Gardenia on the 40th floor with spectacular views of the city. Also on the 40th floor is Top of Akasaka, one of the city's best cocktail lounges with a view.

Services: 24-hour room service, same-day laundry and dry-cleaning service, babysitting, free newspaper.

Facilities: Business center, travel desk, souvenir shop, florist.

ANA HOTEL TOKYO, 1-12-33 Akasaka, Minato-ku 107, Tokyo. Tel. 03/3505-111, or toll free 800/44-ANA HOTELS in the U.S. and Canada. Fax 03/3505-1155. 903 rms, 27 suites. A/C MINIBAR TV TEL **Station:** Roppongi, Akasaka, Kamiyacho, Toranomon, or Kokkai Gijido-mae (then a 15-minute walk).

$ **Rates:** ¥25,000–¥35,000 ($227–$318) single; ¥34,000–¥38,000 ($309–$345) double or twin; from ¥38,000 ($345) executive floor double; from ¥60,000 ($545) suite. Extra bed ¥4,000 ($36). AE, DB, DC, JCB, MC, V.

A gleaming white building rising 37 stories high above the crossroads of Roppongi, Akasaka, Toranomon, and Kasumigaseki, the ANA Hotel is in the heart of the city. Since its opening in 1986, it has given the older deluxe hotels stiff competition, wooing away valued business clients because of its location and its services. The second-floor lobby is impressive and spacious, with cool, cream-colored marble and a fountain. The lobby lounge is a favorite among Tokyoites for people-watching. Restaurants, rooms, and even corridors are superbly decorated with artwork and vases.

Rooms are large, with views of Tokyo Bay, Mt. Fuji, or the Imperial Palace, and come with TV and pay video, well-stocked refrigerator, and minibar. Its 34th floor features a special executive floor, which offers the services of a concierge, free buffet breakfast, and an evening cocktail hour.

Dining/Entertainment: The Rose Room is an intimate French restaurant, while the Unkai serves the best of Japanese cuisine. You can also dine on seafood, Chinese dishes, sushi, and teppanyaki, and the Astral Bar on the 37th floor offers live music and a spectacular view of the city.

Services: Room service (to 2am), same-day laundry service, free newspapers delivered twice daily.

Facilities: Outdoor swimming pool (fee: ¥2,000/$18), sauna (men only), business center, a travel desk, shopping arcade, barbershop and beauty salon, babysitting room.

CAPITOL TOKYU, 2-10-3 Nagata-cho, Chiyoda-ku 100, Tokyo. Tel. 03/3581-4511, or toll free 800/888-1199 in the U.S. and Canada. Fax 03/3581-5822. 459 rms and suites. A/C MINIBAR TV TEL **Station:** Kokkai Gijido-mae (then a one-minute walk).

$ Rates: ¥26,000–¥38,000 ($236–$345) single; ¥37,000–¥43,000 ($336–$391) double or twin; from ¥95,000 ($864) suite. Extra bed ¥4,500 ($40.90). Children under 18 stay free in parents' room. AE, DC, JCB, MC, V.

Built just before the 1964 Olympics, this hotel served as the Tokyo Hilton until 1984, when the Tokyu hotel chain took over the management and the Hilton moved to a new home in Shinjuku. A cozy establishment, it's a small hotel by Tokyo's standards, and has the unique ability to make foreign guests feel that they are in the Orient and at home all at the same time. With more than 982 full-time employees, service is premium. There are, for example, no cigarette machines in the hotel—instead, guests are requested to ask any hotel employee to fetch them a pack of cigarettes. The hotel boasts a meticulously pruned Japanese garden complete with a pond and golden carp and is within walking distance of the moat-encircled Imperial Palace. If you stay here, be sure to check out Hie Shrine, next door.

Double and twin rooms are comfortably large. There are also 50 single rooms available, though the least expensive ones are fairly small. Rooms come with traditional shoji screens; the best of the rooms overlook a small garden. You can't go wrong staying here.

Dining/Entertainment: The Keyaki Grill, famous for its steaks and continental cuisine, has some of the most attentive waiters in the world, but if it's a view of the garden you want, head for the Origami Restaurant or the Tea Lounge (the latter serves Sunday brunch). There's also a very popular Chinese restaurant, a bar, and a lounge.

Services: 24-hour room service, in-house doctor and dentist, free newspaper, same-day laundry service, babysitting.

Facilities: Outdoor swimming pool, steam bath, barbershop, beauty salon, shopping arcade, travel agency.

NEW OTANI, 4-1 Kioi-cho, Chiyoda-ku 102, Tokyo. Tel. 03/3265-1111, or toll free 800/421-8795 in the U.S. and Canada. Fax 03/3221-2619. 1,800 rms and suites. A/C MINIBAR TV TEL **Station:** Akasaka-mitsuke (then a three-minute walk) or Yotsuya (then about a five-minute walk).

$ Rates: ¥30,000–¥38,000 ($272–$345) single; ¥30,000–¥44,000 ($272–$400) double or twin; from ¥60,000 ($545) suite. AE, DC, JCB, MC, V.

Japan's largest hotel has so many facilities that it seems like a city in itself. In fact, it's so big that there are two information desks, to assist lost souls searching for a particular restaurant or one of the shops in its meandering shopping arcade. If you like quiet, small hotels, this isn't the place for you, as it's constantly abuzz with both Japanese and foreigners. Its 400-year-old Japanese garden, perhaps the most spectacular hotel garden in Tokyo, sprawls over 10 acres of ponds, waterfalls, bridges, bamboo groves, and manicured bushes.

Rooms are divided between the main building, built in time for the Olympics and recently renovated, and a 40-story tower. Rooms are comfortable and offer the extras of TV with remote control and English-language cable with CNN, hairdryers, shojilike screens on the windows, and bathroom scales in most rooms. There are also no-smoking rooms.

Dining/Entertainment: With more than 35 restaurants and bars, it's no problem finding a place to eat and drink. Most expensive is La Tour d'Argent, one of Tokyo's most exclusive restaurants, but there's also Trader Vic's, as well as a teppanyaki restaurant called Sekishin-tei in the middle of the garden. For the best view of the garden, however, head for the Garden Lounge for a coffee or cocktail.

Services: 24-hour room service, free newspaper, same-day laundry service.

Facilities: Shopping arcade with 120 stores and boutiques, medical offices, a post office, health club, sauna, indoor and outdoor swimming pools (fee charged), tennis courts, business center, chapel with daily services, tea-ceremony room, travel agency, art museum, beauty parlor, barbershop, babysitting room.

SHINJUKU

CENTURY HYATT, 2-7-2 Nishi-Shinjuku, Shinjuku-ku 160, Tokyo. Tel. 03/3349-0111, or toll free 800/233-1234 in the U.S. and Canada. Fax 03/3344-5575. 786 rms and suites. A/C MINIBAR TV TEL **Station:** Shinjuku (then a 10-minute walk).

$ Rates: ¥30,000–¥38,000 ($272–$345) single; ¥35,000–¥42,000 ($318–$382) double or twin; from ¥65,000 ($591) suite. Extra bed ¥4,000 ($36). Discounts for longer stays. AE, DC, JCB, MC, V.

Located on Shinjuku's west side, this 28-story hotel features an impressive, seven-story-high atrium lobby with massive chandeliers and an inlaid marble floor. The service is excellent and the staff is used to the many foreigners who pass through its doors.

Its adequately sized rooms are attractively appointed in soft pastels, and the bathrooms feature bright lights that are great for shaving or applying makeup. The single rooms have windows at such an angle in the corner that you can hardly see out of them; the twins are better, with big windows letting in lots of sunshine. The higher-priced rooms are on the executive floors, the Regency Club, offering complimentary breakfast and evening cocktails.

Dining/Entertainment: The hotel's 12 bars and restaurants include the well-known Hugo's with its steak teppanyaki, the French Chenonceaux, and Japanese and Chinese restaurants. On the 27th floor is Rhapsody, featuring light jazz nightly and a view of the city.

Services: 24-hour room service, same-day laundry service, babysitting arrangements, free newspaper, free shuttle bus to Shinjuku Station, in-house doctor.

Facilities: Indoor swimming pool on the 28th floor with views of the city (fee: ¥1,500/$13.65), sauna, business center, shopping arcade, travel agency, beauty salon, barbershop.

TOKYO HILTON INTERNATIONAL, 6-6-2 Nishi-Shinjuku, Shinjuku-ku 160, Tokyo. Tel. 03/3344-5111, or toll free 800/HILTONS in the U.S. and Canada. Fax 03/3342-6094. 807 rms. A/C MINIBAR TV TEL **Station:** Shinjuku, west exit (then a 10-minute walk).

$ Rates: ¥28,000–¥37,000 ($254–$336) single; ¥35,500–

¥46,000 ($322–$418) double or twin; ¥60,000–¥80,000 ($545–$727) Japanese-style room; from ¥75,000 ($682) suite. Extra person ¥6,000 ($55). Children stay free in parents' room. AE, DC, JCB, MC, V.

One of west Shinjuku's newer hotels, the Hilton relocated here in 1984. The largest Hilton in the Asia/Pacific area, its S-shaped, 38-story structure offers rooms facing either Shinjuku's skyscrapers (a pretty sight at night) or (on rare clear days) Mt. Fuji. Room rates are based on both size and location, with the more expensive floors higher up. There are three executive floors (the higher-priced singles and doubles listed above) offering VIP services such as separate check-in and complimentary breakfast and cocktails. As with all Hiltons, all its rooms reflect the traditional native style in decor: shoji screens instead of curtains and simple yet elegant furniture. There's a no-smoking floor.

Dining/Entertainment: Of the hotel's seven restaurants and bars, the Imari is its showcase, offering grilled foods, seafood, and fine vintage wines. Other dining facilities include Japanese and Chinese restaurants. St. George's Bar offers draft beer, buffet lunches, and carvery items in the tradition of an English pub, with music entertainment in the evening.

Services: 24-hour room service, free shuttle bus to Shinjuku Station every 10 minutes, same-day laundry service, babysitting.

Facilities: An excellent fitness center, tennis courts, indoor swimming pool (fee: ¥1,500/$13.65), sauna, business center, shopping arcade, beauty salon.

OTHER LOCATIONS

FOUR SEASONS HOTEL CHINZAN-SO, 2-10-8 Sekiguchi, Bunkyo-ku 112, Tokyo. Tel. 03/3943-2222, or toll free 800/332-3442 in the U.S., 800/268-6282 in Canada. Fax 03/3943-2300. 286 rms and suites. A/C MINIBAR TV TEL **Station:** Edogawabashi, Mejiro, or Ikeburkuro.

$ Rates: ¥29,000–¥67,000 ($263–$609) single; ¥33,000–¥67,000 ($300–$609) double or twin; from ¥45,000 ($409) Club Floor double; from ¥60,000 ($545) suite. Extra bed ¥4,000 ($36.30) AE, DC, JCB, MC, V.

A bit off the beaten track, the Four Seasons, set in the 17-acre, 100-year-old Chinzan-so Garden, is utterly inviting after a bustling day in Tokyo. The stunning room interiors and public spaces created by American designer Frank Nicholson make this, in my opinion, the most beautiful European-style hotel in Japan, yet it's less expensive than other Tokyo hotels in its category. Harmony is achieved by complimentary color schemes and garden views from private to public spaces. Overstuffed, elegantly upholstered furnishings are backed by Oriental art, including Japanese woodblock prints.

The smallest room features a king-size bed and is twice the size of most Japanese hotel rooms. All guest rooms offer satellite television, VCRs, a minimum of three telephones, facsimile and personal computer outlets, private safes, scales, terrycloth robes, special shaving/makeup mirrors, and bidet/toilets that are separate from the marble-and-brass bathrooms.

Dining/Entertainment: You have your choice of nine restaurants and bars, including Yang Yuan Zhai, the first overseas outlet of the famous Beijing restaurant Diaoyutai, where heads of state dine, and Bice, featuring hand-picked ingredients and pasta made daily.

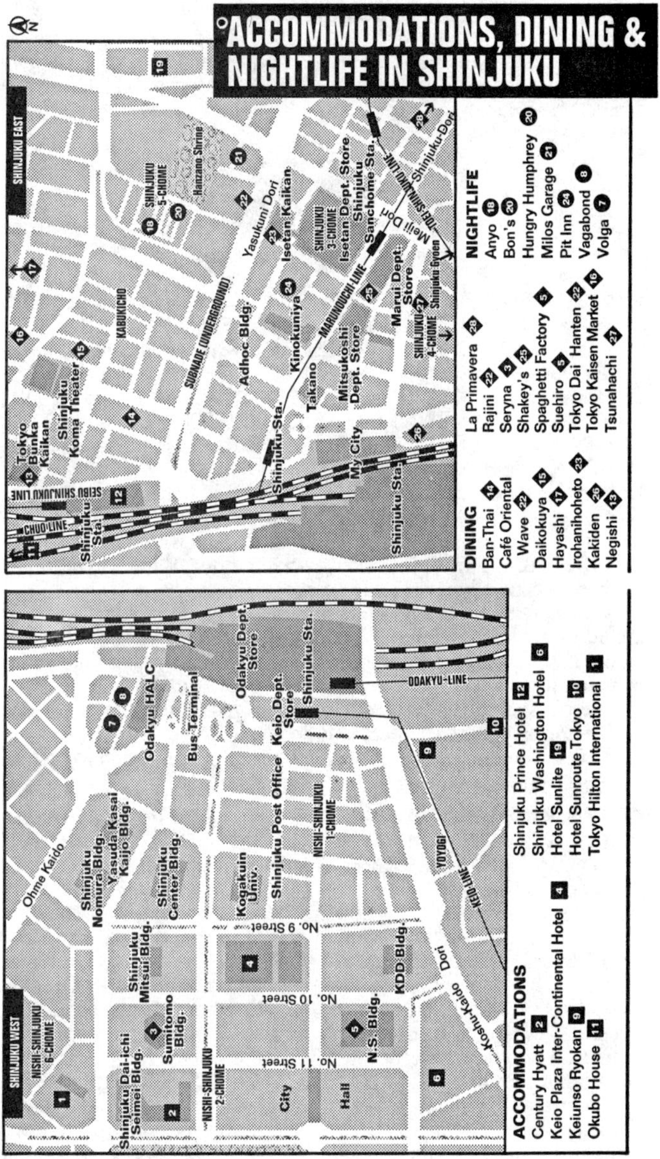

Services: Business center, 24-hour room service, 24-hour laundry, 24-hour multilingual concierge (probably the most helpful I've ever experienced), complimentary shoeshine, your choice of free newspaper (including *USA Today*), complimentary limo service to anywhere in Tokyo (weekdays from 8am to 5pm), complimentary in-room fax machine use, complimentary deluxe bus service to rail and subway stations.

Facilities: Elegant boutiques, amphitheater conference room with simultaneous interpretation facilities, aesthetic salon, spa featuring gorgeous indoor pool, sauna, steam room, Jacuzzi, fitness gym with English-language instruction, Japanese hot springs bath (spa fee: ¥5,000/$45.45).

2. EXPENSIVE

GINZA & HIBIYA

GINZA DAI-ICHI HOTEL, 8-13-1 Ginza, Chuo-ku 104, Tokyo. Tel. 03/3542-5311. Fax 03/3542-3030. 810 rms and suites. A/C MINIBAR TV TEL **Station:** Shimbashi (then a five-minute walk).

$ Rates: ¥18,000–¥22,500 ($164–$204) single; ¥23,000–¥33,000 ($209–$300) twin; ¥29,000 ($263) double; ¥39,000 ($354) triple; ¥88,000 ($800) suite. Extra person ¥3,300 ($30). AE, DC, JCB, MC, V.

Located on the southern edge of Ginza, this is a chain hotel offering comfortable, though unexciting, rooms with tiny bathrooms and televisions that carry CNN broadcasts. Rooms with the best views face Tokyo Bay. The lobby is on the second floor. What you're paying for here is basically its great location.

Dining/Entertainment: The hotel's four restaurants and bars include French and Japanese restaurants on the 15th floor with good views of Tokyo Bay by day and the lights of Ginza by night. Its French restaurant, Lumière, specializes in lobsters and steaks, while its Japanese restaurants offer sukiyaki, shabu-shabu, tempura, and sushi.

Services: Room service, laundry service.

Facilities: Shopping arcade, beauty shop, barbershop, sauna, massage salon, travel agency.

GINZA NIKKO HOTEL, 8-4-21 Ginza, Chuo-ku 104, Tokyo. Tel. 03/3571-4911. Fax 03/3571-8379. 112 rms. A/C MINIBAR TV TEL **Station:** Shimbashi, Ginza, or Hibiya (then a five-minute walk).

$ Rates: ¥17,000–¥19,000 ($155–$173) single; ¥27,000–¥30,000 ($245–$272) twin; ¥29,000 ($263) double. Extra bed ¥3,300 ($30). AE, DC, JCB, MC, V.

This small hotel on the southern edge of Ginza is more than a quarter of a century old, making it one of the oldest hotels in the area. In an attempt to upgrade itself from a business hotel to one attracting tourists, it was recently renovated. Rooms are small but pleasant and come with the usual stocked fridge, TV with video, and hot-water pot with tea. Although not nearly as grand or sophisticated as the hotels listed below, it's a good choice if you like small hotels and want to be near the Ginza—its location on Sotobori Dori Avenue can't be beat.

Dining/Entertainment: The Ginza Nikko offers one coffee shop and one bar.

Services: Free newspaper, laundry service.

MITSUI URBAN HOTEL GINZA, 8-6-15 Ginza, Chuo-ku 104, Tokyo. Tel. 03/3572-4131. Fax 03/3572-4254. 252 rms. A/C TV TEL **Station:** Shimbashi (then a one-minute walk).

$ Rates: ¥14,000–¥16,000 ($127–$145) single; ¥21,000–¥24,000 ($190–$218) double; ¥24,000–¥31,000 ($218–$281) twin. Extra person ¥3,300 ($30). AE, DC, JCB, MC, V.

$ Because of its location near Ginza and the Kasumigaseki and Marunouchi business districts, this hotel caters to both business travelers and tourists and is a cross between a business hotel and a regular hotel. It's attractive, with a lobby on the second floor, served by a friendly staff. The modern guest rooms are small, but bathrooms are larger than in other business hotels and come with hot water for tea, alarm clock, radio, cotton yukata, and TV offering pay adult entertainment. I suggest taking a room away from the highway overpass that runs beside the hotel.

Dining/Entertainment: There are five restaurants, bars, and lounges. Of these, Munakata is my favorite, a pleasant Japanese restaurant offering reasonably priced mini-kaiseki lunches.

Services: Room service, laundry service.

RAMADA RENAISSANCE GINZA TOBU HOTEL, 6-14-10 Ginza, Chuo-ku 104, Tokyo. Tel. 03/3546-0111, or toll free 800/228-2828 in the U.S. Fax 03/3546-8990. 204 rms, 9 suites. A/C MINIBAR TV TEL **Station:** Higashi Ginza (then a one-minute walk) or Ginza (then a four-minute walk).

$ Rates: ¥18,000–¥22,000 ($164–$200) single; ¥31,000 ($281) twin; from ¥70,000 ($636) suite. AE, DC, JCB, MC, V.

Small and personable, this Ramada-affiliated hotel is located on Showa Dori Avenue behind the Matsuzakaya department store. It employs a full-time staff of 250 employees to serve its guests, 40% of whom are foreigners. No tour groups are accepted, which means you never have to deal with masses huddled at the front counter. In addition to the usual laundry rope in the bathroom, massage shower head, and free *Japan Times* delivered in the morning, all rooms come equipped with hairdryers, three telephones, bilingual TV with CNN, and a radio/music system with—get this—44 different music channels, and there are even stereo speakers in the bathroom. There are even hookups for fax machines, which you can use free of charge. And if you feel like splurging, there is one special executive floor called Ramada Renaissance where guests enjoy free continental breakfast and cocktails.

Dining/Entertainment: The hotel has five restaurants and bars, including an upscale French restaurant, a Japanese restaurant, a bar, and a coffee shop open 24 hours a day.

Services: 24-hour room service, newspaper delivery, free use of fax machines.

Facilities: Travel and business center, hairdressing salon.

NEAR TOKYO STATION

PALACE HOTEL, 1-1-1 Marunouchi, Chiyoda-ku 100, Tokyo. Tel. 03/3211-5211, or toll free 800/44-UTELL in the U.S., 800/223-0888 in the U.S. and Canada. Fax 03/3211-6987. 395 rms and suites. A/C MINIBAR TV TEL **Station:** Otemachi (then a one-minute walk) or Tokyo Station (then a seven-minute walk).

$ Rates: ¥23,000–¥24,000 ($209–$218) single; ¥28,000–¥56,000 ($254–$509) twin; ¥33,000–¥45,000 ($300–$409) double; from ¥100,000 ($909) suite. Extra person ¥3,300 ($30). AE, DC, JCB, MC, V.

Because of its proximity to Tokyo's business district, this is a favorite among foreign business travelers, who make up more than half its guests. Located across the street from the Imperial Palace's East Garden, this small, personable hotel was built in 1961. The most expensive twins are large, face the gardens, and have balconies. Rooms are comfortable, with large windows and woodblock prints adorning the walls, and there are two no-smoking floors.

Dining/Entertainment: Of its seven restaurants serving Chinese, Japanese, French, and Italian food, the French Crown Restaurant on the 10th floor is the best, offering superb views of the Imperial Palace.

Services: 24-hour room service, free newspaper, laundry service.

Facilities: Business center, shopping arcade, barbershop, beauty salon.

AKASAKA

AKASAKA TOKYU HOTEL, 2-14-3 Nagatacho, Chiyoda-ku 100, Tokyo. Tel. 03/3580-2311, or toll free 800/822-0016 or 800/624-5068 in the U.S. Fax 03/3580-6066. 535 rms. A/C MINIBAR TV TEL **Station:** Akasaka-mitsuke (then a one-minute walk).

$ Rates: ¥21,000–¥26,000 ($190–$236) single; ¥32,000 ($290) double; ¥31,000–¥44,000 ($281–$400) twin. AE, DC, JCB, MC, V.

Built in 1969 and easily recognizable by its candy-striped exterior, this older hotel boasts an 89% average occupancy, attributed in part to its ideal location but with prices that are lower than the neighboring deluxe hotels. The lobby is on the third floor, and rooms were recently renovated to include such features as hairdryers, clotheslines in the bathrooms, shoji screens and window panels that slide shut for complete darkness even in the middle of the day, pushbutton phones, and televisions with remote control, pay movies, and cable with CNN broadcasts. There are 200 single rooms, but the lower-priced ones are pretty small. Try to get a twin or double room facing Akasaka—windows can open, a rarity in Tokyo.

Dining/Entertainment: The hotel has more than 14 bars and restaurants, including the French restaurant Gondola on the 14th floor with a view of glittering Akasaka.

Services: Room service (to midnight), laundry service (Mon–Fri).

Facilities: Shopping arcade.

SHINJUKU

KEIO PLAZA INTER-CONTINENTAL HOTEL, 2-2-1 Nishi-Shinjuku, Shinjuku-ku 160, Tokyo. Tel. 03/3344-0111, or toll free 800/222-KEIO in the U.S. Fax 03/3345-8269. 1,485 rms. A/C MINIBAR TV TEL **Station:** Shinjuku (then a few minutes' walk).

$ Rates: ¥22,000–¥25,000 ($200–$227) single; ¥28,000–¥40,000 ($254–$363) double or twin; from ¥75,000 ($682) suite. Extra person ¥4,500 ($41). AE, DC, JCB, MC, V.

This hotel has the distinction of being the first skyscraper constructed in Japan, and at 47 stories it's still Tokyo's tallest hotel. Built in 1971, its brilliant white exterior is composed of precast concrete panels, the first application of this technique in Japan. One of Tokyo's largest hotels, it bases room rates on size rather than location, so ask for a room higher up where the view is better. Unfortunately, the recent completion of Tokyo's new city hall blocked the hotel's view of Mt. Fuji. Rooms come with TV with CNN cable broadcasts, remote control, and in-house pay movies, as well as radio, hairdryer, and a phone in the bathroom. There's a no-smoking floor.

Dining/Entertainment: The Keio has more than 20 restaurants and bars. Top of the line is Ambrosia, which offers continental food with a view. Other restaurants specialize in steaks, seafood, Chinese cuisine, sukiyaki, teppanyaki, and kaiseki. For relaxation, Polestar, on the 45th floor, offers an unparalleled view of Tokyo.

Services: Room service, medical and dental services, free newspaper, laundry service.

Facilities: Outdoor swimming pool, sauna, shopping arcade, travel center, beauty parlor, business center, babysitting room.

ROPPONGI

ROPPONGI PRINCE HOTEL, 3-2-7 Roppongi, Minato-ku 106, Tokyo. Tel. 03/3587-1111, or toll free 800/542-8686 in the U.S. Fax 03/3587-0770. 216 rms. A/C MINIBAR TV TEL **Station:** Roppongi (then a 10-minute walk).

$ Rates: ¥21,500 ($195) single; ¥24,000–¥27,000 ($218–$245) twin; ¥25,000–¥27,000 ($227–$245) double. AE, DC, JCB, MC, V.

The 1984 opening of the Roppongi Prince was a welcome event in this neighborhood, which still woefully lacks hotels even though it's a major nightlife district. It attracts mainly young Japanese vacationers aged 20 to 25, and caters to them with a young and cheerful staff, modern designs, and bold colors. The hotel is built around an inner courtyard, which features an outdoor swimming pool with a heated deck—a solar mirror on the hotel's roof directs the sun's rays down on the sunbathers below. Rooms are small, but are bright and colorful and come with the usual desks, clocks, and radios. A good place to be if you want to be close to the action in Roppongi.

Dining/Entertainment: There are Italian, tempura, sushi, and steak restaurants, as well as a coffee shop, bar, and lobby lounge.

Services: Room service, laundry service, free newspaper.

Facilities: Outdoor heated swimming pool open year-round (fee: ¥2,000/$18).

NEAR SHINAGAWA STATION

HOTEL PACIFIC MERIDIEN, 3-13-3 Takanawa, Minato-ku 108, Tokyo. Tel. 03/3445-6711, or toll free 800/543-4300 in the U.S. and Canada. Fax 03/3445-5733. 954 rms and suites. A/C MINIBAR TV TEL **Station:** Shinagawa (then a one-minute walk).

$ Rates: ¥22,000–¥25,800 ($200–$235) single; ¥25,000–¥34,000 ($227–$309) double or twin; from ¥52,000 ($473) suite. Extra bed ¥3,300 ($30). AE, DC, JCB, MC, V.

Located across the street from Shinagawa Station, this graceful and dignified hotel is built on grounds that once belonged to Japan's imperial family. Its coffee lounge looks out onto a peaceful and tranquil garden, and its Blue Pacific lounge, on the 30th floor, has dynamite views of Tokyo Bay. Approximately 40% of the hotel guests are foreigners.

Rooms are of adequate size, and since rates are based on room size rather than height, ask for a room on one of the top floors boasting views of Tokyo Bay. All rooms come with TV with remote control and English-language cable with CNN broadcasts, hairdryer, and clothesline in the bathroom.

Dining/Entertainment: The 11 restaurants and bars in the hotel offer Japanese, Chinese, and excellent French cuisine. Its Blue Pacific lounge, on the 30th floor, has great views.

Services: Room service (to midnight), free newspaper, same-day laundry service, babysitting.

Facilities: Outdoor swimming pool (free to hotel guests), sauna (for men only), shopping arcade, travel agency, barbershop and beauty salon.

MIYAKO HOTEL TOKYO, 1-1-50 Shiroganedai, Minato-ku 108, Tokyo. Tel. 03/3447-3111, or toll free 800/336-1136 in the U.S. Fax 03/3447-3133. 408 rms and suites. A/C MINIBAR TV TEL **Station:** Takanawadai (then an eight-minute walk) or Meguro (then take the free shuttle bus).

$ **Rates:** Western-style rooms, ¥22,000–¥24,000 ($200–$218) single; ¥27,000–¥38,000 ($245–$345) twin; ¥28,000–¥38,000 ($254–$345) double; ¥37,000 ($336) triple; from ¥75,000 ($682) suite. Japanese-style rooms, ¥27,000 ($245) single; ¥31,000 ($281) double. Extra bed ¥3,300 ($30). AE, DC, JCB, MC, V.

Located within an eight-minute taxi ride from Shinagawa Station, this is a cousin of the famous Miyako Hotel in Kyoto. It was designed by Minoru Yamasaki, architect of the World Trade Center in New York and the Century Plaza in Los Angeles. The lobby overlooks 5.5 acres of lush gardens that once belonged to the father of a foreign prime minister. The hotel's rooms are large, with floor-to-ceiling windows that have views of either the hotel's own garden, the garden next door, or Tokyo Tower. There are five Japanese-style rooms. Japanese account for 70% of its guests, and although the hotel is a bit inconveniently located, it offers a free shuttle bus to and from Meguro Station and to Ginza. This hotel is one of my favorites in Tokyo.

Dining/Entertainment: The Miyako has nine restaurants, bars, and cocktail lounges. La Clé d'Or serves continental fare with a view of the hotel's garden, as does the Japanese restaurant Yamatoya Sangen. You can't go wrong at the Yamatoya Sangen—it serves a wide variety of Japanese cuisine, including shabu-shabu, tempura, kaiseki, sushi, and eel.

Services: Room service (to midnight), same-day laundry service, free newspaper, complimentary shuttle bus.

Facilities: Health club with large indoor swimming pool great for swimming laps and sauna (fee: ¥2,000/$18.20), shopping arcade, barbershop, travel agency, medical clinic.

ASAKUSA

ASAKUSA VIEW HOTEL, 3-17-1 Nishi-Asakusa, Taito-ku 111, Tokyo. Tel. 03/3847-1111. Fax 03/3842-2117. 341 rms. A/C MINIBAR TV TEL **Station:** Tawaramachi (then an eight-minute walk).

$ **Rates:** ¥16,500–¥18,500 ($150–$168) single; ¥23,000–¥31,000 ($209–$281) double; ¥28,000–¥34,000 ($254–$309) twin; ¥35,000 ($318) triple; ¥45,000 ($409) Japanese-style double; from ¥32,000 ($290) suite. AE, DC, JCB, MC, V.

Looking out of place amid this historic district's older buildings, this is the only modern, upper-range hotel in Asakusa. It's a good place to stay if you prefer Tokyo's old downtown to the spanking newness of its business districts or busy nightlife areas. The lobby exudes cool elegance, with a marble floor, atrium, and chandeliers that hint at art deco. Rooms are very pleasant and contemporary, and bay windows let in plenty of sunshine. Rooms that face the front have views of the famous Sensoji Temple. There are eight Japanese-style rooms which sleep up to five people.

Dining/Entertainment: You have your choice of basement bars and restaurants or facilities on the top floors. French cuisine, served in the style of Japanese kaiseki with an eye on taste and texture, is featured in Makie on the 27th floor. Less formal but with great views of the city is the Belvedere, on the 28th floor, which serves a popular lunch buffet daily.

Services: Room service, free newspaper, darning and stitching service, laundry service.

Facilities: Indoor swimming pool with a ceiling opened in summer (fee: ¥3,000/$27.25), sauna, massage, jet bath, fitness gym, shopping arcade, Japanese-style public bath with wooden tubs (fee: ¥500/$4.55).

OTHER LOCATIONS

SHIBA PARK

TOKYO PRINCE HOTEL, 3-3-1 Shibakoen, Minato-ku, 105. Tel. 03/3432-1111. Fax 03/3434-5551. 484 rms. A/C MINIBAR TV TEL **Station:** Kamiyacho or Onarimon (then a 5-minute walk), or Hammamatsucho (then a 10-minute walk).

$ **Rates:** ¥23,000–¥25,000 ($209–$227) single; ¥24,000–¥35,000 ($218–$318) double or twin; from ¥70,000 ($636) suite.

Built in 1964 for the Tokyo Olympic Games and set in Shiba Park, the Tokyo Prince is next to Zozoji Temple and Tokyo Tower. The central location makes it possible to walk to Roppongi for nightlife (the walk home is sobering) or to Hibiya or the Tokyo Trade Center on business. Service is that of a small, luxury hotel. Not only do they offer no-smoking rooms, but a no-smoking lounge with an up-close view of Tokyo Tower. All the spacious, beautifully updated rooms feature view windows that open, two phones, modern litho art, and marble bath areas with nonsteam mirrors.

Dining/Entertainment: Bars and restaurants were under renovation when I was last there, but among the many are the fine French restaurant Beaux Séjours, the Prince Villa in the Garden, the no-smoking lounge Tower View (see "The Bar Scene" section in this book) and in summer, the Garden Restaurant, a great outdoor beer garden (see "Specialty Dining," in Chapter 5).

Services: Same-day laundry service, 24-hour room service, complimentary newspaper.

Facilities: Executive business center, meeting rooms, outdoor pool in summer (fee: ¥1,000/$9.10).

KANDA

HILLTOP HOTEL, 1-1 Surugadai, Kanda, Chiyoda-ku 101, Tokyo. Tel. 03/3293-2311. Fax 03/3233-4567. 75 rms. A/C MINIBAR TV TEL **Station:** Jimbocho (then a five-minute walk), or Ochanomizu or Shin-Ochanomizu (then an eight-minute walk).

$ Rates: ¥15,000–¥20,000 ($136–$182) single; ¥23,000–¥25,000 ($209–$227) double; ¥23,000–¥30,000 ($209–$272) twin. Extra bed ¥3,300 ($30). AE, DC, JCB, MC, V.

As its name implies, the Hilltop Hotel sits atop a hill, north of the Imperial Palace near a university. If you're going to the hotel by taxi, it might help to call the hotel by its Japanese name, Yamanoue, which means "hilltop." An old-fashioned, unpretentious hotel with character, its main building dates back to 1937, and together with its newer annex contains a total of only 75 rooms. A far cry from Tokyo's newer and flashier hotels, this place hasn't changed much in decades, which may be just what you're looking for, and was the favorite haunt of writers, including Japanese novelist Yukio Mishima.

Its rooms are fairly small, and although nothing fancy, they're pleasant and come with cherrywood furniture, fringed lampshades, velvet curtains, radio and clock, mahogany desks, and old-fashioned heaters with intricate grillwork. The hotel's brochure maintains that "oxygen and negative ions are circulated into the rooms and its refreshing atmosphere is accepted by many, including prominent individuals, as most adequate for work and rest." I'm not exactly sure what that means, but it probably doesn't do any harm.

Dining/Entertainment: The hotel's seven restaurants, all tastefully decorated, offer steaks, Italian, Chinese, and Japanese cuisine. There are three bars.

Services: Room service (to 2am), same-day laundry service.

NEAR TOKYO CITY AIR TERMINAL

ROYAL PARK HOTEL, 2-1-1 Nihombashi-Kakigara-cho, Chuo-ku 103, Tokyo. Tel. 03/3667-1111, or toll free 800/223-0888 in the U.S. and Canada. Fax 03/3665-7212. 450 rms and suites. A/C MINIBAR TV TEL **Station:** Suitengumae (underneath the hotel).

$ Rates: ¥22,000 ($200) single; ¥28,000–¥45,000 ($254–$409) double; ¥30,000–¥42,000 ($272–$382) twin; ¥40,000 ($363) Japanese-style room; executive floor ¥25,000 ($227) single, ¥34,000 ($309) twin; from ¥75,000 ($682) suite. Extra bed ¥4,500 ($41). AE, DC, JCB, MC, V.

Opened in 1989, the Royal Park Hotel is located to the east of Tokyo Station (10 minutes away via taxi), not far from the Tokyo Stock Exchange and Japan's financial center. Next door is the Tokyo City Air Terminal (TCAT), main terminus for the Airport Limousine Bus which shuttles passengers to and from the Narita airport (the hotel is connected to the TCAT by an enclosed walkway).

As for the hotel itself, it's spacious, with a two-story atrium lobby, and offers up-to-date guest rooms equipped with radio, hairdryer, cotton kimono, and a remote-control 60-channel television that provides stock-market quotations, currency-exchange rates, airline schedules, 24-hour CNN news updates, movies, and access to guests' messages and bills. The best rooms, in my opinion, are the twins that face the Sumida River. There are two executive floors, each offering complimentary breakfast and cocktails, as well as Gucci-brand amenities.

Dining/Entertainment: The hotel's 10 restaurants and bars include the French Palazzo restaurant, the Sumida teppanyaki restaurant, and the Orpheus Sky Lounge, located on the 20th floor with stunning views of the city.

Facilities: Fitness club with indoor swimming pool, gym, massage, and sauna (fee: ¥3,300/$30); business center; beauty parlor and barbershop; shopping arcade.

3. MODERATE

GINZA & HIBIYA

GINZA CAPITAL HOTEL, 3-1-5 Tsukiji, Chuo-ku 104, Tokyo. Tel. 03/3543-8211. Fax 03/3543-7839. 572 rms. A/C TV TEL **Station:** Shintomicho (then a two-minute walk).

$ Rates (including tax and service charge): Main building, ¥8,800 ($80) single; ¥14,500–¥15,600 ($132–$142) twin. Annex, ¥9,300–¥10,500 ($85–$95) single; ¥15,800 ($144) double or twin; ¥20,000 ($182) triple. AE, DC, JCB, MC, V.

The Ginza Capital Hotel, along with its newer annex, called the New Ginza Capital Hotel, is within a 10-minute walk of Ginza. A modern and efficient business hotel with a friendly staff, its rooms are clean and bright even though they're minuscule. If being able to look out a window is a big deal to you, stay away from rooms in the annex that face north—they have a glazed covering about a foot out from the building so you can't see anything (heaven knows why). Single rooms in the annex face another building and are dark. Otherwise, rooms in the annex are a bit more modern, but are the same size as those in the older building. All rooms come with the usual tea-making facility, cotton yukata, alarm clock, radio, and TV with adult movies. The annex has both a Western and a Japanese restaurant; the main building has a Western restaurant.

HOTEL GINZA DAI-EI, 3-12-2 Ginza, Chuo-ku 104, Tokyo. Tel. 03/3545-1111. Fax 03/3541-2882. 101 rms. A/C TV TEL **Station:** Higashi-Ginza (then a few minutes' walk).

$ Rates (including tax and service charge): ¥10,500 ($96) single; ¥16,000–¥18,000 ($145–$164) double or twin. AE, DC, JCB, V.

A red-brick building located several blocks behind the Matsuya department store past Showa Dori Avenue, this is a typical business hotel with minuscule rooms, but a plus is that its windows open. There's a Chinese restaurant, and a sauna (for men only).

NEAR TOKYO STATION

HOLIDAY INN TOKYO, 1-13-7 Hatchobori, Chuo-ku 104, Tokyo. Tel. 03/3553-6161. Fax 03/3553-6040. 120 rms. A/C MINIBAR TV TEL **Station:** Hatchobori (then a three-minute walk).

$ Rates: ¥17,000–¥22,000 ($155–$200) single; ¥22,400 ($204) double. Extra person or bed ¥2,200 ($20). Children under 12 stay free in parents' room. AE, DC, JCB, MC, V.

Americans are on familiar turf here; in fact, as many as 30% of its guests are American, mainly individual travelers. Similar to Holiday Inns back home, this red-brick building is located on Shin Ohashidori Avenue, about a five-minute taxi ride from either Tokyo Station or the

Tokyo City Air Terminal. Rooms, fairly large for Tokyo, are what you'd expect, with the usual desks, clocks, radios, and TVs with remote control and English cable, including CNN. All beds are double size or larger, even in the twin rooms. There is one Western restaurant and a bar, and the outdoor rooftop swimming pool, open only from July to September, is free to hotel guests. Babysitters are available on request, and a free *Japan Times* is delivered to your room in the morning.

TOKYO CITY HOTEL, 1-5-4 Nihombashi-honcho, Chuo-ku 103, Tokyo. Tel. 03/3270-7671. Fax 03/3270-8930. 266 rms. A/C TV TEL **Station:** Mitsukoshi-mae (then a two-minute walk) or Tokyo Station (then a five-minute taxi ride).

$ Rates (including tax and service charge): ¥7,900 ($72) single; ¥11,500 ($105) double; ¥13,400 ($122) twin. AE, JCB, MC, V.

This is a fine, no-nonsense business hotel in the heart of Tokyo, not far from the Mitsukoshi department store. Although the single rooms are quite small, the twin rooms are adequate. Its one restaurant serves Western food.

AKASAKA

AKASAKA SHANPIA HOTEL, 7-6-13 Akasaka, Minato-ku 107, Tokyo. Tel. 03/3586-0811, or 03/3583-1001 for reservations. Fax 03/3589-0575. 232 rms. A/C TV TEL **Station:** Akasaka (then about a five-minute walk).

$ Rates (including tax and service charge): ¥9,800–¥11,000 ($89–$100) single; ¥16,700 ($152) twin; ¥19,800 ($180) double. AE, DC, JCB, MC, V.

This business hotel has primarily singles—202 of them—a sure sign that it caters to Japanese businessmen. Rooms are minuscule in size, and since the single beds are tiny, you'll probably want to spring for a double bed if you're tall. However, there are only 18 twin-bedded rooms and 12 with double beds. Only twins and doubles come with stocked refrigerators and hairdryers. Signs in all guest rooms, which have windows that open, remind guests to ROCK THE DOOR. Facilities include one restaurant that serves both Japanese and Western food, and a bar.

AKASAKA YOKO HOTEL, 6-14-12 Akasaka, Minato-ku 107, Tokyo. Tel. 03/3586-4050, or 03/3586-8341 for reservations. Fax 03/3586-5944. 245 rms. A/C TV TEL **Station:** Akasaka (then a five-minute walk).

$ Rates (including tax and service charge): ¥8,900–¥9,800 ($81–$89) single; ¥13,000–¥15,500 ($118–$141) twin. AE, MC, V.

A pleasant, small business hotel, this place with a handy location about halfway between the nightlife of Roppongi (about a 15-minute walk) and Akasaka caters primarily to Japanese. For a couple of dollars more in each category you can get a slightly larger room, which may be worth it if you're claustrophobic. The bathrooms are barely large enough for one person. The hotel has a coffee shop, as well as vending machines that dispense beer and soda.

HOTEL TOKYU KANKO, 2-21-6 Akasaka, Minato-ku 107, Tokyo. Tel. 03/3582-0451, or 03/3583-4741 for reservations. Fax 03/3583-4023. 48 rms. A/C TV TEL **Station:** Roppongi or Akasaka (then about a 15-minute walk).

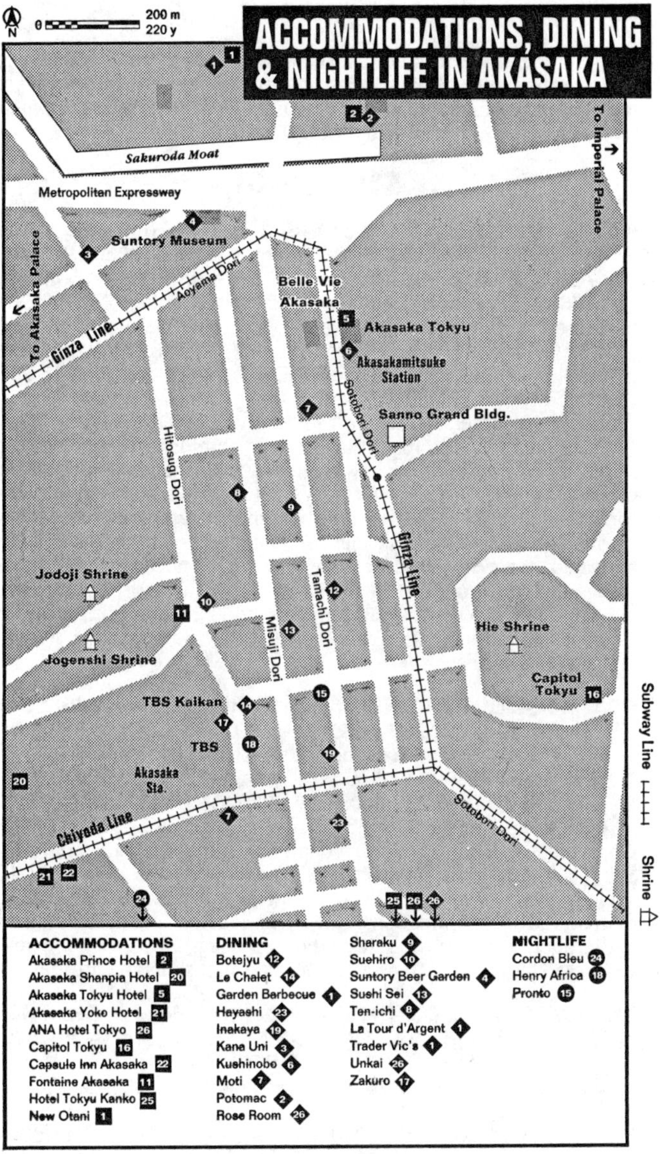

$ Rates: ¥7,700–¥10,200 ($70–$93) single; ¥15,400 ($140) double or twin. Extra bed ¥2,200 ($20). AE, DC, JCB, MC, V.

Located across from the ANA Hotel and down a small side street, this older business hotel was built at the time of the 1964 Olympics. It shows its age and is a bit worn in places, but is still popular because of its location. Rooms are larger than in some other business hotels, and bathrooms are tiled, not fitted with the usual plastic walls and fixtures. The cheapest singles have showers instead of tubs and are a bit drab; they face an inner courtyard and have glazed windows. If you like the light of day, it might be worth springing for the single with bathtub. There's a coffee shop and a Japanese restaurant which serves reasonably priced tempura and yakitori.

SHINJUKU

HOTEL SUNLITE, 5-15-8 Shinjuku, Shinjuku-ku 160, Tokyo. Tel. 03/3356-0391. Fax 03/3356-1223. 197 rms. A/C TV TEL **Station:** Shinjuku Sanchome (then about a 5-minute walk) or Shinjuku Station (then a 15-minute walk).

$ Rates (including tax and service charge): Annex, ¥8,600–¥9,000 ($78–$82) single; ¥14,200 ($129) twin. Main building, ¥9,500 ($86) single; ¥15,400 ($140) double; ¥16,000 ($145) twin. AE, JCB, MC, V.

This business hotel, located east of Shinjuku Station on Meiji Dori (Avenue), consists of a main building and an older annex across the street. The best rooms are twins in the main building located on corners, since they have windows on two walls and are bright. All rooms are cheerful and clean, but those in the annex are small and its singles are minuscule. Feelings of claustrophobia are somewhat mitigated, however, by the fact that all windows can be opened. Some rooms contain minibars. Incidentally, if you like staying out late, beware: Doors here close at 2am and don't reopen until 5:30am. There is one combination bar-lounge and one restaurant serving Western food.

HOTEL SUNROUTE TOKYO, 2-3-1 Yoyogi, Shibuya-ku 151, Tokyo. Tel. 03/3375-3211. Fax 03/3379-3040. 538 rms. A/C TV TEL **Station:** Shinjuku (then a two-minute walk).

$ Rates: ¥13,000–¥14,000 ($118–$127) single; ¥16,000–¥17,000 ($145–$155) double; ¥17,000–¥24,000 ($155–$218) twin. Extra bed ¥3,300 ($30). AE, DC, JCB, MC, V.

Conveniently located just a couple of minutes' walk south of Shinjuku Station, this hotel attracts a large foreign clientele and calls itself a "city hotel," but its rooms resemble a business hotel rather than tourist accommodations. Guest rooms are small but clean, cozy, and attractive. It has three restaurants serving Italian, Chinese, and Japanese cuisine, as well as a pub and a small shopping arcade.

SHINJUKU PRINCE HOTEL, 1-30-1 Kabuki-cho, Shinjuku-ku 160, Tokyo. Tel. 03/3205-1111, or toll free 800/542-8686 in the U.S. Fax 03/3205-1952. 571 rms. A/C TV TEL **Station:** Seibu Shinjuku (beneath the hotel) or Shinjuku (then a five-minute walk).

$ Rates: ¥15,000–¥16,000 ($136–$145) single; ¥17,000–¥32,000 ($155–$290) double or twin. Extra person ¥3,000 ($27). AE, DC, JCB, MC, V.

This smart-looking, streamlined brick building has a great location, right on top of the Seibu Shinjuku Station and just a five-minute walk northeast of Shinjuku Station, making it a good place to stay if you want to be near the nightlife of Kabuki-cho. The lower 10 floors of this high-rise include shopping arcades and restaurants, while the 10th through 24th floors hold the guest rooms. The cheapest rooms are small, but all rooms offer a great view of Shinjuku; some have minibars. Those facing Shinjuku Station have double-paned windows to shut out noise. Facilities include 10 restaurants and bars, and services include 24-hour room service, same-day laundry service, no-smoking floors, and free English-language newspapers on request. All in all, a good choice in a moderately priced business hotel.

SHINJUKU WASHINGTON HOTEL, 3-2-9 Nishi-Shinjuku, Shinjuku-ku 160, Tokyo. Tel. 03/3343-3111. Fax 03/3342-2575. 1,638 rms. A/C MINIBAR TV TEL **Station:** Shinjuku (then about a 10-minute walk).

$ Rates: ¥12,600–¥14,500 ($115–$132) single; ¥17,000–¥24,000 ($155–$218) double; ¥17,600–¥40,000 ($160–$363) twin; ¥26,500–¥36,500 ($240–$331) triple. AE, DC, JCB, MC, V.

If you like electronic gadgetry and the benefits of the space age, you might like staying here. Opened in West Shinjuku in 1984, with an annex added in 1987, this huge white building reminds me of an ocean liner—even the hotel's tiny windows resemble a ship's portholes. It has an interesting interior design with a lot of open spaces, and everything is bright and white. Make your way up to the third-floor lobby, where a row of machines provide automated check-in and check-out. There are also humans around to help you with the process. There are no bellboys, however, or room service. Upon check-in you'll receive a "card key," resembling a credit card, which also activates the bedside controls for such things as the TV, radio, and room lights. The guest rooms remind me of cabins in a ship and are small, but with everything you need. The annex has its own check-in counter, and if you're staying here you'll be treated to the Japanese version of the French bidet—toilets that release a jet

FROMMER'S COOL FOR KIDS: HOTELS

Holiday Inn Tokyo (*see p. 95*) This American chain hotel will seem familiar to kids, who will appreciate the rooftop swimming pool. Parents will appreciate that the pool is free of charge to hotel guests, that children under 12 can stay free in their parents' room, and that babysitting is available.

Tokyo Hilton International (*see p. 85*) This modern hotel in the heart of Shinjuku offers a family plan, with no extra charge for children who occupy the same room as their parents. In addition, babysitting is available, and the hotel's in-house movies and indoor swimming pool are sure to keep teenagers happy.

National Children's Castle (*see p. 101*) The absolute best place for children, complete with an indoor/outdoor playground and activity rooms for all ages, offering everything from building blocks to computer games.

Sakura Ryokan (*see p. 105*) This modern, Japanese-style inn offers a large family room that sleeps up to eight people in traditional Japanese style, on futons laid out on tatami mats.

spray into the air with a push of a button. There are more than 20 bars and restaurants in the hotel complex, as well as a shopping arcade and a sauna (for men only).

NEAR SHINAGAWA STATION

MIYAKO INN TOKYO, 3-7-8 Mita, Minato-ku 108, Tokyo. Tel. 03/3454-3111. Fax 03/3454-3397. 403 rms. A/C MINIBAR TV TEL **Station:** Tamachi, Mita, or Sengakuji (then a six-minute walk).

$ Rates: ¥10,500–¥13,500 ($95–$123) single; ¥15,000–¥16,000 ($136–$145) double; ¥16,000–¥22,000 ($145–$200) twin. AE, DC, JCB, MC, V.

Rising 14 stories high in southern Tokyo, this is a combination business and city hotel. Rooms on the top floor have the best views and face either Tokyo Bay or Tokyo Tower in the distance. Each room comes with the usual refrigerator, TV with extra charges for movies, cotton yukata, alarm clock, hot-water Thermos, and tea. Differences in room rates are based on the size of the room and the bed. There are Japanese, Western, and Chinese restaurants.

SHINAGAWA PRINCE HOTEL, 4-10-30 Takanawa, Minato-ku 108, Tokyo. Tel. 03/3440-1111, or toll free 800/542-8686 in the U.S. Fax 03/3441-7092. 1,273 rms. A/C TV TEL **Station:** Shinagawa (then a one-minute walk).

$ Rates: ¥9,500 ($86) single; ¥14,600 ($133) double; ¥14,300–¥24,000 ($130–$218) twin. AE, DC, JCB, MC, V.

Catering to Japanese businessmen during the week and to students on weekends and holidays, this gleaming-white hotel consists of a main building with 1,016 single rooms and an annex with 257 twins and doubles. If you're staying in the main building, ask for a room above the 10th floor, where you have a view of either mountains on the west side or the sea on the east. Annex rooms have the extra benefit of a minibar, but the views are unexciting. Facilities include 12 restaurants and bars and an adjoining sports center with indoor tennis courts, bowling lanes, and a fitness center (fee charged).

ROPPONGI

HOTEL IBIS, 7-14-4 Roppongi, Minato-ku 106, Tokyo. Tel. 03/3403-4411. Fax 03/3479-0609. 182 rms. A/C MINIBAR TV TEL **Station:** Roppongi (then a one-minute walk).

$ Rates (including tax and service charge): ¥13,000–¥16,000 ($118–$145) single; ¥19,500–¥26,000 ($173–$236) double; ¥22,000–¥27,000 ($200–$245) twin; ¥29,000 ($263) triple. AE, DC, JCB, MC, V.

This is about as close as you can get to the nightlife of Roppongi. Located just a minute's walk from Roppongi Crossing, Roppongi's main intersection, it caters to businessmen and to couples who come to Roppongi's discos and don't make (or don't want to make) the last subway home. The lobby, up on the fifth floor, has a spare, minimalist look, and rooms were all recently renovated and modernized and come with trendy furniture, windows that can be opened, and TV with English cable and CNN. The Sky Restaurant, on the 13th floor, is an inexpensive French restaurant offering good views of the surrounding area.

HARAJUKU & AOYAMA

KODOMO NO SHIRO HOTEL (National Children's Castle), 5-53-1 Jingumae, Shibuya-ku 150, Tokyo. Tel. 03/3797-5677. Fax 03/3406-7805. 27 rms. A/C TV TEL **Station:** Omotesando (then a 7-minute walk) or Shibuya (then a 10-minute walk).

$ Rates (including tax and service charge): ¥6,300 ($57) single; ¥13,000–¥14,000 ($118–$127) twin; from ¥17,400 ($158) Japanese-style room. AE, DC, JCB, MC, V.

The National Children's Castle is a great place to stay if you're with children. In addition to a small hotel on the seventh and eighth floors, this complex boasts an indoor/outdoor sophisticated playground for children, complete with a clinic and restaurants. Hotel guests range from businesspeople to families and young college students. Rooms, mainly twins, are simple, with large windows to let in the sunshine. The most expensive twins, which face toward Shinjuku, have the best views. Note that the hotel's three singles don't have windows, but you can pay extra to stay in a twin. There are also three Japanese-style rooms, available for three or more people and great for families wishing to experience the traditional Japanese lifestyle. Since rooms are limited, it's best to make reservations at least six months in advance, especially if you plan on being in Tokyo in the summer. The front desk is on the seventh floor. Note that there's an 11pm curfew and that check-in isn't until 3pm.

PRESIDENT HOTEL, 2-2-3 Minami Aoyama, Minato-ku 107, Tokyo. Tel. 03/3497-0111. Fax 03/3401-4816. 210 rms. A/C MINIBAR TV TEL **Station:** Aoyama-Itchome (then a one-minute walk).

$ Rates: ¥14,000–¥15,000 ($127–$136) single; ¥18,000 ($164) double; ¥18,000–¥23,000 ($164–$209) twin. AE, DC, JCB, MC, V.

This hotel is one of the best deals in town. Although a small hotel, it offers some of the same conveniences as the larger and more expensive hotels (like TV with CNN and room service) and has a great location between Akasaka, Shinjuku, and Roppongi. The lobby is pleasingly elegant but unpretentious and has a somewhat European atmosphere, with a reading corner with a supply of English-language magazines and newspapers. Approximately half the hotel guests are foreigners. Rooms are small but clean, comfortable, and pleasant, with the extras of a hairdryer, hot water for tea, radio, and cotton yukata. There are two very good restaurants, one Japanese and one French.

OTHER LOCATIONS

AKIHABARA

AKIHABARA WASHINGTON HOTEL, 1-8-3 Kanda, Sakumacho, Chiyoda-ku 101, Tokyo. Tel. 03/3255-3311. Fax 03/3255-7343. 312 rms. A/C MINIBAR TV TEL **Station:** JR Akihabara station (then a one-minute walk).

$ Rates: ¥10,500–¥16,000 ($95–$145) single; ¥18,700 ($170) twin; ¥26,000 ($236) double. AE, DC, JCB, MC, V.

This relatively new business hotel is located on the edge of Akihabara, Japan's largest retail electronics district. Rooms are modern and bright, though tiny and offering no view whatsoever. The eighth floor is a so-called woman's floor, but the only difference I can see is the addition of a small plant and hairdryer in each room. Still, this is the first business hotel I've seen that acknowledges the existence of women. There's also a no-smoking floor. Facilities include five restaurants and bars.

NEAR THE IMPERIAL PALACE

FAIRMONT HOTEL, 2-1-17 Kudan-Minami, Chiyoda-ku 102, Tokyo. Tel. 03/3262-1151. Fax 03/3264-2476. 208 rms. A/C MINIBAR TV TEL **Station:** Kudanshita (then a 10-minute walk).

$ Rates: ¥11,000–¥23,000 ($100–$209) single; ¥20,000–¥25,000 ($182–$227) double or twin. Extra bed ¥3,300 ($30). AE, DC, JCB, MC, V.

A good choice in this category, the Fairmont has a beautiful location on a quiet street opposite the northwest end of the Imperial Palace moat, which is lined with cherry trees—a real treat when the blossoms burst forth in spring. Guests like the Fairmont because it's a small, older hotel (built in 1952) and because it's conveniently located near the heart of the city, and yet it's away from the hustle and bustle of downtown Tokyo. For joggers, the circular moat is popular for traffic-free running. The more expensive rooms are larger and face the moat—and are definitely worth it during cherry-blossom season. All rooms have TV with English cable and CNN broadcasts. One of the hotel's restaurants, the Brasserie de la Verdure, has a view of the moat, while the French restaurant Cerisiers looks out onto a pleasant small garden with a waterfall. As extra services, the hotel offers free newspapers, room service (to 10:30pm), and laundry service.

MEGURO

GAJOEN KANKO HOTEL, 1-8-1 Shimo-Meguro, Meguro-ku 153, Tokyo. Tel. 03/3491-0111. Fax 03/3495-2450. 98 rms. A/C MINIBAR TV TEL **Station:** Meguro (then a four-minute walk).

$ Rates: ¥10,000 ($91) single; ¥17,000–¥22,000 ($155–$200) double or twin; ¥26,000 ($236) family room for three, ¥35,000 ($318) for four. AE, DC, JCB, MC, V.

This may be the closest thing Tokyo has to the tradition of an old, grand hotel. A rather eccentric-looking, quaint hotel tucked away in Meguro, it was built in the 1930s. In its early years it served as a hospital; American army personnel were stationed here for 10 years after World War II. After decades of neglect, it was renovated in 1986 and a new wing was added. It has a charming, decidedly Oriental atmosphere, with wood paneling and Japanese murals on its lobby ceiling and intricately inlaid shell and mother-of-pearl designs in its two old elevators. Rooms come in a variety of shapes, sizes, and prices, but I prefer the old-fashioned rooms in the main building to those in the new wing. The best, and most expensive, rooms are the corner twins where you'll be treated to lots of windows, a mural on the high ceiling over the bed, and large tiled bathrooms. In Tokyo's zeal for modernization, it's a wonder this place has survived. Facilities include French and Chinese restaurants and a barbershop, and there's a same-day laundry service.

KANDA

TOKYO YMCA HOTEL, 7 Mitoshiro-cho, Kanda, Chiyoda-ku 101, Tokyo. Tel. 03/3293-1911. Fax 03/3293-1926. 40 rms (all with bath). A/C TV TEL **Station:** Shin-Ochanomizu (then a three-minute walk), Ogawamachi (then a two-minute walk), or Awajicho (then a five-minute walk).

$ Rates: ¥11,000 ($100) single; ¥17,000–¥22,000 ($155–$200) twin. 10% discount for YMCA members. No credit cards.

Where else but Tokyo would there be a YMCA priced as expensively as a regular hotel? However, this place is spanking new, modern, and spotless, with an atmosphere better than most business hotels in this category. Fully carpeted, it has one Western restaurant, a pharmacy, and a beauty salon, and there's laundry service. Both men and women are accepted, and rooms (which are mostly singles) come with hot water and tea, cotton yukata, and bilingual TV with remote control. Vending machines dispense beer and soft drinks. The front doors are locked at midnight.

Ryokan

SHIMIZU BEKKAN (1), 1-30-29 Hongo, Bunkyo-ku 113, Tokyo. Tel. 03/3812-6285. 21 rms (2 with bath). A/C MINIBAR TV TEL **Station:** Hongo Sanchome (then about an eight-minute walk, but it's best to arrive by taxi).

$ Rates (per person, including tax and service charge): ¥9,000 ($82) room without bath or meals, ¥10,000 ($91) room with breakfast only, ¥13,500 ($123) room with dinner and breakfast. Room with bath ¥1,000 ($9) per person extra. No credit cards.

This ryokan is accustomed to foreigners and offers a variety of choices depending on how many meals you wish to eat and whether you want your own private bathroom. Meals are served in your room, and there are separate public baths for men and women.

A NOTE ON JAPANESE SYMBOLS

Many hotels, restaurants, and other establishments in Japan do not have signs showing their names in English letters. The Appendix lists the Japanese symbols for all such places appearing in this guide. Each establishment name in Japanese symbols is numbered, and the same number appears in an oval in the text following the boldfaced establishment name. Example: **Suehiro** (7) means that the restaurant's name is no. 7 in the Japanese symbol list.

4. BUDGET

SHINJUKU

RYOKAN

KEIUNSO RYOKAN, 2-4-2 Yoyogi, Shinjuku-ku 151, Tokyo. Tel. 03/3370-0333. 20 rms (all with toilet only). A/C TV TEL A/C TV **Station:** Shinjuku, the south exit (then a three-minute walk).

$ Rates: ¥6,500 ($59) single; ¥5,500 ($50) per person double or triple. JCB.

This is one of the least expensive places to stay in the vicinity of Shinjuku Station, but the English-speaking woman who runs the place expressed some reluctance about taking in foreigners who had never stayed in a ryokan before. Another disadvantage to staying here is that guests are requested to leave during the day from 10am to 5pm; and check-in is at 4:30pm and check-out 9am. However, this place has such a good location that it's worth a try. The rooms are Japanese style, with their own toilet, but the bath is communal.

OKUBO HOUSE, 1-11-32 Hyakunincho, Shinjuku-ku 169, Tokyo. Tel. 03/3361-2348. 76 beds (no rooms with bath). **Station:** Shin-Okubo (then about a two-minute walk).

$ Rates: ¥1,700 ($15.45) bed in men's dormitory, ¥1,800 ($16.35) bed in women's dormitory; ¥3,300 ($30) single; ¥4,500–¥4,900 ($41–$45) double. No credit cards.

Judging from the number of old Tokyo hands who stayed here when they first arrived in the city, this place has been around forever. It's not a member of the Japanese Inn Group; the people who run this place are sometimes curt and gruff, and check-in isn't until 5pm. What's more, you have to leave during the day from 9:30am to 5pm and the front doors are locked at 11pm. Still, it's cheap and you might try it if the other ryokan in this category are full. The private rooms are the smallest I've seen—just two- or three-tatami-mat rooms—but at least they have windows. The majority of beds here are dormitory style, separated for men and women. Children are not accepted. Cotton yukata and Japanese tea are provided, but there's no kitchen or meals. There are separate public baths for men and women.

This place is located one station north of Shinjuku Station on the Yamanote Line. To reach it, turn left out of Shin-Okubo's only exit, then turn left again on the first side street, which runs parallel to the train tracks. Okubo is on this street, with a sign in English.

ASAKUSA

ASAKUSA PLAZA HOTEL, 1-2-1 Asakusa, Taito-ku 111, Tokyo. Tel. 03/3845-2621. Fax 03/3841-8862. 70 rms (all with bath). A/C TV TEL **Station:** Asakusa (then about a one-minute walk).

$ Rates: ¥5,500–¥7,000 ($50–$64) single; ¥9,500–¥10,500 ($86–$95) double; ¥10,000–¥12,500 ($91–$114) twin; ¥15,000 ($136) triple. AE, JCB, MC, V.

If you prefer to stay in the old downtown district of Asakusa, this simple business hotel is located just a few minutes' walk from the famous Sensoji Temple and is a red-brick building right on the main thoroughfare of Asakusa. Almost half its rooms are singles; the cheapest do not have windows. The cheapest doubles have a semi-double bed, which is between single and full size. Otherwise, rooms are simple but adequate and come with hot-water pot and tea and cotton yukata. The lobby is on the second floor, and there's one Western-style restaurant specializing in seafood.

RYOKAN

KIKUYA RYOKAN, 2-18-9 Nishi Asakusa, Taito-ku 111, Tokyo. Tel. 03/3841-6404. Fax 03/3841-6404. 10 rms (5 with bath). A/C TV **Station:** Tawaramachi (then an eight-minute walk).

$ Rates: ¥4,600 ($42) single without bath, ¥5,500–¥6,500 ($50–$59) single with bath; ¥7,800 ($71) double without bath, ¥8,300–¥8,800 ($75–$80) double with bath; ¥11,000 ($100) triple without bath, ¥12,000 ($109) triple with bath. AE, MC, V.

A modern red-brick building, this friendly establishment is located just off Kappabashi Dori Avenue (which is lined with shops selling those plastic-food displays you see in restaurants throughout Japan). Sensoji Temple is about a 10-minute walk away. The front doors close at midnight, and there's a communal refrigerator where you can store food and drinks (only rooms with private bathroom have refrigerators). It's a member of the Japanese Inn and Welcome Inn Groups.

RYOKAN MIKAWAYA BEKKAN, 1-31-11 Asakusa, Taito-ku 111, Tokyo. Tel. 03/3843-2345. Fax 03/3843-2348. 12 rms (none with bath). A/C TV **Station:** Asakusa (then a few minutes' walk).

$ Rates: ¥5,700 ($52) single; ¥10,500 ($95) double. AE, MC, V.

Located just off Nakamise Dori, a colorful, shop-lined pedestrian street leading to the famous Sensoji Temple, this is a great place to stay for visitors in search of old Japan. Owned by Katsuo Tobita, who speaks good English, it has been a ryokan for more than half a century and has a miniature courtyard with a goldfish pond where guests can sit outside in fine weather. The 12 tatami rooms come with coin-operated TV, floor cushions with backrests, and Japanese-style vanity mirrors. A member of the Japanese Inn Group, for ¥900 ($8.20) it offers both a Japanese breakfast or a Western-style breakfast of eggs, toast, salad, fruit, and coffee. The front doors are closed at 11:30pm and guests are requested to leave their rooms from 10am to noon daily for cleaning.

SAKURA RYOKAN, 2-6-2 Iriya, Taito-ku 110, Tokyo. Tel. 03/3876-8118. Fax 03/3873-9456. 16 rms (6 with bath). A/C TV TEL **Station:** Iriya (then a five-minute walk).

$ Rates: ¥5,500 ($50) single without bath, ¥6,500 ($59) single with bath; ¥9,900 ($90) double without bath, ¥11,000 ($100) double with bath; ¥12,000 ($109) triple without bath. AE, MC, V.

This modern, concrete establishment, a member of the Japanese Inn Group, is located just off the Kappabashi Dori and Kototoi Dori intersection, about a 10-minute walk from Sensoji Temple. The reception is on the second floor and the owner speaks English. A combination business/tourist hotel, it has both Japanese and foreign guests and rooms are spotless. All rooms have sinks and alarm clocks, and guests have use of a coin laundry and an elevator. Half the rooms are Western style with and without private bathroom, while all the Japanese-style rooms are without private bath. There's one Japanese-style room large enough for a family of six or seven people, complete with a terrace. Japanese breakfasts are available for ¥700 ($6.35), while Western-style breakfasts cost ¥600 ($5.45).

UENO

HOTEL OHGAISO, 3-3-21 Ikenohata, Taito-ku 110, Tokyo. Tel. 03/3822-4611. Fax 03/3823-4340. 85 rms (all with bath). A/C MINIBAR TV TEL **Station:** Nezu (then a three-minute walk), or Keisei (Skyliner) Ueno Station, Ikenohata exit (then a seven-minute walk).

$ Rates: ¥7,800 ($71) single; ¥14,000 ($127) twin. AE, DC, JCB, MC, V.

Located near Ueno Park just north of Shinobazu Pond, this hotel is rather unimaginative, but the rooms are clean and inexpensive and come with desk, refrigerator, radio, coin-operated TV, and clock. The front doors are locked at 2am. Its one restaurant serves both Japanese- and Western-style breakfasts, as well as tempura, sashimi, and sukiyaki.

RYOKAN

KATSUTARO, 4-16-8 Ikenohata, Taito-ku 110, Tokyo. Tel. 03/3821-9808. Fax 03/3821-4789. 7 rms (4 with bath). A/C TV **Station:** Nezu (then a 5-minute walk), or Keisei (Skyliner) Station, Ikenohata exit (then a 10-minute walk).

$ Rates: ¥4,600 ($42) single without bath; ¥8,100 ($74) double without bath, ¥9,200 ($84) double with bath; ¥11,500 ($105) triple without bath, ¥13,800 ($125) triple with bath. AE, MC, V.

A great area to stay in if you want to get away from the glitter and neon of Tokyo is this neighborhood northwest of Ueno Park, where you'll find this and the following three ryokan. Rooms here are quite large and have coin-operated TVs, but try to avoid rooms that face the main street, as these can be quite noisy. The building itself is more than 35 years old, and at least half its guests are Japanese. In addition to the usual Japanese tea available at all Japanese inns and most hotels, this member of the Japanese Inn Group also offers free coffee throughout the morning and afternoon. A continental breakfast costs ¥400 ($3.65), while a Japanese breakfast is ¥800 ($7.25).

RYOKAN SAWANOYA, 2-3-11 Yanaka, Taito-ku 110, Tokyo. Tel. 03/3822-2251. Fax 03/3822-2252. 12 rms (2 with bath). A/C TV TEL **Station:** Nezu, Nezu Kosaten exit (then a seven-minute walk).

$ Rates: ¥4,400–¥4,600 ($40–$42) single without bath; ¥8,000 ($73) double without bath, ¥8,800 ($80) double with bath; ¥10,800 ($98) triple without bath, ¥12,500 ($114) triple with bath. AE.

Although this Japanese Inn Group member is relatively modern looking and unexciting, it's surrounded by a delightful part of old Tokyo—narrow streets lined with potted plants and bonsai, temples and old wooden houses tucked behind walls with wood gates, mom-and-pop shops selling everything from Japanese paper to rice crackers. To help in your exploration of the area, the ryokan will give you a map outlining places of interest. As for the ryokan itself, it's a good place to meet other travelers and exchange information. The best rooms are those on the third floor because each has its own small balcony, and all rooms have coin-operated TVs, heaters, and sinks. Instant coffee and tea are available all day, and facilities include a beer- and soda-vending machine, a coin-operated washing machine and dryer (with free laundry detergent), a communal refrigerator, and a public bath. A breakfast of toast and fried eggs is available for ¥300 ($2.75) and a Japanese breakfast goes for ¥900 ($8.20). Highly recommended.

SUIGETSU, 3-3-21 Ikenohata, Taito-ku 110, Tokyo. Tel. 03/3822-4611. Fax 03/3823-4340. 66 rms (24 with bath). A/C MINIBAR TV TEL **Station:** Nezu (then a three-minute walk), or Keisei (Skyliner) Station, Ikenohata exit (then a seven-minute walk).

$ Rates: ¥6,500 ($59) single without bath, ¥18,000 ($164) single with bath; ¥11,400 ($104) double without bath, ¥20,000 ($182) double with bath; ¥14,400 ($131) triple without bath, ¥28,000 ($254) triple with bath. AE, MC, V.

This ryokan is located behind the Hotel Ohgaiso, a Western-style hotel (see above). They are under the same management but have separate front desks. Catering mainly to Japanese families and tour groups, this large establishment resembles a hotel more than it does a traditional ryokan, and rooms come with coin-operated TVs with adult video, refrigerators, safes, mirrors, and tables. Although a few rooms are available with private bath, they are much more expensive than those without. In any case, there are three public baths: one for women, one for men, and one for families. A restaurant serves Japanese food and Japanese- and Western-style breakfasts.

YAMANAKA RYOKAN, 4-23-1 Ikenohata, Taito-ku 110, Tokyo. Tel. 03/3821-4751. Fax 03/3821-4770. 13 rms (all with bath). A/C MINIBAR TV TEL **Station:** Nezu (then a 3-minute walk) or JR Ueno (then a 20-minute walk).

$ Rates: ¥7,000 ($63) single; ¥14,000 ($127) double; ¥21,000 ($190) triple. No credit cards.

This member of the Welcome Inn Group is located in a residential district in a two-story ferroconcrete building, but is close to Ueno Park attractions. They serve a mixture of Chinese, Western, and Japanese food at meals. Breakfast is ¥1,000 ($9.10) and dinner costs ¥2,000 ($18.20).

HARAJUKU & AOYAMA

ASIA CENTER OF JAPAN, 8-10-32 Akasaka, Minato-ku, 107. Tel. 03/3402-6111. Fax 03/3402-0738. 172 rms (100 with bath). A/C TV TEL **Station:** Aoyama-1-chome or Nogizaka (then a three-minute walk).

$ Rates (including tax and service charge): ¥5,000 ($45) single without bath, ¥5,900–¥6,900 ($54–$63) single with bath; ¥6,600–¥7,200 ($60–$65) twin without bath, ¥10,000–¥11,400 ($91–$104) twin with bath; ¥9,300 ($85) double with bath; ¥13,200 ($120) triple with bath. No credit cards.

This is the top choice in this category if you're looking for cheap Western-style accommodations in the center of town. The only problem is that it's so popular it's often fully booked. Everyone from businessmen to students to travelers to foreigners teaching English stay here. (I know one teacher who has lived here for years.) Resembling a college dormitory, it offers basic rooms with no frills, and the singles are so small you can almost reach out and touch all four walls. Rooms have coin-operated TVs. An inexpensive cafeteria serves breakfasts averaging ¥600 ($5.45), lunches for ¥850 ($7.70), and dinners at ¥1,500 ($13.65). It's about a 15-minute walk to Roppongi, where all the night action is.

OTHER LOCATIONS

RYOKAN

KIMI RYOKAN, 2-36-8 Ikebukuro, Toshima-ku 171, Tokyo. Tel. 03/3971-3766. 41 rms (none with bath). A/C TEL **Station:** Ikebukuro, west exit (then a five-minute walk; the tiny police post located to your right as you exit the station has maps that will guide you to Kimi).

$ Rates: ¥4,500 ($41) single; ¥7,000 ($64) double; ¥7,500 ($68) twin. No credit cards.

This place is a legend. It's owned by three brothers of the Minato family, who speak excellent English and began attracting foreign visitors in the late 1970s. In 1986 Kimi underwent a complete remodeling and was transformed from a rambling, wooden structure to a modern, five-story concrete building with whitewashed walls, wooden corridors, and tatami-style guest rooms. The place is spotlessly clean, and although it's modern in every sense of the word, care has been given to add such Japanese touches as sliding screens. Traditional Japanese music plays softly in the hallways. Catering exclusively to foreigners, Kimi attracts backpackers, English teachers, the middle-aged, families, and those in search of more permanent homes. There's a bulletin board with various jobs available (mainly as English teachers). Although it's not a member of the Japanese Inn Group, this place is so popular that there's usually a waiting list to get in. Facilities include a lounge with TV, a vending machine for drinks, and a pay phone from which you can make international calls. Free tea is available throughout the day. The Minato family is to be commended. If only Tokyo had other such places!

RYOKAN FUJI, 6-8-3 Higashi-Koiwa, Edogawa-ku 133, Tokyo. Tel. 03/3657-1062. Fax 03/3657-1062. 9 rms (all with bath). A/C TV **Station:** JR Koiwa (then a 6-minute walk) or Keisei Koiwa (then a 10-minute walk).

$ Rates: ¥6,500 ($59) single; ¥12,000 ($109) double; ¥18,000 ($164) triple. No credit cards.

Located in a modern two-story building in a residential district, this ryokan, a member of the Welcome Inn Group, is a bit out of the way, but comes highly recommended by a reader from Belgium. Although the older lady who runs the place doesn't speak English, she makes up for it with kindness. Japanese-style meals—breakfast for ¥1,000 ($9.10) and dinner for ¥2,000 ($18.20)—are served.

SANSUISO, 2-9-5 Higashi Gotanda, Shinagawa-ku 141, Tokyo. Tel. 03/3441-7475. Fax 3449-1944. 9 rms (2 with bath). A/C TV **Station:** Gotanda (then a five-minute walk).

$ Rates: ¥4,700 ($43) single without bath, ¥5,000 ($45) single with bath; ¥8,000 ($73) double without bath, ¥8,400 ($76) double with bath; ¥11,000 ($100) triple without bath. AE, V.

The friendly and accommodating couple who run this place don't speak any English but they have a poster with all pertinent questions, such as how many nights you are staying. The ryokan, a member of the Japanese Inn Group, is very clean and rooms come with the usual hot water and tea bags, cotton yukata and towel, mirror, heater, and coin-operated TV. Some rooms have Japanese toilet and bath. There's a midnight curfew.

SUZUKI RYOKAN, 7-15-23 Yanaka, Taito-ku, Tokyo. Tel. 03/3821-4944. 10 rms (3 with bath). A/C TV **Station:** Nippori (then a couple minutes' walk).

$ Rates (including tax): ¥3,800 ($35) single without bath, ¥4,400 ($40) single with bath; ¥7,700 ($70) double without bath, ¥8,800 ($80) double with bath. No credit cards.

This simple ryokan is located in a historic and quaint part of Tokyo called Nippori that is known for its many shrines, temples, and the Yanaka cemetery. A typical Japanese house with traditional woodwork throughout and a pebbled hallway, it offers simple rooms. While no English is spoken, it is a member of the Welcome Inn Group.

THE Ys

YMCA ASIA YOUTH CENTER, 2-5-5 Sarugaku-cho, Chiyoda-ku 101, Tokyo. Tel. 03/3233-0611. Fax 03/3233-0633. 55 rms (all with bath). A/C TV TEL **Station:** Suidobashi (then a 5-minute walk) or Jimbocho (then a 10-minute walk).

$ Rates (including tax and service charge): ¥7,500 ($68) single; ¥13,000 ($118) twin; ¥17,500 ($159) triple. YMCA member discount ¥500 ($4.55). No credit cards.

This relatively new and modern-looking concrete structure accepts men and women of any age. Rooms are simple, like a college dormitory, and facilities include an indoor swimming pool (fee: ¥1,000/$9.10). Japanese or Western breakfasts are ¥1,000 ($9.10), lunches start at ¥1,000 ($9.10), and dinners start at ¥1,500 ($13.65). There's a midnight curfew and laundry service is available.

TOKYO YWCA SADOWARA HOSTEL ②, 3-1-1 Ichigaya Sadowara-cho, Shinjuku-ku 162, Tokyo. Tel. 03/3268-7313. Fax 03/3268-4452. 20 rms (18 with toilet only, 2 with bath). A/C TEL **Station:** Ichigaya, Ichigaya exit (then a seven-minute walk).

$ Rates (including tax and service charge): ¥6,000 ($55) single with toilet only; ¥12,000 ($109) twin with toilet only, ¥14,000 ($127) twin with bathroom. No credit cards.

This YWCA is located in a modern, spotless building. In addition to female travelers, it also accepts married couples, but only for one of its two twins that also have private bathroom and kitchenette. All rooms have a sink. For communal use there's an iron and ironing board, kitchen, and refrigerator. The front door closes at 11pm.

HOSTELS

TOKYO INTERNATIONAL YOUTH HOSTEL, 1-1 Kagura-kashi, Shinjuku-ku 162, Tokyo. Tel. 03/3235-1107. 138 beds. **Station:** Iidabashi, west exit (then a one-minute walk).

$ Rates: ¥3,000 ($27.25) per person for members, ¥3,700 ($34) for nonmembers. Breakfast ¥400 ($3.65) extra; dinner, ¥800 ($7.25). No credit cards.

Opened in 1984, this is definitely the best place in its price range. The lobby is on the 18th floor of the new Central Plaza Building, and the rooms are new, spotlessly clean, and modern, and offer a great view of Tokyo. The best thing is that you don't even need a youth hostel card to stay here. All rooms are dormitory style, with two, four, or five bunk beds to a room. Rooms are very pleasant, with big windows and wooden and metal bunk beds of modern design. Each bed has its own curtain you can draw around for privacy. Officially you can stay here a maximum of three days, although if there are vacancies you can stay longer. The place is so popular in summer, however, that it's necessary to make reservations about three months in advance. Curfew is 10:30pm, and the hostel is closed during the day from 10am to 3pm. A plus, however, is the free use of a washer and dryer.

TOKYO YOYOGI YOUTH HOSTEL, National Olympic Memorial Youth Center, 3-1 Yoyogi-Kamizono, Shibuya-ku 151, Tokyo. Tel. 03/3467-9163. 75 beds. **Station:** Sangubashi (then about a five-minute walk).

$ Rates: ¥2,300 ($21) per person. No credit cards.

Accepting only youth-hostel members, this youth hostel is located on the west side of Meiji Shrine Outer Garden in an enclosed complex of buildings surrounded by a fence. The whole compound housed American occupation troops after World War II and was later used to accommodate athletes during the 1964 Olympics. The youth hostel is in Building 14, and there's a large Japanese-style bath in a neighboring building. No meals are served, but there are cooking facilities. The hotel is closed during the day from 10am to 5pm, and the front gate closes at 10pm.

CAPSULE HOTELS

For a novel experience, stay at one of these capsule hotels, where bed units are stacked on top of each other the length of a corridor. Don't expect much privacy. Note that they're *for men only*.

AKASAKA

CAPSULE INN AKASAKA, 6-14-1 Akasaka, Minato-ku 107, Tokyo. Tel. 03/3588-1811. 288 beds. A/C TV **Station:** Akasaka (then a three-minute walk).

$ Rates: ¥4,400 ($40) per person. No credit cards.

Located just off Akasaka Dori Avenue in the heart of Akasaka, this capsule hotel for men only offers a sauna and public bath. Each capsule unit has a color TV, radio, and alarm clock. Check-in is after 5pm, and check-out is at 10am.

FONTAINE AKASAKA, 4-3-5 Akasaka, Minato-ku 107, Tokyo. Tel. 03/3583-6554. 367 beds. A/C TV **Station:** Akasaka Station (then a two-minute walk) or Akasaka-mitsuke (then a five-minute walk).

$ Rates: ¥5,300 ($48) per person. AE, DC, JCB, MC, V.

A large blue building in the heart of Akasaka's nightlife on Hitosugi Dori near the TBS Building, it offers a sauna, public bath, no-smoking floors, and vending machines selling everything from beer and instant noodles to toothbrushes. Its English brochure says sternly that "Persons whose bodies are tattooed are requested to keep out" (tattoos are associated with Japanese gangsters). Also, "Dead drunks are requested to keep out." Ah, the joys of Japanized English. Check-in is after 5pm; check-out is at 10am.

CHAPTER 5

TOKYO DINING

Tokyo's social life revolves around its restaurants and bars. Little wonder, considering the fact that apartments are often far from the city center and so small that entertaining at home is almost unheard of. Restaurants serve as places for socializing, meeting friends, and entertaining business associates, as well as excuses for drinking a lot of beer, sake, and whiskey. There are an estimated 45,000 restaurants in Tokyo, from stand-up noodle shops at train stations to rustic farmhouses serving traditional country foods to chic French restaurants to pizzerias.

The biggest problem facing the hungry foreigner is ordering, simply because many restaurants in Tokyo don't have English menus. However, many restaurants display plastic-food models of their most popular dishes, either in a glass case outside the restaurant or just inside the front door. Sushi, tempura, daily specials, spaghetti—they're all there in mouth-watering plastic replicas, along with the corresponding prices.

Unfortunately, not all restaurants have plastic display cases, including many of Tokyo's most authentic and exclusive Japanese restaurants. In fact, you'd miss some of the best the city has to offer if you limited your dining experiences only to those restaurants with plastic displays. The best thing to do is to look at what people around you are eating and order what looks best. An alternative is simply to order the "set course" (a fixed-price meal), also referred to as "seto" or simply "course." At lunchtime, many Japanese restaurants also offer the ever-popular teishoku, or daily lunch special. These are usually an entire meal with soup, rice, appetizer, and main dish. In Western restaurants the lunch special is usually called the "set lunch." You can help keep costs down, therefore, by eating your big meal in the middle of the day. Even a restaurant that may be too expensive at dinnertime may be perfect for a lunchtime splurge, when specials cost as little as a fourth of what a dinner would be. Thus even if you're a budget traveler, don't neglect the listings of medium-priced restaurants. The usual time for teishoku is from about 11 or 11:30am to 2pm, although many restaurants offer set dinner as well.

Although Japanese food is varied, healthy, and delicious, even the most dedicated Japanophile starts craving Western food after a while. I have therefore included some non-Japanese restaurants. The most popular Western restaurants are French and Italian, which can be rather expensive. Other international cuisines more reasonably priced include Mexican, Chinese, Thai, and American.

For the simplicity of organization, I've divided Tokyo's restaurants according to location and then by price.

PRICE RANGES For those restaurants in the "Very Expensive" category, expect to spend more than ¥10,000 ($90.90) for a meal, not including drinks. Meals at an "Expensive" restaurant generally run ¥6,000 to ¥10,000 ($54.55 to $90.90), while those in the "Moderate" price range average ¥3,000 to ¥6,000 ($27.25 to $54.55). Budget restaurants are those that offer meals for less than ¥3,000 ($27.25).

Remember, however, that these prices are only guidelines and that you can dine more cheaply at lunch. Don't neglect the lunch prices in the more expensive categories. Even if you're on a budget, you can usually eat lunch at the moderately priced restaurants for as little as ¥1,500 ($13.65).

DINING ON A BUDGET If you're restricted by a tight budget, you can still manage to eat quite well in Tokyo, despite the horror stories you may have read about the high prices of everything from coffee to fruit. The secret, of course, is to eat like the Japanese, since Western establishments tend to be more expensive. Many of Tokyo's most colorful, noisy, and popular restaurants fall into the inexpensive category, frequented by the city's huge working population as they catch a quick lunch or socialize after hours. Be sure to read over the nightlife chapter, Chapter 9, "Tokyo Nights," since there are a number of bars and nightspots listed there that serve food. In fact, Japanese bars are often the cheapest places around for an inexpensive but hearty meal.

Although noodle establishments and other quick-food Japanese-style places offer rock-bottom choices, you can save even more money by avoiding restaurants altogether. There are all kinds of prepared foods you can buy, and some of them are complete meals in themselves, perfect for picnics in the park or right in your hotel room.

Best-known perhaps is the **obento (box lunch),** commonly sold on express trains, on train station platforms, and at counter windows of tiny shops throughout Tokyo. Costing usually between ¥500 and ¥1,500 ($4.55 and $13.65), the basic obento contains a piece of meat (generally fish or chicken), rice, and pickled vegetables. Sushi lunchboxes are also available.

Department stores sell **prepared foods** in their basement food-and-produce sections, including such items as tempura, yakitori, sushi, salads, and desserts. There are numerous samples available and some travelers have been known to "dine" in department-store basements for free. In addition, most department stores have inexpensive restaurants, usually on one of the top floors. Since they almost always have plastic food displays, ordering is easy.

Other good sources for inexpensive meals are **street vendors.** They sell a variety of foods, including oden, okonomiyaki, and fried noodles. And finally, if you find yourself in real financial woes, you can always subsist on "cup noodle," which you can buy in any food store. Eaten by poor students and salarymen who don't have the time to sit down to a real meal, it's a dried soup that springs to life (well, sort of) when you add hot water, which is usually readily available in hotel and ryokan guest rooms. It comes in a variety of choices such as curry or chili tomato and usually costs less than ¥300 ($2.75). Eat too much of it, though, and you'll probably disintegrate.

Although technically Chinese fast-food restaurants, **ramen shops** are also cheap places for a meal. Serving what I consider to be generic Chinese noodles, soups, and other dishes, ramen shops can be found everywhere in Tokyo, easily recognizable by their red signs, flashing lights, and quite often pictures of various dishes displayed at the front door. In addition to noodle and vegetable soup, you can also get such things as fried noodles or (my favorite) gyoza, which are fried pork dumplings. What these places lack in atmosphere is made up for in price, with most dishes averaging about ¥500 to ¥900 ($4.55 to $8.20).

In case you're interested, Japan also has American **fast-food chains** such as McDonald's, Wendy's, and Kentucky Fried Chicken (now simply KFC), as well as Japanese hamburger-and-fries chains—Morninaga, Lotteria, and First Kitchen among them.

TAXES Keep in mind that restaurants will add a 3% consumption tax to bills totaling less than ¥7,500 ($68). For bills costing ¥7,500 and more, both the 3% consumption tax and a 3% local tax will be added to your bill. In addition, many first-class restaurants, as well as hotel restaurants, will add a 10% to 15% service charge in lieu of tipping.

Keep in mind, too, that last order for most restaurants is a half hour before the actual closing time.

1. GINZA & HIBIYA

VERY EXPENSIVE

JAPANESE FOOD

KINSEN ③, 4-4-10 Ginza. Tel. 3561-8708.

Cuisine: KAISEKI. **Reservations:** Recommended at lunch, required at dinner. **Station:** Ginza (then a one-minute walk).

$ Prices (including tax and service charge): Set dinners ¥11,000–¥15,800 ($100–$144); set lunches ¥2,500–¥7,500 ($22.70–$68.20). AE, JCB, MC, V.

Open: Lunch daily 11:30am–2pm; dinner daily 5–9pm.

A modern kaiseki restaurant in the heart of Ginza, Kinsen is on Harumi Dori Avenue on the fifth floor of the Ginza Kintetsu Building, just across the street from Jena Bookstore. There's no English menu, but various set meals are available; simply choose one to fit your budget. Lunches range from obento lunch boxes to mini-kaiseki courses, while dinner is primarily kaiseki, artistically arranged on a variety of small dishes.

SUSHIKO ④, 6-3-8 Ginza. Tel. 3571-1968.

Cuisine: SUSHI. **Reservations:** Required. **Station:** Ginza or Hibiya (then less than a five-minute walk).

$ Prices: Set meals ¥10,000–¥15,000 ($90.90–$136.35). No credit cards.

Open: Lunch Mon–Sat 11:30am–2pm; dinner Mon–Sat 5-9:30pm. **Closed:** Hols.

If money is no object, you have plenty of it on hand (no credit or charge cards accepted here), and you're in pursuit of exclusive sushi shops, your search will eventually take you to this tiny restaurant, which looks rather plain and ordinary on the outside but is about as exclusive as you can get, with seating at the counter for only 11 customers. Owned by a fourth-generation restaurateur, this establishment doesn't display its fish as in most sushi bars, but rather keeps the fish freshly refrigerated until the moment it meets the swift blade of the expert chefs. I wish that all those who claim they don't like sushi could afford to try it here.

NON-JAPANESE FOOD

MAXIM'S, 5-3-1 Ginza. Tel. 3572-3621.

Cuisine: FRENCH. **Reservations:** Recommended. **Station:** Ginza (then a one-minute walk).

$ Prices: Main dishes average ¥5,000–¥11,000 ($45.45–$100); set dinners ¥22,000 ($200); set lunches ¥6,000–¥9,000 ($54.55–$81.80). AE, DC, JCB, MC, V.

Open: Lunch Mon–Sat 11:30am–3pm; dinner Mon–Sat 5:30–11pm.

Only in Japan would you find a top-class restaurant in the third basement of the Sony Building. An exact copy of Paris's famous Maxim's, which opened its doors in 1893, the Japanese imitation is faithful to the art nouveau style, and its small dining room is one of the most romantic in town—very French, with gilded mirrors, cut-glass panels, mahogany paneling, and crimson cushions. Service is discreet and professional, as waiters bring in goose-liver pâté, sole cooked in French vermouth, sautéed tenderloin with truffle sauce, roast duckling with peaches, or grilled prime rib of Kobe beef. The average à la carte meal costs around ¥15,000 ($136.35). The set lunch and set dinner change daily. For dinner, men are required to wear a suit and tie.

EXPENSIVE

JAPANESE FOOD

GINZA BENKAY, 7-2-17 Ginza. Tel. 3573-7335.

Cuisine: VARIED JAPANESE. **Reservations:** Recommended at dinner. **Station:** Yurakucho or Hibiya (then a few minutes' walk).

$ Prices: Set dinners ¥7,000–¥20,000 ($63.65–$181.80); set lunches ¥1,500–¥4,400 ($13.65–$40). AE, DC, JCB, MC, V.

Open: Lunch Mon–Sat 11:30am–2pm; dinner Mon–Sat 5–9:30pm (last order). **Closed:** Hols.

Most Japanese restaurants specialize in only one or two types of cuisine, but this pleasant second-floor restaurant serves set meals of teppanyaki, sushi, shabu-shabu, kaiseki, and lunchboxes, each served

---

A NOTE ON JAPANESE SYMBOLS

Many hotels, restaurants, and other establishments in Japan do not have signs showing their names in English letters. The Appendix lists the Japanese symbols for all such places appearing in this guide. Each establishment name in Japanese symbols is numbered, and the same number appears in an oval in the text following the boldfaced establishment name. Example: **Suehiro** (7) means that the restaurant's name is no. 7 in the Japanese symbol list.

FROMMER'S SMART TRAVELER: RESTAURANTS

VALUE-CONSCIOUS TRAVELERS SHOULD TAKE ADVANTAGE OF THE FOLLOWING:

1. The teishoku, or daily special, offered by Japanese restaurants for lunch or even the whole day, and usually a complete meal.
2. Lunchtime menus offered by most expensive and medium-range restaurants, at prices much lower than dinner menus, making lunchtime a good time for a splurge.
3. Set courses, which are fixed-price meals usually offered for both lunch and dinner.
4. Inexpensive Japanese restaurants serving noodles, sushi, pork cutlets, and other Japanese fare, which are generally cheaper than restaurants serving Western cuisine.
5. Take-out counters throughout the city, including most train stations, selling sushi and obento box lunches.
6. Coffee shops, which often offer a "morning service" consisting of coffee, a small salad, boiled egg, and toast for less than ¥500 ($4.55).
7. Drinking establishments, especially yakitori-ya, which offer a variety of dishes and snacks at low prices.

QUESTIONS TO ASK IF YOU'RE ON A BUDGET

1. Is there a teishoku, daily special, or set course? Since these are complete meals, they're usually cheaper than ordering à la carte.
2. If the menu is only in Japanese, how much is the price of beer or other alcoholic drinks? Drinks can really add to the bill.
3. Is there a table charge or snack charge? Some bars and drinking establishments charge extra for such things, so ask before sitting down.

in its own special dining area and available in a variety of price ranges. You will be asked what you would like to eat upon entering and then be ushered off to the appropriate room. Lunch is the most economical time to dine, when you can order an assorted plate of sushi, a small kaiseki lunchbox, or a teppanyaki course. With a cool decor of stone-and-pebble floor, bamboo, wood, and shoji screens, it's located across from the International Arcade on the Ginza side, just a few minutes' walk from the Tourist Information Center. The English-speaking manager is very accommodating to foreigners. There's another Ginza Benkay located in the basement of the President Hotel in Aoyama (tel. 3402-0246), open the same hours.

KAMON, on the 17th floor of the Imperial Hotel, 1-1-1 Uchisaiwai-cho. Tel. 3504-1111.

Cuisine: TEPPANYAKI. **Reservations:** Not required. **Station:** Hibiya (then a one-minute walk).

$ Prices: Set dinners ¥9,000–¥20,000 ($81.80–$181.80); set lunches from ¥3,000 ($27.25). AE, DC, JCB, MC, V.

Open: Lunch daily 11:30am–2:30pm; dinner daily 5:30–9:30pm.

The interior of Kamon, which means "Gate of Celebration," is like a statement on Tokyo itself—traditionally Japanese, yet ever so high-tech. The steak, seafood, and vegetables grilled before your eyes are mouth-watering good and, of course, the service is imperial.

OHMATSUYA (5), 5-4-18 Ginza. Tel. 3571-7053.

Cuisine: GRILLED FOODS. **Reservations:** Required. **Station:** Ginza (then about a three-minute walk).

$ Prices: Set dinners ¥5,500–¥7,500 ($50–$68.20). AE, DC, V.

Open: Dinner only, Mon–Sat 5–10pm.

I know it doesn't look very promising from the outside, but go up the stairs to the second floor and you're instantly greeted by waitresses clad in countryside costumes and by an atmosphere that evokes the feeling of an old farmhouse. Little wonder: Part of the decor was brought from a 17th-century samurai house in northern Japan. Even the style of cooking is traditional: Customers grill their own food over a hibachi and charcoal flame. Sake is served in a length of bamboo and is drunk from bamboo cups. Set dinners include such delicacies as grilled fish, skewered pieces of meat, and vegetables. This establishment is a true find—and an easy one to find at that. It's located on Sony Street, the small side street behind the Sony Building. As you walk from Sony, the restaurant will be on your left in a stone-and-tile building called the IN Building.

SHABUSEN (6), Core Bldg. 2F, 5-8-20 Ginza. Tel. 3571-1717.

Cuisine: SHABU-SHABU/SUKIYAKI. **Reservations:** Not required. **Station:** Ginza (then a one-minute walk).

$ Prices: Dishes ¥350–¥1,000 ($3.20–$9.10); set dinners ¥3,800–¥5,500 ($34.55–$50); set lunches ¥1,200–¥2,200 ($10.90–$20). AE, MC, V.

Open: Daily 11am–9:30pm.

Under the management of Zakuro, this is a fun restaurant where you can cook your own sukiyaki or shabu-shabu in a boiling pot in front of you as you sit at a counter. Orders are being shouted back and forth among the staff, service is rapid, and the place is lively. There's an English menu complete with cooking instructions, so it's user-friendly. I had the special shabu-shabu dinner for ¥5,500 ($50) with appetizer, tomato "super dressing" salad, beef, vegetables, rice porridge, and dessert—and it was more than I could eat.

SUEHIRO (7), 6-11-1 Ginza. Tel. 3571-9271.

Cuisine: STEAKS/SUKIYAKI. **Reservations:** Required. **Station:** Ginza (then about a five-minute walk).

$ Prices: Set dinners ¥5,500–¥25,000 ($50–$227); set lunches ¥1,000–¥8,800 ($9.10–$80). AE, DC, JCB, MC, V.

Open: Daily 11am–10pm. Bay of Ginza, lunch daily 11am–2pm; dinner daily 5–10:30pm.

Suehiro is a successful steak-and-sukiyaki chain, established in 1933 and claiming to be the first restaurant in Tokyo to serve sukiyaki. With 17 locations in Japan served by its own cattle ranches for Matsuzaka beef, it recently updated and upgraded this main store, located behind the Matsuzakaya department store. A shiny new building complete with an information counter on the main floor, it offers several floors of dining. Most formal and expensive is the European-style dining hall on the seventh floor, which serves Matsuzaka beef steaks and teppanyaki. The sixth floor specializes in shabu-shabu and sukiyaki and features a traditional Japanese decor. Least expensive is the Bay of Ginza in the basement, which offers French cuisine with steaks as the main course. There are daily specials, best of which are the set steak dinners starting at ¥5,500 ($50).

TEN-ICHI, 6-6-5 Ginza. Tel. 3571-1949.

Cuisine: TEMPURA. **Reservations:** Recommended at lunch, required at dinner. **Station:** Ginza (then a few minutes' walk).

$ Prices: Set dinners ¥8,500–¥15,000 ($77.25–$136.35); set lunches ¥7,000–¥10,000 ($63.65–$90.90). AE, DC, JCB, MC, V.

Open: Mon–Sat 11:30am–9:30pm, Sun noon–9pm.

Located on Namiki Dori Street in the heart of Ginza's nightlife, this is the main shop of a restaurant chain that first served tempura in Tokyo more than 50 years ago and helped this style of cooking gain worldwide recognition by serving important foreign customers.

Today Ten-ichi still has one of the best reputations for delicately fried foods, and there are more than 10 branches in Tokyo, including several others in the Ginza and Hibiya area. There's a branch in the Sony Building on the intersection of Harumi Dori Avenue and Sotobori Dori Avenue (tel. 3571-3837), as well as a branch in the Imperial Hotel's Tower basement (tel. 3503-1001). Hours for all are the same.

MODERATE

JAPANESE FOOD

BENIHANA OF NEW YORK, 6-3-7 Ginza. Tel. 3571-9060.

Cuisine: TEPPANYAKI. **Reservations:** Recommended. **Station:** Hibiya (then a 5-minute walk) or Ginza (then a 10-minute walk).

$ Prices: Set dinners ¥4,500–¥20,000 ($40.90–$181.80); set lunches ¥1,800–¥3,300 ($16.35–$30). AE, DC, JCB, MC, V.

Open: Mon–Sat 11am–10pm, Sun and hols 11am–8pm.

I'm not sure how to categorize this restaurant, since it's an Americanized version of a Japanese steak house. With about 50 such restaurants in the United States, most Americans are familiar with Benihana and consider it Japanese food. However, the restaurant in Tokyo calls itself Benihana of New York, and what's more, all that theatrical bravado and karate-style knife chops are an American tradition and have very little to do with Japanese food preparation methods. In any case, teppanyaki steak courses are the specialty here, along with side dishes of seafood that might include lobster, squid, shrimp, scallops, and mussels. I suppose in the end it all tastes the same, regardless of the fanfare.

GINZA DAIMASU (8), 6-9-6 Ginza. Tel. 3571-3584.

Cuisine: VARIED JAPANESE. **Reservations:** Not required. **Station:** Ginza (then a two-minute walk).

$ Prices: Main dishes ¥1,000–¥2,800 ($9.10–$25.45); set dinners ¥3,000–¥5,000 ($27.25–$45.45); set lunches ¥1,800–¥2,800 ($16.35–$25.45). DC, JCB, MC, V.

Open: Daily 11:30am–9:30pm.

This 60-year-old restaurant has a simple, modern decor with Japanese touches. Experienced, kimono-clad waitresses will serve you artfully arranged dishes from the English menu. My Fukiyose-zen set meal—many delicate dishes served in three courses—included beautiful tempura delicacies served in an edible basket and a menu (in Japanese) explaining what I was eating. You'll recognize it because it's across from the Matsuzakaya department store and has a plastic food display in the front window. Lunch is served until 3pm.

KUSHI COLZA ⑨, 6-4-18 Ginza. Tel. 3571-8228.
Cuisine: YAKITORI/KUSHIYAKI. **Reservations:** Recommended. **Station:** Hibiya (then a 5-minute walk) or Ginza (then a 10-minute walk).
$ Prices: Appetizers ¥500–¥650 ($4.55–$5.90); set dinners ¥3,300–¥4,500 ($30–$40.90). AE, DC, MC, V.
Open: Dinner only, Mon–Fri 5–10pm, Sat–Sun 5–9pm.

Kikkoman, a well-known brand of soy sauce in Japan, maintains several restaurants, including this one which specializes in yakitori and kushiyaki (a similar style of grilled meats and vegetables served on skewers). This place is small, informal, and pleasant, with an open counter where you can watch the chefs prepare your food. An English menu lists three set dinners, which consist of various skewered filets of beef, fish, eel, or pork, along with an appetizer, salad, soup, and dessert. A la carte selections for skewered specialties average ¥320 to ¥750 ($2.90 to $6.80) per skewer. Try the asparagus wrapped with bacon, gingko nuts, or salad with soy sauce dressing.

RANGETSU, 3-5-8 Ginza. Tel. 3567-1021.
Cuisine: SUKIYAKI/SHABU-SHABU/KAISEKI/OBENTO. **Reservations:** Recommended. **Station:** Ginza (then about a three-minute walk).
$ Prices: Set dinners ¥7,500–¥18,000 ($68.20–$163.65); set lunches ¥1,700–¥4,000 ($15.45–$36.35). DC, JCB, MC, V.
Open: Mon–Sat 11:30am–10pm, Sun and hols 11:30am–9pm.

Located on Chuo Dori Avenue across from the Matsuya department store, this well-known Ginza restaurant has been dishing out sukiyaki, shabu-shabu, traditional box lunches, and steaks for more than four decades. They use only Matsuzaka beef (bought whole and then carved up by the chefs), which ranges from the costlier fine-marbled beef to the cheaper cuts with thick marbling. There are also various crab dishes (including a crab sukiyaki), kaiseki, sirloin steaks, and eel dishes. An especially good deal are the obento box lunches, available day and night, and the various set meals of tempura or steak offered for lunch. In the basement is a sake bar, with more than 80 different kinds of sake from all over Japan, which you can also order with your meal.

SUSHI SEI ⑩, 8-2-13 Ginza. Tel. 3572-4770 or 3571-2772.
Cuisine: SUSHI. **Station:** Hibiya (then about a five-minute walk).
$ Prices: Sushi à la carte ¥100–¥300 (90¢–$2.75); set lunches (basement only) ¥1,000–¥1,500 ($9.10–$13.65). AE, DC, JCB, MC, V.
Open: Lunch Mon–Sat noon–2pm; dinner Mon–Sat 5–10:45pm. **Closed:** Hols.

If you're hungering for mouth-watering sushi, this is a dependably good, medium-priced chain of sushi bars serving tender cuts of raw fish, making it a natural for both the novice and appreciative sushi fans. The ground-floor sushi bar serves sushi only à la carte—most dinners average about ¥5,000 ($45.45) per person. The basement is the place to go if you want one of its three lunch teishoku. The chef will prepare your food and place it on a raised platform on the counter in front of you, which serves as your plate. Look for this restaurant near the elevated tracks of the Yamanote Line.

NON-JAPANESE FOOD

ATTORE, in the Hotel Seiyo, 1-11-2 Ginza. Tel. 3535-1111.
Cuisine: ITALIAN. **Station:** Ginza (then a five-minute walk) or Ginza-Itchome (then a two-minute walk).
$ Prices: Appetizers ¥700–¥4,000 ($6.35–$36.35); pasta ¥1,400–¥3,200 ($12.70–$29.10); main dishes ¥2,400–¥4,400 ($21.80–$40); set lunches ¥1,700–¥9,000 ($15.45–$81.80). AE, DC, JCB, MC, V.
Open: Daily 11am–10pm.

Although located in one of the Ginza's most exclusive and expensive hotels, this basement Italian restaurant offers reasonably priced cuisine. Its dining room is modern, cheerful, and pleasant, separated from the open kitchen by a pane of clear glass. It offers a variety of pasta and main dishes, from whole-wheat spaghetti with mushrooms and oven-baked spinach gnocchi with tomato sauce to calamari stuffed with shrimp. For that special splurge, there's a second dining hall with a slightly more expensive but more elaborate menu, including more seafood and meat dishes.

KUJAKU-CHO [Peacock Hall], in the Ginza Tokyo Hotel, 5-15-9 Ginza. Tel. 3541-2411.
Cuisine: CHINESE. **Reservations:** Recommended at lunch. **Station:** Higashi-Ginza (then less than one-minute walk).
$ Prices: Dishes ¥1,800–¥3,000 ($16.35–$27.25); set dinners ¥8,500 ($77.25); lunch buffet ¥3,800 ($34.55); set lunches ¥3,600–¥5,600 ($32.70–$50.90). AE, DC, JCB, MC, V.
Open: Lunch daily 11:30am–2pm; dinner daily 5–10pm.

This Chinese restaurant is a popular place for informal business lunches in the Ginza. Simply decorated, with the addition of screens to give it a semblance of privacy, it has a good buffet lunch, as well as set lunches that range from noodle and rice dishes to more elaborate fare. Dinner is more expensive, with more than 100 items on its menu of mainly Cantonese and Szechuanese fare.

BUDGET

JAPANESE FOOD

ATARIYA (11), 3-5-17 Ginza. Tel. 3564-0045.
Cuisine: YAKITORI. **Station:** Ginza (then a three-minute walk).
$ Prices: Yakitori courses ¥1,500–¥2,700 ($13.65–$24.55); individual skewers ¥150–¥400 ($1.35–$3.65). No credit cards.
Open: Dinner only, Mon–Sat 5–10pm (last order).

The fact that it's open only at night and serves yakitori makes this technically a drinking establishment, but I mention it here because it's a good choice for inexpensive dining as well. Since its yakitori course includes most parts of the chicken (liver, gizzard, and skin), you may wish to order your favorites à la carte from the English menu. My favorites include tsukune (ground chicken on a skewer) and nabemono mizutaki (chicken with vegetables in a broth). A lively, fun place, it's located on the side street that runs behind the Wako department store (Suzuran Street), in the direction of Nihombashi.

DONTO ⑫, 1-7-1 Yurakucho. Tel. 3201-3021.

Cuisine: NOODLES/TEMPURA/OBENTO/SASHIMI. **Station:** Hibiya (then a one-minute walk).

$ Prices: A la carte dishes ¥500–¥8,000 ($4.55–$72.70); set dinners ¥3,600–¥7,500 ($32.70–$68.20); set lunches ¥800–¥1,500 ($7.25–$13.65). AE, DC, JCB, MC, V.

Open: Lunch Mon–Sat 11am–2:30pm; dinner Mon–Sat 5–10pm. **Closed:** Hols.

This inexpensive restaurant is right across the street from the Tourist Information Center in Hibiya, in the basement of the Denki Building. Take off your shoes as you enter the restaurant and put them into one of the lockers—but remember which one, because the outside is inscribed only in Japanese. This restaurant is popular with the local working crowd and is pleasantly decorated with shoji screens, wooden floors, and an open kitchen. Choose what you want from the plastic display case, which shows everything from noodles and sashimi to tempura and kaiseki. Highly recommended.

MUNAKATA, in the Mitsui Urban Hotel, 8-6-15 Ginza. Tel. 3574-9356.

Cuisine: MINI-KAISEKI/OBENTO/TEMPURA. **Station:** Shimbashi (then a 2-minute walk) or Hibiya (then about a 10-minute walk).

$ Prices: Mini-kaiseki lunch ¥3,000 ($27.25); tempura set meal ¥1,300 ($11.80). AE, DC, JCB, MC, V.

Open: Lunch daily 11:30am–4pm; dinner daily 5–10pm.

Kaiseki cooking is one of the most expensive meals you can have in Japan, but there are some lunch specials here that make it quite reasonable. This basement restaurant is cozy, with slats of wood and low lighting that give customers a sense of privacy. In addition to mini-kaiseki meals, there are also tempura courses available night and day and various obento lunchboxes. A great place for lunch.

OTAKO ⑬, 8-6-19 Ginza. Tel. 3571-0751.

Cuisine: ODEN. **Station:** Ginza (then a five-minute walk).

$ Prices: A la carte ¥150–¥500 ($1.35–$4.55). AE, DC, JCB, MC, V.

Open: Mon–Sat 4pm–12:30am.

Located on Namiki Dori, a small street in the heart of Ginza's nightlife district, this clean and friendly establishment has been dishing out its own oden (a traditional stew made of vegetables, fish cakes, tofu, and other ingredients simmered for hours in a sweetened stock) for more than 60 years. The Japanese eat it on cold winter days, but it's available here year-round. There's an English menu describing the various kinds of oden, from those with potatoes to those with meatballs wrapped in cabbage. You can also order a plate of various sashimi (sashimi moriawase).

YAKITORI UNDER THE TRACKS, under the Yamanote Line tracks in Hibiya.

Cuisine: YAKITORI. **Station:** Hibiya or Yurakucho (then a few minutes' walk).

$ Prices: Skewers ¥150–¥400 ($1.35–$3.65). No credit cards.

Open: Evenings only, variable.

This is not the name of a restaurant but rather a place. Underneath an arch of the railway tracks not far from the Imperial Hotel are about a dozen tiny yakitori stalls, open only in the evenings and catering to a rather boisterous working class, mainly men.

The atmosphere is one of prewar Japan, somewhat an anomaly in the otherwise chic Ginza. The place is definitely worth a visit for those seeking a different kind of experience. If you order simply "yakitori," you'll get white chicken meat, but tsukune (ground chicken) and other parts of the chicken, as well as beer and sake, are also available.

NON-JAPANESE FOOD

CHIANG MAI, 1-2-8 Yurakucho. Tel. 3580-0456.

Cuisine: THAI. **Station:** Hibiya (then about a one-minute walk).

$ **Prices:** Dishes ¥1,500–¥2,700 ($13.65–$24.55). No credit cards.

Open: Sun–Fri 11:30am–11pm.

This tiny, second-floor restaurant serving food of northern Thailand is located on a small street behind the Tourist Information Center in Hibiya. The menu is rather limited.

SHAKEY'S, 3-5-8 Ginza. Tel. 3563-2008.

Cuisine: PIZZA. **Station:** Ginza (then about a three-minute walk).

$ **Prices:** All-you-can-eat pizza ¥600 ($5.45). No credit cards.

Open: All-you-can-eat lunch Mon–Sat 11am–2pm.

If you want to gorge yourself on pizza, this is the best deal in town, an all-you-can-eat pizza lunch. Be prepared for a few surprises—especially pizza with corn or squid—but basically it's what you'd expect. While the pizza won't win any gourmet awards, it's a good place for gluttons. There are several Shakey's in Tokyo. This one is on Chuo Dori Avenue.

2. TSUKIJI

VERY EXPENSIVE

JAPANESE FOOD

TAMURA (14), 2-12-11 Tsukiji. Tel. 3541-2591.

Cuisine: KAISEKI. **Reservations:** Recommended at lunch, required at dinner. **Station:** Tsukiji (then about a one-minute walk).

$ **Prices:** Set dinners from ¥30,000 ($272); set lunches ¥6,500–¥11,000 ($59–$100). AE, DC, JCB, MC, V.

Open: Lunch daily noon–2pm; dinner daily 6–10pm (last order at 7:30pm).

This modern kaiseki restaurant has a friendly staff of smiling and bowing kimono-clad waitresses and hostesses who will make you feel as though they've been waiting just for you. Although the menu is only in Japanese, they'll help you decide what to order, but since there are only set meals your budget will probably decide for you. Lunch is the most economical time to come, when it's popular with Japanese housewives. You have your choice of either tatami seating or tables and chairs.

MODERATE

JAPANESE FOOD

TENTAKE ⑮, 6-16-6 Tsukiji. Tel. 3541-3881.
Cuisine: FUGU. **Station:** Tsukiji (then about a seven-minute walk).
$ Prices: Main dishes ¥1,000–¥4,900 ($9.10–$44.55); fugu set meals ¥9,000–¥13,500 ($81.80–$122.70). No credit cards.
Open: Daily noon–10pm. **Closed:** Sun Apr–Sept, first and third Wed Oct–Mar.

People who really know their fugu, or blowfish, will tell you that the only time to eat it is from October through March, when it's fresh. At Tentake you can enjoy fugu all year round, however, and it's a popular place with the Tsukiji working crowd. The menu is in Japanese only, but things you might want to try include the fugu sashimi for ¥2,000 ($18.20) or the fugu-chiri for ¥3,500 ($31.20). The latter is a do-it-yourself meal whereby you cook fugu, cabbage, dandelion leaves, and tofu in a pot of boiling water in front of you. There are also fugu set meals if you feel like going all out on blowfish, as well as tempura, eel, and crab dishes. The restaurant, a white-and-black mortar building, is located on Harumi Dori Avenue next to a bridge (from Tsukiji Station, walk away from Ginza). Before you eat here, be sure to read the description of, and caution about, fugu in "Food and Drink" in Chapter 1.

BUDGET

JAPANESE FOOD

EDOGIN ⑯, 4-5-1 Tsukiji. Tel. 3543-4401.
Cuisine: SUSHI. **Station:** Tsukiji (then a three-minute walk).
$ Prices: Set dinners ¥1,100–¥10,000 ($10–$90.90); lunch teishoku ¥1,000 ($9.10). AE, DC, MC, V.
Open: Mon–Sat 11am–9:30pm.

Since it's near Tsukiji's famous fish market, you can be sure the sushi is fresh, but there's nothing aesthetic about the place—the lights are bright, it's packed with locals, and it's noisy and busy, with waitresses constantly bustling around. What this means, of course, is that people come for the sushi. The menu is in Japanese only, but there's a glass case outside with some of the dishes displayed. As an alternative, look at what people around you are eating, or if it's lunch, order one of the teishoku. The address above is for Edogin's main restaurant, located just off the Harumi and Shin-Ohashi intersection, recognizable by a string of Japanese lanterns adorning its facade. Actually there are four Edogin sushi restaurants in Tsukiji, all within walking distance of one another, any one of which offers a good meal. Ask anyone in the neighborhood to point you in the right direction.

SUSHI DAI ⑰, Tsukiji Fish Market. Tel. 3542-1111.
Cuisine: SUSHI. **Station:** Tsukiji (then about a 10-minute walk).
$ Prices: Sushi à la carte ¥200–¥1,000 ($1.80–$9.10); sushi seto ¥2,000 ($18.20). No credit cards.
Open: Mon–Sat 5am–2pm. **Closed:** Hols.

Sushi for breakfast? Located right on the grounds of the Tsukiji Fish Market, this sushi bar boasts some of the freshest fish in town and consists of just one counter, usually filled with people who work in the market or its vicinity. This is one of the few places I've seen Japanese drink beer in the morning when they weren't on holiday (but heck, these people have been up since long before the crack of dawn). The easiest thing to do is order the seto, a set sushi course which usually comes with tuna, eel, shrimp, and other morsels of sushi, along with rolls of tuna and rice in seaweed (onigiri). Sushi Dai is nestled in a barrack of a building with other tiny shops and restaurants.

To find it, cross the bridge that leads to the market grounds and then take an immediate right, walking past the various small shops selling knives and fish-related cooking objects, and then your first left. To your right will be the barracks. Sushi Dai is located in Building 6 on the third alley, and is the third shop on the right side. Look for the blue curtains outside its front door.

3. NEAR TOKYO STATION

VERY EXPENSIVE

NON-JAPANESE FOOD

CROWN RESTAURANT, in the Palace Hotel, 1-1-1 Marunouchi. Tel. 3211-5211.

Cuisine: FRENCH. **Reservations:** Recommended. **Station:** Otemachi (then a one-minute walk) or Tokyo Station (then a seven-minute walk).

$ Prices: Appetizers ¥1,500–¥4,900 ($13.65–$44.55); main courses ¥5,500–¥22,000 ($50–$200). AE, DC, JCB, MC, V.

Open: Daily 11:30am–11pm.

Elegant dining with a view is what you get at this high-class French restaurant. Decorated in royal blue and featuring beautiful flower arrangements and three walls of windows, it offers a great view of the Imperial Palace, its surrounding garden, and Tokyo Tower (ask for a window seat when making your reservation). It specializes in seafood and steaks, including such house specialties as lobster thermidor, sole, and grilled tournedos with foie gras madeira sauce. There's live music from 6pm, and after dinner you can retire for a drink at the lounge next door. Coat and tie are required.

4. AKASAKA

VERY EXPENSIVE

JAPANESE FOOD

GARDEN BARBECUE, in the New Otani Hotel, 4-1 Kioi-cho. Tel. 3265-1111.

Cuisine: TEPPANYAKI. **Reservations:** Recommended. **Station:** Akasaka-mitsuke (then about a three-minute walk) or Yotsuya (then about a five-minute walk).

$ Prices: A la carte dishes ¥1,800–¥9,000 ($16.35–$81.80); set

FROMMER'S COOL FOR KIDS: RESTAURANTS

Hard Rock Café (*see p. 144*) This internationally known establishment should pacify grumbling teenagers. They can munch on hamburgers, gaze at famous guitars and other rock 'n' roll memorabilia, and most important, buy that Hard Rock Café T-shirt.

Johnny Rockets (*see p. 144*) When your kids start asking for "real food," take them here for the best burgers in town and singing waitresses that are sure to keep everyone entertained.

Shakey's (*see pp. 121 and 157*) When nothing but pizza will satisfy, head for one of these chain pizza parlors for an all-you-can eat bargain lunch.

dinners ¥8,500–¥17,000 ($77.25–$154.55); set lunches ¥4,400–¥7,000 ($40–$63.65). AE, DC, JCB, MC, V.
Open: Lunch daily noon–2pm; dinner daily 6–9pm.

Located in the midst of the New Otani Hotel's famous 400-year-old garden, this teppanyaki restaurant consists of three glass-enclosed pavilions, all with the same menu of Kobe beef, fish, lobster, and vegetables cooked on a grill right in front of you. If you order salad, try the soy-sauce dressing—it's delicious.

INAKAYA (18), 3-12-7 Akasaka. Tel. 3586-3054.
Cuisine: GRILLED FOODS. **Reservations:** Accepted only until 7pm. **Station:** Between Akasaka and Akasaka-mitsuke (then about a five-minute walk from both).
$ **Prices:** Average meal ¥11,000 ($100). AE, DC, JCB, MC, V.
Open: Dinner only, daily 5–11pm.

Whenever I'm playing hostess to foreign visitors in Tokyo I always take them to one of the city's three Inakaya restaurants (the other two are in Roppongi), and they've never been disappointed. The drama of the place alone is worth it. Customers sit at a long counter, on the other side of which are mountains of fresh vegetables, beef, and seafood. And in the middle of all that food are male cooks seated in front of a grill, ready to cook whatever you order in the style of robatayaki. To order, simply point to what you want. Your waiter, ready to bring you more rounds of beer or sake, shouts out your order, which is repeated by all the other waiters in unison, with the result that there is always this excited yelling going on. Sounds strange, I know, but it's actually a lot of fun. Food offerings may include yellowtail, red snapper, sole, king crab legs, giant shrimp, steak, meatballs, gingko nuts, potatoes, eggplant, and asparagus, all piled high in wicker baskets and ready for the grill. Sometimes there are tiny, crunchy crabs you eat whole—they tickle all the way down. I suppose the only drawback is that you don't know the prices of anything you're ordering, but be prepared to spend at least ¥10,000 to ¥15,000 ($90.90 to $136.35) per person, including drinks, tax, and service charge, and you won't be disappointed.

TEN-ICHI, Misuji Dori, Akasaka 3-chome. Tel. 3583-0107.
Cuisine: TEMPURA. **Reservations:** Recommended at dinner. **Station:** Akasaka or Akasaka-mitsuke (then about a five-minute walk).
$ Prices: Set dinners ¥11,000–¥16,500 ($100–$150); set lunches ¥6,500–¥10,000 ($59–$90.90). AE, DC, JCB, MC, V.
Open: Mon–Sat 11:30am–9:30pm.

This is the Akasaka branch of one of Tokyo's best-known and oldest tempura establishments. The set dinner for ¥11,000 ($100) includes deep-fried prawns and other seafoods, vegetables, salad, rice, miso soup, fruit, and pickled vegetables (refer to the Ten-ichi restaurant in Ginza for more information).

UNKAI, in the ANA Hotel Tokyo, 1-12-33 Akasaka. Tel. 3505-1111.
Cuisine: KAISEKI/VARIOUS TRADITIONAL FOODS. **Reservations:** Recommended at dinner. **Station:** Roppongi, Akasaka, Kamiyacho, or Toranomon (all within a 15-minute walk).
$ Prices: A la carte dishes ¥1,000–¥6,500 ($9.10–$59); set dinners ¥12,000–¥22,000 ($109.10–$200); set lunches ¥6,000–¥12,000 ($54.55–$109.10). AE, DC, JCB, MC, V.
Open: Lunch daily 11:30am–2:30pm; dinner daily 5–10pm.

With its stone pathway leading through the restaurant and a replica of a thatch-roofed house built as a facade into one of the walls, the atmosphere is one of a country village—a very refined and elegant country village. The restaurant overlooks a pond and waterfall and is one of the quietest, most dignified places for a meal in town. The food, which ranges from kaiseki to shabu-shabu, is excellent and worth the price, but you can dine for about half the price of dinner if you come for lunch. Try the reasonably priced tempura lunch or à la carte selections of tempura, sashimi, seasonal vegetables, and other dishes.

ZAKURO (19), in the basement of the TBS Kaikan Bldg., 5-3-3 Akasaka. Tel. 3582-6841.
Cuisine: SHABU-SHABU/SUKIYAKI/TEPPANYAKI. **Reservations:** Recommended. **Station:** Akasaka, TBS exit (then a one-minute walk).
$ Prices: Set dinners ¥8,800–¥16,000 ($80–$145.45); set lunches ¥1,700–¥6,500 ($15.45–$59). AE, DC, JCB, MC, V.
Open: Daily 11am–10pm (last order).

Popular with businessmen in the area for its Kobe beef, this restaurant offers shabu-shabu, sukiyaki, teppanyaki, tempura, and steaks. For lunch it also offers an obento lunchbox, as well as inexpensive sukiyaki. With its English menu, ordering is no problem.

NON-JAPANESE FOOD

ROSE ROOM, in the ANA Hotel Tokyo, 1-12-33 Akasaka. Tel. 3505-1111.
Cuisine: FRENCH. **Reservations:** Recommended. **Station:** Roppongi, Akasaka, Kamiyacho, or Toranomon (within a 15-minute walk).
$ Prices: Main courses ¥5,000–¥10,500 ($45.45–$95.45); set dinners ¥16,000–¥20,000 ($145.45–$181.80); set lunches ¥5,500–¥11,000 ($50–$100). AE, DC, JCB, MC, V.

Open: Lunch daily 11:30am–2:30pm; dinner daily 5–10pm.

Small and intimate with a huge vase of roses as its focal point, the Rose Room is about as romantic as you can get. Simple yet elegant, it serves fanciful creations that change twice a year but may include such selections as beluga caviar, turtle soup lightly seasoned with curry, lobster, rack of lamb, grilled salmon, chicken and steak. After dinner, you may wish to retire to the Astral lounge up on the 37th floor, where you have a spectacular view of the city.

LA TOUR D'ARGENT, in the New Otani Hotel, 4-1 Kioi-cho. Tel. 3239-3111.

Cuisine: FRENCH. **Reservations:** Required. **Station:** Akasaka-mitsuke (then a three-minute walk) or Yotsuya (then a five-minute walk).

$ Prices: Appetizers and soups ¥4,000–¥20,000 ($36.35–$181.80); main dishes ¥7,500–¥15,500 ($68.20–$140.90). AE, DC, JCB, MC, V.

Open: Dinner only, daily 5:30–9:30pm (last order).

Related to La Tour d'Argent in Paris, this French restaurant is one of Tokyo's most expensive. You enter through an impressive hallway with a plush interior and displays of tableware used in the Paris restaurant through the centuries. The dining room looks like a Parisian drawing room, with an elegance a bit too overstated for my taste. The service, however, is superb and the food is excellent. The specialty here is duckling; it meets its untimely end in Brittany at the tender age of three weeks and is then flown to Japan. Other dishes on the menu, which changes with the seasons, may include sea bass, medallions of veal in a light curry sauce, young pigeon, beef tenderloin, or fricassee of lobster and morels. For appetizers, try either the duck or goose foie gras.

EXPENSIVE

JAPANESE FOOD

HAYASHI (20), on the fourth floor of the Sanno Kaikan Bldg., 2-14-1 Akasaka. Tel. 3582-4078.

Cuisine: GRILLED FOODS/RICE CASSEROLES. **Reservations:** Required at dinner. **Station:** Akasaka (then a one-minute walk).

$ Prices: Set dinners ¥6,000 and ¥10,000 ($54.55 and $90.90); lunch ¥1,000 ($9.10). AE, DC, JCB, MC, V.

Open: Lunch Mon–Fri 11:30am–2pm; dinner Mon–Sat 5:30–11pm.

This is one of the most delightful of the country-style restaurants in Tokyo and one I would recommend to all my readers. Serving home-style country cooking, this cozy, rustic-looking restaurant specializes in grilled food, which you cook yourself over your own square hibachi. Altogether there are 10 grills in this small place, some of them surrounded by tatami mats and others by wooden stools or chairs. As the evening wears on, the one-room main dining area can get quite smoky, but the owner of the restaurant is of the philosophy that fires burning in grills bring people more in touch with their basic feelings, helping them to relax and open their hearts.

For dinner, only two set meals are offered, which change with the seasons but may include such items as sashimi and vegetables, chicken, scallops, and gingko nuts. Remember, even the cheaper set meal for ¥6,000 ($54.55) will end up being closer to ¥8,800 ($80) by the time you add drinks, tax, and service charge. The more expensive meal includes such items as oysters, abalone, or fresh fish. For lunch, only one meal is served, oyakodomburi. Literally "parent and child," it's a simple rice dish with egg and chicken on top and offers an inexpensive way to experience this great restaurant. It's located just off the Akasaka Dori and Misuji Dori intersection.

NON-JAPANESE FOOD

TRADER VIC'S, in the New Otani Hotel, 4-1 Kioi-cho. Tel. 3265-4708.

Cuisine: SEAFOOD/STEAKS/INTERNATIONAL. **Station:** Akasaka-mitsuke (then a three-minute walk) or Yotsuya (then a five-minute walk).

$ Prices: Appetizers and soups ¥1,500–¥2,500 ($13.65–$22.70); main dishes ¥4,500–¥9,000 ($40.90–$81.80); set lunches ¥3,500–¥4,500 ($31.20–$40.90); Sun brunch ¥6,000 ($54.55). AE, DC, JCB, MC, V.

Open: Lunch daily 11:30am–2:30pm; dinner daily 5–10pm.

Part of an American chain operating out of California, this restaurant probably needs no introduction. The decor, as always, is Polynesian, and its extensive dinner menu offers salads, seafood, Chinese dishes, curries, steaks, and chicken. The lunch menu includes lighter fare such as sandwiches. For an all-out Sunday splurge, come for its champagne brunch.

MODERATE

KUSHINOBO (21), on the third floor of the Akasaka Plaza Bldg., 2-14-3 Nagata-cho. Tel. 3581-5056.

Cuisine: KUSHIKATSU. **Station:** Akasaka-mitsuke (then a one-minute walk).

$ Prices: Skewers à la carte ¥150–¥500 ($1.35–$4.55) per skewer; set lunches ¥1,000–¥2,200 ($9.10–$20). AE, DC, JCB, MC, V.

Open: Lunch daily 11:30am–2pm; dinner daily 5–10pm.

This kushikatsu restaurant, located in the building that connects to the Tokyu Hotel and on the same floor as the hotel lobby, is small, with just one U-shaped counter around the open kitchen. Serving delicious skewers of shrimp, vegetables, and meat deep-fried in oil, it's so popular that customers will wait in line to eat here. For lunch you can order one of the set courses that includes a fixed amount of skewers, soup, pickled vegetables, and rice, but for dinner the best thing to do is to order the Omakase course, or cook's choice, with the cook supplying skewer after skewer until you simply say stop. I've been able to put away skewers of mint leaf, beef, mushroom, fish, asparagus, chicken, crab, shrimp, green pepper, and pumpkin before crawling away from the table. You'll have various sauces in which to dip your skewered goodies, including soy sauce, mustard, and vinegar. Most Omakase dinners average ¥5,000 ($45.45).

There's another Kushinobo restaurant in the heart of Akasaka at 3-10-17 Akasaka (tel. 3586-7390) and one in Shubuya at 33-12 Shibuya, on the second floor of the J&R Building.

SUEHIRO (7), 3-16-7 Akasaka. Tel. 3585-9855.

Cuisine: STEAKS/SUKIYAKI/SHABU-SHABU. **Station:** Akasaka or Akasaka-mitsuke (then a five-minute walk).

$ Prices: Steaks from ¥1,300 ($11.80); sukiyaki or shabu-shabu ¥5,000 ($45.45); set lunches ¥700–¥3,000 ($6.35–$27.25). AE, DC, JCB, MC, V.
Open: Daily 11am–9pm. **Closed:** Hols.

Suehiro is a chain of steak houses, this one less expensive than other branches. Head for the first floor for inexpensive lunches and meals; the second floor is more refined and serves tenderloin and sirloin steaks, sukiyaki, and shabu-shabu. One of the most popular dishes is ishiyaki steak, which is grilled in front of you on a stone plate, beginning at ¥1,700 ($15.45) for 200 grams. It's located on Hitosugi Dori Street.

SUSHI SEI ⑩, 3-11-14 Akasaka. Tel. 3586-6446.
Cuisine: SUSHI. **Station:** Akasaka or Akasaka-mitsuke (then a five-minute walk).
$ Prices: Set lunches ¥1,300–¥2,000 ($10.90–$18.20); dinners average ¥5,000 ($45.45) and up. AE, DC, JCB, MC, V.
Open: Lunch Mon–Sat 11:45am–2pm; dinner Mon–Sat 4:45–10:30pm. **Closed:** Hols.

Described earlier in the Ginza section, Sushi Sei is a chain of medium-priced sushi bars. An evening of eating and drinking here won't cost more than ¥6,000 ($54.55), but if that's too formidable, take the easy way out and come for lunch, when you can order a seto, or set meal, which comes with six pieces of sushi and six pieces of makizushi.

NON-JAPANESE FOOD

KANA UNI, 1-1-16 Moto-Akasaka. Tel. 3404-4776.
Cuisine: FRENCH. **Reservations:** Required. **Station:** Akasaka-mitsuke (then less than a five-minute walk).
$ Prices: Soups and appetizers ¥1,000–¥3,800 ($9.10–$34.55); main courses ¥2,000–¥5,300 ($18.20–$48.20). AE, DC, JCB, MC, V.
Open: Dinner only, Mon–Sat 6pm–2am, Sun 6–11:30pm. **Closed:** Hols.

This cozy, intimate French restaurant/bar is owned and managed by a brother and sister who speak excellent English and love to have foreign guests. In fact, because the place is a little hard to find, someone will come and show you the way if you call from Akasaka-mitsuke Station. Open since 1966, it features live jazz nightly and is one of the few restaurants in Akasaka still serving food after midnight. The English menu lists sliced raw tenderloin, steaks, beef stew, grilled fish, sautéed scallops, and poached filet of sole with sea-urchin sauce. After dinner, relax with cocktails and enjoy the ambience.

LE CHALET, in the basement of the Shimizu Bldg., 3-14-9 Akasaka. Tel. 3584-0080.
Cuisine: FRENCH. **Reservations:** Recommended. **Station:** Akasaka (then a one-minute walk).
$ Prices: Appetizers and soups ¥1,000–¥2,500 ($9.10–$22.70); main dishes ¥2,200–¥3,100 ($20–$28.20); set dinners ¥4,900–¥8,500 ($44.55–$77.25); set lunches ¥1,600–¥3,600 ($14.55–$32.70). AE, DC, JCB, MC, V.
Open: Lunch daily 11:30am–2pm; dinner daily 5:30–9pm.

Decorated in an opulent pink and red, this is a pleasant and modestly priced French restaurant in the heart of Akasaka. The ¥4,900 ($44.55) dinner includes an hors d'oeuvre, soup, fish, a meat dish, dessert, and coffee. The set lunches are a particularly good bargain. Since seating is only for 30 customers, it's safest to make a reservation.

POTOMAC, in the Akasaka Prince Hotel, 1-2 Kioicho Chiyoda-ku. Tel. 3234-1111.
Cuisine: STEAK/AMERICAN. **Reservations:** Not required. **Station:** Akasaka-mitsuke (then a one-minute walk).
$ Prices: Steak meal $10 (based on daily exchange rate); main dishes ¥1,800–¥3,200 ($16.35–$29.10); salad bar ¥800 ($7.25); set dinner ¥3,800 ($34.55). AE, DC, JCB, MC, V.
Open: Dinner only, daily 6pm–1am.

A traditional American restaurant, Potomac has the best deal in town: steak, vegetables, and bread or rice for U.S. $10, based on the daily exchange rate. The serve-yourself salad bar for just ¥800 ($7.25) and dinners such as beef in red wine or scallops in herb sauce with salad, bread, dessert, and coffee for ¥3,800 ($34.55) are bargains. Service is—as with all Prince hotels—excellent.

BUDGET

JAPANESE FOOD

BOTEJYU, 3-10-1 Akasaka. Tel. 3584-6651.
Cuisine: OKONOMIYAKI. **Station:** Akasaka or Akasaka-mitsuke (then a five-minute walk).
$ Prices: Dishes ¥1,000–¥4,500 ($9.10–$40.90); teishoku ¥800–¥1,250 ($7.25–$11.35). AE, DC, JCB, MC, V.
Open: Daily noon–10:15pm.

This simple second-floor restaurant on Tamachi Dori specializes in okonomiyaki, a Japanese-style pizza/pancake topped with cabbage and a meat such as pork, squid, or shrimp. It also serves fried noodles (yakisoba), tofu steak, and its own creation called tororoyaki, which is a yam okonomiyaki. Its teishoku, available until 3pm, are a great deal and include a main dish such as okonomiyaki, rice, soup, and salad. Dinner is more expensive, but you can eat like a king here for less than ¥3,000 ($27.25).

HAYASHI (20), on the fourth floor of the Sanno Kaikan Bldg., 2-14-1 Akasaka. Tel. 3582-4078.
Cuisine: RICE CASSEROLES. **Station:** Akasaka (then a one-minute walk).
$ Prices: Lunch ¥1,000 ($9.10). No credit cards.
Open: Lunch Mon–Fri 11:30am–2pm.

This country-style restaurant was described at length as an expensive restaurant, but I mention it again here simply because I don't want those of you on a budget to miss it. It's expensive at night, but anyone can afford it at lunch, when only one dish is served. It's called oyakodomburi (rice with chunks of chicken and omelet on top) and includes pickled vegetables, clear soup, and tea. Not to be missed.

SHARAKU (22), 3-10-4 Akasaka. Tel. 3582-0333.
Cuisine: SUSHI. **Station:** Akasaka or Akasaka-mitsuke (then a five-minute walk).
$ Prices: Set meals ¥1,600–¥2,700 ($14.55–$24.55). AE, DC, JCB, MC, V.

Open: Mon–Fri 6pm–3am, Sat 6pm–1:30am. **Closed:** Hols. Located on Tamachi Dori (look for the sign for Lollipop, a dance club in the same building), this sushi bar offers take-out as well as inexpensive sushi courses starting at ¥1,600 ($14.55). If you go all out for dinner and order à la carte and drinks, the bill will probably come to about ¥4,500 ($40.90) per head.

NON-JAPANESE FOOD

MOTI, 3-8-8 Akasaka. Tel. 3582-3620.
Cuisine: INDIAN. **Station:** Akasaka (both restaurants within a few minutes' walk).
$ **Prices:** Curries ¥1,100–¥1,500 ($9.10–$13.65); tandoori from ¥1,700 ($15.45); lunch courses ¥990 ($9). AE, JCB, MC, V.
Open: Daily 11:30am–10pm.

This second-floor Indian restaurant is so popular that there are two in Akasaka alone. The other is at 2-14-31 Akasaka (tel. 584-6640), and there are two more in Roppongi. All serve vegetable, mutton, and chicken curries, as well as tandoori. An especially good deal are the set lunches, served until 2:30pm, which give you a curry, along with Indian bread (nan), and tea or coffee.

5. SHINJUKU

VERY EXPENSIVE

JAPANESE FOOD

SERYNA, on the 52nd floor of the Shinjuku Sumitomo Bldg., 2-6-1 Nishi-Shinjuku. Tel. 3344-6761.
Cuisine: SHABU-SHABU/SUKIYAKI/TEPPANYAKI. **Reservations:** Recommended at dinner. **Station:** Shinjuku, west exit (then about a seven-minute walk).
$ **Prices:** Main dishes ¥6,500–¥12,000 ($59–$109.10); set dinners ¥10,000–¥20,000 ($90.90–$181.80); set lunches ¥2,200–¥5,000 ($20–$45.45). AE, DC, JCB, MC, V.
Open: Daily 11:30am–9:30pm.

A branch of Seryna in Roppongi, this pleasant restaurant is perched high above Shinjuku in one of the city's best-known skyscrapers, offering great views of the surrounding area. An English menu lists Kobe steaks, shabu-shabu, sukiyaki, and teppanyaki. Lunches are especially reasonable, making it a good place to stop off if you're exploring the west side of Shinjuku.

EXPENSIVE

JAPANESE FOOD

KAKIDEN (23), 3-37-11 Shinjuku. Tel. 3352-5121.
Cuisine: KAISEKI. **Reservations:** Recommended at lunch, required at dinner. **Station:** Shinjuku, east exit (then a one-minute walk).

$ Prices: Set dinners ¥7,000–¥35,000 ($63.65–$318); set lunches ¥4,400 ($40). AE, DC, JCB, MC, V.
Open: Daily 11am–9pm (last order).

Although located on the eighth floor of a rather uninspiring building on the east side of Shinjuku Station next to My City shopping complex, Kakiden has a relaxing teahouse atmosphere, with low chairs, shoji screens, bamboo trees, and soothing traditional Japanese music playing softly in the background. It's related to a restaurant in Kyoto founded more than 260 years ago as a catering service for the elite. The menu is in Japanese only, so simply pick one of the kaiseki set meals to fit your budget. Menus change with the seasons according to what's fresh and available. The set lunch is available until a late 5pm.

MODERATE

JAPANESE FOOD

HAYASHI (20), 2-22-5 Kabuki-cho. Tel. 3209-5672.
Cuisine: GRILLED FOODS. **Reservations:** Recommended. **Station:** Shinjuku, east exit (then about a 10-minute walk, on the northern edge of Kabuki-cho).
$ Prices: Set dinners ¥5,000–¥7,000 ($45.45–$63.65). AE, JCB.
Open: Dinner only, Mon–Sat 5–11pm. **Closed:** Hols.

With a rustic interior imported intact from the mountain region of Takayama, this country-style restaurant specializes in Japanese set meals cooked over your own hibachi grill. Women in kimonos and traditional clothing oversee the cooking operations like mother hens, taking over if customers seem the least bit hesitant. A small, cozy place with only five hibachi grills, it offers four set meals. I chose the menu for ¥5,000 ($45.45), which included sashimi, yakitori, tofu steak, scallops cooked in their shells, shrimp, and vegetables, all grilled one after the other. Watch your alcohol intake here—drinks can really add to your bill.

SUEHIRO (7), on the 29th floor of the N.S. Bldg., 2-4-1 Nishi-Shinjuku. Tel. 3343-3982.
Cuisine: STEAKS/SHABU-SHABU/SUKIYAKI. **Station:** Shinjuku Station, west exit (then about an eight-minute walk).
$ Prices: Set dinners ¥3,500–¥7,000 ($31.20–$63.65); set lunches ¥1,100–¥7,000 ($10–$63.65). AE, DC, JCB, V.
Open: Daily 11:30am–10pm.

Although its name is Suehiro, it's no relation to the famous Suehiro in Ginza. It does, however, offer steaks, shabu-shabu, and sukiyaki at very reasonable prices, with lots of options on the size of your beef portion and number of side dishes. Since it's also on the 29th floor, it also offers dining with a view. By the way, there are several other restaurants on the same floor.

TSUNAHACHI (24), 3-31-8 Shinjuku. Tel. 3352-1012.
Cuisine: TEMPURA. **Reservations:** Recommended. **Station:** Shinjuku, east exit (then a five-minute walk).
$ Prices: Tempura à la carte ¥350–¥1,000 ($3.20–$9.10) per piece; teishoku ¥1,200–¥2,000 ($10.90–$18.20). AE, JCB, V.
Open: Daily 11am–10pm.

First opened in 1923, this chain of tempura restaurants now has 40 branch restaurants in Japan, including three in Shinjuku Station alone. This main shop on the east side of Shinjuku Station is one of the largest, and its least expensive set meal includes deep-fried shrimp, three kinds of fish, a vegetable, and a shrimp ball.

NON-JAPANESE FOOD

LA PRIMAVERA, 2-5-15 Shinjuku. Tel. 3354-7873.

Cuisine: ITALIAN. **Reservations:** Recommended, especially at dinner. **Station:** Shinjuku Gyoen-mae or Shinjuku-Sanchome (then about a four-minute walk).

$ Prices: Pastas and pizzas from ¥1,500 ($13.65); main dishes ¥1,500–¥2,500 ($13.65–$22.70); set dinners ¥5,000 ($45.45); set lunches ¥1,200–¥3,000 ($10.90–$27.25). AE, DC, JCB, MC, V.

Open: Lunch Mon–Sat 11:30am–2pm; dinner Mon–Sat 5–10:30pm.

Opened in 1985, this Italian restaurant serves great food and has reasonable prices, and its bread is among the best in town. An intimate locale with only half a dozen tables, it offers pizzas, pastas, and dishes of steak, scallops, and fish. Customers are requested to order more than one dish per person for dinner. Set lunches include steak, stew, homemade sausage, or pasta.

RAJINI, on the second floor of the Oriental Wave Building, 5-17-13 Shinjuku. Tel. 3203-2878.

Cuisine: ASIAN. **Reservations:** Not required.

$ Prices: Main dishes ¥550–¥1,300 ($5–$11.80). AE, DC, JCB, V.

Open: Dinner only, daily 5pm–midnight.

This chic-interiored restaurant serves "Oriental crossover" food. The colonial feel and green silk-moiré upholstered seating of the Oriental Wave Café downstairs is repeated. There's a live piano bar Monday through Friday to add to the atmosphere, and cocktails run ¥600 to ¥1,500 ($5.45 to $13.65). Dishes range from chicken salad for ¥700 ($6.35) and Basque chicken for ¥800 ($7.25) to Thai seafood nabe (stew) for ¥1,300 ($11.80). There is no English menu; however, gaijin waiters will help you in native English. An average meal for two, with cocktails, comes to ¥8,000 ($72.70).

TOKYO DAI HANTEN, on the third floor of the Oriental Wave Bldg., 5-17-13 Shinjuku. Tel. 3202-0121.

Cuisine: CHINESE. **Reservations:** Recommended. **Station:** Shinjuku Sanchome (then a two-minute walk).

$ Prices: Appetizers ¥1,600–¥5,000 ($14.55–$45.45); main dishes ¥2,000–¥5,500 ($18.20–$50); dim sum ¥600 ($5.45). AE, DC, JCB, MC, V.

Open: Daily 11am–10pm.

Tokyo Dai Honten is a branch of an old established Chinese restaurant in Shinjuku, with six floors for dining (the fourth through eighth floors are for banquets). With an English menu and gaijin waiters, you'll have no trouble dining here on braised whole fish or rolled fried prawns. Sample the dim sum wagon for delicacies like sweet beans and deep-fried pork dumplings.

TOKYO KAISEN MARKET, 2-36-1 Kabukicho, Shinjuku. Tel. 5273-8301.

Cuisine: FISH/ASIAN. **Reservations:** Recommended. **Station:** Shinjuku (then a five-minute walk).

$ Prices: Appetizers and soup ¥700–¥2,800 ($6.35–$25.45);

main dishes ¥1,000–¥6,000 ($9.10–$59); set dinners ¥5,500–¥7,000 ($50–$63.65). AE, JCB, DC, MC, V.
Open: Dinner only, Mon–Fri 5–11pm (last order), Sat–Sun and hols noon–11pm.

The ground floor of this multilevel, open-beam warehouse-style restaurant is a real fish market with tanks and white tiles. Catch your dinner and they'll cook it any way you like for ¥800 ($7.25). It's also a drinking establishment (if you come after 7pm without a reservation, you'll find yourself waiting in the high-tech bar), where beer starts at ¥400 ($3.65) and cocktails at ¥800 ($7.25). A selection of sashimi (moriawase) is ¥1,980 ($18), Chinese-style lobster is ¥3,800 ($34.55), and five kinds of tofu for two go for ¥1,200 ($10.90). Also, deep-fried salmon in sweet-and-sour sauce is not to be missed. Although there's an English menu, daily fresh specials are on the blackboard, so ask for a translation.

BUDGET

JAPANESE FOOD

DAIKOKUYA (25), on the fourth floor of the Naka-Dai Bldg., 1-27-5 Kabuki-cho. Tel. 3202-7272.
Cuisine: SHABU-SHABU/SUKIYAKI. **Station:** Shinjuku, east side (then about a 10-minute walk).
$ **Prices:** All-you-can-eat meals ¥1,800–¥2,500 ($16.35–$22.70). No credit cards.
Open: Dinner only, Mon–Fri 5–11pm, Sat–Sun and hols 3–11pm.

(S) Truly a place for gluttons, especially those who can put away mountains of food in a short amount of time. Diners are clocked in for two-hour time limits, during which it's all they can eat of either shabu-shabu or sukiyaki, which are barbecued on tabletop grills. Shabu-shabu, for example, costs ¥2,500 ($22.70) per person; add ¥900 ($8.20) per person and it's all the beer, whiskey or shochu you can drink as well. Needless to say, this place is very popular with students and young office workers and can be quite lively and rowdy. It's strangely decorated with heavy wooden pillars and beams and pseudo cave walls—perhaps in deference to more barbaric times when people chowed down unrestrainedly.

IROHANIHOHETO (26), 3-15-15 Shinjuku. Tel. 3359-1682.
Cuisine: YAKITORI/VARIED. **Station:** Shinjuku-Sanchome (then about a 5-minute walk) or Shinjuku (then less than a 10-minute walk).
$ **Prices:** Dishes ¥350–¥450 ($3.20–$4.10); set dinners ¥2,800–¥3,800 ($25.45–$34.55). No credit cards.
Open: Sun–Thurs 5–11:30pm, Fri–Sat 5pm–4am.

(S) This is actually one of a chain of drinking establishments, but its menu is so varied, extensive, and cheap that most people eat here as well. Extremely popular with university students, it bills itself as an "Antique Pub," the meaning of which becomes even less clear once you're inside. The main hall looks imitation barn to me, with rafters, hurricane lamps, and glass lanterns everywhere, but most people seem oblivious to the decor as they dine on yakitori, fried noodles, potato salad, sashimi, grilled meatballs, nikujaga (potato-and-meat stew), fried tofu, oden (a tofu, fishcake, and vegetable stew), and dozens of other dishes. The menu of Japanese and Western food is only in Japanese, but there are pictures. This restaurant with the impossible name is located on Shinjuku's east side, on Yasukuni Dori Avenue on the sixth floor of a building next to Isetan Kaikan.

NEGISHI ㉗**, 2-45-2 Kabuki-cho. Tel. 3232-8020.**
Cuisine: OXTAIL SOUP/BOILED WHEAT WITH GRATED YAM. **Station:** Shinjuku or Seibu Shinjuku (then a few minutes' walk north).
$ Prices: Dishes ¥550–¥800 ($5–$7.25); lunch teishoku ¥900–¥1,500 ($8.20–$13.65). No credit cards.
Open: Mon–Sat 11am–10:30pm, Sun and hols 11am–9:30pm.

It would be easy to overlook this hole-in-the-wall with just a counter and a few tables, but that would be a shame because then you'd miss its healthy, low-calorie foods. It specializes in oxtail soup, mugi-toro (boiled wheat with grated yam), and grilled ox tongue (low in calories and fat, but rich in protein). It's located on Shinjuku's east side, near America Boulevard, on a tiny side street that runs beside Green Plaza.

NON-JAPANESE FOOD

BAN-THAI, 1-23-14 Kabuki-cho. Tel. 3207-0068.
Cuisine: THAI. **Reservations:** Recommended at dinner. **Station:** Shinjuku (then about a seven-minute walk).
$ Prices: Appetizers and salads ¥1,000–¥1,500 ($9.10–$13.65); main dishes ¥1,100–¥1,900 ($10–$17.25); set meals ¥3,500–¥6,000 ($31.20–$54.55). AE, MC, JCB, V.
Open: Mon–Fri noon–1am, Sat–Sun 11am–1am.

Thai food has surged in popularity in recent years, and riding the crest of the wave is Ban-Thai, which offers more than 40 authentic Thai dishes and has a Thai staff. Live music is featured from 6pm. There are many pork, shrimp, chicken, and beef dishes from which to choose, but my own personal favorites are the cold and spicy meat salad, the chicken soup with coconut and lemon grass, and the pat Thai (Thai-style fried rice).

This third-floor restaurant lies hidden in the seediest part of Kabuki-cho, on a neon-lit pedestrian lane that connects the Koma Building with Yasukuni Dori. Look for the numbers of the address on the building. Take the Exit 3 from the subnade and you'll come out at the small pedestrian street with a red archway; Ban-Thai is halfway down on your left.

Note that if you make a reservation there's a ¥1,000 ($9.10) table charge, and since portions are not large, if you order several and add beers to that, your tab can become quite high.

SHAKEY'S, 3-30-11 Shinjuku. Tel. 3341-0322.
Cuisine: PIZZA. **Station:** Shinjuku-Sanchome (then a one-minute walk).
$ Prices: All-you-can-eat pizza lunch ¥650 ($5.90). No credit cards.
Open: Lunch only, daily 11am–2pm.

The best place in town to gorge yourself on pizza for lunch, Shakey's offers a great all-you-can-eat pizza lunch. It's located on Shinjuku Dori Avenue, across the street from the Isetan department store.

SPAGHETTI FACTORY, on the 29th floor of the N.S. Bldg., 2-4-1 Nishi-Shinjuku. Tel. 3348-1393.
Cuisine: SPAGHETTI. **Station:** Shinjuku, west exit (then an eight-minute walk).

$ **Prices:** Dishes ¥1,000–¥1,500 ($9.10–$13.65). No credit cards.
Open: Daily 11:30am–9pm (last order).

Spaghetti with a view is what you get at this informal eatery on the 29th floor of this Shinjuku skyscraper. It offers more than 60 dishes of pasta with a wide variety of sauces and toppings, from traditional meat sauce to short-necked clam and spicy Chinese cabbage or eggplant with bacon and soy sauce. Portions are large, and there's tabasco and parmesan on the tables to spice things up. Be forewarned, however, that during my last visit the young Japanese staff working here seemed overly fond of Japanese pop music at high decibels.

6. ROPPONGI

Because Roppongi is such a popular nighttime hangout for young Tokyoites, it boasts a large number of both Japanese and Western restaurants. Be sure, too, to read the recommendations in Chapter 9, "Tokyo Nights," since many bars also serve food.

To find the location of the following establishments, stop by the police box (*koban*) right on Roppongi Crossing (Roppongi's main intersection, Roppongi Dori Avenue and Gaien-Higashi Dori Avenue), where you'll find a map of the area.

VERY EXPENSIVE

JAPANESE FOOD

INAKAYA (18), 7-8-4 Roppongi. Tel. 3405-9866.
Cuisine: GRILLED FOODS. **Reservations:** Accepted until 7pm. **Station:** Roppongi (then less than a five-minute walk to each restaurant).
$ **Prices:** Meals average ¥12,000 ($109.10). AE, DC, JCB, MC, V.
Open: Daily 5pm–5am.

Whenever I play hostess to foreign visitors in Tokyo, Inakaya is where I take them. Although definitely tourist-oriented, it's fun, lively, and the food is great. Refer to the Akasaka section, above, for more information on these unique restaurants specializing in grilled foods. There's another at 5-3-4 Roppongi (tel. 3408-5040); reservations are accepted here until 7pm.

SERYNA, 3-12-2 Roppongi. Tel. 3403-6211.
Cuisine: SHABU-SHABU/SUKIYAKI/TEPPANYAKI. **Reservations:** Required. **Station:** Roppongi (then a two-minute walk).
$ **Prices:** Set dinners ¥12,000–¥20,000 ($109.10–$181.80). AE, DC, JCB, MC, V.
Open: Dinner only, Mon–Sat 5–10:30pm (last order), Sun 5–9:30pm (last order).

Japanese entertaining first-time visitors to Japan often bring them here, in the belief that steak is more palatable to the foreign tongue than raw fish (there's even a Seryna in New York). There are English menus and the food features Kobe beef. This large, modern establishment, recently renovated, actually contains four different restaurants, all under the same roof and management. Seryna Honkan is the main restaurant and serves shabu-shabu and sukiyaki. Saraebo, on the third floor, specializes in yaki-shabu and Chinese cuisine. Mon Cher Ton Ton, in the basement, serves Kobe beef, shrimp, fish, shellfish and vegetables grilled teppanyaki style right before your eyes. Kani Seryna specializes in crab and seafood dishes, including crab shabu-shabu, Maine lobster, and steamed fish. Seryna also offers ishiyaki, in which beef is cooked at your table on a heated stone.

TAKAMURA (28), 3-4-27 Roppongi. Tel. 3585-6600.

Cuisine: KAISEKI. **Reservations:** Required (for lunch, the day before at the latest). **Station:** Roppongi (then about a five-minute walk).

$ Prices: Set dinners ¥16,500–¥22,000 ($150–$200); set lunches ¥13,000 or ¥15,000 ($118.20 or $136.35). AE, DC, JCB, MC, V.

Open: Lunch Mon–Sat noon–3pm; dinner Mon–Sat 5–10:30pm (last order 8pm).

This traditional kaiseki restaurant is a must for everyone who can afford it. Located away from frenetic Roppongi, this wonderful 50-year-old house is like a peaceful oasis that time forgot. Each of the eight rooms is different, with windows overlooking miniature gardens and bamboo, and with charcoal hearths built into the floor. But it's the food that's the crowning jewel; seasonal kaiseki food is arranged so artfully that you almost hate to destroy it. Specialties may include quail, sparrow, or duck, grilled on the hearth of your own private tatami room by gracious, kimono-clad hostesses. Only set meals are offered, which, by the time you add drinks, tax, and service charge, may well run up to ¥30,000 ($272) for dinner. Lunch is available only to parties of four or more, but you must make reservations at least a day in advance. There are two entrances to Takamura, marked by wooden gates complete with little roofs. The sign is in Japanese only, but look for the credit cards. Taxi drivers should have no problem finding it. Seating, by the way, is on the floor.

EXPENSIVE

JAPANESE FOOD

FUKUZUSHI (29), 5-7-8 Roppongi. Tel. 3402-4116.

Cuisine: SUSHI. **Reservations:** Recommended, especially for dinner. **Station:** Roppongi (then about a four-minute walk).

$ Prices: Set dinners ¥6,500–¥11,000 ($59–$100); set lunches ¥2,500 ($22.70). AE, DC, JCB, MC, V.

Open: Lunch Mon–Sat 11:30am–2pm; dinner daily 5:30–11pm. **Closed:** Hols.

With 7,000 sushi bars in Tokyo, I'd be hard-pressed to say which one is tops. Some people, however, swear that this is a contender for the best sushi in town. At any rate, it certainly is one of the classiest, with an entrance through a small courtyard and an interior of red and black. Its English menu opens like a fan and offers a variety of choices of sashimi and nigiri-zushi. Although dinner can be very expensive, averaging ¥10,000 ($90.90) per person, lunch is quite reasonable. This restaurant is tucked underneath Spago's restaurant, behind the Roi Building and Hard Rock Café.

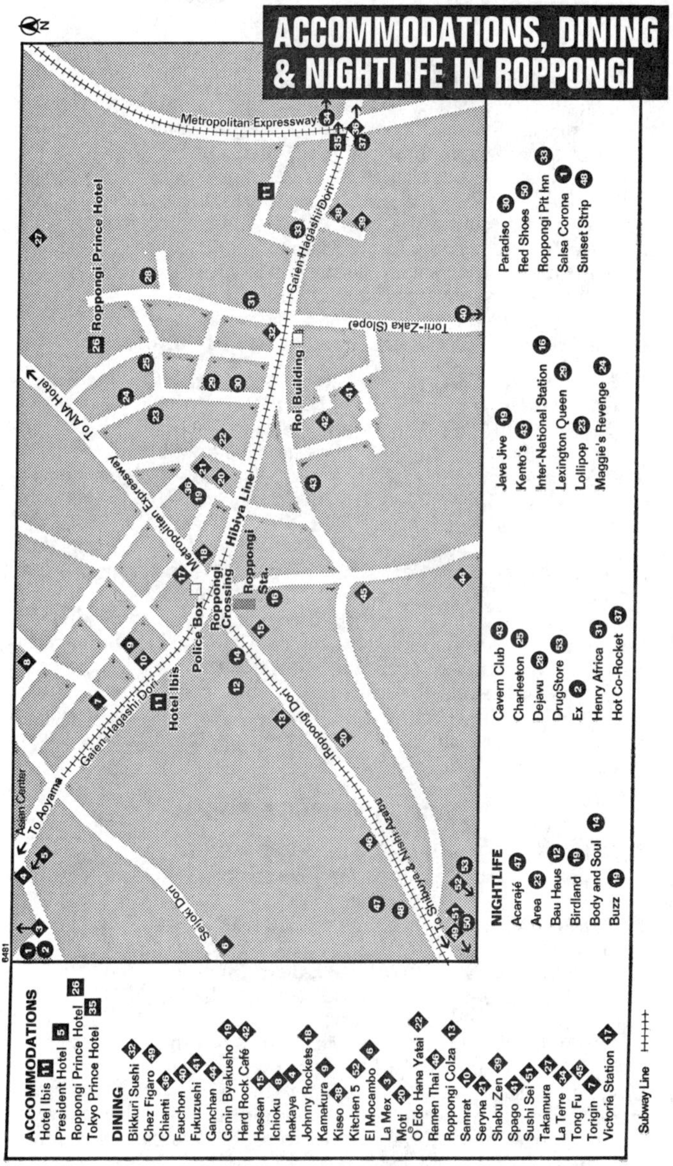

KISSO, in the basement of the Axis Bldg., 5-17-1 Roppongi. Tel. 3582-4191.

Cuisine: KAISEKI. **Reservations:** Required at dinner. **Station:** Roppongi (then about a four-minute walk).

$ Prices: Set dinners ¥10,000–¥15,000 ($90.90–$136.35); set lunches ¥2,300–¥3,800 ($20.90–$34.55). AE, DC, JCB, MC, V.

Open: Lunch Mon–Sat 11:30am–2pm; dinner daily 5:30–9pm (last order).

How appropriate that this very modern kaiseki restaurant is located in the Axis Building, which contains shops specializing in interior design. Even Kisso has a shop up on the third floor, selling Japanese gourmet cookware such as ceramics, utensils, and lacquerware of contemporary design. The restaurant, located in the basement, is simple but elegant, with sprigs of flowers, heavy tables, and soft lighting. The food only comes in set courses, served (as you might guess) in beautifully lacquered bowls, trays, and ceramic plates. I love eating here because to me Kisso represents all the best that is modern Japan—understated elegance in a successful marriage between the contemporary and the traditional.

To reach it, walk from Roppongi Crossing on Gaien-Higashi Dori toward Tokyo Tower; the Axis Building will be on your right.

ROPPONGI COLZA, in the basement of the Clover Bldg., 7-15-10 Roppongi. Tel. 3405-5631.

Cuisine: TEPPANYAKI. **Reservations:** Recommended at dinner. **Station:** Roppongi (then a one-minute walk).

$ Prices: Appetizers ¥1,500–¥3,300 ($13.65–$30); main dishes ¥2,200–¥7,500 ($20–$68.20); set dinners ¥8,800–¥15,000 ($80–$136.35); set lunches ¥1,600–¥4,400 ($14.55–$40). AE, DC, JCB, MC, V.

Open: Lunch Mon–Sat 11:30am–2pm, Sun and hols noon–3pm; dinner Mon–Sat 5–10pm, Sun and hols 5–9pm.

Teppanyaki steaks and seafood, flavored with Kikkoman condiments, are the specialty here, and the beef used is Matsuzaka. Set meals include various cuts of beef and seafood such as scallops, scampi, sole, or turbot, along with side dishes and dessert, and there's an English menu. It's located in a basement, on the right side of Roppongi Dori Avenue as you walk from Roppongi Crossing toward Shibuya.

NON-JAPANESE FOOD

SPAGO, 5-7-8 Roppongi. Tel. 3423-4025.

Cuisine: CALIFORNIAN. **Reservations:** Required. **Station:** Roppongi (then a four-minute walk).

$ Prices: Appetizers ¥2,000–¥2,600 ($18.20–$23.65); pizza and pasta ¥2,200–¥2,700 ($20–$24.55); main dishes ¥3,300–¥4,200 ($30–$38.20). AE, DC, JCB, MC, V.

Open: Dinner only, daily 5:30–10:30pm (last order).

This trendy restaurant serves Californian cuisine created by its owner, Wolfgang Puck, an Austrian-born chef who has a similar restaurant in Los Angeles. The atmosphere is bright, airy, and cheerful, very Californian, with huge bouquets of flowers, potted palms, ferns, white walls, and a colorful mural. The innovative menu changes every three months to reflect what's in season, but examples of what has been offered in the past include spicy fettuccine with grilled shrimp and fresh basil; sliced breast of duck with Japanese oba leaves and plum wine sauce; angel-hair noodles with goat cheese, broccoli, and thyme; grilled spicy chicken with garlic and Italian parsley; pizza with duck sausage, kohlrabi, mushroom, tomato, and sage; and roasted baby lamb with a cabernet, mustard, and rosemary sauce. It also offers homemade ice cream and the largest selection of Californian wines in town. It's located behind the Roi Building and Hard Rock Café.

TONG FU, 6-7-11 Roppongi. Tel. 3403-3527.

Cuisine: CHINESE. **Reservations:** Required. **Station:** Roppongi (then about a two-minute walk).

$ Prices: Main courses ¥2,000–¥4,500 ($18.20–$40.90); set dinners ¥7,700–¥14,000 ($70–$127.25); set lunches ¥1,300–¥3,300 ($11.80–$30). AE, DC, JCB, MC, V.

Open: Lunch Mon–Sat 11:30am–2pm (last order); dinner Mon–Sat 5–10:30pm (last order); hols 11:30am–10:30pm.

This trendy Chinese restaurant features bright-colored tablecloths of lime-green, orange, purple, or yellow, ceiling fans, and a fantasy-provoking mural. Its food is Shanghainese with a twist and includes shark's-fin soup, shrimp in chili sauce, Beijing duck, crabmeat omelet, simmered chili tofu and eggplant, and shredded pork. There's a small bar where you can wait for your table or adjourn after dinner for a drink. It's located on the small diagonal street leading downhill beside Almond Coffee Shop, on the right side.

MODERATE

JAPANESE FOOD

GONIN BYAKUSHO (30), on the fourth floor of the Roppongi Square Bldg., 3-10-3 Roppongi. Tel. 3470-1675.

Cuisine: GRILLED FOODS/OBENTO. **Reservations:** Recommended at dinner. **Station:** Roppongi (then a three-minute walk).

$ Prices: A la carte dishes ¥650–¥6,000 ($5.45–$54.55); set dinners ¥6,000–¥7,500 ($54.55–$68.20); set lunches ¥1,000–¥3,800 ($9.10–$34.55). AE, DC, JCB, MC, V.

Open: Lunch Mon–Sat 11:30am–2pm; dinner Mon–Sat 5–10pm (last order). **Closed:** Hols.

Gonin Byakusho means "five farmers," and the atmosphere here is that of a country farmhouse with heavy beams, thick wooden tables, and a huge hearth and oven—all of which comes as a surprise since it's located on the fourth floor of a building dominated by discos. Take off your shoes at the entrance to the restaurant and deposit them in a locker. Most of the food here is charcoal-broiled, with set dinners that include grilled fish, shrimp, or lobster, sashimi, and vegetables. Lunches range from tempura and sashimi to elaborate lunchboxes. A la carte items on the English menu include yakitori, fresh seafood, charcoal-broiled shrimp, assorted sashimi, and nabemono (a pot of boiled chicken and vegetables). Dinner à la carte will probably run about ¥5,000 ($45.45) per person.

HASSAN (31), 6-1-20 Roppongi. Tel. 3403-8333.

Cuisine: SHABU-SHABU/KAISEKI. **Reservations:** Required for kaiseki. **Station:** Roppongi (then a one-minute walk).

$ Prices: Shabu-shabu ¥4,900–¥7,000 ($44.55–$63.65); kaiseki ¥8,000–¥13,000 ($72.70–$118.20); set lunches ¥2,700–¥6,300 ($24.55–$57.25). AE, DC, JCB, MC, V.

Open: Lunch daily 11:30am–2pm; dinner daily 4:30–9:30pm (last order).

Shabu-shabu and kaiseki are the specialties of this modern basement restaurant, with various options listed on its English menu. If you plan on eating kaiseki, however, you must make reservations. Seating is either in chairs or on tatami, waitresses wear kimonos, and recorded koto (Japanese zither) music plays in the background.

Hard to believe that hectic Roppongi Crossing is right outside. To reach the restaurant, walk from Roppongi Crossing on Roppongi Dori toward Shibuya; it will be almost immediately on your left, below a bookstore.

SHABU ZEN (32), **5-17-16 Roppongi. Tel. 3585-5388.**

Cuisine: SHABU-SHABU/SUKIYAKI. **Reservations:** Recommended. **Station:** Roppongi (then a five-minute walk).

$ Prices: Shabu-shabu or sukiyaki ¥4,800–¥8,000 ($43.65–$72.70). AE, DC, JCB, MC, V.

Open: Dinner only, daily 5pm–midnight.

Various options of shabu-shabu (beef or seafood) and sukiyaki are all colorfully depicted in this restaurant's English menu. For ¥4,800 ($43.65) per person, you can eat all the shabu-shabu or sukiyaki you can consume. There's also an all-you-can-eat seafood shabu-shabu for ¥8,000 ($72.70) per person. The shabu-shabu set meal includes an unlimited amount of meat and vegetables, plus two appetizers, sashimi, egg custard, salad, and dessert. Shabu-Zen is located behind the Axis Building, on Gaien-Higashi Dori in the direction of Tokyo Tower.

SUSHI SEI (10), **3-2-9 Nishi Azabu. Tel. 3401-0578.**

Cuisine: SUSHI. **Station:** Roppongi (then a 10-minute walk).

$ Prices: Sushi à la carte ¥150–¥400 ($1.35–$3.65); set lunches ¥1,000–¥2,000 ($9.10–$18.20). AE, DC, JCB, MC, V.

Open: Lunch daily 11:45am–2pm; dinner daily 4:45–10:30pm.

Closed: Second and third Wed of every month.

The Nishi Azabu branch of this popular chain of sushi bars is simple: just a long counter with stools for about 25 people sitting elbow to elbow and a few tables. Behind a glass counter you can see what's fresh and available, but it's easiest to come for lunch and order the seto, or set course, consisting of six pieces of sushi and six pieces of makizushi. Dinner is à la carte only, with most checks averaging about ¥5,000 ($45.45).

This Sushi Sei is located on Terebi Asahi Dori, which is the first large intersection you come to if you're walking on Roppongi Dori in the direction of the Shibuya. Take a left; the restaurant will soon be on your right, up on the second floor.

NON-JAPANESE FOOD

CHEZ FIGARO, 4-4-1 Nishi Azabu. Tel. 3400-8718.

Cuisine: FRENCH. **Reservations:** Recommended. **Station:** Roppongi (then a 15-minute walk).

$ Prices: Main dishes ¥4,500–¥5,000 ($40.90–$45.45); set dinners ¥6,500 ($59); set lunches ¥2,500–¥3,500 ($22.70–$31.20). AE, DC, JCB, MC, V.

Open: Lunch Mon–Sat noon–2pm; dinner Mon–Sat 6–9pm (last order).

This small and cozy place, popular with both foreigners and Japanese, has been serving traditional French cooking since 1969. Its specialties include homemade pâté, escargots, saffron-flavored fish soup, stuffed quail with grapes, pepper steak, and braised sweetbreads with mushrooms. Expect to spend at least ¥7,000 ($63.65) for dinner.

It's located in Nishi Azabu: From Roppongi Crossing, walk toward Shibuya on Roppongi Dori until you come to Gaien-Nishi

Dori (the second major intersection, at the bottom of a hill), where you turn left. After about four minutes you'll see Chez Figaro on your right.

CHIANTI, 3-1-7 Azabudai. Tel. 3583-7546.

Cuisine: ITALIAN. **Reservations:** Recommended at dinner. **Station:** Roppongi (then less than a 10-minute walk).

$ Prices: Appetizers ¥1,000–¥2,000 ($9.10–$18.20); main dishes ¥3,500–¥4,400 ($31.20–$40). AE, DC, JCB, MC, V.

Open: Daily 11:30am–1:45am.

One of Tokyo's oldest Italian restaurants, Chianti was established in 1960 by two Japanese who had been living in Europe and who wanted to introduce Western food to the Japanese. Meals, therefore, are geared slightly toward the Japanese palate and cannot compete with those served in Tokyo's newer and more authentic Italian restaurants that have opened in the past decade. Still, it's a good moderately priced restaurant in Roppongi and its menu includes such perennial favorites as grilled chicken in spicy tomato sauce, veal scaloppine sautéed with vegetables, veal cutlet milanese, Hungarian beef stew, and braised veal shank in tomato sauce. Dining is either on the second floor, where it's the requisite red-and-white checkered tablecloth in an informal atmosphere, or in the basement, where it's more formal and intimate, better for couples. On the ground floor is a coffee shop where you can have inexpensive snacks, salads, and sandwiches. The restaurant is located on the right side of Gaien-Higashi Dori, in the direction of Tokyo Tower and past the big intersection.

EL MOCAMBO, 1-4-38 Nishi-Azabu, Minatoku. Tel. 5410-0468.

Cuisine: LATIN AMERICAN. **Station:** Roppongi (then a 15-minute walk down Seijoki Dori; it's across from Stars and Stripes).

$ Prices: Dishes ¥500–¥2,500 ($4.55–$22.70). AE, JCB, MC, V.

Open: Sun–Thurs 6pm–midnight, Fri–Sat 6pm–2am.

South American music (live on Tuesday with a ¥1,000/$9.10 cover charge), staff, and menu make this a haven for south-of-the-border aficionados. Although it's in the second basement, high windows look on a central courtyard and the Aztec-modern decor includes ceiling fans and interesting art. Try the Peruvian pork specialty cooked with sweet potato (¥1,580/$14.35) or the tacos you make at your table with fresh flour tortillas and filling of your choice, like bistec con cebollitas, cecina de puerco, or chorizo, each for ¥500 ($4.55). Drinks include beers from Peru, Mexico, and Panama for ¥650 ($5.90) and the house specialty Caipirinha (a Brazilian fresh fruit and rum cocktail), for ¥1,000 ($9.10).

LA MEX, 1-15-23 Minami Aoyama. Tel. 3470-1712.

Cuisine: MEXICAN. **Reservations:** Required at dinner. **Station:** Nogizaka (then a 1-minute walk) or Roppongi (then a 10-minute walk).

$ Prices: Appetizers ¥400–¥700 ($3.65–$6.35); main dishes ¥1,200–¥2,700 ($10.90–$24.55). AE, DC, JCB, MC, V.

Open: Lunch Mon–Sat 11:45am–2pm; dinner Mon–Sat 6–10:30pm, Sun 5–10:30pm.

Tex-Mex, L.A.-Mex and some nouvelle Mexican dishes attract Mexican-food lovers to this popular eatery, decorated in hot-pink adobe. Tostadas, tacos, enchiladas, chimichangas, burritos, flautas, mole poblano, and chile relleño are the standard fare, but there are also oysters (in season), burritos with teriyaki seasoning, spiced shrimp, and steak with Mexican sauce. There are three types of Mexican beer (Corona, Carta Blanca, and Bohemia), and, of course, margaritas and piña coladas.

LA TERRE, 1-9-20 Azabu-Dai, Minatoku. Tel. 3583-9682.
Cuisine: FRENCH. **Reservations:** Recommended. **Station:** Kamiyacho (then walk about three minutes toward Tokyo Tower, turn right at the Reiyukai Temple, and go up the stairs; it's on your left).
$ Prices: Appetizers ¥2,000–¥2,600 ($18.10–$23.65); main dishes ¥2,800–¥4,200 ($25.45–$38.20); set dinners ¥6,000–¥10,000 ($54.55–$90.90); set lunches ¥2,000–¥4,000 ($18.20–$36.35). AE, DC, JCB, V.
Open: Lunch Mon–Sat 11:30am–2pm; dinner Mon–Sat 6–8:30pm (last order). **Closed:** Hols.

Wanting to keep it all to themselves, some of my friends asked me not to mention this hidden-away French bistro with outdoor seating. Since a 10% service charge is added to your bill at night, the lunch specials are especially good deals. My lunch for ¥2,500 ($22.70) included potage du jour (pumpkin soup), canard aux poivres verts, baskets of fresh French bread and butter, gâteau, and tea.

VICTORIA STATION, 4-9-2 Roppongi. Tel. 3479-4601.
Cuisine: STEAKS/HAMBURGERS. **Reservations:** Recommended. **Station:** Roppongi (then a one-minute walk).
$ Prices: Main dishes ¥1,500–¥4,000 ($13.65–$36.35); set dinners ¥3,000–¥4,600 ($27.25–$41.80); set lunches ¥800–¥2,000 ($7.25–$18.20). AE, DC, JCB, MC, V.
Open: Mon–Sat 11am–midnight, Sun and hols 11am–11pm.

This member of an American chain needs no introduction. It specializes in roast prime rib and steaks and has one of the best salad bars in town. A hamburger (served only for lunch) with a trip to the salad bar is only ¥1,400 ($12.70). If you opt for one of the dinner courses, your main dish will come with soup, a trip through the salad bar, bread, and coffee. If you're interested mainly in beverages or lighter dishes, there's a cocktail bar upstairs with its own menu offering chicken, teriyaki steaks, and sandwiches, as well as a salad bar. Victoria Station is located close to Roppongi Crossing almost catercorner from the Almond Coffee Shop.

BUDGET

JAPANESE FOOD

BIKKURI SUSHI, 3-14-9 Roppongi. Tel. 3403-1489.
Cuisine: SUSHI. **Station:** Roppongi (then about a three-minute walk).
$ Prices: Dishes ¥150–¥500 ($1.35–$4.55). No credit cards.
Open: Daily 11am–5am.

This is a conveyor-belt sushi establishment. That is, customers sit at a counter, on top of which is a moving conveyor belt with plates of various sushi. Customers simply help themselves to whichever plates strike their fancy, which makes dining a cinch because you don't have to know the names of anything. The white plates are ¥150 ($1.35), while the colored plates go up to ¥500 ($4.55). When you pay your bill, the cashier counts the number of plates you've taken. One of the cheapest places to eat in this popular nightlife district, it's located on the road leading to Tokyo Tower, on the left-hand side of the street across from the Roi Building.

GANCHAN ㉝, 6-8-23 Roppongi. Tel. 3478-0092.

Cuisine: YAKITORI. **Station:** Roppongi (then a five-minute walk).

$ Prices: Yakitori skewers ¥200–¥300 ($1.80–$2.75); yakitori seto ¥3,000 ($27.25). JCB, V.

Open: Mon–Sat 6pm–3am, Sun and hols 6pm–midnight.

This tiny yakitori-ya is owned by a friendly and entertaining man who can't speak English worth a darn but keeps trying with the help of a worn-out Japanese-English dictionary he keeps behind the counter. He also keeps an eclectic cassette collection; I never know whether to expect Japanese pop tunes or Simon and Garfunkel. Seating is just along one counter with room for only a dozen or so people. Although one could easily spend ¥4,000 ($36.35) for food and beer ordered from the English menu, the cheapest way to dine is to order the yakitori seto, which comes with salad and soup and eight skewers of such items as chicken, beef, meatballs, green peppers, and bacon-wrapped asparagus. If you're still hungry, order individual skewers or such items as tofu steak, pork-and-leek ravioli, or stewed meat and vegetables. Located on the small side street beside the Almond Coffee Shop, it's at the bottom of the hill on the right before the big intersection; look for the big white paper lantern outside its door.

ICHIOKU ㉞, 4-4-5 Roppongi. Tel. 3405-9891.

Cuisine: JAPANESE ORIGINALS. **Station:** Roppongi (then a four-minute walk).

$ Prices: Dishes ¥700–¥1,400 ($6.35–$12.70). No credit cards.

Open: Dinner only, Mon–Sat 5–11pm, Sun and hols 5–10pm.

A tiny, cozy place with only eight tables, this is one of my favorite restaurants for casual dining. Its food is difficult to describe or categorize—maybe you could call it Japanese nouvelle cooking. There's tuna-and-ginger sauté, mushroom sauté, shrimp spring rolls, tofu steak, and cheese gyoza (a fried pork dumpling with cheese melted on it). The English menu is glued onto each table underneath clear glass, and customers are expected to fill out their own orders. The place is tucked away on a side street; look for the Japanese flag and purple neon sign on its facade.

KAMAKURA, 4-10-11 Roppongi. Tel. 3405-4377.

Cuisine: YAKITORI. **Station:** Roppongi (then less than a two-minute walk).

$ Prices: Yakitori skewers ¥170–¥300 ($1.55–$2.75); yakitori set courses ¥3,000–¥7,000 ($27.25–$63.65). AE, DC, JCB, MC, V.

Open: Dinner only, Mon–Sat 6–11pm.

Technically a drinking establishment, but much more refined than most yakitori-ya, this basement restaurant is decorated with black walls, paper lanterns, and sprigs of fake but cheerful spring blossoms, with traditional koto music playing softly in the background. Its English menu lists skewers of shrimp, meatballs, squid, eggplant, mushrooms, and more. It's located across from the Ibis Hotel, down a side street.

O EDO HANA YATAI ㉟, 3-13-12 Roppongi. Tel. 3478-4212.

Cuisine: JAPANESE/CHINESE/ETHNIC. **Station:** Roppongi

(then a two-minute walk toward Tokyo Tower and turn left at the second street).

$ Prices: Dishes ¥130–¥900 ($1.20–$8.20). AE, DC, JCB, V.
Open: Dinner only, daily 5–11:30pm.

A lively *matsuri* (festival) atmosphere make dining here at *yatai* ("outdoor street" stalls) fun. Stroll by the individual yatai and choose okonomi-yaki for ¥500 ($4.55) or dim sum for ¥450 ($4.10) or assorted nigiri sushi for ¥900 ($8.20) or chicken with garlic Indian style for ¥700 ($6.35) and the waitress will bring it to your table. There's an English menu and you can see what's being cooked for you at the yatai. It's also a drinking establishment, where beer starts at ¥480 ($4.35), sake at ¥600 ($5.45), and shochu and cocktails at ¥450 ($4.10).

TORIGIN (36), 4-12-6 Roppongi. Tel. 3403-5829.
Cuisine: YAKITORI/RICE CASSEROLES. **Station:** Roppongi (then a two-minute walk).

$ Prices: Yakitori skewers ¥130–¥270 ($1.20–$2.45); kamameshi ¥750–¥900 ($6.80–$8.65). No credit cards.
Open: Lunch Mon–Sat 11am–2:30pm; dinner Mon–Sat 5–10pm.

This no-frills establishment is part of a chain of yakitori-ya and is typical of the smaller Japanese restaurants all over the country. An English menu includes grilled gingko nuts, green pepper, quail eggs, and chicken, as well as various kamameshi, a rice casserole cooked and served in its own little pot and topped with such ingredients as chicken, bamboo shoots, mushroom, crab, salmon, or shrimp.

NON-JAPANESE FOOD

HARD ROCK CAFE, 5-4-20 Roppongi. Tel. 3408-7018.
Cuisine: AMERICAN. **Station:** Roppongi (then a three-minute walk).

$ Prices: Appetizers ¥650–¥1,500 ($5.90–$13.65); main dishes ¥1,500–¥4,200 ($13.65–$38.20). AE, DC, JCB, MC, V.
Open: Mon–Thurs 11:30am–2am, Fri–Sat 11:30am–4am, Sun and hols 11:30am–11:30pm.

Every American teenager knows about the Hard Rock Café (or at least is owner of a Hard Rock Café T-shirt), so if you have one in tow you might bring him or her to Tokyo's version of this world-famous hamburger joint dedicated to rock 'n' roll. It features guitars, records, and other memorabilia on the walls, as well as hamburgers, salads, sandwiches, steak, barbecued pork ribs, and fajitas. The music, by the way, is loud. T-shirts are sold in a kiosk across the street.

JOHNNY ROCKETS, 3-11-10 Roppongi. Tel. 3423-1955.
Cuisine: HAMBURGERS. **Station:** Roppongi (then a one-minute walk).

$ Prices: ¥600–¥1,300 ($5.45–$11.80); set lunches ¥1,000 ($9.10). No credit cards.
Open: Sun–Fri 11am–11pm, Sat 11am–5am.

Quite simply, the best burgers in town. At ¥900 ($8.20), they're also rather steep, but when nothing else will do these are so huge that they'll definitely hit the spot. Perched on the second floor of a building on Roppongi Crossing, Johnny Rockets is decorated like an American '50s diner, and when certain songs come up on the jukebox, the waitresses all stop to sing and dance in unison, just like in the movies. Seating is on a first-come, first-served basis at counters, and no smoking is allowed. Other goodies on the menu include sandwiches, fries (including fries topped with chili), malts, shakes, floats, and pie à la mode. From 11am to 2pm daily, a fixed-price lunch is offered that includes a hamburger, fries and a drink.

KITCHEN FIVE, 4-2-15 Nishi-Azabu. Tel. 3409-8835.

Cuisine: MEDITERRANEAN/ETHNIC. **Reservations:** Not accepted. **Station:** Roppongi or Hiroo (then a 15-minute walk).

$ Prices: Dishes ¥950–¥2,200 ($8.65–$20). No credit cards.

Open: Dinner only, Tues–Sat 6–9:45pm (last order). **Closed:** Hols and end of July to early Sept.

If it's true that cooking with love is the best spice, then perhaps that's why Yuko Kobayashi's 9-year-old, 16-seat restaurant is so popular (get there before 7pm to get a seat), though she refuses to be written about or to advertise. She goes to market every morning to fetch ingredients for such dishes as coxinhas de galinha, stuffed eggplant, fritata de verdure, moussaka, and tajin. Every summer Kobayashi goes off to search for recipes in Sicily, South America, or North Africa. The love for what she does shines in her black eyes as she cooks, serves, and walks you through the menu of daily dishes displayed. From Nishi-Azabu Crossing, head toward Hiroo and turn right opposite the gas station. Highly recommended.

MOTI, 6-2-35 Roppongi. Tel. 3479-1939.

Cuisine: INDIAN. **Station:** Roppongi (then a three-minute walk).

$ Prices: Curries ¥1,100–¥1,800 ($10–$16.35); set lunch ¥990 ($9). AE, DC, JCB, MC, V.

Open: Daily 11:30am–10pm.

This place is packed at lunchtime, when set lunches with a choice of vegetable, chicken, or mutton curry, along with Indian bread (nan), and tea or coffee, are served until 2:30pm. There's also a wide selection of other curries, as well as tandoori. It's on the left side of Roppongi Dori as you walk from Roppongi Crossing toward Shibuya. A second Roppongi location is Moti Darbar on the second floor of the Roppongi Plaza Building, 3-12-6 Roppongi (tel. 5410-6871).

RAMEN TAI, 1-8-4 Nishi Azabu. Tel. 3405-5576.

Cuisine: CHINESE. **Station:** Roppongi (5-minute walk).

$ Prices: ¥450–¥950 ($4.10–$8.65). No credit cards.

Open: Mon–Thurs 11am–4am, Fri 11am–5am, Sun 11am–7pm.

Inexpensive food in the middle of the night? Head for this ramen shop, located on the right side of Roppongi Dori as you walk in the direction of Shibuya. Its menu has pictures showing what's available, including various kinds of ramen (noodle soup), gyoza (fried dumplings), and noodle dishes.

7. ASAKUSA

EXPENSIVE

JAPANESE FOOD

MUGITORO (38), 2-2-4 Kaminarimon. Tel. 3842-1066.

Cuisine: YAMS. **Reservations:** Recommended. **Station:** Asakusa (then less than a two-minute walk).

$ Prices: Set dinners ¥6,000–¥13,000 ($54.55–$118.20); set lunches ¥3,500 ($31.20). AE, DC, JCB, MC, V.

Open: Daily 11:30am–8:30pm (last order).

Popular with middle-aged Japanese housewives, this restaurant specializes in tororo-imo, which is yam, considered a health food in Japan. Founded about 60 years ago but now housed in a new building, it serves yams in a variety of ways from a Japanese menu that changes monthly.

From Kaminarimon Gate, walk south on Edo Dori Avenue with your back to the temple until you reach the first big intersection. Komagatabashi Bridge will be to your left, and Mugitoro is located right beside the bridge and a tiny playground. Look for the big white lanterns hanging outside.

KUREMUTSU (37), 2-2-13 Asakusa. Tel. 3842-0906.

Cuisine: GRILLED FOOD/KAISEKI. **Reservations:** Required. **Station:** Asakusa (then about a five-minute walk).

$ Prices: Set meals from ¥8,000 ($72.70); kaiseki from ¥9,000 ($81.80). No credit cards.

Open: Dinner only, Fri–Wed 4–10pm.

Located just southeast of Sensoji Temple, Kuremutsu is actually a tiny house, tucked behind an inviting courtyard with a willow tree and an entrance lit with lanterns. Inside it's like a farmhouse in the countryside, filled with farm implements, old chests, masks, cast-iron teakettles, hibachis, and other odds and ends. Traditionally dressed waitresses serve fresh fish, the restaurant's specialty, as well as platters of assorted sashimi and kaiseki. The menu is only in Japanese and since only cash is accepted, make sure you know what you've ordered. Easiest is to order one of the set meals.

MODERATE

JAPANESE FOOD

ICHIMON (39), 3-12-6 Asakusa. Tel. 3875-6800.

Cuisine: VARIED JAPANESE. **Station:** Tawaramachi (then a 7-minute walk) or Asakusa (then about a 15-minute walk).

$ Prices: Meals average ¥5,000 ($45.45). No credit cards.

Open: Dinner only, Mon–Sat 5:30–10:30pm (last order).

Ichimon takes its name from *mon,* which was the lowest piece of currency used by common people during the Edo Period. Ichimon means "one mon." At any rate, this drinking establishment has a unique system whereby each customer is required to purchase ¥5,000 ($45.45) worth of mon, issued here in wooden tokens, which are then used to pay for your sake and meal. It's usually enough to cover the cost of a couple flasks of sake, a tray of appetizers, and a dish or two that might include sashimi, steak, nabe (a one-pot stew of meat and vegetables), or chicken. Mon you don't use can be exchanged for the real thing when you leave. The establishment is cozy and decorated like an old farmhouse, with wooden beams and shoji screens. The specialty of the house is its 45 different kinds of sake. When you order some, a basket filled with sake cups is brought to your table so you can select the one you want to drink from. A fun place to end a day in Asakusa.

KOMAGATA DOJO (40), 1-7-12 Komagata. Tel. 3842-4001.

ACCOMMODATIONS & DINING IN ASAKUSA

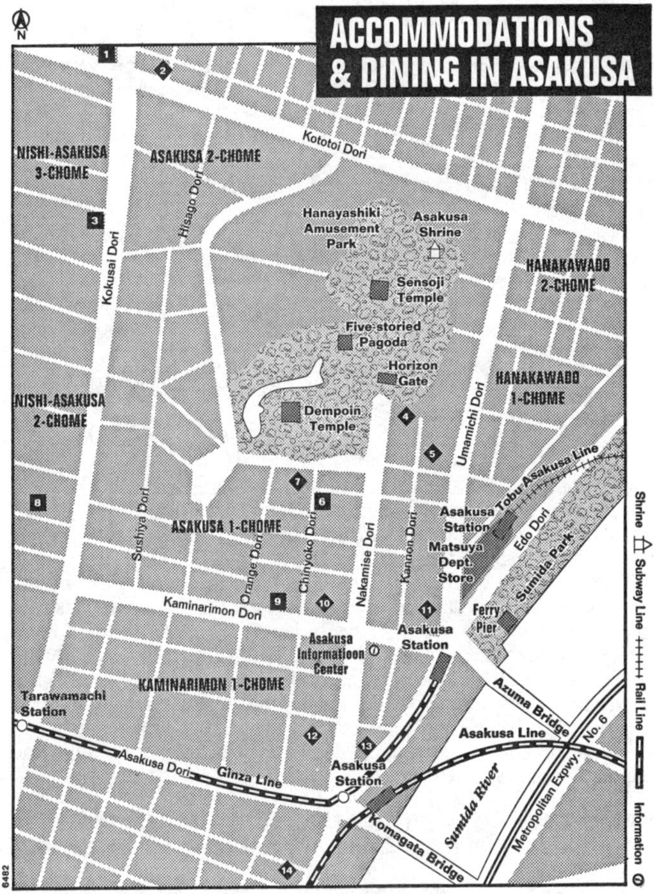

ACCOMMODATIONS
- Asakusa Plaza Hotel 9
- Asakusa View Hotel 3
- Kikuya Ryokan 8
- Ryokan Miyakawa Bekkan 6
- Sakura Ryokan 1

DINING
- Chinya 10
- Daikokuya 7
- Ichimon 2
- Kamiya Bar 11
- Keyaki 5
- Mugitoro 13
- Komagata Dojo 14
- Kuremutsu 4
- Namiki 12

Cuisine: DOJO. **Reservations:** Recommended at dinner. **Station:** Asakusa (then about a three-minute walk).

$ Prices: Dishes ¥300–¥1,500 ($2.75–$13.65); set dinners from ¥4,700 ($42.70); teishoku ¥3,600 ($32.70). DC, JCB, MC, V.

Open: Daily 11am–9pm.

Following a tradition spanning more than 185 years, this old-style dining hall specializes in dojo, a tiny river fish similar to a sardine but resembling a miniature eel. It's served in a variety of styles, from grilled to stewed, and various teishoku are available anytime. The dining area is simply one large room of tatami mats, with waitresses moving quietly about dressed in kimonos. It's a scene right out of the Edo Period.

To reach the restaurant, walk south with your back to Kaminarimon Gate past the Bank of Tokyo. The restaurant, a large, old-fashioned house on a corner with blue curtains at its door, will be on your right.

BUDGET

JAPANESE FOOD

CHINYA (41), 1-3-4 Asakusa. Tel. 3841-0010.
Cuisine: SHABU-SHABU/SUKIYAKI. **Station:** Asakusa (then less than a minute's walk).
$ Prices: ¥2,900–¥6,000 ($26.35–$54.55). DC, JCB, MC, V.
Open: Thurs–Tues 11:30am–9:30pm.

Established in 1880, Chinya is an old sukiyaki restaurant with a new home in a seven-story building. It's located to the left of the Kaminarimon if you stand facing the famous Sensoji Temple; look for the sukiyaki sign. Its entrance is open-fronted; you'll see a man waiting to greet customers. Instead of entering here, look for the smaller doorway to the left of this main entrance, which leads to a much cheaper restaurant in the basement, a one-room informal eatery offering inexpensive plates of sukiyaki and shabu-shabu. Seating is around a counter, where you can watch the cooks at work. If you feel like splurging with a meal in more relaxed surroundings, the main restaurant upstairs offers a very good shabu-shabu or sukiyaki set lunch for ¥2,500 ($22.70), available until 3pm and including soup and side dishes.

DAIKOKUYA (25), 1-38-10 Asakusa. Tel. 3844-1111.
Cuisine: TEMPURA. **Station:** Asakusa (then about a five-minute walk).
$ Prices: ¥1,450–¥1,800 ($13.20–$16.35). No credit cards.
Open: Thurs–Tues 11:30am–8:30pm.

This is Asakusa's best-known restaurant for inexpensive tempura. A simple establishment that bustles with waiters and waitresses rushing around filling orders, it's especially favored for its tempura ebi (shrimp), kisu (smelt), and kaki (oysters).

To reach it, take the small street that passes by the south side of Dempoin Temple (also spelled Demboin Temple); Daikokuya is at the first intersection, a white building on the corner with a Japanese-style tiled roof and front sliding door.

KAMIYA BAR, 1-1-1 Asakusa. Tel. 3841-5400.
Cuisine: VARIED JAPANESE/WESTERN. **Station:** Asakusa (then less than a minute's walk).
$ Prices: ¥250–¥1,400 ($2.25–$12.70). No credit cards.
Open: Wed–Mon 11:30am–9:30pm (last order).

You can't get more casual than this large establishment, founded in 1880 and serving both Japanese and Western fare. Very much a place for the locals, it can be quite noisy and crowded, filled with office workers and housewives during the day and groups of carousing salarymen at night. The first and second floors offer Western food, including fried chicken, smoked salmon, spaghetti, fried shrimp, and hamburger steak. I think you're better off, however, heading for the third floor, which serves Japanese food ranging from udon noodles and yakitori to tempura and sashimi. Although the menus are only in Japanese, there are extensive plastic-food display cases. A plain, brown-tile building, Kamiya Bar is located almost on top of the Asakusa subway station not far from Kaminarimon Gate.

KEYAKI (42), 1-34-5 Asakusa. Tel. 3844-9012.
Cuisine: EEL. **Station:** Asakusa (then a few minutes' walk).
$ Prices: A la carte dishes ¥550–¥10,000 ($5–$90.90); lunch teishoku ¥1,200–¥1,800 ($10.90–$16.35). No credit cards.
Open: Lunch Tues–Sun 11:30am–2pm; dinner Tues–Sun 5–10pm.

Put all your prejudices about eels aside and head for Keyaki, located on the second street that parallels Nakamise Dori Avenue to the east; look for the brown flag with an eel on it and for the fish tank just inside the door. Small, with just a counter, a couple of tables, and an adjoining tatami room, it offers a good eel teishoku, as well as tempura or sashimi courses. Try the house specialty, a sake called ginjo-shu.

NAMIKI (43), 2-11-9 Kaminarimon. Tel. 3841-1340.
Cuisine: NOODLES. **Station:** Asakusa (3-minute walk).
$ Prices: ¥550–¥1,600 ($5–$14.55). No credit cards.
Open: Fri–Wed 11:30am–7:30pm.

Asakusa's best-known noodle shop, this is a one-room place with tatami and tables and an English menu. Since it's a small establishment, don't linger once you've finished your meal if there are people waiting for a table (the Japanese consider it rude). To reach it, take the road that leads south with your back to Sensoji Temple and Kaminarimon Gate. Namiki is a brown building on the right side of the street with some bamboo trees by the front door.

8. UENO

EXPENSIVE

JAPANESE FOOD

IZU'EI (44), 2-12-22 Ueno. Tel. 3831-0954.
Cuisine: EEL. **Station:** JR Ueno Station (then a three-minute walk).
$ Prices: Dishes ¥1,500–¥3,000 ($13.65–$27.25); set meals ¥7,000–¥15,000 ($63.65–$136.35). AE, DC, JCB, MC, V.
Open: Daily 11am–9:30pm.

This modern yet traditionally decorated restaurant, specializing in eel, has a history stretching back 260 years to the Edo Period. It boasts its own charcoal furnace in the mountains of Wakayama Prefecture, which produces the best charcoal in Japan—the charcoal used in grilling eel is considered one of the most important factors in the quality of the eel itself. There's no English menu, but there is a plastic display case outside and a pamphlet with pictures. I personally like the unagi donburi, rice with strips of grilled eel on top. Tempura and sushi are also available. It's located across the street from

Shinobazu Pond and the Shitamachi Museum, next to Kentucky Fried Chicken (now simply KFC).

BUDGET

NON-JAPANESE FOOD

MAHARAJA, on the third floor of the Nagafuji Bldg. Annex, 4-9-6 Ueno. Tel. 3835-0818.
Cuisine: INDIAN. **Station:** JR Ueno Station (then a two-minute walk).
$ Prices: Appetizers and soups ¥450–¥1,800 ($4.10–$16.35); main dishes ¥1,100–¥1,800 ($10–$16.35); set lunches ¥850–¥1,200 ($7.70–$10.90). No credit cards.
Open: Daily 11am–9:30pm.

For inexpensive Indian food, head for this spotless, modern restaurant located in a shiny white building between busy Chuo Dori Avenue and the Ameyokocho shopping street. Decorated in cool peach and pink, with etched mirrors and lots of brass, it offers curries and tandoori, at prices lower than in Roppongi and other more upscale neighborhoods.

9. HARAJUKU & AOYAMA

VERY EXPENSIVE

NON-JAPANESE FOOD

MANIN, 2-22-12 Jingumae. Tel. 3478-3778.
Cuisine: ITALIAN. **Reservations:** Recommended. **Station:** Harajuku, Meiji-Jingumae, or Gaienmae (then a 10-minute walk).
$ Prices: Main dishes ¥4,500–¥8,000 ($40.90–$72.70); set dinners ¥12,000–¥18,000 ($109.10–$163.65). AE, DC, JCB, MC, V.
Open: Dinner only, Mon–Sat 6–10pm. **Closed:** Hols.

You must have both money and an appreciation for starkness and space to enjoy dining in this very modern Italian restaurant. With one of the most unusual interior designs I've ever seen, its dining area is in a basement at the bottom of a long, wide flight of stairs and features a 30-foot-high ceiling, massive black beams, red velvet and mahogany walls, a black floor, and white tablecloths. All in all, it's rather like dining in the world's most expensive fallout shelter. For appetizers, try the tomato-and-garlic scallops, followed by risotto with squid, red snapper grilled with clam sauce, or grilled veal.

EXPENSIVE

NON-JAPANESE FOOD

L'ORANGERIE DE PARIS, on the fifth floor of the Hanae Mori Bldg., 3-6-1 Kita-Aoyama. Tel. 3407-7461.
Cuisine: FRENCH. **Reservations:** Recommended at lunch, required at dinner. **Station:** Omotesando (then a one-minute walk).
$ Prices: Appetizers and soups ¥3,000–¥4,000 ($27.25–$36.35); main dishes ¥3,000–¥8,000 ($27.25–$72.70); set din-

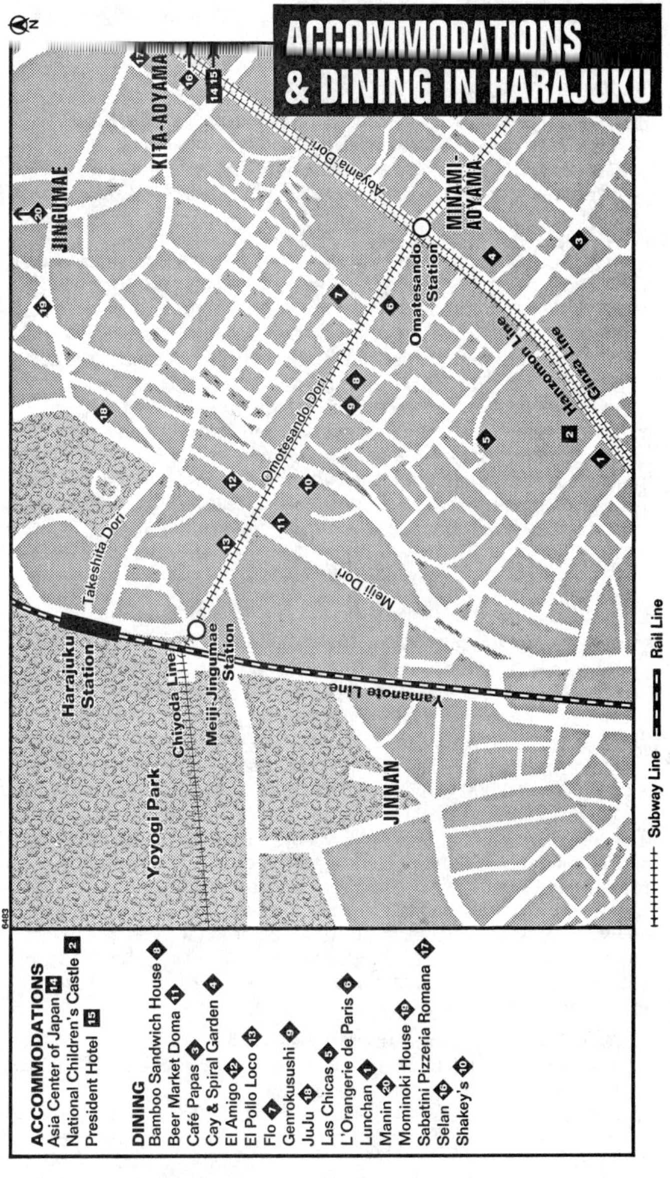

ners ¥8,800 ($80); set lunches ¥4,400 ($40). AE, DC, JCB, MC, V.

Open: Lunch daily 11am–2:30pm; dinner Mon–Sat 5:30–9:30pm.

Located on chic Omotesando Dori, this Tokyo branch is related to the Parisian restaurant of the same name. Its menu changes with the seasons, while set dinners and lunches change every two weeks. Popular with Tokyo's well-heeled foreign population, it's in the building designed by architect Kenzo Tange that houses fashion designer Hanae Mori's entire collection. Check out the front shop windows—they're always interesting.

SABATINI, in the basement of the Suncrest Bldg., 2-13-5 Kita-Aoyama. Tel. 3402-3812.
Cuisine: ITALIAN. **Reservations:** Recommended at dinner. **Station:** Gaienmae (then a two-minute walk on Aoyama Dori Avenue).
$ Prices: Appetizers and soups ¥1,500–¥2,800 ($13.65–$25.45); pasta ¥1,800–¥3,400 ($16.35–$30.90); main dishes ¥3,000–¥8,200 ($27.25–$74.55); set lunches ¥4,900 ($44.55). AE, DC, JCB, MC, V.
Open: Lunch daily 11:30am–2:30pm; dinner daily 5:30–11pm.

This Italian restaurant is owned by three brothers who have had a restaurant in Rome for more than 30 years. They take turns overseeing the Tokyo store, so one of them is always here, serving food or helping out in the kitchen. With its furniture and tableware and strolling musicians, the restaurant looks as if it had been moved intact from Italy. Only the Japanese waiters remind you that you're in Tokyo. Its menu includes soups, pasta, seafood (including fresh lobster), veal, steak, lamb, and a variety of vegetables.

MODERATE

NON-JAPANESE FOOD

CAY & SPIRAL GARDEN, in the basement of the Spiral Bldg., 5-6-23 Minami Aoyama. Tel. 3498-5790.
Cuisine: THAI. **Reservations:** Recommended. **Station:** Omotesando (then a one-minute walk).
$ Prices: Appetizers and soups ¥1,000–¥2,000 ($9.10–$18.20); main dishes ¥3,000–¥4,000 ($27.25–$36.35); set dinners ¥5,000–¥9,000 ($45.45–$81.80). AE, DC, JCB, MC, V.
Open: Dinner only, Mon–Sat 6–11pm. **Closed:** Hols.

The Spiral Building is one of Aoyama Dori Avenue's most modern and fashionable buildings, and in its basement is this trendy Thai restaurant. Decorated with artwork and plants, the restaurant even serves as a venue for music a few evenings a month, for which there's an extra admission charge. Its food, toned down for Japanese palates, includes roast-beef salad, hot-and-sour shrimp soup, deep-fried fish with coconut sauce, grilled chicken Thai style, fried duck with lime sauce, and Thai curries.

FLO, 4-3-3 Jingumae. Tel. 5474-0611.
Cuisine: FRENCH. **Reservations:** Not required. **Station:** Omotesando (then a three-minute walk).
$ Prices: Appetizers ¥950–¥3,200 ($8.70–$29.10); main dishes ¥2,200–¥3,800 ($20–$34.55); set dinners ¥5,000–¥6,000 ($45.45–$54.55); set lunches ¥2,000–¥3,000 ($18.20–$27.25). AE, DC, JCB, MC, V.
Open: Lunch daily 11:30am–3pm; dinner daily 5–11:30pm.

French restaurateurs have opened this beautiful bistro with French staff and authentic bistro food. The menu may include dishes such as choucroute (the Alsatian version of sausage and cabbage) or soupière de homard à la bretonne (Brittany-style lobster soup). We had *La Formule Déjeuner* (set lunch) with potage crème de Saint-Jacques (scallop soup), confit de canard (duck) with roasted new potatoes in bacon-and-mushroom sauce for ¥2,000 ($18.20). Besides an extensive wine list, they serve all the typical and irresistable French desserts from mille feuille to crème brûlée which cost from ¥480 to ¥780 ($4.35 to $7.10).

LA PATATA, 2-9-11 Jingumae. Tel. 3403-9664.
Cuisine: ITALIAN. **Reservations:** Recommended at dinner. **Station:** Gaienmae (then about a 10-minute walk).
$ Prices: Appetizers ¥2,200–¥3,000 ($20–$27.25); pasta ¥1,500 ($13.65); main dishes ¥3,000–¥5,000 ($27.25–$45.45). AE, DC, JCB, MC, V.
Open: Lunch Tues–Sun noon–2pm; dinner Tues–Sun 6–10:30pm.

This Italian restaurant, specializing in seafood, is cheerful with lots of windows, plants, and warm, blond furniture, reminding me of health-food restaurants in the States. The dinner menu includes a fish of the day, broiled shrimp, sole, lamb, sliced veal, and beef filet. It's located on a street with the intimidating name of Killer Dori Avenue.

LUNCHAN, 1-2-5 Shibuya. Tel. 5466-1398.
Cuisine: AMERICAN. **Reservations:** Required only for Sun brunch. **Station:** Omotesando (then a 7-minute walk) or Shibuya (then a 10-minute walk).
$ Prices: Appetizers ¥1,400–¥1,800 ($12.70–$16.35); main dishes ¥1,600–¥2,800 ($14.55–$25.45); set lunches ¥1,200–¥1,400 ($10.90–$12.70). AE, D, DC, JCB, MC, V.
Open: Daily 11am–11pm; brunch Sun 11am–3pm.

Chef David Chiddo is actually in the open kitchen creating his original recipes in this contemporary, airy, mauve-and-teal bistro. Choose dishes like pizza al Il Forno (the hot Santa Monica and soon-to-be-in-Roppongi pizzeria), Bangkok-style grilled chicken, or herb-crusted fish. A wide selection of lunch specials are offered, including real sandwiches—that is, with all the trimmings. Easy to find, it's across the side street from the National Children's Castle.

SABATINI PIZZERIA ROMANA, in the basement of the Suncrest Bldg., 2-13-5 Kita-Aoyama. Tel. 3402-2027.
Cuisine: ITALIAN. **Reservations:** Recommended. **Station:** Gaienmae (then a one-minute walk).
$ Prices: Appetizers and soups ¥1,000–¥1,800 ($9.10–$16.35); pasta and pizza ¥1,300–¥1,600 ($11.80–$14.55); main dishes ¥2,700–¥4,400 ($24.55–$40); set lunches ¥2,300–¥3,800 ($20.90–$34.55). AE, DC, JCB, MC, V.
Open: Lunch daily 11:30am–2:30pm; dinner daily 5:30–11pm.

Owned by three brothers from Rome who also operate an expensive Italian restaurant in the same building, this pizzeria offers the closest thing to real Italian pizza in town. Many ingredients are flown in from Italy, including olive oil, huge slabs of parmesan and other cheeses, as well as the restaurant's large wine selection; they even shipped in a pasta machine. In addition to its pizzas, the restaurant serves spaghetti, lasagne, fettuccine, and meat dishes. All you need order, however, is a pizza. It's at the intersection of Aoyama Dori Avenue and Killer Dori Avenue.

SELAN, 2-1-19 Kita-Aoyama. Tel. 3478-2200.
Cuisine: NOUVELLE JAPANESE/FRENCH. **Reservations:** Recommended. **Station:** Gaienmae or Aoyama-Itchome (then a five-minute walk).
$ Prices: Appetizers and soups ¥700–¥3,200 ($6.35–$29.10); main dishes ¥1,400–¥3,000 ($12.70–$27.25); set dinners ¥5,000 ($45.45). AE, JCB, MC, V.

Open: Lunch daily 11:30am–2:30pm; dinner daily 6–10pm.

It looks like a French restaurant with its pink interior, chandeliers, sidewalk seating, and menu offering such fare as steaks, chicken, fish, lobster, and duck. However, the food is cooked using Japanese ingredients and thus may be classified as "nouvelle japonaise" cuisine. In any case, it's a successful marriage between French and Japanese cooking, with such innovative dishes as flounder stuffed with chopped shrimp and calamari and topped with sea urchin and vegetables, or seared bonito salad with soy sauce, garlic, and oil dressing. Little wonder that this is fast becoming one of Tokyo's most popular mealtime retreats. The ground floor serves as a café, with artwork adorning the wall and wicker chairs, while more formal dining is upstairs where large windows overlook a tree-lined street.

BUDGET

JAPANESE FOOD

GENROKUSUSHI (45), 5-8-5 Jingumae. Tel. 3498-3968.

Cuisine: SUSHI. **Station:** Meiji-Jingumae (then a one-minute walk) or Omotesando (then a five-minute walk).

$ **Prices:** Sushi ¥120 or ¥240 ($1.10 or $2.20) per plate. No credit cards.

Open: Daily 11am–9pm.

Genrokusushi is another one of those budget sushi bars where plates are brought to customers via a conveyor belt that moves along the counter. Customers help themselves to whatever strikes their fancy. Plates cost either ¥120 or ¥240, and to figure the bill the cashier simply counts the number of plates the customer took from the conveyor belt. There are also take-out sushi boxes starting at ¥400 ($3.65), which you might want to eat in nearby Yoyogi Park. Genrokusushi is located on Omotesando Dori Avenue close to the Oriental Bazaar.

NON-JAPANESE FOOD

ANDERSEN, 5-1-26 Minami Aoyama. Tel. 3407-4833.

Cuisine: SANDWICHES. **Station:** Omotesando (then a one-minute walk).

$ **Prices:** Salads ¥250–¥400 ($2.25–$3.65); sandwiches ¥650–¥1,000 ($5.90–$9.10). No credit cards.

Open: Daily 10am–10pm. **Closed:** Third Mon of each month.

This popular bakery has a self-serve deli in its basement, offering a variety of sandwich spreads to go with its freshly baked bread. Chicken salad, roast beef, smoked salmon, or ham and cheese are just some of the options, and there are also about half a dozen choices in salads.

BAMBOO SANDWICH HOUSE, 5-8-8 Jingumae. Tel. 3406-1828.

Cuisine: SANDWICHES. **Station:** Omotesando or Meiji-Jingumae (then a three-minute walk).

$ **Prices:** Sandwiches ¥450–¥800 ($4.10–$7.25). No credit cards.

Open: Daily 11am–9pm.

A great place to go if you crave a decent yet inexpensive sandwich, this cheerful and informal restaurant is housed in what used to be a private residence and is located just off

Omotesando Dori on a side street near the Paul Stuart shop. It offers more than 20 sandwich fillings, and you have your choice of white or rye bread. It's probably the only place in town to offer a bottomless cup of coffee for a mere ¥220 ($2), a price that hasn't changed in more than a dozen years. What's more, it boasts outdoor seating.

BEER MARKET DOMA, in the basement of the Ga-Z Bldg., 6-5-3 Jingumae. Tel. 3498-7251.

Cuisine: ASIAN. **Station:** Meiji-Jingumae (then a one-minute walk) or Harajuku (then a three-minute walk).

$ **Prices:** ¥500–¥2,000 ($4.55–$18.20). No credit cards.

Open: Lunch daily 11:30am–2pm; dinner daily 5–11:30pm.

This is one of my favorite places for a meal in Harajuku. I like it for its food, its prices, and its atmosphere. "Doma" means an "earth-floored room," and this restaurant is true to its name with its earthen floor, clay walls, and silk cloth draped from the ceiling to make it look like a Mongolian nomad's tent. The menu lists Chinese, Japanese, Thai, and other Asian cuisines, along with pao dishes. Pao foods, originally from the Middle East, feature morsels of beef or fish wrapped in lettuce. In addition to its table-service menu, it has a cafeteria with a dozen or so dishes ranging from salads, soups, and entrées to desserts, most priced under ¥800 ($7.25). A true find, it's located just off the intersection of Omotesando and Meiji Dori.

CAFE PAPAS, 6-11-1 Minami-Aoyama. Tel. 3400-0884.

Cuisine: WESTERN. **Station:** Omotesando (then a 10-minute walk).

$ **Prices:** Dishes ¥900–¥1,200 ($8.20–$10.90); sandwiches ¥800–¥1,000 ($7.25–$9.10); set lunches ¥1,000 ($9.10). No credit cards.

Open: Mon–Fri 11:30am–10pm, Sat–Sun 11:30am–8pm.

Opened by fashion biggies Bigi Co., this New England boathouse-style café is connected to a shop selling the Papas, Mademoiselle, and Non-Non Bigi labels. There's a menu with dishes such as homemade roast beef, spaghetti, and pizza available from 6pm, but at lunch (until 2pm) you have to choose from the two set meals, like Provençal-style chicken or goulash. Lunch comes with spaghetti and rice, salad, and coffee or tea (iced in summer). There's an English menu, but lunch specials are on a chalkboard in Japanese only—a good chance to strike up a conversation. On Saturday and Sunday, only sandwiches are served at lunch. Café Papas is on the right-hand side, about halfway down Koto Dori (Antique Avenue), the street once known for its antiques shops, but now getting more and more fashion-oriented.

EL AMIGO, 4-30-2 Jingumae. Tel. 3405-9996.

Cuisine: MEXICAN. **Station:** Meiji-Jingumae (then a one-minute walk).

$ **Prices:** Dishes ¥600–¥1,000 ($5.45–$9.10); set meals ¥3,000 ($27.25). AE.

Open: Dinner only, Mon–Fri 6pm–midnight, Sat–Sun 5pm–midnight.

Located off Omotesando Dori on a side street beside Wendy's hamburger shop, this is one of the cheapest Mexican restaurants in town. To cut corners they use cabbage instead of lettuce, but otherwise it's the usual tacos and enchiladas, margaritas, and

Mexican beer. There's an outdoor patio of sorts, below street level and smothered in plants.

EL POLLO LOCO, 1-13-12 Jingumae. Tel. 3408-4024.
Cuisine: CHICKEN. **Station:** Harajuku or Meiji-Jingumae (then a one-minute walk).
$ Prices: ¥350–¥2,000 ($3.20–$18.20). No credit cards.
Open: Daily 10am–10pm.

A fast-food chain from the shores of California on Omotesando Dori, El Pollo Loco specializes in charcoal-broiled chicken served with tortillas and mild salsa, along with such side dishes as coleslaw, corn on the cob, rice, and potato salad. There are also curry-chicken burgers and Oriental chicken burgers.

JUJU (46), 3-23-6 Jingumae. Tel. 3470-9630.
Cuisine: NOUVELLE JAPANESE. **Station:** Meiji-Jingumae (then about a four-minute walk).
$ Prices: Appetizers ¥600–¥1,000 ($5.45–$9.10); main dishes ¥1,000–¥1,400 ($9.10–$12.70); set dinners ¥4,000 ($36.35). AE, V.
Open: Dinner only, Mon–Sat 5pm–midnight.

A tiny, one-room establishment with only a few tables and counter seating, this Oriental-looking restaurant specializes in original creations of Chinese, Japanese, and French food, which is served on Asian plates and dishes and is eaten with chopsticks. Its English menu includes homemade pickled vegetables, tofu salad, steamed chicken with sesame sauce, and beef served with seaweed. Try the homemade dumpling for an appetizer. It's located on the right side of Meiji Dori if you walk north from its intersection with Omotesando, up on the second floor.

LAS CHICAS, 5-47-6 Jingumae. Tel. 3407-6865.
Cuisine: ETHNIC. **Station:** Omotesando (then a five-minute walk).
$ Prices: Dishes ¥1,100–¥1,500 ($10–$13.65); set lunches ¥1,000–¥1,200 ($9.10–$10.90). No credit cards.
Open: Daily 11:30am–10pm (last order 9:30pm).

Opened by fashion house Vision Network, Las Chicas is the café of a complex housing interior goods, world music compact discs, coffee-table books, and of course, the latest in fashion. Foreign waiters and cooks and Las Chicas chic draw foreigners and the fashion/design business crowd. Large-portion dishes are eclectic, like Thai pork salad, salmon steak with herbs and pumpkin, and chick pea curry. It's also a good spot for espresso, fruit smoothies, wine and beer, and homemade desserts, like kiwi custard tart or carrot cake for ¥600 ($5.45). My special lunch for ¥1,100 ($10) was a plate piled with alu gobi curry, banana raita, millet, crispy Indian cracker-bread, salad, and homemade herb bread. Las Chicas reminds me of a '60s health-food restaurant, but (thank heavens) with '90s interior style.

To get here, take the Kinokuniya exit of the Omotesando subway and head down Route 246 toward Shibuya, taking a right at City Bank; Las Chicas is down this small street.

MOMINOKI HOUSE, 2-18-5 Jingumae. Tel. 3405-9144.
Cuisine: NOUVELLE JAPANESE/FRENCH. **Station:** Harajuku or Meiji-Jingumae (then a 15-minute walk).
$ Prices: Dishes ¥1,000–¥2,000 ($9.10–$18.20); set lunches ¥850–¥1,300 ($7.70–$11.80). No credit cards.
Open: Mon–Sat 11am–10pm (last order), hols 3–10pm.

The food of Mominoki House is so unique I'm not sure how to classify it. Although the menu (written only in Japanese on a huge blackboard) is French, the dishes are the special creations of the chef, who uses lots of soy sauce, ginger, and Japanese vegetables. Suffice it to say that it's in a category by itself and is somewhat of a rarity in Tokyo. Serving macrobiotic foods, this alternative restaurant features hanging plants and split-level dining, allowing for more privacy than one would think possible in such a tiny place. Its collection of recorded jazz music is extensive and on weekends there's live music. The menu changes according to what's fresh and what the chef himself feels like eating, but dishes may include tofu steak, duck, sole, escargots, eggplant gratin (baked in a delicious white sauce), salads, and homemade sorbet. There's a small English menu listing house specialties, but be sure to ask the chef about the daily specials on the blackboard (he speaks English well). Its lunch teishoku is an especially good deal, including brown rice, miso soup, salad, fish or other main course, and a glass of wine. There's also a vegetarian teishoku. Because the restaurant is a bit difficult to find, you might want to come by taxi.

SHAKEY'S, 6-1-10 Jingumae. Tel. 3409-2405.
Cuisine: PIZZA. **Station:** Meiji-Jingumae (then a few minutes' walk).
$ Prices: All-you-can-eat pizza lunch ¥650 ($5.90). No credit cards.
Open: Lunch only, Mon–Sat 11am–2pm. **Closed:** Public hols.

Like other Shakey's around town, this location on Omotesando near the Oriental Bazaar offers a buffet of all the pizza you can consume for lunch, a great bargain. Be aware, however, that it can be packed on Saturday, so get here early if you don't want to fight the crowds of teenagers.

ZEST, 6-7-18 Jingumae. Tel. 3409-6268.
Cuisine: AMERICAN/MEXICAN. **Station:** Meiji-Jingumae (then a few minutes' walk).
$ Prices: Appetizers and salads ¥600–¥1,500 ($5.45–$13.65); main dishes ¥1,800–¥3,000 ($16.35–$27.25). AE, DC, MC, V.
Open: Daily 11:30am–5am.

A good place to hang out in Harajuku, Zest serves burgers, sandwiches, salads, and Mexican fare ranging from burritos to tacos. The tacos are outrageously expensive—three shells cost ¥700 ($6.35), with an extra ¥1,000 ($9.10) for each filling. However, the grub is good and may hit the spot when nothing else will. Besides, you don't have much choice in Harajuku if you're hungry past midnight.

10. SHIBUYA

MODERATE

NON-JAPANESE FOOD

SEIYO HIROBA (47), on the fifth floor of the Prime Bldg., 2-29-5 Dogenzaka. Tel. 3770-1781.
Cuisine: MEDITERRANEAN. **Reservations:** Recommended. **Station:** Shibuya (then about a two-minute walk).

$ **Prices:** Dinner buffet ¥5,500 ($50); lunch buffet ¥2,200 ($20). AE, DC, JCB, MC, V.
Open: Lunch daily 11:30am–2pm; dinner daily 6–10pm.

All-you-can-eat lunch or dinner buffets are rare in Tokyo (the idea of piling a plate with food is alien to the Japanese), but this place would stand out even with competition. Its buffet offers a great selection of Mediterranean-influenced French and Spanish cuisine, with an emphasis on fish, salads, and vegetables, and in the evenings there's even free entertainment, ranging from guitar music to pantomime. The restaurant bills itself as a "resort restaurant," the idea being that customers should feel as though they've embarked on a mini-vacation just by dining here. The dining area's spaciousness, turquoise lighting, potted palms, and candlelit tables make the place look romantic even in the middle of the day.

BUDGET

JAPANESE FOOD

IROHANIHOHETO (26), 1-19-3 Jinnan. Tel. 3476-1682.
Cuisine: YAKITORI/VARIED. **Station:** Shibuya (then about a 10-minute walk).
$ **Prices:** ¥350–¥500 ($2.25–$4.55). No credit cards.
Open: Daily 5pm–4am.

A boisterous drinking establishment that offers inexpensive dining, this place is so popular with university students that you may have to wait for a place to sit. The atmosphere is a Japanese perception of American country, with hurricane lamps and wooden beams in what could be described as barn decor. The extensive menu of Japanese and Western fare is in Japanese only, but there are pictures, making it easy to order. There's yakitori, oden, potato-and-meat stew (nikujaga), sashimi, fried noodles, potato salad, and lots more. It's located about halfway down on the road that leads between Parco I and II to the elevated train tracks, in the basement of a modern building.

TENMI (48), 1-10-6 Jinnan. Tel. 3496-9703.
Cuisine: MACROBIOTIC VEGETARIAN. **Station:** Shibuya (then about a five-minute walk).
$ **Prices:** Dishes ¥400–¥800 ($3.65–$7.25); set dinners ¥1,000–¥1,600 ($9.10–$14.55); set lunches ¥700–¥1,600 ($6.35–$14.55). AE, DC, JCB, MC, V.
Open: Lunch Mon–Fri 11:30am–2:30pm; dinner Mon–Fri 5–8:30pm, Sat 11:30am–7pm, Sun and hols 11:30am–6pm.
Closed: Second and third Wed of every month.

Located on the second floor above a health-food store, Tenmi serves traditional Japanese macrobiotic vegetarian food, including various vegetable, tofu, noodle, and rice combinations and set menus. I found the ¥1,100 ($9.10) set lunch of brown rice, an assortment of boiled vegetables, seaweed, and miso soup very satisfying. It's located near the TEPCO Electric Energy Museum.

NON-JAPANESE FOOD

THE PRIME, 2-29-5 Dogenzaka. Tel. 3770-0111.
Cuisine: INTERNATIONAL. **Station:** Shibuya (then a two-minute walk).

$ **Prices:** ¥500–¥1,000 ($4.55–$9.10); set lunches ¥500–¥900 ($4.55–$8.20). No credit cards.
Open: Daily 11:30am–10pm.

Opened a few years back by the Seibu conglomerate, the Prime is a great building filled with restaurants and amusements, including movie theaters, a dance and aerobics studio, and a concert and theater ticket agency. The second floor is a large cafeteria, with various counters offering dishes from around the world, including pizza, bagels, sandwiches, Indian curries, Chinese dishes, sushi, salads, and pasta. In the basement of the Prime are a number of noodle shops serving Chinese, Singaporean, Kyushu, and Hokkaido noodles.

11. OTHER LOCATIONS

DAIKANYAMA

MODERATE

CHEZ LUI, 17-22 Daikanyama-cho. Tel. 3461-9550.
Cuisine: FRENCH. **Reservations:** Recommended. **Station:** Daikanyama (then a two-minute walk).
$ **Prices:** Main dishes ¥1,000–¥2,200 ($9.10–$20); set dinners ¥3,000–¥8,000 ($27.25–$72.70); set lunches ¥1,700–¥3,000 ($15.45–$27.25). AE, DC, MC, V.
Open: Lunch daily 11:30am–2:30pm; dinner daily 6–9:30pm (last order).

A famous, yet unassuming restaurant, Chez Lui has long been frequented by fashion and movie nobs. I last saw actor Tora (Atsumikiyoshi) dining here—alone. The decor is French provincial and the menu includes côte d'agneau rôti provençal and escalope de saumon Chez Lui, each ¥2,200 ($20). Chez Lui is up the hill from Daikanyama Station (on the right side of the station if you're coming from Shibuya) on Hachiman Dori (Avenue). Turn right at Hachiman Dori and continue down two blocks; it's on your right. They also run a pâtisserie/traiteur across the street from the restaurant and next to the post office.

TABLEAUX, in the basement of the Sunroser Daikanyama Bldg., 11-6 Sarugaku-cho. Tel. 5489-2201.
Cuisine: INTERNATIONAL. **Reservations:** Not required.
$ **Prices:** Appetizers ¥1,000–¥2,800 ($9.10–$25.45); main dishes ¥1,300–¥4,800 ($11.80–$43.65); set lunches ¥1,800 ($16.35). AE, DC, JCB, MC, V.
Open: Lunch Mon–Sat 11:30am–2pm, Sun 11:30am–2:30pm; dinner Sun–Thurs 5:30–10:30pm, Fri–Sat 5:30–11pm; tea lounge Mon–Fri 2–5:30pm.

Designer Margaret O'Brien created a rich Russian tearoom atmosphere using bead-fringed curtains, gilt mirrors, chandeliers, stars and moons, animal-skin and velvet upholstery, and deep colors. The food is good and reasonable despite the avant-garde setting and clientele. For the health-conscious, there's fish or charcoal-grilled free-range chicken. For the rest, order terrine de foie gras with shiitake mushrooms for ¥1,900 ($17.25), crab ravioli in lobster sauce for ¥1,400 ($12.70), or calzone of the day for ¥1,000 ($9.10). An English menu and a staff dying to speak English make ordering easy.

After dining, try the set offering of coffee/tea and cake for ¥500 ($4.55). Your selection of herb and black teas will be ceremoniously offered from a cigar box. You might want to come just for tea and enjoy the interior design.

BUDGET

RED THUNDER CAFE, 24-1 Sarugaku-cho. Tel. 3462-4750.

Cuisine: TEX-MEX/NATIVE AMERICAN.

$ Prices: Appetizers ¥580–¥780 ($5.25–$7.10); dishes ¥800–¥1,500 ($7.25–$13.65); set meals ¥1,800–¥2,000 ($16.35–$18.20). AE, JCB, MC, V.

Open: Daily noon–4am.

Rough wood, horse blankets, and other Wild West trappings, plus Harleys parked in front, create this biker (the completely innocent variety) cum Southwest café/saloon featuring faux-mud walls. The roof rolls back to create outdoor seating. Appetizers from nachos (¥780/$7.10) to chili con carne with fried Idaho potato (¥580/$5.25) go down well with beer or magaritas for ¥700 to ¥800 ($6.35–$7.25). The chicken with mole sauce for ¥1,200 ($10.90) and Navajo fry bread ¥650 ($5.90) are popular.

NEAR AKIHABARA

MODERATE

KANDAGAWA (49), 2-5-11 Soto, Kanda. Tel. 3251-5031.

Cuisine: EEL. **Reservations:** Required. **Station:** Akihabara (then about a five-minute walk).

$ Prices: Appetizers and soups ¥500–¥800 ($4.55–$7.25); main dishes ¥2,500–¥3,500 ($22.70–$31.20). No credit cards.

Open: Lunch Mon–Sat 11:30am–2pm; dinner Mon–Sat 4:30–8pm. **Closed:** National hols.

I can't imagine a more beautiful, old-fashioned, and traditional setting than that afforded by this wonderful restaurant. Famous since the Edo Period for its eel dishes, this restaurant is located in a Japanese-style wooden house, hidden behind a wooden gate as in days of yore and reminiscent of a Japanese inn with its long wooden corridors and tatami rooms. Dining is either in a large tatami dining room or in one of the seven private tatami rooms.

The menu, in Japanese only, offers side dishes of soup, rice, and Japanese pickles, and such main dishes as kabayaki (broiled and basted eel), unaju (broiled eel on rice with a sweet sauce), shiroyaki ("white" eel, broiled without soy sauce or oil), and umaki (eel wrapped in an omelet). There's also grilled eel's liver, and sashimi. Expect to spend a minimum of ¥7,500 ($68.20) per person including drinks, appetizers, tax, and service. Since no one here speaks English, it's best to have a Japanese make your reservation, at which time you should order the dishes you'd like to be served. This is a great place for a splurge.

BUDGET

YABU-SOBA (50), 2-10 Awajicho, Kanda. Tel. 3251-0287.

Cuisine: NOODLES. **Station:** Awajicho (then about a 5-minute walk) or Akihabara (then about a 10-minute walk).

$ **Prices:** ¥600–¥1,500 ($5.45–$13.65). No credit cards.
Open: Tues–Sun 11:30am–7pm.

Soba (noodle) shops are usually simple affairs, sometimes offering no more than a stand-up counter at which to dine. This, however, is one of Tokyo's most famous noodle places, established in 1880. Surrounded by a wooden gate and with a small bamboo and rock garden, the house features shoji screens, a wooden ceiling, and a dining area with tatami mats and tables. You'll find the restaurant filled with middle-aged businessmen and housewives, and if you come during lunchtime you may have to wait for a seat. There's a menu in English, featuring hot and cold noodles, and noodles with shredded yam, topped with crispy shrimp tempura, or served with grilled eel. Listen to the woman sitting at a small counter by the kitchen—she sings out orders to the chef as well as hellos and good-byes to customers. Yabu-Soba is located between Awajicho and Akihabara Stations, near Sotobori Dori and Yasukuni Dori Avenues.

NEAR ICHIGAYA STATION

MODERATE

CARMINE, 1-19 Saiku-cho, Shinjuku-ku. Tel. 3260-5066.
Cuisine: ITALIAN. **Reservations:** Required. **Station:** Ichigaya (then a 12-minute walk) or Kagurazaka (then an 8-minute walk).
$ **Prices:** Appetizers ¥1,000–¥1,500 ($9.10–$13.65); pasta ¥1,000 ($9.10); set dinners ¥3,500–¥5,000 ($31.28–$45.45); set lunches ¥1,800–¥2,500 ($16.35–$22.70). No credit cards.
Open: Lunch Mon–Sat noon–2pm; dinner Mon–Sat 6–10pm.

This tiny Italian restaurant is out in the boonies as far as most Tokyoites are concerned, and yet people flock here because the food is great and the prices are almost shockingly low. Carmine Cozzolino is the chef and gregarious host, who received his training in the Tuscany style of cooking in Florence. Specialties include the antipasto misto del giorno, the penne al salmone or al gorgonzola, the scaloppine al marsala and the filetto di manzo all scalogno. The four-course set dinner for ¥3,500 ($31.20) is a steal; there's also a set lunch for as little as ¥1,800 ($16.35). The one-room dining hall is minuscule, simply decorated with artwork supplied by one of Carmine's friends. Since there arc only 48 seats, you won't get more than your foot in the door without a reservation. Take a taxi from either station listed above.

IKEBUKURO

BUDGET

MEKONG, in the New Matsumoto Bldg., 3-26-5 Nishi-Ikbukuro. Tel. 3988-5688.
Cuisine: THAI. **Station:** Ikebukuro, west exit (Exit 1B).
$ **Prices:** Appetizers ¥1,000–¥1,500 ($9.10–$13.65); dishes ¥1,000–¥2,000 ($9.10–$18.20). AE, JCB, MC, V.
Open: Lunch daily 11:30am–2:30pm; dinner daily 5–11pm.

This small and unpretentious basement restaurant serves dependably good and inexpensive Thai specialties, including shrimp and fish dishes, spicy beef salad, and pat Thai (a noodle dish and possibly the restaurant's best recommendation). My only complaints are that the tables are too close to each other for comfort and that the menu is in

Japanese only, although it does have photographs of each dish. The food makes these inconveniences worth it.

MEGURO

BUDGET

TONKI (51)**, 1-1-2 Shimo Meguro, Meguro-ku. Tel. 3491-9928.**

Cuisine: TONKATSU. **Station:** Meguro, west exit (then a one-minute walk).

$ Prices: ¥650–¥1,100 ($5.90–$10); set meal ¥1,600 ($14.55). JCB, V.

Open: Wed–Mon 4–11pm (last order 10:30pm). **Closed:** The third Mon of each month.

This is one of the best-known tonkatsu (pork cutlet) restaurants in town, so popular that you'll probably have to wait for a seat at the U-shaped counter. An English menu lists its two specialties, the hirekatsu (a filet cut of lean pork) and the rosukatsu (loin cut), either one of which is available in a set meal that includes soup, rice, pickled vegetables, and as much tea and cabbage as you want. Kushikatsu, skewered meat with onions, is also available. The open kitchen behind the counter takes up most of the space in the restaurant, and as you eat you can watch the dozen or so cooks scrambling around turning out orders. Never a dull moment. Tonki is on the side street that runs beside the Mitsui Bank—look for the blue curtains in front of the restaurant's glass sliding doors.

NEAR SHINAGAWA STATION

VERY EXPENSIVE

YAMATOYA SANGEN, in the Miyako Hotel, 1-1-50 Shiroganedai. Tel. 3445-0058.

Cuisine: VARIED JAPANESE. **Station:** Takanawadai (then an eight-minute walk).

$ Prices: Set dinners ¥16,000–¥20,000 ($145.45–$181.80); set lunches ¥2,500–¥12,000 ($22.70–$109.10). AE, DC, JCB, MC, V.

Open: Lunch daily 11:30am–2pm; dinner daily 5–9:30pm.

Although Japanese restaurants usually specialize in only one type of cooking, this hotel restaurant serves a variety of foods, from shabu-shabu, tempura, kaiseki, and sushi to eel. This is a good place to come if there are several of you and you can't make up your mind what you want to eat. If you've been intimidated by the thought of eating eel, this may be the best place to try it for the first time, although note that it's available only at lunch. The restaurant overlooks the hotel's Japanese garden and is simply decorated with shoji screens and slats of wood.

TAKADANOBABA

BUDGET

RAJPUT CURRY RESTAURANT, 4-13-12 Takadanobaba. Tel. 3360-8372.

Cuisine: INDIAN/PAKISTANI. **Station:** Takadanobaba (then a couple minutes' walk).

$ Prices: Dishes ¥1,000–¥1,500 ($9.10–$13.65); set lunch ¥900 ($8.20). No credit cards.

Open: Lunch Tues–Sun noon–3pm; dinner Tues–Sun 5–10pm. **Closed:** Lunch on hols.

$ This second-floor dining hall is about as casual as you can get, with just a counter, a few tables, and a television showing Pakistani videos as the only adornments. Its English menu includes mutton curry, chicken dahl, sag chicken (chicken with spinach), and potato cauliflower. Diners can choose how hot they want each dish using a rating of −3 to 7+ (−3 is very sweet, 1 is medium, while 7 is Muslim hot). Beer is inexpensive, making this a great place for a hot, inexpensive meal.

12. SPECIALTY DINING

BEER GARDENS

If you're in Tokyo during the summer months, you should take advantage of the very popular beer gardens. These sprout up all over the city when the weather turns warm, often atop office buildings. In addition to the two places below, another good place for an outdoor beer is Hibiya Park, located across from the Imperial Hotel, where there are various beer gardens and bars, open from about April to October daily from 11am to 8pm.

GARDEN RESTAURANT, in the Tokyo Prince Hotel, 3-3-1 Shibakoen. Tel. 3432-1111.

Cuisine: TEPPANYAKI. **Reservations:** Not required. **Station:** Kamiyacho or Onarimon (then a 5-minute walk) or Hammamatsucho (then a 10-minute walk).

$ **Prices:** Dishes ¥600–¥1,200 ($5.45–$10.90); set dinners ¥6,500, ¥7,500, and ¥10,000 ($59, $68.70, and $90.90). AE, DC, JCB, MC, V.

Open: May to mid-Sept, daily 5:30–9:30pm. **Closed:** Mid-Sept to Apr.

In a lovely garden setting, this lively beer garden offers three set dinner courses. The A course for ¥7,500 ($68.70) is all you can drink, teppanyaki steak, lamb, vegetables, sausages, soybeans, Chinese fried noodles, salad, and fruit. The B course is the same as the A, but Japanese steak is used. The C course is the same as the A, but with only one drink. Or you can order à la carte such dishes as yakitori, soybeans, and steak for ¥600 to ¥1,200 ($5.45 to $10.90). Beer starts at ¥750 ($6.80) and whiskey and cocktails run ¥700 to ¥1,000 ($6.36 to $9.10). I've seen this place crowded even in the pouring rain, with diners quite happy under the awnings.

HANEZAWA BEER GARDEN, 3-12-15 Hiro, Shibuya-ku. Tel. 3400-6500.

Cuisine: JAPANESE BARBECUE. **Reservations:** Required. **Station:** Ebisu, Omotesando, or Shibuya (then take a taxi).

$ **Prices:** Appetizers ¥440–¥750 ($4–$6.80); main dishes ¥5,000–¥6,000 ($45.45–$54.55). No credit cards.

Open: Apr–Sept, daily 5–9pm (last order). **Closed:** Oct–Mar.

This is a lovely place, one of my favorites for outdoor dining and drinks. A garden spread under trees and paper lanterns, it looks traditionally Japanese and serves sukiyaki, shabu-shabu, Mongolian barbecue that's cooked at your table, and a variety of snacks and other dishes. Note that if you want shabu-shabu or sukiyaki, however, you should notify the restaurant the day before. A mug of foaming beer costs ¥500–¥900 ($4.55–$8.20).

SUNTORY BEER GARDEN, on the rooftop of the Suntory Bldg., 1-2-3 Moto-Akasaka. Tel. 3401-4367.
Cuisine: JAPANESE BARBECUE. **Reservations:** Recommended. **Station:** Akasaka-mitsuke (then a one-minute walk).
$ Prices: Appetizers ¥500–¥700 ($4.55–$6.35); main dishes ¥1,300–¥2,400 ($11.80–$21.80). No credit cards.
Open: June–Aug, Mon–Sat 5–9pm (last order). **Closed:** Public hols and Sept–May.

With a great view of surrounding Akasaka, this rooftop beer garden is better and more sophisticated than most, with real palms and bushes circling the dining area instead of the usual plastic that seems to plague most beer gardens. Even more astounding, there's no Astroturf! In addition to its draft Suntory beer, which starts at ¥630 ($5.70) for a mug, it also offers a barbecue of sirloin, beef, or ram you grill at your own table, as well as the usual beer snacks listed on an English menu.

Purchase what you want from the ticket booth, sit down, and then hand the waiter your ticket.

DINING WITH A VIEW

There are so many tall hotels and skyscrapers in Tokyo that dining with a view is easy to come by. For a view of the Imperial Palace, head for the 10th floor of the Palace Hotel, where the **Crown Restaurant** offers elegant French dining against a dramatic backdrop.

In Shinjuku, restaurants on the upper floors of skyscrapers with views of the surrounding city include **Seryna,** serving shabu-shabu, sukiyaki, and teppanyaki; **Suehiro,** which also offers steaks, shabu-shabu, and sukiyaki; and the **Spaghetti Factory,** which offers more than 60 different kinds of pasta dishes and should prove a delight with kids.

Much closer to the ground is the **Garden Barbecue,** a teppanyaki restaurant featuring glass walls smack dab in the middle of the New Otani Hotel's 400-year-old garden.

LIGHT, CASUAL & FAST FOOD

There are **ramen (Chinese noodle) shops** all over Tokyo, easily recognizable by their red signs, flashing lights, and pictures of various dishes displayed by the front door. In addition to ramen you can also order gyoza (fried dumplings), fried noodles, and Chinese fast food. Since ramen shops are found on almost every corner in Tokyo, it seems pointless to single any out, but if you want specific addresses there is one in Roppongi that's easy to find. If you walk from Roppongi Crossing toward Tokyo Tower, within a minute there will be a ramen shop on your left at 3-14-10 Roppongi (tel. 3408-9190). Look for the red signs and pictures (outside by the door) of the various dishes served.

There are also many **obento** establishments throughout the city, usually tiny hole-in-the-walls selling take-out sushi or box meals. Every neighborhood has such places; train stations are another good place to look. You can also find take-out food at every department store food section, usually located in the basement.

COFFEE/TEA SHOPS

Tokyo has many fine coffee and tea shops, serving a variety of beverages and comestibles. The greatest concentration of sidewalk cafés is in fashionable Harajuku. Outdoor or indoor, these cafés—like cafés the world over—are great for people-watching. Some of the most popular are recommended below.

CAFE DE ROPE, 6-1-8 Jingumae. Tel. 3406-684.

Cuisine: COFFEE SHOP. **Station:** Meiji-Jingumae (then about a two-minute walk) or Harajuku (then a three-minute walk).

$ Prices: Coffee ¥600 ($5.45); beer from ¥650 ($5.90).

Open: Daily 11am–11pm.

Close to the Meiji–Omotesando Dori intersection, the oldest outdoor café in Harajuku has long been a place popular with Tokyo's "beautiful people." In the wintertime a plastic tarp and heaters keep the place in operation. In addition to beer, cocktails, and coffee, there are also cakes and sandwiches.

CAFE ORIENTAL WAVE, 5-17-13 Shinjuku. Tel. 3203-2881.

Cuisine: COFFEE SHOP. **Station:** Shinjuku-sanchome (then a five-minute walk) or Shinjuku (then a seven-minute walk).

$ Prices: Tea, coffee, cakes, ice cream, or desserts ¥600–¥1,000 ($5.45–$9.10). No credit cards.

Open: Daily 11am–11pm.

More than a Café Oriental Wave is a whole building of Oriental-style dining, with Rajini and Tokyo Daihanten, listed above, upstairs. The interior feels colonial with green silk moiré high-backed sofas; you'll be served from ultmate-design sugar bowls and teapots. Right on Yasukuni Dori, near the small street leading to Hanazono Jinja (shrine), it's a great place to watch people go by its glass front. To me this is what Tokyo, lacking in other cultural attractions, is all about—avant-garde design and interiors.

DEMEL, in the Quest Bldg., 1-13-12 Jingumae. Tel. 3478-1251.

Cuisine: COFFEE SHOP. **Station:** Meiji-Jingumae or Harajuku (then about a one-minute walk).

$ Prices: Coffee ¥1,000 ($9.10).

Open: Daily 11am–11pm.

In a relatively new building called Quest, you'll find the exclusive Demel, modeled after Vienna's famous coffee shop. It's not a sidewalk café, but if it's raining or you feel like splurging, come here for sinful desserts.

FAUCHON, 1-7-5 Azabu-Juban. Tel. 5474-2101.

Cuisine: TEA SHOP/EPICERIE. **Station:** Roppongi (then a 15-minute walk).

$ Prices: Tea and coffee ¥600 ($5.45); sandwiches and salads ¥700–¥1,000 ($6.35–$9.10). AE, JCB, V.

Open: Mon–Sat 10am–8pm, Sun and hols 10am–6pm.

When you can't live another minute without an authentic croissant (¥170/$1.55) or pain au raisin (¥150/$1.35) or café au lait (¥600/$5.45), head for this Tokyo branch of the famous Parisian épicerie. Tea lovers will be thrilled to know that your brew is served in the pot with a strainer and timer and you can choose from Earl Grey to the à la vanille to peppermint for ¥600 ($5.45). Sandwiches like croque-monsieur (served on pain de mie for ¥1,000/$9.10) are also offered, as are Fauchon chocolates, cookies, canned goods, pâté, and spices.

From Roppongi, head toward Tokyo Tower, turn right at the Roi Building down Torii-zaka (slope) and left at the first large cross street; Fauchon is on the second street on your right.

LAURA ASHLEY, on the fourth floor of Tokyu Honten, 2-24-1 Dogenzaka, Shibuya-ku. Tel. 3477-3111.

Cuisine: TEA. **Station:** Shibuya (then a five-minute walk).

$ Prices: Tea and coffee ¥700 ($6.35); high tea ¥1,500 ($13.65); sandwiches ¥600–¥1,200 ($5.45–$10.90).

Open: Wed–Mon 10am–6:30pm.

Laura Ashley–clad pinafored waitresses and Laura Ashley tablecloths and dishes set the mood for this tea room. Scones for ¥400 ($3.65) and cakes for ¥600 ($5.45) may be ordered with your tea or coffee, or go all out for the high tea, served with sandwiches, cakes, and scones. On the fourth floor of the main Tokyu department store, its next to Bunkamura—literally "culture village," a complex of museum, theaters, a bookstore, and shops.

DESSERTS

TATSUTANO, 7-8-7 Ginza. Tel. 3571-1850.

Cuisine: TRADITIONAL DESSERTS/KAMAMEISHI. **Station:** Ginza.

$ Prices: Desserts ¥700–¥800 ($6.35–$7.25); kamameishi ¥1,200 ($10.90). No credit cards.

Open: Daily noon–8pm.

If you'd like to try a traditional Japanese dessert, one place in Ginza is famous for anmitsu, which is beans, molasses, sweet-bean paste, and gelatin for ¥700 ($6.35). Across from the Matsuzakaya department store on Chuo Dori, this 100-year-old purveyor has two floors—the window seats upstairs are great for people-watching. Another traditional dessert, oshiruko, a hot sweet-bean porridge, costs ¥800 ($7.25). Downstairs are counters where you can order desserts to take home with you. If you're hungry for something more substantial, they serve reasonably priced kamameishi (rice caserole) for ¥1,200 ($10.90) and zosui (rice porridge) for ¥1,080 ($9.80).

BREAKFAST/BRUNCH

Sunday brunch is a favorite pastime of Tokyo's expatriate community, but it has caught on only in places where Westerners hang out—Tokyo's hotels and the cosmopolitan area of Aoyama. Below are some of the city's best brunch spots, all of which feature buffets.

AKASAKA

TEA LOUNGE, in the Capitol Tokyu Hotel, 2-10-3 Nagatacho. Tel. 3581-4511.

Reservations: Recommended Sat–Sun. **Station:** Kokkai Gijido-mae (then a one-minute walk).

$ Price: Breakfast ¥2,600 ($23.65) per person. AE, DC, JCB, MC, V.

Open: Breakfast Mon–Fri 7–10:30am, Sat–Sun 7am–noon.

Located just off the lobby with a view of a traditional Japanese garden, the Tea Lounge is casual and pleasant, with seating on sofas and overstuffed chairs.

TRADER VIC'S, in the New Otani Hotel, 4-1 Kioi-cho. Tel. 3265-4707.

Reservations: Recommended. **Station:** Akasaka-mitsuke (then a three-minute walk).

$ Prices: Brunch ¥6,000 ($54.55) per person. AE, DC, JCB, MC, V.

Open: Brunch Sun and hols 11:30am–2:30pm.

If you like champagne for breakfast, this is the place, since it includes as much as you want of the bubbly stuff in the price of its buffet. The spread here includes fresh fish, meats, salads, and desserts in addition to breakfast foods.

SHINJUKU

MARBLE LOUNGE, in the Tokyo Hilton International, 6-6-2 Nishi-Shinjuku. Tel. 3344-5111.

Reservations: Recommended Sun and hols. **Station:** Shinjuku, west exit (then a 10-minute walk).

$ Prices: Breakfast Mon–Sat ¥3,300 ($30); brunch Sun and hols ¥4,400 ($40). AE, DC, JCB, MC, V.

Open: Breakfast Mon–Sat 6:30–11am, Sun and hols 11am–2pm.

Dishes from the United States, Switzerland, Japan, and Indonesia are served in this Sunday buffet, including a German-Swiss porridge, a light stew of tofu with Japanese leeks, cheeses, croissants, omelets, bacon, hash-brown potatoes, and more. On other days, breakfast features waitress service.

HARAJUKU & AOYAMA

BRASSERIE D, on the second floor of the Suzuki Glass Bldg., 3-5-14 Kita Aoyama, Minato-ku. Tel. 3470-0203.

Reservations: Required. **Station:** Omotesando (then a two-minute walk).

$ Prices: Brunch ¥7,000 ($63.65) per person. AE, DC, JCB, MC, V.

Open: Brunch Sun and hols noon–2:30pm.

This restaurant serves a very reasonable Sunday brunch, giving you a choice of beer, wine, kir, or juice, and a choice of omelet, croque, or eggs Benedict. On the buffet table are a variety of salads, side dishes, and desserts. From the nearest subway station, Omotesando, as you walk toward Gaienmae, you'll find Brasserie D on the left side of Aoyama Dori Avenue.

LUNCHAN, 1-2-5 Shibuya. Tel. 5466-1398.

Cuisine: AMERICAN. **Reservations:** Recommended. **Station:** Omotesando (then a 7-minute walk) or Shibuya (then a 10-minute walk).

$ Prices: Brunch ¥2,500 ($22.70). AE, D, DC, JCB, MC, V.

Open: Brunch Sun 11am–3pm.

Lunchan, a combination of the words "lunch" and the affectionate Japanese *chan,* is the perfect light-and-airy place to have brunch. For ¥2,500 ($22.70) per person you can have your choice of a glass of champagne, mimosa, bloody Mary, or juice; muffin, danish, croissant, bagel, or toast; coffee or tea; and dishes such as eggs Benedict, spinach and mushroom omelet, smoked bagel plate, or Grand Slam pancakes. American chef David Chiddo has created original recipes for this trendy bistro.

L'ORANGERIE DE PARIS, on the fifth floor of the Hanae Mori Bldg., 3-6-1 Kita-Aoyama. Tel. 3407-7461.
Reservations: Required. **Station:** Omotesando (then a one-minute walk).
$ **Prices:** Brunch ¥4,000 ($36.35) per person. AE, DC, JCB, MC, V.
Open: Brunch Sun 11:30am–2:30pm.
This Sunday brunch seems to attract half the foreign population of Tokyo. A place to see and be seen, it's located on Omotesando Dori.

SPIRAL GARDEN, in the Spiral Bldg., 5-6-23 Minami Aoyama. Tel. 3498-5791.
Reservations: Recommended. **Station:** Omotesando (then a one-minute walk).
$ **Prices:** Brunch ¥3,500 ($31.20) per person. AE, DC, JCB, MC, V.
Open: Brunch Sun 11am–2pm.
Also in Omotesando but on the other side of Aoyama Dori Avenue, Spiral is in a beautifully designed white building that opened in 1985 and houses galleries, a concert hall and theater, a shop on the second floor that specializes in well-designed kitchenware and household gadgets, and several restaurants. Spiral Garden offers a brunch which includes a choice of cocktails and one egg dish and a trip to the buffet. My one complaint is that the eggs almost always arrive cold, but a consolation is the live classical music that accompanies you as you eat.

LATE NIGHT

Tokyo's nightlife districts are your best bet for a meal after midnight. In Shinjuku, **Irohanihoheto,** a popular student hangout serving inexpensive dishes and snacks, is open until 4am on weekend nights, while **Ban-Thai,** a Thai restaurant, is open until 1am every night of the week. In Roppongi, where the action goes on until dawn, good places for a late-night meal include **Inakaya,** a robatayaki open daily until 5am; **Bikkuri Sushi,** a conveyor-belt sushi bar open daily until 5am; the **Hard Rock Café,** serving American food on weekends until 4am; **Johnny Rockets,** an imitation '50s diner, serving great hamburgers and open on Saturday night until 5am; **Ramen Thai,** a ramen shop open until 4am Monday through Thursday and until 5am on Friday and Saturday; and **Samrat,** an Indian restaurant open daily until 5am.

PICNIC FARE & WHERE TO EAT IT

All department stores have food sections in their basements where you can buy precooked foods ready for take-out. Salads, chicken, pickled vegetables, fish, sushi, and a variety of Western and Japanese food are usually available, as well as fruit and drinks. Similarly, take-out counters throughout the city and at train stations sell obento lunchboxes, complete meals that include a main dish such as fish, along with side dishes ranging from rice to pickled vegetables.

The best place for a picnic in crowded Tokyo is at one of its large parks, including Ueno and Yoyogi Parks. Popular with families, they are especially crowded on weekends.

CHAPTER 6

WHAT TO SEE & DO IN TOKYO

Many Westerners grow up with a highly romanticized view of Japan, picturing it like a woodblock print—charming, mysterious, and ancient.

What a shock, then, to come to Tokyo. In a country known around the world for its appreciation of the aesthetic, Tokyo is disappointingly unimpressive. Some foreigners, unable to reconcile their unrealistic expectations with the cold facts of reality, summarily dismiss Tokyo as a monstrosity of the 20th century and go off in search of the "real" Japan. What they don't realize is that beneath Tokyo's concrete shell is a cultural life left very much intact.

In fact, Tokyo is the best place in the world for taking in Japan's performing arts such as Kabuki and such diverse activities as the tea ceremony and flower arranging.

SUGGESTED ITINERARIES

The one thing to remember in planning your sightseeing itinerary is that the city is huge and it takes time to get from one end to the other. Plan your days so you cover it neighborhood by neighborhood, coordinating sightseeing with dinner and evening plans. To help you get the most out of your stay, the suggested itineraries below will guide you to the most important attractions. Note, however, that some attractions are closed one day of the week, so plan your days accordingly. In addition, you must enter museums and gardens at least 30 minutes before closing time.

IF YOU HAVE ONE DAY Start by getting up in the wee hours of the morning (if you've just flown in from North America, you'll be suffering from jet lag anyway and will find yourself wide awake by 5am) and head for the Tsukiji Fish Market, Japan's largest wholesale fish market (closed Sunday and holidays). Be brave and try a breakfast of the freshest sushi you'll ever have. By 9am you should be on the Hibiya Line on your way to Ueno, where you should race to the Tokyo National Museum, the country's largest and most important museum (closed Monday). From there you should head to Asakusa for lunch in one of the area's traditional Japanese restaurants, followed by a walk on Nakamise Dori (good for souvenirs) to Sensoji Temple. In the afternoon you might want to go to Ginza for some shopping, followed by dinner in a restaurant of your choice.

IF YOU HAVE TWO DAYS Get up early in the morning of your first day to go to the Tsukiji Fish Market to eat sushi for breakfast.

? DID YOU KNOW . . . ?

- Tokyo has been the capital of Japan only since 1868; before that, Kyoto served as capital for more than 1,000 years.
- 10% of Japan's total population lives in Tokyo, 12 million residents.
- Tokyo's workers commute to work an average of 90 minutes one-way.
- Tokyo has some of the most expensive land in the world: In fashionable Aoyama near Harajuku, one square meter of commercial real estate costs about ¥16.5 million (about $150,000).
- Shinjuku Station handles the most train and subway passengers in all of Japan, more than one million people a day; more than 60 exits lead out of the station.
- Sunshine City, a 60-story skyscraper in Ikebukuro, is one of Japan's tallest buildings (790 ft.) and claims to have the fastest elevators in the world, whisking passengers to the top floor in 35 seconds.
- Tokyo Disneyland, which opened in 1983, is 1½ times larger than Disneyland in California and had received 129 million visitors by March 1993.

Next, head for the nearby Hama Rikyu Garden, which opens at 9am (closed Monday). It's about a 20-minute walk from Tsukiji or a short taxi ride away. After touring the gardens, board the ferry which departs directly from the garden for a trip up the Sumida River to Asakusa, where you can visit Sensoji Temple and shop along Nakamise Dori, followed by lunch in a traditional Japanese restaurant. If you'd like to spend several hours touring this older section of Tokyo, see Chapter 7 for a recommended walking tour of Asakusa.

By late afternoon you should try to be in Ginza, particularly if there's a Kabuki play being staged in Kabukiza theater (evening shows run from about 4:30 to 9pm). Otherwise, Ginza is good for shopping, art galleries, and restaurants. (See Chapter 7 for suggestions of things to do in Ginza, and Chapter 5 for a list of Ginza's restaurants.) After dinner, drop in on one of Ginza's bars or yakitori-ya locales.

Start the second day with a trip to Ueno, where you can spend the morning wandering through Ueno Park and visiting the Tokyo National Museum (described later in this chapter, and in the walking tour in Chapter 7). For lunch, board the Yamanote Line and go to Shinjuku Station, where on the west side are a number of tall skyscrapers with restaurants on their top floors, offering panoramic views of the city while you dine (see Chapter 5). After lunch, reboard the Yamanote Line and go two stations south to Harajuku, where you can visit Meiji Jingu Shrine, Tokyo's most famous Shinto shrine; the Ota Memorial Museum of Art with its collection of woodblock prints; and the Oriental Bazaar, a great shop for souvenirs (see the walking tour in Chapter 7). Devote the rest of your afternoon to shopping, visiting more museums, or other attractions. Spend the evening in one of Tokyo's famous nightlife districts such as Shinjuku or Roppongi.

IF YOU HAVE THREE DAYS Spend the first two days as outlined above. On the third day, head for Kamakura, one of Japan's most important historical sites. Located an hour south of Tokyo by train, Kamakura served as capital back in the 1100s and is packed with temples and shrines.

IF YOU HAVE FIVE DAYS OR MORE Consider yourself lucky. Spend the first three days as outlined above. Devote the fourth day to pursuing your own interests, such as visiting the Tokyo Stock Exchange, a trip to one of Tokyo's numerous specialty museums or a sumo stable, an appointment with an acupuncturist, shopping, or following one of the recommended walking tours outlined in Chapter 7. This may be the evening to spend in wild partying, staying out until the first subways start running at 5am (suggestions on where to party are given in Chapter 9).

On the fifth day, you might visit Nikko, approximately two hours north of Tokyo, to see the sumptuous mausoleum of Tokugawa Ieyasu, the shogun who succeeded in unifying Japan in the 1600s or you might consider a two-day trip to Hakone, famous for its open-air sculpture museum. Hakone also has some of the best old-fashioned Japanese inns near Tokyo, and if the weather is clear, it also offers great views of Mt. Fuji. See Chapter 10 for more excursions.

1. THE TOP ATTRACTIONS

Among Tokyo's many temples, shrines, and museums, the most important are Sensoji Temple, Meiji Jingu Shrine, and the Tokyo National Museum. Traditional entertainment, such as Kabuki or sumo wrestling, also ranks top among things to do in Tokyo.

THE TOP MUSEUM

TOKYO KOKURITSU HAKUBUTSUKAN (Tokyo National Museum), Ueno Park, Taito-ku. Tel. 3822-1111.

If you go to only one museum during your stay in Japan, the Tokyo National Museum should be it. Not only is it Japan's largest museum, it's also the largest repository of Japanese art in the world. It has a bit of everything and is the place to see antiques from Japan's past—old kimono, samurai armor, priceless swords, lacquerware, pottery, scrolls, screens, ukiyoe (woodblock prints), and more. Altogether the museum has about 86,000 items in its collections, including more than 10,000 paintings, 1,000 sculptures, 15,500 metalworks, 3,000 swords, 3,700 pieces of lacquerware, 27,000 archeological finds, and 7,500 works of foreign Eastern art. Needless to say, its collections are much too large to display all at once, so only about 4,000 items are shown at any one time and are changed on a rotating basis. No matter how many times you visit the museum you'll always see different things.

The museum encompasses four main buildings. The **Main Gallery (Honkan),** straight ahead as you enter the main gate, is the most important. Among the items to be found here are Buddhist sculptures dating from about 538 to 1192, armor and helmets, swords, textiles, ceramics from prehistoric times, paintings, calligraphy, and scrolls.

The **Gallery of Eastern Antiquities (Toyokan)** houses art and archeological artifacts from Asian countries outside Japan: Egyptian relics, stone reliefs from Cambodia, embroidered wall hangings and cloth from India, Korean bronze and celadon, Buddhas from Pakistan, Thai and Vietnamese ceramics, and Chinese art, including jade, glass, stone reliefs, paintings, calligraphy, mirrors, lacquerware, ceramics, and bronzes.

The **Hyokeikan Gallery** contains archeological relics of Japan,

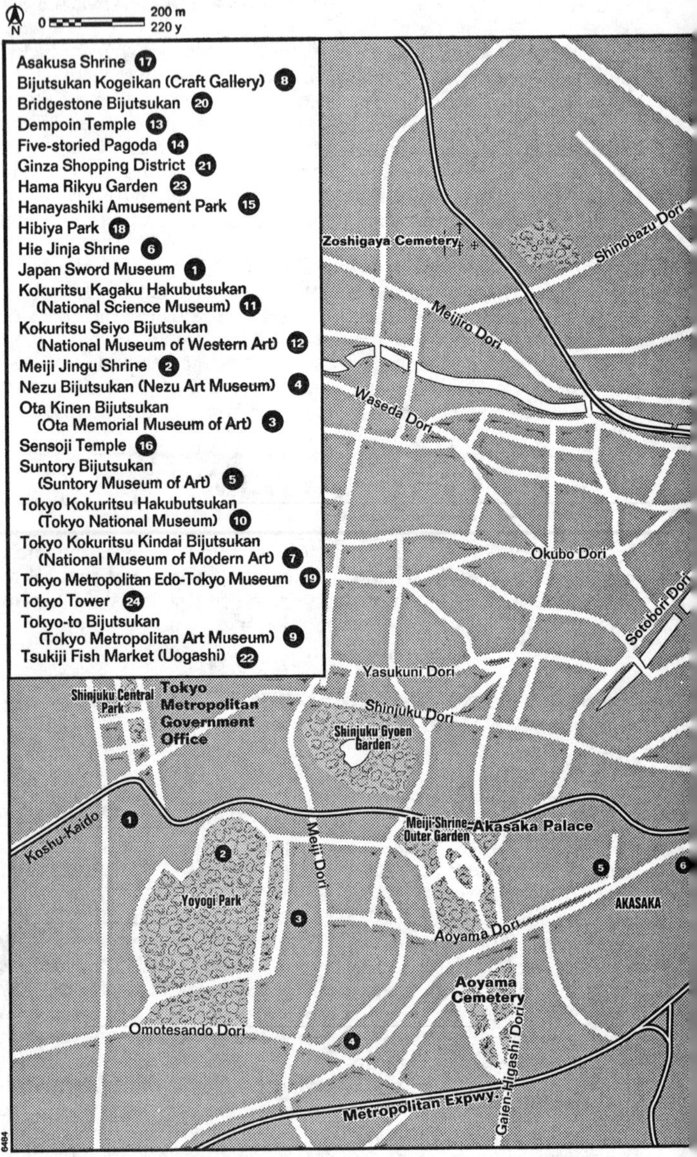

including pottery and objects recovered from ancient burial mounds. One room is devoted to items used in daily life by the Ainu, an indigenous ethnic group native to Japan's northern island of Hokkaido.

The fourth building is the **Gallery of Horyuji Treasures,** which houses treasures from the Horyuji Temple in Nara, including gilt bronze Buddhist statuettes, religious objects, and paintings. This building is open only on Thursday, and only then if the weather is dry, since wet weather would damage the fragile contents inside.

Admission: ¥400 ($3.65).

TOKYO ATTRACTIONS

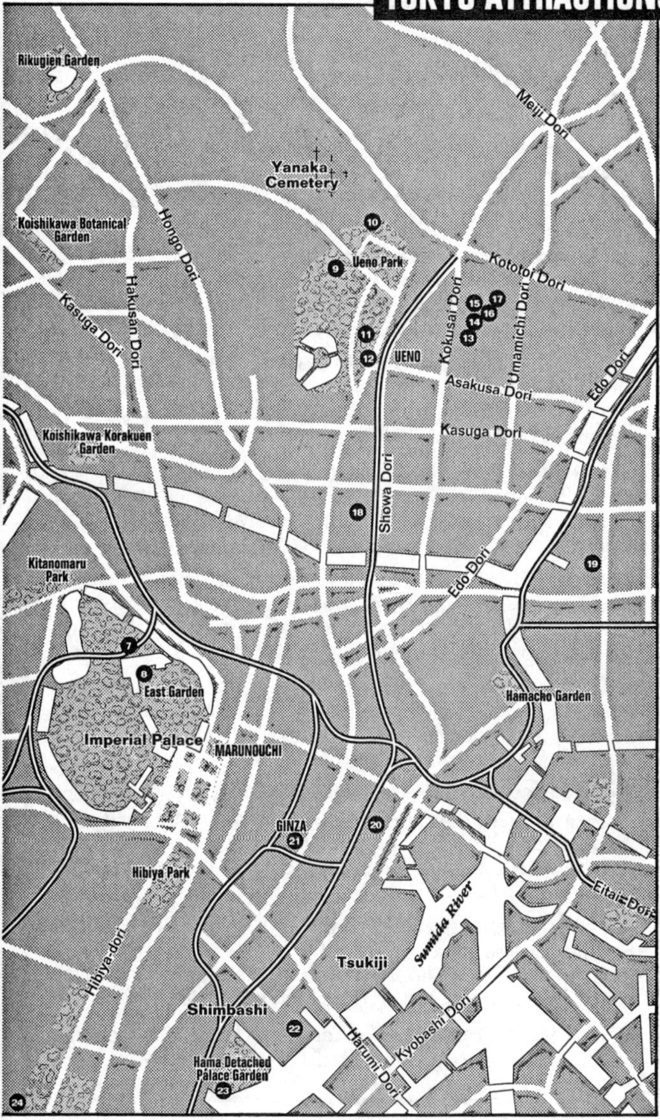

Open: Tues–Sun 9am–4:30pm (you must enter by 4pm). **Station:** Ueno (then about a seven-minute walk).

TEMPLES & SHRINES

MEIJI JINGU SHRINE, 1-1 Kamizonocho, Yoyogi, Shibuya-ku. Tel. 3379-5511.

Although it dates only from this century, Meiji Jingu Shrine is Tokyo's most venerable Shinto shrine. It was built in 1920 in honor of Emperor and Empress Meiji, who are credited with

FROMMER'S FAVORITE TOKYO EXPERIENCES

A Stroll Through Asakusa to Sensoji Temple More than any other place in Tokyo, Sensoji Temple and surrounding Asakusa convey a feeling of old Tokyo.

An Evening in a Yakitori-ya There's no better place to observe Tokyo's army of office workers at play than at a yakitori-ya, a drinking establishment that serves skewered foods and bar snacks. Fun, noisy, and boisterous.

A Kabuki Play at the Kabukiza Theater Watch the audience as they yell their approval; watch the stage for its gorgeous costumes, stunning stage settings, and easy-to-understand dramas of love, duty, and revenge.

Sunday in Harajuku Start with a Sunday brunch; then stroll Omotesando Dori Avenue to where young musicians, dancers, and performers entertain the crowds. Visit Meiji Jingu Shrine, shop the boutiques, and relax at a café.

Tsukiji Fish Market This is Japan's largest fish market, where tuna, salmon, shrimp, squid, octopus, and other creatures from the deep are sold wholesale. The best part of the action is from 4 to 8am; the earlier you get there, the better.

A Day of Sumo Nothing beats watching huge sumo wrestlers, most weighing well over 200 pounds, throw each other around. Matches are held in Tokyo in January, May, and September. Great fun and not to be missed.

Department Store Shopping Tokyo's department stores are cities in themselves—huge, spotless, and filled with more merchandise than you've ever seen in one spot. Seibu in Ikebukuro is the city's largest; the greatest concentration of stores is in Shibuya.

A Spin Through Kabuki-cho Shinjuku's Kabuki-cho has the craziest nightlife in all of Tokyo, with countless strip joints, pornography shops, restaurants, bars, and the greatest concentration of neon you're likely to see anywhere.

Clubs in Roppongi You can party the night away in the madness of Roppongi; most revelers party until dawn.

introducing Japan to the modern age by ushering in the Industrial Revolution. The pathway to the shrine leads through a forest of trees and shrubs, donated by people from throughout the country, and past two large torii built of cypress wood more than 1,700 years old. Meiji Jingu Shrine is *the* place to be on New Year's Eve, when more than two million crowd onto the shrine's grounds to usher in the new year. Note how restrained and simple the architecture of the shrine is—a marked contrast to colorful Sensoji Temple. More information is given in Chapter 7.

Admission: Free.

Open: Daily 9am–5pm (to 4:30pm in winter). **Station:** Harajuku (then a two-minute walk).

SENSOJI TEMPLE, 2-3-1 Asakusa, Taito-ku. Tel. 3842-0181.

No temple in Tokyo is more popular, loved, and visited than Sensoji Temple, the city's oldest temple, also known as the Asakusa Kannon Temple. Founded in A.D. 628, it was destroyed during an air raid in 1945 and rebuilt in 1958. According to popular lore, the temple was erected to enshrine a tiny golden statue of Kannon that was fished out of the nearby Sumida River by two brothers. Kannon is the Buddhist goddess of mercy and happiness and is empowered with the ability to release humans from suffering. Although the statue is still housed in Sensoji Temple, it is never shown to the public. And yet worshippers still flock here, to seek favors of Kannon and to shop at the traditional shops and souvenir stalls that line colorful Nakamise Dori. All in all, a visit to Sensoji Temple and Asakusa is something no visitor to Tokyo should miss. For more information on Sensoji Temple, see the walking tour of Asakusa, described in Chapter 7.

Admission: Free.

Open: Daily 9am–5pm (to 4:30pm in winter). **Station:** Asakusa (then a few minutes walk).

PARKS & GARDENS

In a traditional Japanese landscape garden, nothing is left to chance. Rather, everything from the shape of hills, trees, and bushes to the placement of rocks and waterfalls is skillfully arranged by the gardener in a faithful reproduction of nature, in the belief that even nature can be improved upon. Basically there are three styles of Japanese gardens. The most common uses ponds, hills, and streams to depict nature in miniature. Another uses stones and raked sand or gravel instead of water and is often seen at Zen Buddhist temples. The third style emerged with the tea ceremony and is built around a teahouse with an eye toward simplicity and tranquility.

HAMA RIKYU GARDEN, 1-1 Hamarikyuteien, Chuo-ku. Tel. 3541-0200.

Considered by some to be the best garden in Tokyo, this was once the site of a villa of a former feudal lord where the Tokugawa shoguns practiced falconry. In 1871 possession of the garden passed to the imperial family, and it was opened to the public after World War II. Come here to see how the upper classes enjoyed themselves during the Edo Period. Surrounded by water on three sides, it contains an inner tidal pool, spanned by three bridges draped with wisteria. There are also other ponds, a promenade along the river lined with pine trees, moon-viewing pavilions, and teahouses. Ferries depart from a boarding pier inside the garden's grounds for Asakusa every hour or so between 10:25am (10:15am on weekends and holidays) and 4:05pm; the fare is ¥520 ($4.70) one-way.

Admission: ¥200 ($1.80).

Open: Tues–Sun 9am–4:30pm. **Station:** Shimbashi (then a 10-minute walk).

HIGASHI GYOEN (East Garden), 1-1 Chiyoda, Chiyoda-ku. Tel. 3213-2050.

Located just east of the Imperial Palace, the 53 acres of this formal garden are all that remain of the once-mighty Edo Castle, the stone foundation of which can still be seen on the grounds of the garden. A pleasant and peaceful oasis right in the heart of the city, the garden contains sculpted bushes and a pond framed with wisteria. Since there isn't much to see of the Imperial Palace itself (as home of the imperial family, it's closed to the public), the best thing to do is take a snapshot of the palace from the moat and then visit the garden.

Admission: Free.

Open: Tues–Thurs and Sat–Sun 9am–4pm (you must enter by 3pm). **Station:** Otemachi, Takebashi, or Nijubashi-mae.

SHINJUKU GYOEN, 11 Naitocho, Shinjuku-ku. Tel. 3350-0151.

Whenever the weather turns warm and I have only a few hours to spare, this is where I usually go. Conveniently located in the center of the city, it was formerly the private estate of a feudal lord and then of the imperial family. Its 144 acres make for a wonderful park for strolling, because there are various types of planted gardens ranging from French and English style to Japanese traditional. Walking through this park, one of the city's largest, is like visiting the gardens of several countries.

Admission: ¥160 ($1.45).

Open: Tues–Sun 9am–4:30pm (enter before 4pm). **Station:** Shinjuku Gyoenmae (then a two-minute walk).

UENO PARK, Taito-ku.

Opened in 1873, Ueno Park was the capital's first public park and the site of the nation's first museum and zoo. Today it's one of the largest parks in Tokyo and serves as a cultural mecca with a number of museums, including the Tokyo National Museum, the delightful Shitamachi Museum with its displays of old Tokyo, Ueno Zoo, and Shinobazu Pond, a bird sanctuary. One of the most popular destinations for Japanese families on an outing, it is also Tokyo's most popular viewing spot during the cherry blossom season.

Admission: Park, free; separate admissions to each of its attractions.

Open: Park, daily 24 hours. **Station:** Ueno (then a minute's walk).

2. MORE ATTRACTIONS

TSUKIJI FISH MARKET (UOGASHI)

This huge fish market is Japan's largest, not surprising when you consider that 12 million people live in Tokyo and that the average Japanese eats 80 pounds of seafood a year. The action at Tsukiji Fish Market starts early, around 3am with the arrival of boats from the seas of Japan, from Africa, and even from the waters of North America, laden with enough fish to satisfy the demands of a nation where seafood reigns supreme. The king is tuna, huge and frozen, which is laid out in rows on the ground and numbered. Wholesalers then walk up and down, inspecting the tuna with flashlights and jotting down the numbers of the best-looking ones. By 6am the auctions are well under way, after which the wholesalers transfer their purchases to their own stalls in the market, which they subsequently sell to their regular customers, usually retail stores and restaurants.

The market takes place in a cavernous hangarlike covered building, which means that you can visit it even on a dismal rainy morning.

The wholesale stalls seem to stretch forever, selling salmon, shrimp, mackerel, tuna, sardine, squid, octopus, sea urchin, and countless other varieties of fish. There's a lot going on—men in black rubber boots rushing wheelbarrows and carts through the aisles, hawkers shouting, knives chopping and slicing. This is a good place to bring your camera, but keep clear of the workers as they rush through their jobs, and because the floors are wet, leave your fancy shoes at the hotel.

As you might imagine, this market offers some of the freshest seafood anywhere, making it a good place for a breakfast of sushi. Beside the covered market are rows of barracklike buildings divided into sushi restaurants and shops relating to the fish trade. Sushi Dai (see the Tsukiji section of Chapter 5) offers a seto for ¥2,000 ($18.20).

Admission: Free.

Open: Mon–Sat 3–10am (but the best hours are 4–8am). **Closed:** Hols, New Year's, and Aug 15–16. **Directions:** To reach the fish market, take the Hibiya Line to Tsukiji Station and go out the Honganji Temple exit. Walk along Shin Ohashi Dori, past the modern-looking temple on the left-hand side, cross Harumi Dori, and continue walking on Shin Ohashi under the covered storefronts. Take the first left, and then turn right when you reach the small shrine and walk over the bridge. The market is about a seven-minute walk from the station.

TOKYO STOCK EXCHANGE, 2-1 Nihonbashi-Kabutocho, Chuo-ku. Tel. 3666-0141.

Established in 1878, the Tokyo Stock Exchange now vies with that of New York as one of the busiest in the world. Located in the Nihombashi/Kyobashi district, a commercial area even during the Edo Period, it boasts a fine visitors' center, with a glass-enclosed observation deck from which to watch the frenetic activity on the trading floor. An excellent learning center called Exhibition Plaza has a number of audiovisual displays to enhance the visitor's knowledge of securities and the stock market, with explanations in English. A three-dimensional display, for example, explains the intricacies of what takes place on the trading floor, while a robot demonstrates the various hand signals used by the traders. Computers simulate the actual experience of investing in stock by leading the visitor through various procedures. On the ground floor is a history hall tracing the development of the Japanese securities market.

You can visit on your own, but if you wish to learn more about the exchange there's a free one-hour English-language tour offered Monday through Friday at 1:30pm, but you must reserve in advance.

Admission: Free.

Open: Mon–Fri 9am–4pm. **Closed:** National hols. **Station:** Kayabacho, Exit 11, or Nihombashi, Exit A2 (both a five-minute walk).

MUSEUMS

Note that most museums are closed on Monday and the first three days of the New Year. If Monday happens to be a national holiday, however, most museums will remain open but will close the next day, Tuesday, instead. Call beforehand to avoid disappointment. And remember, you must enter museums at least 30 minutes before the actual closing time.

Though obviously corporate image tools and customer magnets

(and therefore at odds with the real function of museums), don't under estimate the importance of Japanese department store museums and galleries. In Tokyo, 6 of 13 main department stores have museums and all but two have galleries. Combined exhibitions draw 600,000 visitors a year. A 1993 Dalí exhibition at Mitsukoshi drew 250,000 in 35 days compared to the annual attendance rate of 220,000 at the Tokyo National Museum of Modern Art. Also, department stores usually have more to spend than public-endowed museums. When I lived in Tokyo, I made a habit of combining shopping with gallery visits. (Check the *Tokyo Journal* for current exhibitions.)

MUSEUMS OF THE ARTS

BRIDGESTONE BIJUTSUKAN [Bridgestone Museum of Art], on the second floor of the Bridgestone Bldg., 1-10-1 Kyobashi, Chuo-ku. Tel. 3563-0241.

On view at this privately owned museum are changing exhibitions, as well as a collection of French impressionist art and Japanese paintings in the Western style.

Admission: ¥500 ($4.55) adults, ¥400 ($3.65) students, ¥200 ($1.80) children 6–11, free for children under 6.

Open: Tues–Sun 10am–5pm (enter before 5:30pm). **Closed:** During exhibit changes. **Station:** Halfway between Kyobashi and Nihombashi, on Chuo Dori Avenue.

GOTO BIJUTSUKAN [Goto Art Museum], 3-9-25 Kaminoge, Setagaya-ku. Tel. 3703-0661.

This museum houses fine arts and crafts of ancient Japan, China, and other Asian countries, including calligraphy, paintings, ceramics, and lacquerware. Surrounding the museum is a garden with a teahouse.

Admission: ¥500 ($4.55) and up adults, ¥350 ($3.20) students and children 6–11, free for children under 6.

Open: Tues–Sun 9:30am–4:30pm (enter before 4pm). **Closed:** During exhibit changes. **Station:** Kaminoge.

HARA BIJUTSUKAN [Hara Museum of Contemporary Art], 4-7-25 Kita-Shinagawa, Shinagawa-ku. Tel. 3445-0651.

Devoted to contemporary international and Japanese art, this pleasant museum is housed in a Bauhaus-style, art deco building that used to be the Hara family home. The building itself would be worth the trip, and its collection, internationally respected, includes work by most major postwar Western artists and probably every postwar Japanese artist. Highly recommended.

Admission: ¥700 ($6.35) adults, ¥500 ($4.55) students and children 6–11, free for children under 6.

Open: Tues–Sun 11am–5pm. **Station:** Shinagawa (then by taxi).

KOKURITSU SEIYO BIJUTSUKAN [National Museum of Western Art], Ueno Park, Taito-ku. Tel. 3828-5131.

With a main building designed by Le Corbusier, this museum features Western art, with a concentration on works from the late 19th century, including French impressionism. Artists include Renoir, Monet, Sisley, Manet, Delacroix, Cézanne, Degas, El Greco, and Goya, though there are far better collections in Europe. The museum is perhaps most famous for its 50-odd sculptures by Rodin, the third-largest Rodin collection in the world. There are also special exhibits, for which an additional admission is charged.

Admission: ¥400 ($3.65) adults, ¥130 ($1.20) students, ¥70 (65¢) children 6–11, free for children under 6.

Open: Tues–Sun 9:30am–5pm (enter before 4:30pm). **Station:** Ueno (then a five-minute walk).

NEZU BIJUTSUKAN [Nezu Art Museum], 6-5-36 Minami Aoyama, Minato-ku. Tel. 3400-2536.

This museum houses a fine collection of Asian art, including Chinese bronzes, Japanese calligraphy, Korean ceramics, and other artwork. The museum is surrounded by a delightful small garden with several teahouses.

Admission: ¥1,000 ($9.10) adults, ¥700 ($6.35) students and children 6–11, free for children under 6.

Open: Tues–Sun 9:30am–4:30pm. **Closed:** The day following hols, during exhibition changes, and Aug. **Station:** Omotesando (then a 10-minute walk).

OTA KINEN BIJUTSUKAN [Ota Memorial Museum of Art], 1-10-10 Jingumae, Shibuya-ku. Tel. 3403-0880.

This great museum features the private ukiyoe (woodblock print) collection of the late Ota Seizo, who early in life recognized the importance of ukiyoe as an art form and dedicated his life to its preservation. Exhibitions of the museum's 12,000 prints are changed monthly, with descriptions of the displays in English. The museum itself is small but delightful, with such traditional touches as bamboo screens, stone pathways, and even a small tearoom which sells Japanese sweets.

Admission: ¥500–¥800 ($4.55–$7.25) adults, ¥250–¥600 ($2.25–$5.45) students and children 6–11, free for children under 6.

Open: Tues–Sun 10:30am–5:30pm. **Closed:** From the 24th to the end of every month. **Station:** Harajuku or Meiji Jingumae (then a two-minute walk).

SUNTORY BIJUTSUKAN [Suntory Museum of Art], on the 11th floor of the Suntory Bldg., 1-2-3 Moto-Akasaka, Minato-ku. Tel. 3470-1073.

Exhibitions change regularly, and may feature ceramics, screens, glass objects, lacquerware, paintings, or prints, on loan from other museums and collections from around the world.

Admission: ¥900–¥1,000 ($8.20–$9.10) adults, ¥500–¥600 ($4.55–$5.45) students, ¥200–¥300 ($1.80–$2.75) children 6–11, free for children under 6.

Open: Tues–Thurs and Sat–Sun 10am–5pm, Fri 10am–7pm. **Closed:** During exhibit changes. **Station:** Akasaka-mitsuke (then a one-minute walk).

TOKYO KOKURITSU KINDAI BIJUTSUKAN [National Museum of Modern Art], Kitanomaru Koen Park, Chiyoda-ku. Tel. 3214-2561.

This is Japan's best display of modern Japanese art, including paintings, sculpture, prints, watercolors, and drawings, dating from the Meiji Period onward. A few Western artists are also represented.

Admission: ¥400 ($3.65) adults, ¥130 ($1.20) students, ¥70 (65¢) children 6–11, free for children under 6.

Open: Tues–Sun 10am–5pm (enter before 4:30pm). **Station:** Takebashi (then less than a five-minute walk).

TOKYO-TO BIJUTSUKAN [Tokyo Metropolitan Art Museum], Ueno Park, Taito-ku. Tel. 3823-6921.

This museum features modern Japanese works, mainly by 20th-century artists, with temporary exhibitions, as well as changing exhibits of amateur work organized on a local level.

Admission: ¥500–¥800 ($4.55–$7.25).

Open: Tues–Sun 9am–5pm (enter by 4pm). **Closed:** During exhibit changes. **Station:** Ueno (then about a six-minute walk).

SPECIALIZED MUSEUMS

BIJUTSUKAN KOGEIKAN [Crafts Gallery], Kitanomaru Koen Park, Chiyoda-ku. Tel. 3211-7781.

Housed in a Gothic-style brick building constructed in 1910 as headquarters of the Imperial Guard, the Crafts Gallery collects the finest in contemporary crafts, including lacquerware, metalwork, ceramics, textiles, bamboo works, and dolls, which it shows in rotating exhibitions.

Admission: ¥400–¥700 ($3.65–$6.35) adults, ¥130–¥250 ($1.20–$2.25) students, ¥70 (65¢) children 6–11, free for children under 6; more for special exhibits.

Open: Tues–Sun 10am–5pm (enter before 4:30pm). **Station:** Takebashi (then a 10-minute walk).

DAIMYO TOKEI HAKUBUTSUKAN [Daimyo Clock Museum], 2-1-27 Yanaka, Taito-ku. Tel. 3821-6913.

This small museum displays about 50 clocks and watches drawn from its extensive collection of clocks made during the Edo Period, from huge freestanding clocks to small watches that were attached to *obi* (the sash worn with a kimono). Displays change annually.

Admission: ¥300 ($2.75) adults, ¥200 ($1.80) students, ¥100 (65¢) children 6–11, free for children under 6.

Open: Tues–Sun 10am–4pm. **Closed:** July–Sept and Dec 25–Jan 15. **Station:** Nezu (then a 10-minute walk).

FUKAGAWA EDO SHIRYOKAN [Fukagawa Edo Museum], 1-3-28 Shirakawa, Koto-ku. Tel. 3630-8625.

This delightful museum is a reproduction of a 19th-century neighborhood in Fukagawa, a prosperous community on the east bank of the Sumida River during the Edo Period. The hangarlike interior contains an entire neighborhood—11 houses, vegetable and rice shops, a fish store, two inns, and tenement homes. There are lots of small touches and flourishes to make the community seem real and believable—a cat sleeping on a roof, a snail crawling up a fence, a dog relieving itself on a pole, and sounds of birds, a vendor shouting his wares, horse hooves clattering, and a dog barking. Of Tokyo's museums, children would probably like this one best.

Admission: ¥300 ($2.75) adults, ¥50 (45¢) children 6–11, free for children under 6.

Open: Daily 10am–5pm. **Station:** Monzen-Nakacho or Morishita (then a 15-minute walk, or from both stations, bus no. 33 toward Kiyosumi Garden to the Kiyosumi Teien-mae bus stop).

HATAKEYAMA KINENKAN [Hatakeyama Memorial Museum], 2-20-12 Shiroganedai, Minato-ku. Tel. 3447-5787.

This museum's emphasis is on tea-ceremony ceramics and other objects, but it also has paintings, calligraphy, sculpture, and lacquerware from ancient Japan and China.

Admission: ¥500 ($4.55) adults, ¥350 ($3.20) students and children 6–11, free for children under 6.

Open: Apr–Sept, Tues–Sun 10am–5pm; Oct–Mar, Tues–Sun 10am–4:30pm. **Closed:** Last two weeks in Mar, June, Sept, and Dec, and first week in Jan. **Station:** Takanawadai (then a six-minute walk).

KAGU NO HAKUBUTSUKAN [Furniture Museum], on the second floor of the JFC Bldg., 3-10 Harumi, Chuo-ku. Tel. 3533-0098.

Traditional Japanese furniture is preserved and displayed, as well as some antique European furniture.

Admission: ¥400 ($3.65) adults, ¥200 ($1.80) children 6–11, free for children under 6.

Open: Thurs–Tues 10am–4:30pm. **Closed:** Hols. **Station:** Tsukiji or Ginza (then by taxi).

KAMI NO HAKUBUTSUKAN [Paper Museum], 1-1-8 Horifune, Kita-ku. Tel. 3911-3545.

For enthusiasts of traditional Japanese paper, this museum displays products and utensils used in making Japanese paper by hand.

Admission: ¥200 ($1.80) adults, ¥100 (90¢) children 6–11, free for children under 6.

Open: Tues–Sun 9:30am–4:30pm. **Closed:** Hols. **Station:** Oji, across from the south exit.

KOKURITSU KAGAKU HAKUBUTSUKAN [National Science Museum], Ueno Park, Taito-ku. Tel. 3822-0111.

This sprawling complex covers everything from the evolution of life to electronics in Japan, aircraft, and automobiles. Unfortunately not all displays are in English, but the museum is worth visiting for its exhibits relating to Japan, including its displays on the origin and development of the Japanese people, examples of Japanese architecture (no nails were used to join heavy wooden beams), the process of making Japanese lacquerware and paper, a Zero fighter plane from World War II, and an excellent collection of antique Japanese clocks.

Admission: ¥400 ($3.65) adults, ¥70 (65¢) children 6–11, free for children under 6.

Open: Tues–Sun 9am–4:30pm (enter by 4pm). **Station:** Ueno (then about a five-minute walk).

NIPPON MINGEIKAN [Japan Folk Crafts Museum], 4-3-33 Komaba, Meguro-ku. Tel. 3467-4527.

Folk art gathered from around Japan is displayed in this very special museum, including furniture, pottery, and textiles, many dating from the Edo and Meiji eras. Crafts from other Asian and European countries are also on display.

Admission: ¥1,000 ($9.10) adults, ¥500 ($4.55) students, ¥200 ($1.80) children 6–11, free for children under 6.

Open: Tues–Sun 10am–5pm. **Station:** Komaba-Todaimae Station on the Keio-Inokashira Line (then a five-minute walk).

REKIHAKU [National Museum of Japanese History], 117 Jonai-cho, Sakura, Chiba Prefecture. Tel. 043/486-0120.

Although outside of Tokyo and a 70-minute trip away, I've included this museum on a reader recommendation. It's located in the beautiful Sakura Castle Park, where the home of Lord Hotta, an important shogun, once stood. The museum is divided into four galleries showing, respectively, the Paleolithic Era to the Nara Period, the Heian to Azuchi-Momoyama Periods, the Edo Period, and traditional popular culture including Awa puppet heads and fishing gear. In the special exhibit galleries are displayed one-tenth-size models of structures designated "national treasures" or "important cultural assets."

Admission: ¥400 ($3.65) adults, ¥250 ($2.25) high school and college students, ¥110 ($1) children 6–11, free for children under 6.

Open: Tues–Sun 9:30am–4:30pm (enter by 4pm). **Station:** Keisei Sakura on the Keisei Line (then a 15-minute walk) or Sakura on the JR Sobu Line (then a 15-minute bus ride).

SHITAMACHI FUZOKU SHIRYOKAN [Shitamachi Museum], Ueno Park, Taito-ku. Tel. 3823-7451.

Shitamachi means "downtown" and refers to the area of Tokyo in which commoners used to live, mainly around Ueno and Asakusa. There's very little left of old downtown Tokyo, and with that in mind, this museum seeks to preserve for future generations a way of life that was virtually wiped out by the great earthquake of 1923 and then by World War II. There are shops set up as they may have looked back then, including a merchant's shop and a candy shop, as well as a Shitamachi tenement house that was common at the turn of the century. A long narrow building with one roof over a series of dwelling units separated by thin wooden walls, these were the homes of the poorer people, confined to the narrow back alleys. Everyone knew everyone else's business—few secrets could be kept in such crowded conditions as these. The alleyways served as communal living rooms. Children played in them and families sat outside to catch whatever breeze there might be. The museum also displays relics relating to the life of these people, including utensils, toys, costumes, and tools, most of which are not behind glass but are simply lying around so that you can pick them up and examine them more closely. The museum's collections were all donated by individuals, many living in Shitamachi.

Admission: ¥200 ($1.80) adults, ¥100 (90¢) children 6–11, free for children under 6.

Open: Tues–Sun 9:30am–4:30pm. **Station:** Ueno (then about a three-minute walk).

SUGINO GAKUEN ISHO HAKUBUTSUKAN [Sugino Costume Museum], 4-6-19 Osaki, Shinagawa-ku. Tel. 3491-8151.

Clothing of western Europe from around the 18th century, as well as clothing worn in Japan and other Asian countries, is displayed. Included are kimonos, samurai outfits, and costumes worn in Noh dramas and the comic kyogen plays that accompany them.

Admission: ¥200 ($1.80) adults, ¥100 (90¢) children 6–11, free for children under 6.

Open: Mon–Sat 10am–4pm. **Closed:** Hols. **Station:** Meguro (then a seven-minute walk).

SUMO HAKUBUTSUKAN [Sumo Museum], 1-3-28 Yokoami, Sumida-ku. Tel. 3622-0366.

Located in the Kokugikan sumo stadium, it shows the history of sumo since the 18th century, with portraits and mementos of past grand champions.

Admission: Free, but during tournaments you must have sumo tickets to enter the stadium.

Open: Mon–Fri 9:30am–4:30pm. **Closed:** Hols. **Station:** Ryogoku (then a one-minute walk).

TAKO NO HAKUBUTSUKAN [Kite Museum], on the fifth floor of the Taimeiken Bldg., 1-12-10 Nihombashi, Chuo-ku. Tel. 3275-2704.

Kites from countries around the world are on display, including Japan, Brazil, Indonesia, and Malaysia. It's located behind the Nihombashi Tokyu department store.

Admission: ¥200 ($1.80) adults, ¥100 (90¢) children 6–11, free for children under 6.

Open: Mon–Sat 11am–5pm. **Closed:** Hols. **Station:** Nihombashi (then a three-minute walk).

TOKEN HAKUBUTSUKAN [Sword Museum], 4-25-10 Yoyogi, Sumi-da-ku. Tel. 3379-1386.

This museum pays tribute to Japanese swords, with more than 6,000 in its collection. Considered by the Japanese to embody spirits all their own, Japanese swords rank as an art form in the highest degree, and in feudal Japan swordmakers were respected masters.

Admission: ¥515 ($4.70) adults, free for children under 11.

Open: Tues–Sun 9am–4pm. **Station:** Sangubashi, on the Odakyu Line.

TOKYO METROPOLITAN EDO-TOKYO MUSEUM, 1-4-1 Yokoami, Sumida. Tel. 3626-8000.

Located in the heart of Shitamachi (downtown) in a modern, 10-years-in-the-making, very abstract *kura* (rice granary) with an outside escalator (an idea obviously ripped off from Paris's Centre Georges-Pompidou), the Tokyo Metropolitan Edo-Tokyo Museum, opened in mid-1993, is the metropolitan government's too ambitous attempt to present the history, art, disasters, science—everything—of Tokyo from its beginnings to the present. Enter the museum by crossing over a replica of Nihonbashi Bridge; on opposite sides are the Edo and Tokyo zones. Edo, the old name for Tokyo, was the capital of the shoguns from 1603 until 1868. Here the life of shoguns, merchants, and craftspeople is displayed. On the Tokyo side the rapid advances after the Meiji Restoration, the Great Kanto Earthquake, and the bombing raids of World War II are presented. The museum is not limited to display cases; entire reconstructed buildings, scaled-down dioramas, and video presentations are also offered. The museum has collected more than 170,000 items (43% were donated by Tokyoites), but some 90% of the permanent collection cannot be displayed "due to lack of space" despite the seven floors. There's a video library in the basement, which includes 26 English-language videos on topics ranging from folklore to fine arts. From the ticket vendor you can rent a cordless headset for a ¥3,000 ($27.25) refundable deposit for narration in English.

Admission: ¥500 ($4.55) adults, ¥250 ($2.25) students through high school, free for children under 6.

Open: Tues–Thurs and Sat–Sun 10am–6pm, Fri 10am–9pm. **Station:** Ryogoku, on the JR Sobu Line (then a three-minute walk).

SHOWROOMS

AMLUX TOYOTA AUTO SALON, 3-3-5 Higashi-Ikebukuro, Toshima-ku. Tel. 5391-5900.

This is one of the largest automobile showrooms, with five floors of exhibition space boasting the newest of the new. More than 60 cars are on display, from sports cars and racing cars to luxury cars, all open so that potential customers can put themselves in the driver's seat and fidget with the dials. Educational programs include a movie showing the assembly process (viewers wear 3-D glasses to get the full effect), as well as a display using holograms to show what goes into making a car. It's located across from Sunshine City (Tokyo's tallest skyscraper) and Tokyu Hands department store.

Admission: Free.

Open: Tues–Sat 11am–8pm, Sun and hols 10am–7:30pm. **Station:** Ikebukuro, east exit (then a 10-minute walk), or Higashi-Ikebukuro (then a 3-minute walk).

SONY BUILDING, 5-3-1 Ginza. Tel. 3573-2371.

This was one of the first company showrooms in Tokyo and has long been popular as a meeting place for Tokyoites in the Ginza. Showrooms on almost every floor show the latest in Sony products, most touchable, from the Walkman to computers.

Admission: Free.

Open: Daily 11am–7pm. **Station:** Ginza (then a one-minute walk).

TEPCO ELECTRIC ENERGY MUSEUM, 1-12-10 Jinnan, Shibuya-ku. Tel. 3477-1191.

If you find yourself in Shibuya with nothing to do or you're interested in electricity, drop by this new public-service facility of the Tokyo Electric Power Company (TEPCO). Established to teach urban dwellers how electricity is generated, supplied, and consumed, it offers four floors of displays, including a model of a nuclear reactor and a "house of the future" equipped with the latest in appliances and technology. Visitors learn that TEPCO operates 11 nuclear power plants to supply Tokyo and its vicinity with electricity and that, by 1994, nuclear power will account for 40% of TEPCO's power supply. An English-language pamphlet describes the displays.

Admission: Free.

Open: Thurs–Tues 10:30am–6:30pm. **Station:** Shibuya (then a five-minute walk on Koen Dori).

OBSERVATION PLATFORMS

OBSERVATORY, in the Sunshine City Bldg., 3-1-1 Higashi Ikebukuro, Toshima-ku. Tel. 3989-3331.

This 60-story building in the north end of Tokyo is one of the city's tallest. A special elevator—reputedly the fastest in the world—whisks you to its observation deck on the 60th floor in 35 seconds. If you want to forgo the price of the observatory and the fast elevator, take one of the regular elevators to the 59th floor, where you can relax over a cup of coffee at Le Trianon Lounge, open daily from 10am to 2am.

Admission: ¥620 ($5.65) adults, ¥310 ($2.80) children 6–11, free for children under 6.

Open: Daily 10am–8pm. **Station:** Ikebukuro (then a five-minute walk).

TOKYO METROPOLITAN GOVERNMENT OFFICE (TMG), 2-8-1 Nishi-Shinjuku. Tel. 5321-1111.

One of the purposes of the TMG is "a new face to symbolize Tokyo as a world metropolis." This shiny new, architecturally interesting complex of three buildings (TMG No. 1, TMG No. 2, and the Assembly Building) succeeds. The Observatories are located at a height of 656½ feet on the 45th floors of both the North and South Towers of the TMG No. 1 Building, with access from the first floor when ascending. You are requested to get off at the second floor when descending. On the second floor are two history corners, and although the explanations are in Japanese only, the videos and photos are self-explanatory, providing invaluable glimpses into how the city was. The observatory is a large round room making for a 360° view. A café in the center is very reasonable, with offerings such as coffee, ice cream, toast, and cheesecake—all under ¥350 ($3.20). Of course, there's a souvenir shop with soap, perfume, postcards, drinking glasses—all with Tokyo themes. Pick up a bilingual guide to the Observatory at the information desks on the first or second floors.

Admission: Free.

Open: Tues–Fri 9:30am–5:30pm, Sat–Sun and hols 9:30am–7:30pm. **Closed:** Tues when Mon is a hol, and Dec 29–Jan 3. **Station:** Shinjuku.

TOKYO TOWER, 4-2 Shiba Koen, Minato-ku. Tel. 3433-5111.

Built in 1958 and modeled after the Eiffel Tower in Paris, Tokyo Tower is one of the city's most familiar landmarks. Lit up at night and towering 1,089 feet, it has lost its popularity over the decades with the construction of Tokyo's skyscrapers. At any rate, the best time of year to go up is supposedly during Golden Week at the beginning of May. With many Tokyoites gone from the city and most plants and businesses closed down, the air is thought to be the cleanest and clearest at this time, affording views of the far reaches of the city—and exactly how far this city stretches will amaze you. There are two observation decks, one at 492 feet and one at 820 feet.

Admission: Main observatory (493 ft. high), ¥720 ($6.55) adults, ¥410 ($3.70) children 6–11, free for children under 6; top observatory (820 ft. high), ¥1,240 ($11.25) adults, ¥770 ($7) children 6–11, free for children under 6.

Open: Apr–Oct, daily 9am–8pm; Nov–Mar, daily 9am–7pm. **Station:** Onarimon or Kamiyacho.

PACHINKO

No doubt you'll notice pachinko parlors as you walk around Tokyo and anywhere else in Japan. Usually brightly lit and garish, they're packed with upright units similar to pinball machines, with row upon row of Japanese businessmen, housewives, and students sitting intently and quietly in front of them. Popular since the end of World War II, pachinko is a game in which ball bearings are flung into the machine, one after the other, and points are amassed according to which holes the ball bearings fall into. Players control the strength with which the ball is released, but otherwise there's very little to do. Just ¥100 (90¢) gives you 25 ball bearings, which don't last for long. If you're good at it, you win ball bearings back, which you can subsequently trade in for food, cigarettes, watches, calculators, and the like. It's illegal to win money in Japan, but outside many pachinko parlors, along back alleyways, are tiny windows where you can trade in what you won for cash. Police just look the other way.

3. COOL FOR KIDS

TOKYO DISNEYLAND, 1-1 Maihama, Urayasu-shi, Chiba Prefecture. Tel. 0473/54-0001.

On a flight to France I met people whose vacation goal was to "do" all the Disney attractions in the world; they were on their way to EuroDisney. If you have similar goals (or if the kids' vote wins), you will want to visit Tokyo Disneyland. Virtually a carbon copy of the back-home versions, you can find the Jungle Cruise, Pirates of the Caribbean, Haunted Mansion, and Space Mountain. The hottest attractions are the park's newest: Swiss Family Treehouse; Disney Fantasy on Parade, a daytime parade; and Splash Mountain (based on the Disney movie *Song of the South,* it's a journey through swamps and down waterfalls).

Opened in April 1983, Tokyo Disneyland had already entertained some 129 million visitors by March 1993. Tickets for Tokyo Disneyland can be purchased in advance at the Tokyo Disneyland Ticket Center, located near the Yurakucho subway station, and at major travel agencies.

Admission: Disneyland Passport (including entrance and all attractions), ¥4,800 ($43.65) adults, ¥4,400 ($40) junior and high school students, ¥3,300 ($30) children 4–11, free for children under 4. Starlight admission (after 5pm during extended hours), ¥3,800 ($34.55) adults, ¥3,500 ($31.20) junior and high school students, ¥2,300 ($20.90) children 4–11, free for children under 4.

Open: Summer, Mon–Fri 9 or 10am to 7 or 8pm, Sat–Sun 9am–10pm; winter, slightly shorter hours. Schedule subject to change, so call in advance. **Directions:** Shuttle buses depart every 10 or 15 minutes from Tokyo Station (behind the Tekko Building on the Yaesu-guchi side of Tokyo Station), arriving at Disneyland's front gate in 35 minutes; one-way fare is ¥600 ($5.45) for adults, ¥300 ($2.75) for children. You can also take the JR Keiyo Line from Tokyo Station to Maihama Station, from which the park is a few minutes' walk.

HANAYASHIKI, 2-8-1 Asakusa, Taito-ku. Tel. 3842-8780.

Japan's oldest amusement park is northwest of the famous Sensoji Temple in Asakusa. Small by today's comparisons, it offers a small roller coaster and diversions that would appeal to younger children.

Admission: ¥500 ($4.55) adults, ¥300 ($2.75) children.

Open: Wed–Mon 10am–6pm (to 5pm in winter). **Station:** Asakusa (then about a five-minute walk).

KODOMO NO SHIRO [National Children's Castle], 5-53-1 Jingumae, Shibuya-ku. Tel. 3797-5666.

Designed to appeal to children of all ages and located right in the heart of Tokyo, the National Children's Castle is an indoor playground, with various rooms devoted to different activities. A Play Hall features building blocks, jungle gym, table tennis, and football, a large dollhouse, and computer games. There's an art room with supervised instruction, as well as a video room with private cubicles where viewers can make selections from a stocked library of English and Japanese videos, including fairy tales, the "Golden Book" Series, "Sesame Street," and rock videos. On the roof is an outdoor playground.

Admission: ¥400 ($3.65) adults, ¥300 ($2.75) children 6–18, free for children under 6.

Open: Tues–Fri 12:30–5:30pm, Sat–Sun and hols 10am–5:30pm. **Station:** Omotesando, B2 exit (then about a five-minute walk).

UENO DOBUTSUEN (Ueno Zoo), Ueno Park, Taito-ku. Tel. 3828-5171.

Founded in 1882 and the oldest zoo in Japan, the Ueno Zoo is small by today's standards but is still very popular with Japanese families. The main attractions are Japan's only two resident giant pandas, donated by the Chinese government. The zoo also has an aquarium and a large aviary filled with tropical plants.

Admission: ¥400 ($3.65) adults, ¥100 (90¢) children 12–14, free for children under 12 and senior citizens.

Open: Tues–Sun 9:30am–4:30pm (enter by 4pm). **Closed:** Some major hols. **Station:** Ueno (then about a five-minute walk).

INTERNATIONAL AQUARIUM, Sunshine City, 3-1-3 Higashi Ikebukuro. Tel. 3989-3466.

Claiming to be the world's highest aquarium, this 20-year-old attraction is located in the Sunshine City complex in Ikebukuro, on the 10th floor of the World Import Mark Building. It's home to more than 20,000 fish and animals, including dolphins, octopus, eels, piranhas, seahorses, sea otters, seals, giant crabs, and rare species of fish. There are several shows, including performances by sea lions, but this may be the only place on earth that has a fish performance, featuring an electric eel that gives off an electric charge.

Admission: ¥1,440 ($13.10) adults, ¥720 ($6.55) children 4–12, free for children under 4.

Open: Mon–Sat 10am–5:30pm, Sun 10am–6pm. **Station:** Ikebukuro (then about an eight-minute walk) or Higashi-Ikebukuro (then a five-minute walk).

TOSHIMAEN, 3-25-1 Koyama, Nerima, Tokyo. Tel. 3990-3131.

This is an old-timer in the world of amusement parks. Its 50 attractions include a carousel carved by German craftsmen at the turn of the century, four roller coasters, a Japanese-style haunted house with its own assortment of ghosts, a safari ride, and seven swimming pools, including a water slide and an Olympic-size pool, making it a cool place to hang out on a hot summer's day (avoid weekends).

Admission: Entrance and all rides, ¥3,000 ($27.25) adults, ¥2,500 ($22.70) children 6–11, free for children under 6.

Open: Daily 9:30am–4:30pm. **Station:** Nerima, on the Seibu Ikebukuro Line (take the local, not the express, from Ikebukuro), and transfer there to Track 4 for Toshimaen Yuki.

HIBIYA CITY ICE SKATING RINK, in the Hibiya Kokusai Bldg., 2-2-3 Uchisaiwaicho. Tel. 3595-0295.

This has to be one of the best deals in Tokyo, since it's inexpensive fun for the whole family and right in the center of town (practically across from the Imperial Hotel). Lessons are available for children only.

Admission: ¥500 ($4.55); rental skates, ¥600 ($5.45).

Open: Mid-Nov to mid-Mar, Mon–Fri 2–8pm, Sat–Sun 11am–7pm. **Station:** Uchisaiwaicho (in front of the station) or Hibiya (then a few minutes' walk).

YOYOGI KOEN, 2-1 Yoyogi-Kamizono-cho, Shibuya-ku. Tel. 3469-6081.

This is a great park for flying kites (on sale at one of the concessions), feeding the ducks in the pond, and picnics. Near the west end, there are tricycles and bikes for rent free of charge daily from 9am to 4pm and an open area for riding. Adjacent to the shrine, with its famous iris garden, the park is perfect for long walks. (Don't try to take your stroller on the gravel paths inside the shrine.)

Admission: Free.

Open: Daily sunrise–sunset. **Station:** Harajuku or Meiji-Jingumae (then a few minutes' walk).

4. ORGANIZED TOURS

Although this book is designed to make it possible for individual travelers to explore Tokyo on their own, your schedule might make it more advantageous to join a sightseeing tour group. Unsurprisingly, there are a number of tour operators offering English-guided trips of Tokyo and its environs, including such companies as the **Japan Travel Bureau (JTB)** (tel. 3276-7777) and **Japan Gray Line** (tel. 3433-5745 or 3436-6881), with bookings easily made at most tourist hotels. Day tours take in such sights as Tokyo Tower, the Imperial Palace district, Asakusa's Sensoji Temple, Meiji Jingu Shrine, and Ginza. Night tours include such activities as a Japanese dinner, a visit to a Kabuki theater, and a trip to a "geisha party," but keep in mind that it's very touristy. Prices for tours range from about ¥4,500 ($40.90) for a half-day tour to about ¥14,000 ($127.25) for a night tour with dinner.

One tour you might consider joining because you can't do it on your own is the "Industrial Tour" offered by JTB twice a week. Plants toured may include the Japan Airline's maintenance base at Haneda Airport, Isuzu Motors factory, or the Tokyo Stock Exchange. The price of this tour is ¥10,560 ($96), including lunch.

5. SPORTS & RECREATION

Japan's most popular spectator sports are sumo wrestling and baseball. Check the monthly magazine *Tokyo Journal* for information on current sporting events, which may range from an occasional kick-boxing match to pro-wrestling, soccer or golf.

If you'd rather participate in sports yourself, such as swimming or tennis, many first-class hotels have fitness centers, open to the public for fees averaging ¥4,000 ($36.35). Refer to Chapter 4 for hotels with sports facilities.

SUMO

Sumo is a Japanese form of wrestling that has been practiced for about 2,000 years. Good sumo wrestlers, revered as national heroes, are often taller than six feet and weigh well over 200 pounds, their long hair drawn tightly up on their head in a topknot.

Quickly summarized, a sumo match takes place on a sandy-floored ring less than 15 feet in diameter. The object of the match is for one wrestler to force his opponent out of the ring or to cause him to touch the ground with any part of his body other than his feet. This is accomplished by shoving, pushing, slapping, tripping, throwing, and even carrying the opponent. There are as many as 48 various sumo holds, and real fans know all of them.

TOURNAMENTS

Tournaments are held at the Kokugikan in Tokyo three times a year. Even if you don't go to a tournament, you can still watch it on television or listen to it on the American military FEN radio station.

KOKUGIKAN, 1-3-28 Yokoami, Sumida-ku. Tel. 3623-5111.

Tokyo's sumo matches are held in this new stadium completed in 1985. Matches, held in January, May, and September for 15 consecutive days, usually begin around 10am and last until 6pm, with the top wrestlers competing after 4pm. The best seats are ringside box seats, but they're bought out by companies and friends and families of the wrestlers. Usually available are balcony seats, which can be purchased at any Playguide (a ticket outlet in Tokyo, with counters throughout the city) in Tokyo or at the Kokugikan ticket office beginning at 9am every morning of the tournament.

Admission: Tickets, ¥1,500–¥10,000 ($13.65–$90.90).
Station: Ryogoku.

VISITING A SUMO STABLE

If no tournament is going on, you might want to visit a sumo stable to watch the wrestlers train. There are more than 30 stables in Tokyo, many of which are located in Ryogoku close to the sumo stadium. Call first to make an appointment and make sure the wrestlers are in town. In addition to the ones listed here, other sumo stables and their addresses are available at the Tourist Information Center: **Azumazeki Beya,** 4-6-4 Higashi Komagata, Sumida-ku (tel. 3625-0033); **Dewanoumi Beya,** 2-3-15 Ryogoku, Sumida-ku (tel. 3631-0090); **Kasugano Beya,** 1-7-11 Ryogoku, Sumida-ku (tel. 3631-1871); or **Tokitsukaze Beya,** 3-15-3 Ryogoku, Sumida-ku (tel. 3635-0015).

BASEBALL

Introduced into Japan from the United States in 1873, baseball is as popular among Japanese as it is among Americans. Even the annual high school playoffs are avidly followed on television. As with most imports, the Japanese have added their own adaptations. The playing field is smaller, and while a number of Americans are playing ball in Japan, only two foreigners per team are allowed. While playing your hardest is at a premium in the States, such go-for-it tactics as stealing bases or individual excelling are frowned on in Japan. One American player's contract was cancelled because he was with his son who was undergoing a life-or-death operation, instead of at opening day of training camp: The message is clearly "Team first!" Other subtler differences can be heard if you tune in to a game on the radio: It sounds like a football game, complete with cheerleaders. There are two professional leagues, the Central and the Pacific, which play from April to October and meet in final play-offs. Tokyo's teams are the

Central League's Yomiuri Giants and Yakult Swallows and the Pacific League's Nippon Ham Fighters. Advance tickets can be purchased at the stadium or, for Tokyo teams, at any Playguide ticket office in the city.

Local area teams include:

Chiba Lotte Marines, Chiba Marine Stadium, 1 Mihama, Mihama-ku, Chiba City, Chiba Prefecture (tel. 043/296-1189). Station: Kaihin Makuhari Station on the Keiyo Line (then a 15-minute walk).

Nippon Ham Fighters, Tokyo Dome, 1-3 Koraku, Bunkyo-ku, Tokyo (tel. 3811-2111). Station: Suidobashi.

Seibu Lions, Seibu Lions Stadium, 2135 Kami Yamaguchi, Tokorozawa City, Saitama Prefecture (tel. 0429/25-1151). Station: Seibu Kyujomae Station, on the Seibu Sayama Line.

Yakult Swallows, Jingu Stadium, 13 Kasumigaokamachi, Shinjuku-ku, Tokyo (tel. 3404-8999). Station: Gaienmae, on the Ginza Line (then a five-minute walk).

Yokohama Bay Stars, Yokohama Stadium, Yokohama Park, Naka-ku, Yokohama City, Kanagawa Prefecture (tel. 045/661-1251). Station: Kannai Station, on the JR Keihin Tohoku Line.

Yomiuri Giants, Tokyo Dome, 1-3 Koraku, Bunkyo-ku, Tokyo (tel. 3811-2111). Station: Suidobashi.

MARTIAL ARTS

If you're interested in the martial arts, including kendo and aikido, stop by the Tourist Information Center for its list of schools that might allow you to watch their practices or even join them on a monthly basis for instruction.

Otherwise, contact the various federations directly by calling the **International Aikido Federation** (tel. 3203-9236), the **All-Japan Judo Federation** (tel. 3818-4199), the **World Union of Karate-do Organization** (tel. 3503-6637), and the **Japan Kendo Federation** (tel. 3211-5804). All have member schools in Tokyo.

6. CULTURAL EXPERIENCES

This section gives a rundown on the various traditional cultural activities Tokyo has to offer and where to find them. For up-to-date schedules, check either the *Tokyo Journal,* which comes out weekly and is available at foreign-language bookstores, restaurants, and bars, or *Tour Companion's Tokyo City Guide.* Both list current productions for Kabuki, Noh, and Bunraku and when and where they're being staged. Performances are generally in the afternoon and early evening.

KABUKI

Japan's best-known traditional stage art, Kabuki theater still enjoys widespread popularity in Japan. The reason is simple—Kabuki is fun. The plays are usually dramatic, costumes are gorgeous, stage settings can be fantastic, and themes center on conflicts everyone can identify with—love, revenge, and duty.

And contrary to what some Westerners believe, Kabuki is far from being highbrow. In fact, it originated centuries ago as entertainment for the masses, particularly the merchants, in feudal Japan, when a group of women in Kyoto began giving performances of very erotic dances in the 1600s. Needless to say, the dancers were so enthusiastically received that it wasn't long before more troupes of women sprang up. The shogun, deciding the dances were too vulgar, banned all women from the stage. Eventually Kabuki became the domain of all-male companies, so that even today all roles, even those of women, are portrayed by men.

As for Kabuki performances, they've changed little over the past century. Altogether there are more than 300 Kabuki plays, all written before this century. One of the most amusing things about attending a Kabuki performance is watching the audience. Because this has always been entertainment for the masses, the audience can get quite lively, with yells from the spectators, guffaws, and laughter. There are often programs available in English that outline the details of the plot; you can follow the story and get as much enjoyment out of it as everyone around you.

KABUKIZA, 4-12-15 Ginza, Chuo-ku. Tel. 3541-3131, or 5565-6000 for reservations.

This is Tokyo's most famous Kabuki theater. It stages about eight or nine Kabuki productions a year, with each production running close to 25 days. Productions generally begin their run between the first and third of each month; note that there are no shows in August.

There are usually two different plays: Matinees run from 11 or 11:30am to 4pm, and evening performances run from 4:30 or 5pm until about 9pm. It's considered perfectly okay to come for only part of a performance. In addition to English programs explaining the plot, which cost ¥1,000 ($9.10), there are also English-language earphones you can rent for ¥600 ($5.45) that provide a running commentary on the story, the music, actors, stage properties, and other aspects of Kabuki. I strongly suggest that you either buy a program or rent earphones; it will add to your enjoyment of the play immensely.

If you wish to come for only part of a performance (for an hour or so), you can sit up on the fourth floor for as little as ¥500 to ¥1,000 ($4.55–$9.10), depending on the show. No earphones are available here, but you can still buy a program. These seats are on a first-come, first-served basis.

Admission: Tickets, ¥2,000–¥15,000 ($18.20–$136.35), depending on program and seat location; fourth floor, ¥500–¥1,000 ($4.55–$9.10). Advance tickets can be purchased at the Advance Ticket Office, to the right of the Kabukiza's main entrance, from 10am to 6pm. Otherwise, tickets for each day's performance go on sale an hour before the opening of each matinee and evening performance.

Station: Higashi-Ginza (then a one-minute walk).

KOKURITSU GEKIJO [National Theatre of Japan], 4-1 Hayabusacho, Chiyoda-ku. Tel. 3265-7411.

Kabuki and Bunraku (puppet theater) performances are held here several times a year, with English earphone guides available for ¥550 ($5). Kabuki is scheduled throughout the year except during May, September, and December, when Bunraku is being staged instead.

Admission: Tickets, ¥1,500–¥8,000 ($13.65–$72.70).
Station: Hanzomon, Kojimachi, or Nagatacho.

NOH

Noh is the oldest form of theater in Japan. Whereas Kabuki represents extroverted liveliness, Noh is calculated, slow, and restrained. In fact, action can be so slow and tedious that many foreigners find it too tiresome to sit through an entire performance. Worth staying for, however, are the short comic reliefs, called *kyogen,* which are performed between Noh dramas. They make fun of life in the 1600s.

Altogether there are about 240 Noh plays, often concerned with supernatural beings, beautiful women, mentally confused and tormented people, or tragic-heroic epics. As with Kabuki, all the performers are men. Masks are usually worn. There has been so little change in Noh presentations in the past 600 years that its language is too archaic for the Japanese to understand today, which explains in part why Noh does not have the following of Kabuki.

Performances are given in a number of locations throughout Tokyo, with tickets usually ranging between ¥2,000 and ¥5,000 ($18.20 and $45.45). Performances are generally in the afternoon at 1pm or late afternoon at 5 or 6:30pm, but check *Tour Companion, Tokyo Journal,* or *Tokyo Time Out* for exact times.

Hosho Noh-Gakudo, 1-5-9 Hongo, Bunkyo-ku (tel. 3811-5753). Station: Suidobashi (then a five-minute walk).

Kanze Noh-Gakudo, 1-16-4 Shoto, Shibuya-ku (tel. 3469-5241). Station: Shibuya, in the area behind the Tokyu Main Department Store (then a 15-minute walk).

Kita Noh-Gakudo, 4-6-9 Kami-Osaki, Shinagawa-ku (tel. 3491-7773). Station: Meguro (then a 10-minute walk toward Gajoen).

Kokuritsu Noh-Gakudo (National Noh Theater), 4-18-1 Sendagaya, Shibuya-ku (tel. 3423-1331). Station: Sendagaya (then a five-minute walk).

Tessenkai Butai, 4-21-29 Minami Aoyama, Minato-ku (tel. 3401-2285). Station: Omotesando, Exit A4 (then a five-minute walk).

Umewaka Noh-Gakudo, 2-6-14 Higashi-Nakano, Nakano-ku (tel. 3363-7748). Station: Nakano Sakaue Station on the Marunouchi Line (then a five-minute walk) or Higashi-Nakano Station on the JNR Sobu Line (then a seven-minute walk).

Yarai Noh-Gakudo, 60 Yaraicho, Shinjuku-ku (tel. 3268-7311). Station: Kagurazaka, on the Tozai Line, Yarai exit.

BUNRAKU

Bunraku is traditional Japanese puppet theater, but contrary to what you might expect, the dramas are for adults rather than for children. Many dramas now used in Kabuki were first written for the Bunraku stage, with themes centering on love, revenge, sacrifice, and suicide.

Popular in Japan since the 17th century, Bunraku is fascinating to watch because the puppeteers are always right on stage, dressed in black and wonderfully skilled in making their puppets seem like real human beings. The puppets are about three-quarters the size of a human being, and it usually takes three puppeteers to work one puppet. One, for example, is responsible for the head, the facial expressions, and the right arm and hand, while the other puppeteers move the other arm and the legs. A narrator recites the story and speaks all the various parts; he is accompanied by the samisen, a three-stringed Japanese instrument.

Although the main Bunraku theater in Japan is in Osaka, the National Theatre of Japan in Tokyo (listed above under "Kabuki") stages about three Bunraku plays a year, in May, September, and December, usually with two performances daily. Tickets average about ¥4,000 to ¥4,800 ($36.35 to $43.65), and earphones with English explanations are available for ¥650 ($5.90). If you're lucky enough to be in town during one of the performances, don't miss it!

TEA CEREMONY

Tea was brought to Japan from China more than 1,000 years ago. Popular at first with Buddhist priests, who drank it to stay awake during long hours of meditation, it gradually became accepted among the upper classes of Japan. In the 16th century tea drinking was raised to an art with the practice of elaborate tea ceremonies, based on the principles of Zen and the spiritual discipline of the samurai. Developed to free the mind of everyday stress through simplicity of movement and tranquil settings, the tea ceremony became so ritualized that exact strictures were followed in preparing, serving, and consuming the tea.

Today the tea ceremony, *cha-no-yu,* is still practiced in Japan and is regarded as a form of disciplinary training for mental composure as well as a good way to learn etiquette and manners. Although many foreigners may find the frothy green tea too bitter for their taste, watching the process of the tea ceremony can be a fascinating experience. In Tokyo, your best bet for observing the tea ceremony and learning something about it is in several of the city's first-class hotels which offer instruction in English. Since they're often booked by groups, be sure to call in advance to see whether you can participate and to make a reservation.

Chosho-An, in the Hotel Okura, seventh floor, 2-10-4 Toranomon, Minato-ku (tel. 3582-0111). The cost is ¥1,000 ($9.10) for a 30-minute ceremony. It's offered daily from 11am to noon and 1 to 5pm. Station: Toranomon or Kamiyacho (then a 10-minute walk).

Seisei-An, in the Hotel New Otani, seventh floor, 4-1 Kioi-cho, Chiyoda-ku (tel. 3265-1111, ext. 2443). It costs ¥1,000 ($9.10) for a 30-minute ceremony. The program is given Thursday through Saturday from 11am to noon and 1 to 4pm. Station: Yotsuya (then a five-minute walk) or Akasaka-mitsuke (then a three-minute walk).

Toko-An, in the Imperial Hotel, fourth floor, 1-1-1 Uchisaiwaicho, Chiyoda-ku (tel. 3504-1111). The charge is ¥1,100 ($10), and the ceremony is presented Monday through Saturday from 10am to noon and 1 to 4pm (closed holidays). Make a reservation in advance. Station: Hibiya (then a few minutes' walk).

Sakura Kai, Tea Ceremony Service Center, 3-2-25 Shimoochiai, Shinjuku-ku (tel. 3951-9043). Admission (including tea ceremony instruction and flower arranging) is ¥2,700 ($24.55). It's given on

Thursday and Friday from 10am to noon and 1 to 4pm. Station: Mejiro (then a few minutes' walk).

IKEBANA

Whereas a Westerner is likely to put a bunch of flowers into a vase and be done with it, the Japanese consider flower arranging a paramount art and usually utilize only a few blooms in any one piece. Called *ikebana* in Japanese, flower arranging first became popular among the aristocrats during the Heian Period of the 8th to 12th centuries and spread to the common people in the 14th to 16th centuries. In its simplest form, ikebana is supposed to represent heaven, man, and earth.

If you're interested in seeing ikebana, department stores sometimes have special ikebana exhibitions in their galleries. Yasukuni Shrine, located northwest of the Imperial Palace on Yasukuni Dori Avenue, stages ikebana exhibitions throughout the year.

If you're interested in receiving instruction in ikebana, try the schools listed below, where you should call first to make an appointment. More information about ikebana can be obtained from an association called **Ikebana International,** Ochanomizu Square Building, 1-6 Surugadai, Kanda (tel. 3293-8188).

Ichiyo School Nakano, 4-17-5 Nakano (tel. 3388-0141), provides instruction in English at various sites around Tokyo, including the American Club in Minato-ku, and also provides certification. Short-term instruction is available upon request and arrangement. Call for place and time. A series of 10 lessons costs ¥30,000 ($272.70).

Ohararyu Ikebana School, 5-7-17 Minami Aoyama, Minato-ku (tel. 3499-1200), is open Monday through Friday from 10am to noon. Lessons cost ¥1,700 ($15.45). Flower materials are ¥1,500 to ¥2,000 ($13.65 to $18.20) extra. Station: Omotesando.

Sogetsuryu Ikebana School, 7-2-21 Akasaka, Minato-ku (tel. 3408-1126), offers sessions on Tuesday and Thursday at 10am, 1:30pm, and 6pm. Lessons cost ¥10,300 ($93.65) for three classes a month. Flower materials are ¥1,600 ($14.55). Station: Near Aoyama-Itchome, on Aoyama Dori, close to the Canadian Embassy.

ACUPUNCTURE & JAPANESE MASSAGE

There are clinics all over Tokyo for acupuncture *(hari)* and Japanese pressure-point massage *(shiatsu)*, and the staff of your hotel may be able to guide you to the one nearest you. If it's just a massage you want, most first-class hotels have their own massage services. Otherwise, you might try the following clinics:

Kojimachi Rebirth, in the Kur House Building, second floor, 4-2-12 Kojimachi, Chiyoda-ku (tel. 3262-7561), charges a first-time fee of ¥7,500 ($68.20) for acupuncture or shiatsu. The clinic is open Monday through Saturday from 9:30am to 9pm (closed holidays). Station: Kojimachi.

Seibu Shinjuku Ekimae Clinic, in the Chiyoda Building, fourth floor, 2-45-6 Kabuki-cho, Shinjuku-ku (tel. 3209-9217), charges ¥5,000 ($45.45) for acupuncture or shiatsu treatments. It's open

Monday through Friday from 9am to 1pm and 2 to 6pm, and on Saturday from 9am to 1pm and 2 to 3pm (closed holidays). Station: Shinjuku (it's a few minutes' walk northeast, above a pharmacy).

ZAZEN

Zazen, or sitting meditation, is practiced by Zen Buddhists as a form of mental or spiritual training. Laymen meditate to relieve stress and clear the mind. If you'd like to try it yourself, contact the Tourist Information Center in Hibiya for a list of temples that might be offering instruction in English. In addition, check the *Japan Times* to see whether a session of zazen is being organized with instruction in English for foreigners.

The **Eiheiji Temple,** 2-21-34 Nishi-Azabu, Minato-ku (tel. 3400-5232), holds a weekly zazen, on Monday from 7 to 9pm, but instruction is in Japanese only. The cost is ¥100 (90¢). Station: Roppongi (then about a 10-minute walk).

VISITING A PUBLIC BATH

If you won't have any other opportunity to visit a communal bath in Japan, I suggest that you go at least once to a neighborhood *sento* (public bath). Altogether Tokyo has an estimated 2,000 sento, which may sound like a lot but is nothing compared to the 20,000 the city used to have. Ask your hotel staff for the sento nearest you, or visit one listed below. Easily recognizable by a tall chimney and shoe lockers just inside the door, a sento sells everything you might need—soap, shampoo, towels, even underwear. If you want to try an open-air bath, the closest one to Tokyo is in Yumoto, Hakone.

ASAKUSA KANNON ONSEN, 2-7-26 Asakusa, Taito-ku. Tel. 3844-4141.

Located near the famous Sensoji Temple, this one boasts water from a hot spring and has the atmosphere of a real neighborhood bath.

Admission: ¥600 ($5.45).

Open: Fri–Wed 6:30am–6pm. **Station:** Asakusa (then a two-minute walk).

AZABU JUBAN ONSEN, 1-5 Azabu Juban, Minato-ku. Tel. 3404-2610.

The brownish water here comes from a hot spring.

Admission: ¥320 ($2.90).

Open: Wed–Mon 3–11pm. **Station:** Roppongi (then a 10-minute walk).

KAPPA TENGOKU (52), Yumoto, Hakone. Tel. 0460/5-6121.

Located 1½ hours from Shinjuku Station in the heart of Hakone, this is the closest open-air bath to Tokyo. The open-air baths are on a hill directly behind Yumoto Station. From the station, take a right and go under the tracks, and then another immediate right. Walk uphill and then up the stairs.

Admission: ¥500 ($4.55).

Open: Daily 10am–10pm. **Station:** Hakone Yumoto (then a three-minute walk).

CHAPTER 7

STROLLING AROUND TOKYO

1. **AROUND THE IMPERIAL PALACE**
2. **GINZA**
3. **UENO**
4. **ASAKUSA**
5. **HARAJUKU**

Because Tokyo is a jigsaw puzzle of distinct neighborhoods, it makes sense to explore the city section by section. Below are five of Tokyo's most famous neighborhoods, which lend themselves easily to walking tours. For information on sightseeing and attractions outside these neighborhoods, and for additional information on all the museums described below, see Chapter 6, "What to See and Do in Tokyo."

WALKING TOUR 1 — AROUND THE IMPERIAL PALACE

Start: Tourist Information Center (TIC), 1-6-6 Yurakucho.
Finish: Yasukuni Shrine, Yasukuni Dori Avenue.
Time: Allow approximately two hours, not including stops along the way.
Best Times: Tuesday, Wednesday or Thursday, when everything is open.
Worst Times: Monday, when museums are closed; Friday, when the Imperial Palace East Garden is closed; and weekends, when the craft shops are closed.

If you're arriving by subway, take the A4 exit out of Hibiya Station. That will take you to the:

1. **Tourist Information Center,** where you should pick up a map of the city and stock up on pamphlets and brochures of Tokyo if you haven't already done so (see "Orientation," in Chapter 3, for complete information). From there, take a left out of the TIC and walk two short blocks to a large intersection, where you'll find Hibiya Dori Avenue. Catercorner is:
2. **Hibiya Park,** which became the city's first Western-style park in 1903. It contains dogwoods donated by the United States in return for cherry trees given by the Japanese to Washington D.C. It also boasts a number of beer gardens, a pleasant place to while away a sunny afternoon.

   To the east of Hibiya Park is one of Hibiya's landmarks, the:
3. **Imperial Hotel.** Today a modern first-class hotel, it used to be in a much smaller building designed by Frank Lloyd Wright. Pressures of space, however, brought about the grand old hotel's demise, and the original facade is now in Meji Mura, an architectural museum outside Nagoya. The present Imperial Hotel houses expensive boutiques, such as Gucci, Hanae Mori,

WALKING TOUR — AROUND THE IMPERIAL PALACE

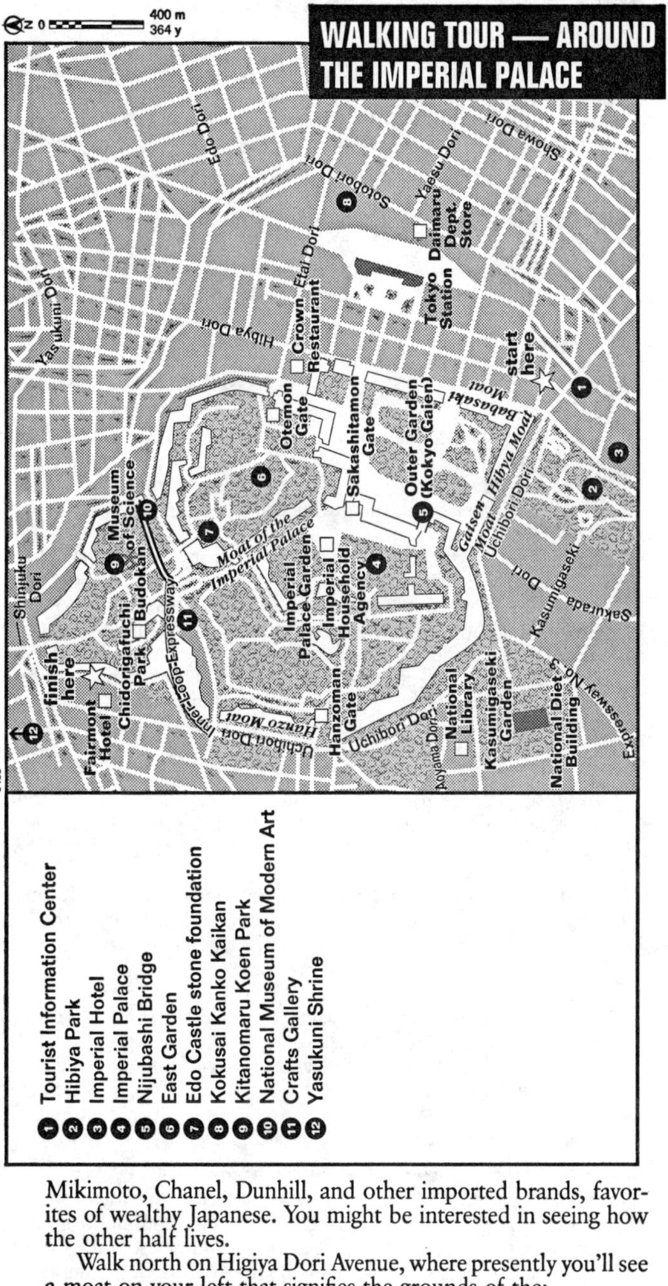

Mikimoto, Chanel, Dunhill, and other imported brands, favorites of wealthy Japanese. You might be interested in seeing how the other half lives.

Walk north on Higiya Dori Avenue, where presently you'll see a moat on your left that signifies the grounds of the:

4. Imperial Palace. Built on the spot where the Edo Castle stood during the days of the Tokugawa Shogunate, the palace was completed in 1888 after the imperial family moved from Kyoto to Tokyo. The present palace, however, isn't the original—that was destroyed, along with almost everything else in the city, during air raids in 1945. The palace was rebuilt in 1968, but its grounds are open to the public only two days a year: on New Year's Day and on the emperor's birthday (Dec. 23).

Yet while they can't see much of the palace, tourists still make brief stops here to pay their respects. Console yourself with a camera shot of the palace taken from the southeast side of:

5. **Nijubashi Bridge,** with the moat and the turrets showing above the trees. The wide moat surrounds the palace and is lined with cherry trees, beautiful in the spring and popular all year round with jogging enthusiasts. It takes about an hour to circle the three miles around the palace if you were to walk at a leisurely pace. But probably the most worthwhile thing to do in the vicinity of the palace is to visit its:
6. **East Garden** (Higashi Gyoen), located just to the east of the palace grounds (see "The Top Attractions," in Chapter 6, for details). It takes about an hour to wander through this pleasant green oasis in the middle of the city. Be sure to stop by the little pond with its wisteria, stepping stones, and croaking frogs.

   Also in the East Garden, you can see what's left of the central keep of old:
7. **Edo Castle:** its stone foundation. Built in the first half of the 1600s, Edo Castle was once the largest castle in the world, with an outer perimeter stretching 10 miles. The central keep towered 168 feet above its foundations, offering an expansive view of Edo. As you stand on top of what's left of the keep's foundation, consider how different things looked back then—a marsh surrounded the Sumida River and a fishing village was where Hibiya now stands. You could see the shore of the bay; what's Ginza today used to be completely under water.

   Take the Otemon-Gate exit from the East Garden (the main exit), and continue walking due east on Etai Dori Avenue, crossing under the elevated railway tracks. Take the next right, which will bring you to the entrance of Tokyo Station. Here, beside the station, is the:
8. **Kokusai Kanko Kaikan** (look for the sign for the Kokusai Kanko Hotel, which is in the same building), where on the first through fourth floors are the tourism promotional offices for almost every prefecture in Japan—each with its own shop selling locally made goods and products. Next door is the:
9. **Daimaru Department Store,** where on the ninth floor you'll find more prefectural shops. Altogether there are 49 of these outlets, offering a more varied collection of Japanese goods than you'll find anywhere else in the country, at very reasonable prices. They're open Monday through Friday from 9am to 5pm (see Chapter 8 for more information).

REFUELING STOPS Like almost every department store in Japan, the **Daimaru Department Store** contains a number of restaurants and coffee shops selling Japanese and Western food and desserts. For elegant dining with a view, there's the **Crown Restaurant,** serving French food on a top floor of the Palace Hotel, 1-1-1 Marunouchi, offering panoramas of the Imperial Palace and East Garden.

After you've had your fill of shopping, return to the palace moat outside the East Garden, and continue following it north as it snakes around the imperial grounds. Northwest of the East Garden lies another park:

10. Kitanomaru Koen Park. Formerly the private grounds of the Imperial Guard, today it boasts two fine museums. Most important is the:

11. National Museum of Modern Art (Tokyo Kokuritsu Kindai Bijutsukan), with its excellent collection of modern Japanese art, dating from the Meiji Period. (See "More Attractions," in Chapter 6, for more information).

Not far from the art museum is the:

12. Crafts Gallery (Bijutsukan Kogeikan), a Gothic-style brick building that features changing exhibitions of contemporary crafts, including exquisitely made lacquerware, ceramics, bamboo works, and more. Its hours are the same as the art museum's.

If you have the time and inclination to cover more in this area, walk through Kitanomaru Koen Park to Yasukuni Dori Avenue, where you should take a left. Within a 10-minute walk, on your right side will be:

13. Yasukuni Shrine, built in 1869 and dedicated to the Japanese war dead. Famous for its cherry blossoms in spring, the shrine is built in classic Shinto style and becomes a center of controversy every August when World War II memorials are held here and the prime minister shows up (some people think it improper that a prime minister should visit a shrine so closely tied to Japan's nationalistic and militaristic past). During any day of the week, you're likely to encounter older Japanese here, paying their respects to friends and families who perished in the war. On the shrine's grounds is a small war museum, with such disturbing displays as a suicide-attack plane (a tiny, primitive thing with enough propellant for only three minutes of flight), a kind of human torpedo (tiny submarines guided by one occupant and loaded with explosives), and various guns and artillery. Ironically enough, on the grounds of the shrine are also display cases that hold temporary exhibitions of ikebana (Japanese flower arrangements).

A FINAL REFUELING STOP To the west of Kitanomaru Koen Park and across the moat is the **Fairmont Hotel,** 2-1-17 Kudan-Minami, which has two moderately priced restaurants. Brasserie de la Verdure offers continental food with a view of the moat, while the French restaurant, Cerisiers, looks out onto a pleasant small garden with a waterfall.

WALKING TOUR 2 — GINZA

Start: Tourist Information Center (TIC), 1-6-6 Yurakucho.
Finish: Kabukiza, 4-12-15 Ginza.
Time: Allow approximately two hours, not including stops along the way.

Best Times: Tuesday through Friday, when most establishments are open.
Worst Times: Monday, when the Nishi Ginza Electric Center is closed; Thursday, when the Nihonshu Center selling sake is closed; Sunday when some galleries and shops are closed; and the last of each month and the whole month of August, when there are no Kabuki productions.

Ginza means "silver mint," a name that goes back to the days of Tokugawa Ieyasu, when the area was reclaimed from the sea and became the home of a silver mint in 1612. After Japan opened itself up to the rest of the world in 1868, Ginza was the first place to become modernized with Western-style buildings, and to display goods from abroad. There were brick buildings, gas streetlamps, and planted trees, a popular place for the upwardly mobile to shop and be seen. Today the Ginza remains the hub of Japan's affluence and the most expensive area in which to shop and entertain.

If you're arriving by subway, take the A4 exit from Hibiya Station. That will take you to the:

1. **Tourist Information Center,** where you should stop if you haven't yet picked up a map of the city. Then take a right out of the TIC, and then another immediate right, following the elevated train tracks. Underneath these tracks is the:
2. **International Arcade,** a long arcade of shops where you can look for such tax-free items as watches, kimonos, Noritake china, woodblock prints, pearls, cameras, and other souvenirs, as well as clothing, shoes, and accessories. Although you can find lower prices elsewhere, this may be a good place to wander through if you're in a rush and don't have time to hunt around. Be sure to have your passport with you so that you qualify for duty-free prices. Stores are open daily from 10am to 6pm.

   Located next to the International Arcade, and also under the tracks, is the:
3. **Nishi Ginza Electric Center,** where you can shop for radios, cassette players, calculators, compact disk players, and televisions. It's open Tuesday through Saturday from 10am to 7pm and on Sunday and holidays) from 10am to 6pm.

   Cross to the other (east) side of the tracks and continue walking three blocks east (away from the elevated train tracks) to a large street called Sotobori Dori Avenue, where you should take a right and walk a few blocks, passing art galleries along the way, until you find the:
4. **Takumi Craft Shop** on your left (if you reach the Ginza Nikko Hotel you've gone too far), located at 8-4-2 Ginza. This crafts store stocks Japanese folk art including ceramics, some kites, umbrellas, lacquerware, textiles, and paper objects. Hours are 11am to 7pm (to 5:30pm on national holidays); closed Sunday.

   Paralleling Sotobori Dori a couple of blocks east is Namiki Dori Street. On this narrow tree-lined lane, art galleries and exclusive boutiques alternate with pubs and hostess bars; you'll find a different atmosphere if you return here at night. Some galleries you might want to drop in on include:
5. **Tokyo Gallery,** on the second floor of the Dai Go Shuwa Building, 8-6-18 Ginza (tel. 3571-1808), specializing in avant-garde art;

WALKING TOUR — GINZA

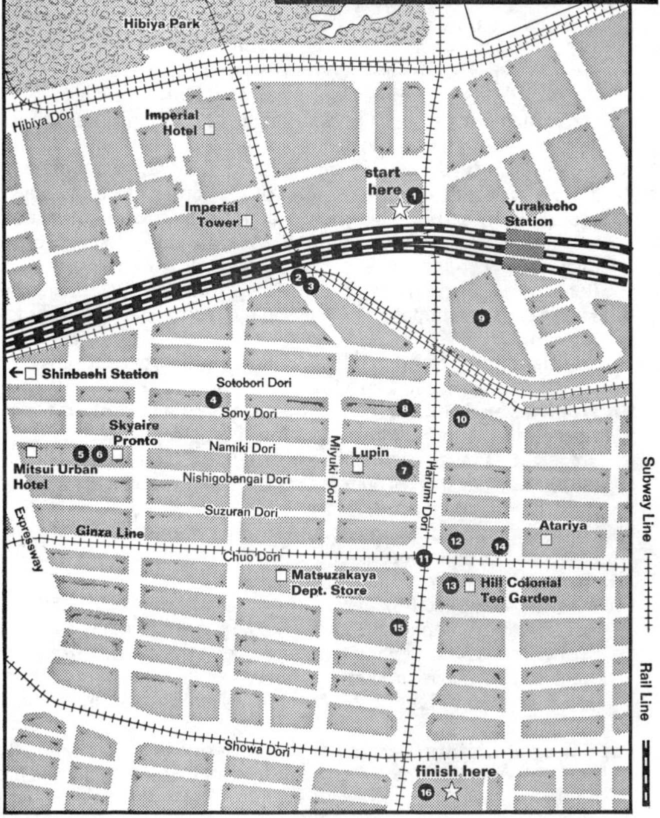

1. Tourist Information Center
2. International Arcade
3. Nishi Ginza Electric Center
4. Takumi Craft Shop
5. Tokyo Gallery
6. S. Watanabe
7. Yoseido Gallery
8. Sony Building
9. Hankyu and Seibu
10. Koban (police box)
11. Ginza 4-chome Crossing
12. Wako department store
13. Mitsukoshi
14. Mikimoto
15. Nihonshu Center
16. Kabukiza

---

6. S. Watanabe, 8-6-19 Ginza (tel. 3571-4684), dealing mostly in modern and old woodcut prints; and:

7. Yoseido Gallery, 5-5-15 Ginza (tel. 3571-1312), specializing in modern Japanese woodblock prints, silk-screens, lithographs, copper plates, and etchings. (See Chapter 8 for more details on these three galleries.)

A REFUELING STOP If you feel like taking a coffee break, a few shops down from S. Watanabe is one of the cheapest places in the Ginza: **Skyaire Pronto,** 8-6-25 Ginza. A coffee shop by day and a bar by night, it offers a cup of coffee for a mere ¥150 ($1.35).

Namiki Dori empties onto Harumi Dori Avenue, a busy street that runs from Hibiya through the heart of Ginza. Turn left here and go two blocks, to the:

8. **Sony Building,** 5-3-1 Ginza (tel. 3573-2371). This place is always crowded because it acts as a meeting place in Ginza, especially in early evening when couples or friends meet after work to go for a meal or drink. As you might expect, Sony displays its products in showrooms on almost every floor. Stop here to see all the latest in everything from the Walkman and Handycam to computers to television. It's open daily from 11am to 8pm.

Catercorner from the Sony Building are two relatively new department stores in Ginza:

9. **Hankyu and Seibu,** located beside each other, both of which opened in the mid-1980s with a lot of fanfare. Altogether there are eight large department stores in the Ginza area. They're closed one day a week, but it's staggered so you can always find department stores open.

To see more department stores, retrace your steps and walk east on Harumi Dori Avenue. You'll notice a smart-looking two-story:

10. **Koban,** or police box. There are koban all over Japan, but this one, with its copper-plated peaked roof and red-and-brown striped walls is larger than most and one of the most stylish. Stop here if you need directions. Otherwise, continue on Harumi Dori until you come to Chuo Dori Avenue. This intersection, called the:
11. **Ginza 4-chome Crossing,** is the heart of Ginza, and the subway station here is serviced by three subway lines—the Hibiya, Ginza, and Marunouchi Lines. The older building with the clock tower is the:
12. **Wako department store,** famous for its innovative shop windows (and high prices). Across the street is:
13. **Mitsukoshi,** another department store, while farther down the area are Matsuya and Matsuzakaya. (See Chapter 8 for more information regarding department stores.) There are also many boutiques and shops along Chuo Dori Avenue, including:
14. **Mikimoto,** 4-5-5 Ginza, Japan's most famous distributor of cultivated pearls, located across the street from Mitsukoshi.

A REFUELING STOP One of my favorite places for a break in Ginza is the **Hill Colonial Tea Garden,** a coffee-and-dessert shop on the second floor of Mitsukoshi department store, which serves tea, coffee, and snacks. It's open daily from 8:30am to 11:30pm.

Back at Ginza Crossing, there's an interesting shop, located just a stone's throw east of the crossing on Harumi Dori Avenue, called the:

15. **Nihonshu Center,** 5-9-1 Ginza, which sells something dear to

my heart—the Japanese rice wine, sake (look for the store's sign that says SAKESPO 101). For only ¥300 ($2.75) you can sample five different kinds of sake, and you even get to keep the cup. What a deal! It's closed on Thursday and holidays, but open the rest of the week from 10:30am to 6:30pm.

Farther east on Harumi Dori, on the right side of the street, is the:

16. Kabukiza, 4-12-15 Ginza, Tokyo's most famous Kabuki theater (see "Cultural Experiences," in Chapter 6, for information on Kabukiza).

FINAL REFUELING STOPS What better way to end the day than at a yakitori-ya, a drinking establishment that sells skewers of chicken and other snacks. **Atariya,** 3-5-17 Ginza, is a lively, fun place with an English menu listing all kinds of yakitori. It's located on the side street that runs beside the Wako department store, not far from Ginza Crossing. If you prefer something quieter, a great bar in the Ginza is **Lupin,** 5-5-11 Ginza, in a small alleyway off Miyuki Dori behind the Ketel German restaurant.

WALKING TOUR 3 — UENO

Start: Ueno Station.
Finish: Ameya Yokocho flea market, along the tracks of the Yamanote Line.
Time: Allow approximately two hours, not including stops along the way.
Best Times: Weekdays, when museums and shops aren't as crowded.
Worst Times: Monday, when the museums are closed.

Located on the northeast end of the Yamanote Line loop, Ueno is one of the most popular places in Tokyo with Japanese families on a day's outing. In contrast to the sophistication of Ginza, Ueno has always been favored by the working people of Tokyo and visitors from Tokyo's rural north. During the Edo Period, the area around Ueno was where merchants and craftsmen lived, worked, and played. Ueno was also site of Kaneiji Temple, which served as the burial ground of the shoguns. Today, Ueno's main drawing card is Ueno Park, the largest park in Tokyo and a cultural mecca with a number of museums, including the prestigious Tokyo National Museum.

You will probably arrive in Ueno by either subway or the JR Yamanote Line. Regardless, make your way to the main entrance of Keisei Ueno Station (terminus of the Skyliner train from the Narita airport). If you wish, stop by one of the many obento counters that stretch along the road between the Keisei Ueno Station and JR Ueno Station. Sushi, sandwiches, and traditional obento can be purchased here for a picnic later in the park, as there are few restaurants in the park itself. At any rate, beside Keisei Ueno Station you'll find a steep flight of stone stairs leading up to an area of trees. This is the south entrance of:

1. **Ueno Park.** Formerly the precincts of Kaneiji Temple, Ueno Park was opened in 1873 as Tokyo's first public park. Although it's the city's largest park, it's small compared to New York's Central Park. But families and school groups come here for a bit of culture, relaxation, and fun. By the way, along with Shinjuku, Ueno is a favorite place for Tokyo's down-and-out population, so don't be surprised if you see a few of them snoozing away on park benches. (Yes, even Tokyo has its homeless people, who are largely ignored by Japanese society, outcasts in a country where hard work and achievement are revered.)

   The busiest time of the year at Ueno Park is in April, during that brief single week of the cherry-blossom season. There's nothing like the blooming of cherry trees to make one feel that spring is finally here, and people flock to Ueno Park to celebrate the birth of the new season, especially on a weekend and in the evenings. But it's not the spiritual communion with nature you might think.

   Employees of every company in Tokyo, it seems, converge on Ueno Park during this week to sit under the cherry trees on plastic or cardboard. They drink sake and beer, and they get drunk and rowdy. The worst offenders are those who sing loudly into microphones accompanied by cassettes playing background music, a hit in Japan known as karaoke music. At any rate, visiting Ueno Park during cherry-blossom season is an experience no one should miss. More than likely you'll be invited to join one of the large groups, and by all means do.

   A landmark near the south entrance to the park is a bronze:

2. **statue of Takamori Saigo,** a samurai born in 1827 near Kagoshima on Kyushu island. Rising through the ranks as a soldier and statesman, he was instrumental in helping restore the emperor to power after the downfall of the Tokugawa Shogunate. He later, however, became disenchanted with the Meiji regime when the rights enjoyed by the samurai class, such as the right to wear swords, were suddenly rescinded. He led a revolt against the government that failed, and ended by taking his own life in ritual suicide. The statue was erected in 1898 and later became the center of controversy when Gen. Douglas MacArthur, leader of the U.S. occupation forces in Japan after World War II, demanded that the statue be removed because of its emotional ties to nationalism. The Japanese people made a large public outcry and MacArthur finally relented. Today the statue, which depicts the stout Saigo dressed in a simple cotton kimono with his hand on his sword, is the best known in Tokyo, if not all of Japan. Also near the park's south entrance is the:

3. **Kiyomizu Kannondo Temple,** which was completed in 1631 in association with Kyoto's temple of the same name. Ueno Park's most famous religious structure, however, is the nearby:

4. **Toshogu Shrine.** Erected in 1651, it's dedicated to Ieyasu Tokugawa, founder of the Tokugawa Shogunate. Stop here to pay respects to the man who made Edo (present-day Tokyo) the seat of his government and thus elevated the small village to the most important city in the country. The pathway leading to the shrine is lined with massive stone lanterns that were donated by the various feudal lords.

   Not far from Toshogu Shrine is the first of Ueno Park's many museums (see "The Top Attractions" and "More Attractions," in Chapter 6, for details on these museums). The:

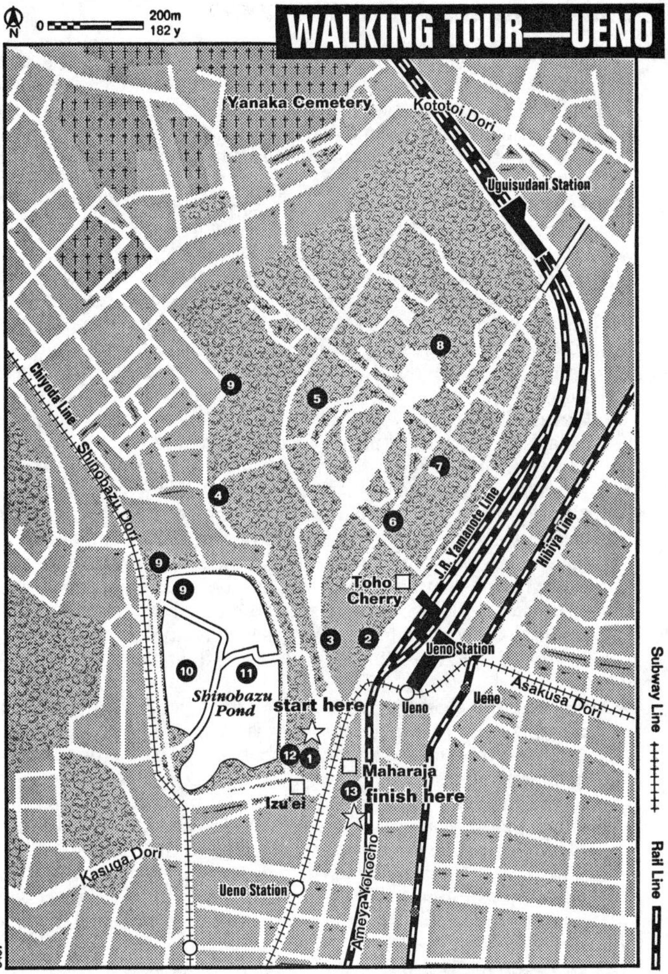

1 Ueno Park
2 Statue of Takamori Saigo
3 Kiyomizu Kannondo Temple
4 Toshogu Shrine
5 Tokyo Metropolitan Art Museum
6 National Museum of Western Art
7 National Science Museum
8 Tokyo National Museum
9 Ueno Zoo
10 Shinobazu Pond
11 Benzaiten Temple
12 Shitamachi Museum
13 Ameya Yokocho

5. **Tokyo Metropolitan Art Museum** (Tokyo-to Bijutsukan) displays modern Japanese works, staging temporary exhibitions.

Across from the art museum, the:

6. **National Museum of Western Art** (Kokuritsu Seiyo Bijutsukan) features works by Western artists, including Renoir, Monet, Sisley, Manet, Delacroix, Cézanne, Degas, El Greco, and Goya, but is probably most famous for its 50-some sculptures by Rodin.

Just north of this museum is the:

7. **National Science Museum** (Kokuritsu Kagaku Hakubutsu-

kan), worth visiting because of its exhibits relating to Japan, including those showing examples of Japanese architecture, the process of making Japanese lacquerware and paper, and an excellent collection of Japanese clocks.

And finally, the fourth and most important museum in this cultural corner of the park is the:

8. **Tokyo National Museum** (Tokyo Kokuritsu Hakubutsukan), Japan's largest museum and the crowning jewel of Ueno Park. In fact, it has the largest collection of Japanese art in the world and is the place to go to see antiques from Japan's past, including lacquerware, pottery, scrolls, screens, ukiyoe (woodblock prints), samurai armor, swords, kimonos, and much more. If you go to only one museum in Tokyo, this should be it!

Assuming you don't spend entire day in museums, head next for the:

9. **Ueno Zoo,** which opened in 1882. It seems rather small by today's proportions, but the Ueno Zoo remains one of the best known in Japan, in part because of its two giant pandas which were donated by the Chinese government. These two celebrities are so popular that there are always long lines to their cages on weekends, and there are all kinds of panda souvenirs you can buy. When one of the zoo's pandas died a few years back, the entire nation went into mourning, until the Chinese quickly sent a replacement. Take the zoo's monorail to the aquarium, where you'll also find a children's zoo and more attractions.

Taking the zoo's southern exit, you will find yourself walking along:

10. **Shinobazu Pond** (you can also get to Shinobazu Pond without entering the zoo by retracing your steps to the south end of the park and then taking a flight of stairs down to the pond). This marshy pond was constructed in the 17th century so that visitors to the various shrines in the area had a nice view of water on which to rest their eyes. Teahouses used to line the pond's banks. Now part of the pond has literally gone to the birds: It's a bird sanctuary. The pond is filled with lotus plants, a lovely sight when they bloom in August. There are small boats for rent in a corner, and on an island in the middle of the pond, connected to the bank with walkways, is the:

11. **Benzaiten Temple,** dedicated to the goddess entrusted with the security of our descendants. At the southeastern edge of Shinobazu Pond is the:

12. **Shitamachi Museum** (Shitamachi Fuzoku Shiryokan). *Shitamachi* means "downtown" and refers to the area of Tokyo where commoners used to live, mainly around Ueno and Asakusa. Displays here include a Shitamachi tenement house, as well as everyday objects used in work and play.

Not far from the Shitamachi Museum, on the other side of Chuo Dori Avenue, is:

13. **Ameya Yokocho,** a narrow shopping street along the west side of, as well as under, the elevated tracks of the Yamanote Line between Ueno and Okachimachi Stations. Originally a wholesale market for candy and snacks, and after World War II a black market in U.S. Army goods, Ameya Yokocho (also referred to as Ameyacho or Ameyoko) today consists of hundreds of stalls and shops selling at a discount everything from fish and vegetables to handbags and clothes. Early evening is the most crowded time as workers rush through on their way home. Some shops close on

Wednesday, but otherwise most shops are open from about 10am to 7pm.

FINAL REFUELING STOPS Across from the Shitamachi Museum, next to Kentucky Fried Chicken, is **Izu'ei,** 2-12-22 Ueno, a modern restaurant that has served eel since the Edo Period. If Indian food is more to your taste, nearby is **Maharaja,** 4-9-6 Ueno, located on the third floor of the Nagafuji Building Annex next to the Ameya Yokocho market. Finally, if the weather is warm, you may wish to end your day at **Toho Cherry,** an informal restaurant with a beer garden at the south end of Ueno Park.

WALKING TOUR 4 — ASAKUSA

Start: Hama Rikyu Garden, near Shimbashi Station.
Finish: Kappabashi Dori.
Time: Allow approximately four hours, including the boat ride.
Best Times: Tuesday through Friday, when the crowds aren't as big.
Worst Times: Monday, when some attractions are closed, and Sunday, when shops on Kappabashi Dori are closed.

If anything remains of old Tokyo, Asakusa is it. Located east of Ueno, it was the heart of old downtown Tokyo (Shitamachi), and it's here that you'll find at least a remnant of the Japan of your fantasies—narrow streets with traditional wooden homes, quaint shops selling all kinds of items, from handmade combs to sweet pastries. Old Japanese women in kimonos shuffle down lanes, bent over their canes, and in front of doors are miniature jungles of potted bonsai.

Asakusa first began as a temple town back in A.D. 628, with the erection of Sensoji Temple. Asakusa is also where many merchants settled when the Tokugawas made Edo the seat of their shogunate government in the 1600s. In those days merchants were considered quite low on the social ladder and were restricted as to where they could live and even what they could wear. Gradually, however, the merchants acquired wealth, and whole new forms of popular entertainment arose to occupy their time. Theaters for Kabuki and Bunraku were built and flourished in Asakusa. Ukiyoe (woodblock prints) became the artistic rage, depicting scenes of daily life in Edo, the stars of Kabuki, and beauties. To the north of Asakusa was Yoshiwara, the most famous geisha and pleasure district in the city. What a sight Asakusa must have been back then, with its carnival atmosphere of stalls, theaters, and amusements, and its lively bustling crowds. In the days of Edo, Asakusa was the busiest part of the city.

Unfortunately, Asakusa was largely reduced to rubble during World War II, and it has not escaped the modernization that swept through Japan in recent decades. However, more than anywhere else in Tokyo, it retains the charm of old downtown Edo.

The most dramatic way to arrive in Asakusa is by boat, just as people used to arrive in the olden days (if you want to forgo the boat ride, take the subway to Asakusa station and start with number 3, below). Start this tour, therefore, by heading first for the:

1. **Hama Rikyu Garden,** 1-1 Hamarikyuteien, located about a 10-minute walk from Shimbashi Station. One of Tokyo's best gardens, it was once the site of a villa of a formal feudal lord and includes an inner tidal pool, a promenade along the Sumida River, pavilions, and tea houses. (See "The Top Attractions," in Chapter 6, for more information.)

   From inside the garden, a:

2. **ferry** departs for Asakusa approximately every hour, making its way along the Sumida River just as in past centuries boats carried wealthy townspeople to the pleasure district of Yoshiwara. Although much of what you see along the river today is only concrete embankments, I recommend the trip because it affords a different perspective of Tokyo—barges making their way down the river, high-rise apartment buildings with laundry fluttering from balconies, warehouses, and superhighways. The boat passes under approximately a dozen bridges during the 35-minute trip, each bridge completely different. Cost of the ferry one-way is ¥560 ($5.10). For information on the ferry and departure schedules, telephone 3841-9178 or 3457-7830.

   Upon arrival in Asakusa, walk from the boat pier a couple of blocks inland, where you'll soon see the colorful Kaminarimon Gate. Across the street from this gate is the:

3. **Asakusa Information Center,** 2-18-9 Kaminarimon (tel. 3842-5566). Open daily from 9:30am to 8pm, it's staffed by English-speaking volunteers until 5pm. Stop here to pick up a map of the area and to ask directions to restaurants and other sights in the area you might be interested in visiting. In addition, that huge Seiko clock you see on its facade is a mechanical music clock, with performances every hour on the hour from 10am to 7pm. Then it's time to head across the street, to the:

4. **Kaminarimon Gate,** unmistakable with its bright-red colors and a huge lantern hanging in the middle. Those statues inside the gate are the gods of thunder and of rain, ready to protect the deity enshrined in the temple.

   Once past the gate, you'll find yourself immediately on a pedestrian lane called:

5. **Nakamise Dori,** which leads straight to the temple. This lane is lined with stalls selling fabrics, shoes, toys, Japanese crackers (called *sembei),* trinkets, bags, umbrellas, Japanese dolls, clothes, fans, masks, and traditional Japanese accessories. How about a brightly decorated straight hairpin? A black hairpiece? A wooden comb? A temporary tattoo in the shape of a dragon? It's a great place for shopping for souvenirs and gifts.

REFUELING STOPS If you're hungry for lunch, there are a number of possibilities in the neighborhood. **Chinya,** 1-3-4 Asakusa, located near Kaminarimon Gate, has been serving sukiyaki since 1880. Nearby is **Namiki,** 2-11-9 Kaminarimon, Asakusa's best-known noodle shop.

At the end of Nakamise Dori as you head toward the temple is another gate, which opens on a square filled with pigeons and a large:

6. **incense burner,** where worshippers "wash" themselves to ward off or help against illness. If, for example, you have a sore

WALKING TOUR — ASAKUSA

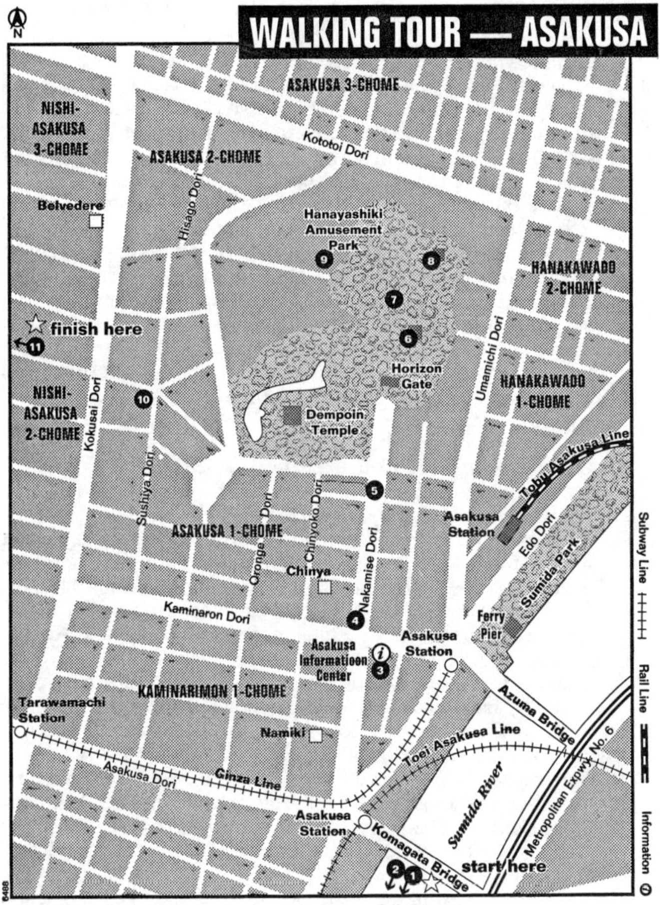

1. Hama Rikyu Garden
2. Ferry
3. Asakusa Information Center
4. Kaminarimon Gate
5. Nakamise Dori
6. Incense burner
7. Sensoji Temple
8. Asakusa Jinja Shrine
9. Hanayashiki
10. France-za
11. Kappabashi Dori

---

throat, be sure to rub some of the smoke over your throat for good measure. But the dominating building of the square is:

7. Sensoji Temple, Tokyo's oldest and most popular temple. Founded in the 7th century, Sensoji Temple is dedicated to Kannon, the Buddhist goddess of mercy, and is therefore popularly called the Asakusa Kannon Temple. According to popular lore, the temple was founded after two fishermen netted the catch of their lives—a tiny golden statue of Kannon. It was enshrined in a temple; word spread, and before long people flocked to Asakusa to worship it. Today the sacred statue is still housed in the temple, carefully preserved inside three boxes, but it's never presented to public view. That doesn't seem to bother the crowds of the faithful who flock to the temple to pay their respects. Inside the temple's main building is a counter where you can buy your fortune by putting ¥100 (90¢) into a wooden box and extracting one of the long wooden sticks inside. The stick will have a number on it, which corresponds to numbers on a set of drawers. Take out the fortune from the drawer which has your number. Although it's written only in Japanese, you can take it to the counter on the left where you can ask for a translation (if the counter is unoccupied, you can also ask at the Asakusa Information Center). If you don't like your fortune, you can negate it by tying it to one of the wires provided or to the twig of a tree.

On the right side of the temple is a shrine, the:

8. **Asakusa Jinja Shrine,** built in commemoration of the two fishermen who found the statue of Kannon.

Northwest of Sensoji Temple is:

9. **Hanayashiki,** a small and kind of corny amusement park that opened about 40 years ago and still draws in the little ones (see "Cool for Kids," in Chapter 6, for more information). But most of the area west of Sensoji Temple (the area to the left if you stand facing the temple) is a small but interesting area of Asakusa popular among Tokyo's older working class. This is where several of Asakusa's old-fashioned pleasure houses remain, including bars, restaurants, strip shows, traditional Japanese vaudeville, and so-called love hotels, which rent out rooms by the hour. One of the most famous strip shows is:

10. **France-za,** 1-43-12 Asakusa (tel. 3841-6631). It's located on a small side street that leads west from Sensoji Temple. With four shows daily, beginning at 11:30am and the last show at 6:30pm, it charges a ¥4,000 ($36.35) entrance fee—and leaves nothing to the imagination.

If you keep walking west, within 10 minutes you'll reach:

11. **Kappabashi Dori Street,** Tokyo's wholesale district for restaurant items. Yes, this is where you can buy models of all that plastic food you've been drooling over in restaurant displays—mugs foaming with beer, ice cream, fish, sushi. There is also kitchenware, lacquerware, rice cookers, and *noren,* the curtains hung outside Japanese restaurants.

A FINAL REFUELING STOP A great place for lunch or to end the day in Asakusa is 28 floors above ground, at the **Belvedere** in the Asakusa View Hotel on Kokusai Dori Avenue. It serves a lunch buffet of Japanese, Western, and Chinese food daily from noon to 2:30pm for ¥3,300 ($30); in the evening you can listen to music while sipping drinks and watching the sun go down. Another good place to end the day is **Ichimon,** 3-12-6 Asakusa, located northeast of the Kokusai Dori and Kototoi Dori intersection. Decorated like an old farmhouse, it specializes in sake and has a unique system in which customers buy ¥5,000 ($45.45) worth of *mon,* wooden tokens, which are traded for food and drinks.

WALKING TOUR 5 — HARAJUKU

Start: At the Omotesando Dori and Aoyama Dori intersection (nearest station: Omotesando).
Finish: Yoyogi Park.
Time: Allow approximately three hours, not including restaurant and shopping stops.
Best Times: Sunday, when you can start with a Sunday brunch and when Omotesando Dori becomes a pedestrian zone and dancers converge on the scene.
Worst Times: On Monday and from the 27th to the end of every month, when the Ota Memorial Museum of Art is closed; on Thursday, when the Oriental Bazaar is closed.

Harajuku is one of my favorite neighborhoods in Tokyo. Sure, I'm too old to really fit in. Anyone older than 25 is apt to feel ancient here, for this is Tokyo's most popular and trendy hangout for Japanese high school and college students. But I like Harajuku for its vibrancy, its sidewalk cafés, its street hawkers and fashionable clothing boutiques. Harajuku is where the young come to see and be seen, and there are Japanese punks, girls dressed in black, and young couples in their fashionable best. Harajuku is also the home of Tokyo's most important Shinto shrine, as well as a woodblock-print museum, an excellent souvenir shop of traditional Japanese items, and a park with wide-open spaces. Formerly the training grounds of the Japanese army and later the residential area of American families during the Occupation, Harajuku was also the site of the 1964 Olympic Village.

If at all possible, come to Harajuku on a Sunday, when the main thoroughfare, Omotesando Dori, becomes a pedestrian promenade. The crowds are the thickest around the Olympic stadium, where anyone who wants to perform can and does.

Start this tour at the intersection of:

1. **Omotesando Dori and Aoyama Dori.** Within a two-minute walk from this intersection are three good places for:

A FANCY BRUNCH STOP Located on the fifth floor of the Hanae Mori Building on Omotesando Dori, **L'Orangerie de Paris** is the most expensive and exclusive brunch spot, attracting the foreign expatriate population. **Spiral Garden,** on Aoyama Dori, is slightly cheaper and more casual. For a more moderately priced French bistro, try **Flo,** located on the second side street on the right-hand side as you descend from the Omotesando Dori and Aoyama Dori intersection. Be sure to make reservations beforehand, since these places are popular. (See Chapter 5 for more details.)

If you have youngsters with you, you might start your tour at the:

2. **National Children's Castle,** a seven-minute walk down Aoyama Dori. Then you can take them to:

AN ALTERNATIVE BRUNCH STOP Across the side street from the Children's Castle is **Lunchan,** the least expensive of the three brunch spots. Or you might try **Las Chicas,** on a small side street off Aoyama Dori (coming from the Children's Castle, turn left at City Bank). Or you might browse down Koto Dori (Antique Avenue), the street in front of Kinokuniya, the international market, and have lunch at the **Café Papas.** Again, make reservations at these popular places. (See Chapter 5 for more details.)

After you've had brunch at one of the above places, head west on Omotesando Dori, where on your left you'll soon see the:

3. **Hanae Mori Building,** 3-6-1 Kita-Aoyama, housing the fashions by this famous designer. Check out the front-window displays—they're always interesting. In the basement of the Hanae Mori Building is the **Antique Market,** with individual stallkeepers selling china, jewelry, clothing, watches, swords, and items from the 1930s. It's open daily from 11am to 8pm. Almost next door is:
4. **Shu Uemura.** A very successful chain of makeup, it features cosmetics, blush, and eyeshadow in incredible rainbow colors. Continuing on Omotesando Dori, you'll soon come to Harajuku's most famous store, the:
5. **Oriental Bazaar,** 5-9-13 Jingumae, one of Tokyo's best places to shop for Japanese souvenirs. Three floors offer antique chinaware, old kimonos, Japanese paper products, fans, jewelry, woodblock prints, screens, and more. If you go to only one souvenir shop in Tokyo, this should be it. Shopping hours are 9:30am to 6:30pm every day except Thursday. Not far from the Oriental Bazaar is:
6. **Vivre 21,** 5-10-1 Jingumae, open daily from 11am to 8pm and boasting boutiques showcasing fashions of designers Kenzo, Takeo Kikuchi, and Kensho Abe.

Also on the left side of Omotesando Dori is:

7. **Kiddy Land,** 6-1-9 Jingumae, which sells gag gifts and a great deal more than just toys. You could spend hours here, but it's often so packed with giggling teenagers that you end up rushing out of here.

REFUELING STOPS There are several inexpensive restaurants near this stretch of Omotesando Dori. **Genrokusushi,** on Omotesando Dori near the Oriental Bazaar at 5-8-5 Jingumae, is a fast-food sushi bar that uses a conveyor belt to deliver plates of food to customers seated at the counter. Also take-out sushi, in case you want to pack yourself a little something to eat later in Yoyogi Park. The **Bamboo Sandwich House,** 5-8-8 Jingumae, located off Omotesando Dori on a side street near the Paul Stuart Shop, offers inexpensive sandwiches and coffee, but my favorite is **Beer Market Doma,** located in the basement of the Ga-Z Building at the intersection of Omotesando and Meiji Dori, which serves a variety of Asian dishes and is decorated like a Mongolian nomad's tent. See Chapter 5 for details on all these places.

The first big intersection you come to on Omotesando Dori is Meiji Dori. If you cross Meiji Dori, you'll arrive almost immediately at:

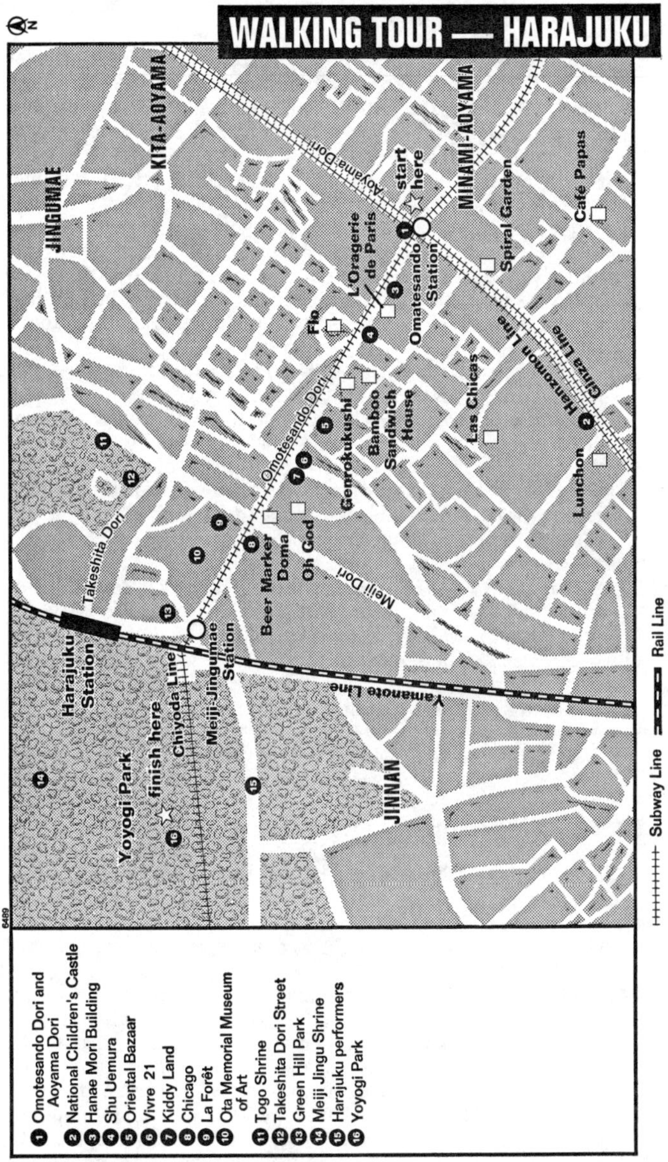

8. Chicago, 6-31-21 Jingumae, which nonetheless stocks hundreds of used and new kimono and yukata in a corner of its basement (see Chapter 8 for complete information). On the corner at the Omotesando and Meiji Dori intersection is:

9. La Forêt, 1-11-6, a fashion department store filled with trendy shoe and clothing boutiques. The lower floors tend to be less expensive—the more exclusive boutiques are higher up. In the basement, check for music scene happenings.

Behind La Forêt is one of my favorite museums, the:

10. **Ota Memorial Museum of Art,** 1-10-10 Jingumae. It features the private ukiyoe (woodblock prints) collection of the late Ota Seizo. Exhibitions of the museum's 12,000 prints are changed monthly. (See "More Attractions," in Chapter 6.)

Return to Meiji Dori and continue going north. If it's the fourth Sunday of the month, you might want to continue walking a few minutes until on your left you see:

11. **Togo Shrine.** A flea market is held on the grounds of the shrine on these days, when everything from old chests, dolls, and inkwells to kitchen utensils and kimonos are for sale, spread out on cloths on a sidewalk that meanders under trees to the shrine. Beginning early in the morning, it usually goes on until about 4pm.

Otherwise, turn left off of Meiji Dori onto the first side street past La Forêt, a pedestrians-only street called:

12. **Takeshita Dori Street.** Lined nonstop with stores, it's often jam-packed with young people—usually Japanese teenagers—who come in from the countryside to hunt for bargains in the shops with doors flung open wide to the crowds. You'll pass record shops, shoe stores, and coffee shops—it's all there if you can only find it through the crowds.

REFUELING STOP At the top of Takeshita Dori (the end closest to Harajuku Station) is a small glass-enclosed café/ flower shop called **Sterling Silver,** located next to McDonald's. Filled with plants and flowers, it's a great refuge from the crowds. Serving coffee, beer, sake, oden, yakitori, and snacks, it's open Monday through Saturday from 11am to 11pm.

At the top end of Takeshita Dori, where you'll see Harajuku Station, turn left. Soon, across from the station, you'll see a small enclosed area called:

13. **Green Hill Park,** where young vendors set up stalls of clothing and accessories. You can find bargains here, though some of the leather-studded items might be too bizarre for the folks back home.

Just past the station, turn right and walk over the bridge above the tracks, where you'll then find yourself at the entrance of:

14. **Meiji Jingu Shrine.** The most venerable shrine in Tokyo, Meiji Jingu Shrine opened in 1920, dedicated to Emperor and Empress Meiji, who were instrumental in opening Japan to the outside world a hundred years ago. A fine example of dignified and refined Shinto architecture, this shrine is made of Japanese cypress topped with green copper roofs. Two large torii built of cypress wood more than 1,700 years old mark the entrance to the shrine on a shaded pathway lined with trees and dense woods. Almost all the 100,000 shrubs and trees on the shrine grounds were donated by people from throughout Japan, which means that you can find flora from all over the country. On the way to the shrine you can stop off at the Iris Garden, spectacular for its irises in late June. A stream meanders through the garden, and if you follow it to its source, you'll find a spring where you can drink the cold water. North of the shrine complex is the Treasure Museum with the garments and personal effects of Emperor Meiji and the empress.

Retrace your steps back to the entrance to the shrine, turn right, and you'll see a wide boulevard that, if it's Sunday, has been closed to traffic and is filled with a mass of people. Here, from about noon to 5pm, are the:

15. Harajuku performers. In what is Tokyo's best free show, everyone from rock 'n' rollers and breakdancers to roller skaters, rock bands, and pantomime artists converges on Omotesando Dori in the shadows of the Olympic stadiums to do their thing on the street. It all started in the 1970s when a group of kids got together and began dancing to music they brought with them on their portable cassette players. Gradually the number of young dancers grew, until by the mid-1980s there were as many as several hundred teenagers dancing in the street, dressed either in styles of the 1950s or in colorful circuslike clothing.

Although today the number of dancers has dwindled, a few diehards are still here, and like most undertakings in Japan, this is group participation, with each group having its own cassette player, music, leader, and costumes. Individual dancing is out, and if by chance you simply joined in, the other dancers would regard you with astonishment and consider you slightly weird. The fun consists in simply wandering about, observing group after group. You might also come across a roller-skating club putting on stunts, young boys performing on trick bicycles, a pantomimist, and, in recent years, lots of rock bands. In this carnivallike atmosphere there are also stalls selling everything from fried noodles to roasted corn on the cob to a kind of Japanese omelet.

Opposite the Olympic stadiums is:

16. Yoyogi Park, a huge expanse of green popular with families, couples, and students. In recent years, it has also become the main Sunday meeting ground of Iranians working in Tokyo.

FINAL REFUELING STOPS After you've seen the Sunday dancers of Harajuku, visited Meiji Jingu Shrine, and fought your way through the crowds, you're probably ready to imbibe a drink or two. Although Tokyo does not have many sidewalk cafés, Harajuku is blessed with several, all on Omotesando Dori Avenue. Closest to the Meiji–Omotesando Dori intersection is **Café de Rope,** 6-1-8 Jingumae, the oldest outdoor café in Harajuku. For an indoor bar in the area, walk past Café de Rope on the small lane beside it to **Oh God,** 6-7-18 Jingumae. It shows free foreign films every night beginning at about 6pm and is decently dark.

CHAPTER 8

SHOPPING A TO Z

I have never seen a people shop as much as the Japanese do. Judging from the crowds that surge through Tokyo's department stores every day, I'm convinced it's the country's number-one pastime. Women, men, couples, and even whole families go on shopping expeditions in their free time, making Sunday the most crowded shopping day of the week.

WHAT TO BUY Tokyo is Japan's showcase for everything the nation produces, from the latest in camera equipment to fashion and sake. Stores both mammoth and miniature are everywhere, offering everything you can and can't imagine. Good buys in traditional Japanese crafts and souvenirs include contemporary, antique, and reproduction woodblock prints (ukiyoe), products made from Japanese paper (washi), toys and kites, bamboo window blinds, Japanese dolls, carp banners, swords, lacquerware, ikebana (flower arranging) accessories, ceramics, fans, masks (including Noh antique and reproduction masks), knives and scissors, sake, and silk and cotton kimonos. If you're searching for antiques, you'll find ceramics and porcelain, furniture (including tansu chests and those wonderful free-standing stairs with drawers built into them), hibachi, lacquerware, netsuke, fans, and much more. And if you love beautifully handcrafted items such as bamboo vases, lacquered trays, and unique tableware, you'll be in absolute heaven.

Japan is also a good place to shop for clothes, whether you have a fortune to spend on Japanese designers or are bargain-hunting for inexpensive designer imitations. Although sizes tend to be smaller than in the West, many Japanese designers create clothing composed of free-flowing lines that seem to fit tall people best.

Although Japan is also famous for its workmanship in electronic products, including cameras, stereo and video equipment, computers, and typewriters, because of the present exchange rate you won't find many bargains here. In fact, you can probably find Japanese electronic products cheaper back home.

You don't have to spend a fortune shopping. In Harajuku, for example, it's possible to buy a fully lined dress of the latest fashionable craze for $50. I can't even count the number of shoes I've bought in Tokyo for a mere $27, and the Japanese produce beautiful synthetic leather handbags that feel and look like real leather and go for a song.

Remember that a 3% consumption tax will be added to the prices marked on goods, but all major department stores and the larger tourist shops will refund the tax on purchases amounting to more than ¥10,000 ($90.90). Ask at the store's information counter (usually located near the main entrance) for the special form to be filled out by the sales clerks and for the location of the refund counter. Be sure to bring your passport.

SALES Department stores have sales throughout the year where you can pick up great bargains on everything from men's suits and electric goods to golf clubs, toys, lingerie, and designer clothing.

There are even sales for used wedding kimonos. The most popular—and crowded—sales are for designer-name clothes, usually held twice a year, in July and December or January. To find out current sales, check the *Tokyo Journal,* the monthly guide to what's going on in the capital.

SHIPPING IT HOME Most first-class hotels in Tokyo provide a packing and shipping service. In addition, most large department stores, as well as tourist shops such as the Oriental Bazaar and antiques shops, will ship your purchases overseas.

If you wish to ship packages yourself, purchase an easy-to-assemble cardboard box at a post office, available in three sizes with the necessary tape and string. Packages mailed abroad cannot weigh more than 20kg (about 44 lb.) and keep in mind that only the larger international post offices accept packages to be mailed overseas. Ask your hotel concierge for the closest international post office.

HUNTING GROUNDS If you have only a few hours to spare for shopping in Tokyo, head for a **department store.** The Ginza and Shibuya have a large concentration of department stores. For things Japanese, the **International Arcade** near the Imperial Hotel offers a wide range of everything from kimonos to watches and chinaware, while the **Oriental Bazaar** in Harajuku is excellent for traditional Japanese items.

Those of you with more time on your hands might want to explore districts in Tokyo that specialize in certain products. **Kanda,** for example, is famous for its used books, including those in English. If you're interested in seeing the latest in electronics, head for **Akihabara.** The **Ginza** is the chic place for clothing boutiques, but it also has a handful of department stores and more art galleries than any other district in Tokyo. Other department store shopping meccas include **Shibuya** and **Shinjuku.** For young, fun, and inexpensive fashion, head for **Harajuku** and Shibuya.

The shops listed below are just a few of the many in Tokyo.

ANTIQUES & CURIOS

ANTIQUE MARKET, in the basement of the Hanae Mori Bldg., Omotesando Dori, 3-6-1 Kita-Aoyama, Minato-ku. Tel. 3406-1021.

Vendors sell European and Japanese antiques, including china, jewelry, clothing, swords, watches, furniture, lamps, lacquerware, woodblock prints, and 1930s art deco and kitsch. Prices are high. Open daily from 11am to 8pm. Station: Omotesando (then a one-minute walk).

HARUMI ANTIQUES, 9-6-14 Akasaka, Minato-ku. Tel. 3403-1043.

Located on a tree-shaded street near the Defense Agency, this basement establishment has antiques from 10 dealers, including china, furniture, dolls, bronzeware, hibachi, and a jumble of odds and ends. Open Monday through Saturday from 10am to 6pm and on Sunday from 11am to 5:30pm. Station: Nogizaka or Roppongi (from Roppongi, walk toward Nogizaka on Gaien-Higashi Dori and take the first right after the Defense Agency).

KATHRYN MILAN, 3-1-14 Nishi-Azabu, Minato-ku. Tel. 3408-1532.

Oriental antiques and folk art are for sale in this small shop, including Japanese furniture, ceramics, paintings, baskets, and hibachi. Open by appointment or on Saturday, Sunday, and national holidays from 10:30am to 6pm. Station: Roppongi.

KOMINGU KOTTOKAN [Tokyo Antiques Hall], 3-9-5 Minami Ikebukuro, Toshima-ku. Tel. 3982-3433 or 3980-8228.

One of the best places in town for one-stop antiques hunting, this building houses more than 35 antiques dealers' stalls. Although most articles are marked, it doesn't hurt to bargain. You could spend hours here, looking over furniture, ceramics, woodblock prints, jewelry, lacquerware, swords, china, hair combs, Japanese army memorabilia, kimonos and fabrics, scrolls and screens, samurai gear, clocks, watches, dolls, and other items too numerous to list. Antiques are both Japanese and Western, and dealers here work the flea markets across the country. Open Friday through Wednesday from 11am to 7pm (but get here before 5pm, since some stalls close early if business is slow). Station: Ikebukuro (then a 10-minute walk; take a right out of the station's east side, walking south on Meiji Dori; the shop will be on your left).

KUROFUNE, 7-7-4 Roppongi, Minato-ku. Tel. 3479-1552.
Owned by an American who has made his home in Japan for more than 20 years, this shop specializes in Japanese antique furniture that has not been refinished but rather was left in its original condition. The stock also includes fabrics, old prints, maps, hibachi, Imari porcelain, and folk art. Open Monday through Saturday from 10am to 6pm; closed holidays. Station: Roppongi.

MAYUYAMA, 2-5-9 Kyobashi, Chuo-ku. Tel. 3561-5146.
One of the best-known names in fine antiques, this distinguished-looking stone building is among the city's oldest antiques shops, established in 1905. It deals in ceramics, pottery, scrolls, and screens from Japan, China, and Korea, at expectedly high prices. Open Monday through Saturday from 10am to 6pm; closed holidays. Stations: Between Kyobashi and Takaracho Stations.

ART GALLERIES

Ginza has the highest concentration of art galleries in Tokyo, with about 250 shops dealing in everything from old woodblock prints to silk screens, lithographs, and contemporary paintings. Refer to the Ginza walking tour in Chapter 7 for more information regarding particular stores. In addition, the *Tokyo Journal*, the city's monthly magazine, lists current exhibitions in more than two dozen galleries in the Ginza alone, as well as exhibitions in other parts of Tokyo.

BOOKS

If you're a bookworm, you'll want to know that there's a whole slew of bookstores along Yasukuni Dori Avenue in Jimbocho, Kanda, including these that deal in books written in English.

KINOKUNIYA BOOKSTORE, 3-17-7 Shinjuku, Shinjuku-ku. Tel. 3354-0131.

Located on Shinjuku Station's east side on Shinjuku Dori Avenue, this store offers a wide selection of books and magazines in English on the sixth floor. With more than 50,000 titles of foreign books and magazines, it also carries a wide selection of publications in other languages, as well as dictionaries and textbooks for those studying Japanese. Open daily from 10am to 7pm; closed the third Wednesday of the month. Station: Shinjuku.

KITAZAWA, 2-5 Jimbocho, Kanda. Tel. 3263-0011.
With an overwhelming selection of books on Japan, this is a good place to come if you're looking for the latest books published about this country or for books not carried by the regular bookstores. It also has old and rare books. Open Monday through Saturday from 10am to 6pm. Station: Jimbocho (then a three-minute walk).

MARUZEN, 2-3-10 Nihombashi, Chuo-ku. Tel. 3272-7211.
This well-known bookstore on Chuo Dori Avenue (across from the Takashimaya department store) has a large selection of foreign books on the second floor, including all the latest books concerning Japan and things Japanese. Open Monday through Saturday from 10am to 7pm, and on holidays from 10am to 6pm. Station: Nihombashi.

OHYA SHOBO, 1-1 Jimbocho, Kanda. Tel. 3291-0062.
Established back in 1882, this is a delightful old bookstore, piled high with rare books and maps. It claims to have the world's largest stock of old Japanese illustrated books, woodblock prints, and maps. Open Monday through Saturday from 10:30am to 6:30pm; closed holidays. Station: Jimbocho (then about a three-minute walk).

TUTTLE BOOK SHOP, 1-3 Jimbocho, Kanda. Tel. 3291-7072.
This shop is the Tokyo branch of a Vermont firm that publishes a wide selection of books on Japan and the Far East. Open Monday through Friday from 10:30am to 6:30pm, and on Saturday and holidays from 11am to 6pm. Station: Jimbocho (then a three-minute walk).

YAESU BOOK CENTER, 2-5-1 Yaesu, Chuo-ku. Tel. 3281-1811.
Located close to Tokyo Station, this five-story bookstore stocks about a million books, including books in English on the fourth floor. Open Monday through Saturday from 10am to 7pm. Station: Tokyo or Kyobashi.

CAMERAS & FILM

YODOBASHI CAMERA, 1-11-1 Nishi Shinjuku, Shinjuku-ku. Tel. 3346-1010.
This ranks as one of the largest camera shops in the world, with around 30,000 items in stock. In addition to cameras it also has watches, calculators, typewriters, and cassette players. Its prices for film are about as good as you'll find in Tokyo. Its tax-free section is on the second floor and even though prices are marked, you can still bargain. Surrounding Yodobashi Camera are a number of other camera shops as well, making this part of Shinjuku a good place to

comparison-shop. Open daily from 9:30am to 8:30pm. Station: Shinjuku (then walk a block west).

USED CAMERAS

CAMERA NO KIMURA, 1-18-8 Nishi Ikebukuro. Tel. 3981-8437.

A good selection of used cameras. Open Monday through Saturday from 8am to 8pm, and on Sunday and holidays from 10am to 7pm. Station: Ikebukuro (then a two-minute walk west).

MATSUZAKYA CAMERA, 1-27-34 Takanawa, Minato-ku. Tel. 3443-1311.

Used Japanese and foreign cameras. Open Monday through Saturday from 10am to 6:30pm, and on Sunday and holidays from 10am to 5:30pm. Station: Shinagawa (then a 20-minute walk).

FILM DEVELOPMENT

EAST WEST SIGMA, 3-2-6 Nishi Azabu, Minato-ku. Tel. 3497-3931.

This is where professionals bring their film for processing. Kodak color slides can be processed within 24 hours. It's located on Terebi Asahi Dori (the first major left if you're walking on Roppongi Dori from Roppongi Crossing in the direction of Shibuya). Open Monday through Friday from 9am to 7pm, and on Saturday from 9am to 5pm; closed holidays and the second and fourth Saturday of every month. Station: Roppongi (then about a six-minute walk).

CASSETTES & COMPACT DISCS

VIRGIN MEGASTORE, in the basement of the Marui 0101 Fashion Bldg., 3-30-16 Shinjuku. Tel. 3353-0038.

Located on Shinjuku Dori Avenue, this store stocks more than 150,000 titles. There are several listening stations so you can hear before buying, and there's even a disc jockey imported from the U.K. who can tell you about the newest hits. Open Thursday through Tuesday from 11am to 8pm. Station: Shinjuku Sanchome.

WAVE, 6-2-27 Roppongi. Tel. 3408-0111.

A branch of the Seibu giant, this is undoubtedly the largest record store in town. An innovative store with a computerized record reference system, it has a comprehensive selection of records, cassettes, videos, and compact discs. On the first floor are headphones where you can select from 200 of the top hits, which is one way to keep abreast of what's hot in the music industry. Come to Wave for jazz, German new wave, reggae, heavy metal, classical, vintage, or the latest in Japanese music. Open daily from 11am to 9pm; closed the first and third Wednesday of every month. Station: Roppongi (then about a three-minute walk; it's located on the left side of Roppongi Dori in the direction of Shibuya).

CRAFTS & TRADITIONAL JAPANESE PRODUCTS

CRAFTS

BINGOYA, 10-6 Wakamatsucho, Shinjuku-ku. Tel. 3202-8778.

Folk art and crafts are sold on six floors of this small building, including traditional toys such as tops and dolls, baskets, handmade paper products, straw boots, items made from cherry bark, chopsticks, pottery, glassware, lacquerware, and fabrics from all over Japan. Open Tuesday through Sunday from 10am to 7pm. Station: Akebonobashi (then a 15-minute walk) or Shinjuku Station, west exit (then bus no. 76 or 74 to the Kawada-cho bus stop).

ZENKOKU DENTOTEKI KOGEIHIN SENTA [Japan Traditional Craft Center], on the second floor of the Plaza 246 Bldg, 3-1-1 Minami Aoyama. Tel. 3403-2460.

Even if you can't afford to buy anything, it's worth a trip to this lovely shop devoted to beautifully crafted traditional items and established to publicize and distribute information on Japanese crafts. In addition to its permanent exhibition, it sells various crafts from all over Japan that are changed on a regular basis. They usually include lacquerware, ceramics, fabrics, paper products, bamboo items, knives, writing brushes, metalwork, some furniture, and more. Crafts include those of traditional design as well as those that are strikingly contemporary. Prices are high but rightfully so. In a corner is a video screen where you can watch videos showing the making of Japanese swords, lacquerware, woodblock prints, and other traditional crafts. Open Friday through Wednesday from 10am to 6pm. Station: Gaienmae (then a three-minute walk; it's located on the corner of Gaien-Nishi Dori and Aoyama Dori Avenue above a Haägen-Dazs ice-cream parlor).

KOKUSAI KANKO KAIKAN and DAIMARU DEPARTMENT STORE, 1-8 Marunouchi, Chiyoda-ku. Tel. 3215-1181.

There's no other place in Japan quite like these two buildings. Located right beside each other practically on top of Tokyo Station, they contain tourism promotional offices for every prefecture in Japan—each of which also sells its own special goods and products. Altogether there are 49 of these little shops, spread along the first through fourth floors of the Kokusai Kanko Kaikan Building (look for the sign of the Kokusai Kanko Hotel in the same building), and on the ninth floor of the Daimaru department store. You won't find such a varied collection anywhere else in Japan; and prices are very reasonable, lower than at department stores. What's more, hardly anyone ever seems to shop here, so you don't have to deal with the crowds that plague other stores. Shop for Bizen pottery from Okayama, clay ningyo dolls from Fukuoka, or noren (shop curtains) from Tochigi, or coral jewelry from Okinawa. Lacquerware, pottery, glassware, paper products, sake, kokeshi dolls, bamboo ware, pearls, china, and everything else Japan produces can be found right here. Open Monday through Friday from 9am to 5pm. Station: Tokyo Station (then less than a minute's walk from the Yaesu north exit).

ORIENTAL BAZAAR, 5-9-13 Jingumae. Tel. 3400-3933.

This shop with its Oriental-looking facade of orange and green is much more souvenir- and tourist-oriented than the other shops listed here, but it also offers one of the largest selections of traditional Japanese products in town. Its three floors of souvenir and gift items include cotton and silk kimonos (including great bargains in used kimonos), woodblock prints (antique, reproduction, and contemporary), paper products, fans, Japanese swords, lamps and vases, Imari and Kutani porcelain, sake sets, Japanese dolls, pearls, hibachi, chopsticks, and even antiques. If you're looking for something inexpensive to buy for office co-workers, neighbors, or friends, I recommend the Japanese paper wallets (good for checkbooks) which cost only ¥100 (90¢) apiece; they're in a corner of the basement. Other good gift buys include cardboard coasters with scenes of famous woodblock prints, chopsticks, fans, and small prints, all of which are inexpensive and easy to pack. This store will also ship things home for you. Open Friday through Wednesday from 9:30am to 6:30pm. Station: Hara-juku or Meiji-Jingumae (then a few minutes' walk on Omotesando Dori).

CLOISONNE

ANDO, 5-6-2 Ginza. Tel. 3572-2261.

Opened in 1880, this shop has probably the largest selection of cloisonné in town, including jewelry, vases, and plates. It's located on Harumi Dori Avenue in the heart of the Ginza. Open Monday through Saturday from 9am to 6pm; closed holidays. Station: Ginza.

JAPANESE DOLLS

Japanese dolls range from elegant creatures with delicately arranged coiffures and silk kimonos to plain, wooden dolls called kokeshi. In Tokyo, Edo Dori is known as Doll Town, as both sides of this avenue are lined with doll shops, including these two:

KYUGETSU, 1-20-4 Yánagibashi, Taito-ku. Tel. 3861-5511.

Founded in 1830, this is one of the biggest doll shops in Japan. Open Monday through Friday from 9:15am to 6pm. Station: In front of Asakusabashi.

YOSHITOKU DOLLS, 1-9-14 Asakusabashi, Taito-ku. Tel. 3863-4419.

This shop, one of the area's largest, has been here since 1711 and sells a variety of Japanese dolls, including Hakata (fired-clay painted dolls representing traditional characters) and kokeshi, as well as souvenirs and some antiques, including masks and Kabuki figures. If you're looking for a geisha or sumo wrestler doll, this is a good place to come. Open Monday through Friday from 9:30am to 6pm, and on Saturday, Sunday, and holidays from 9:30am to 6:30pm. Station: Asakusabashi (then a one-minute walk).

FANS

ARAI BUNSENDO, Nakamise Dori, Asakusa. Tel. 3844-9711.

This 100-year-old stall on colorful Nakamise Dori (about halfway down, on the west side) sells paper dance fans, including special orders for Kabuki stars. Open daily from 10:30am to 6pm; closed Sunday after the 20th of every month. Station: Asakusa.

FIGURES

SUKEROKU, Nakamise Dori, Asakusa. Tel. 3844-0577.

This tiny shop sells handmade figures of traditional Japanese characters, from mythological figures to priests, farmers, entertainers, and animals, including the many castes from the Edo Period ranging from peasants to feudal lords. Most are in the ¥3,000 to ¥5,000 ($27.25 to $45.45) price range, though some are much higher than that. A truly unique shop, it's located on Nakamise Dori, the next to the last shop on the right as you walk from Kaminarimon Gate toward Sensoji Temple. Open Friday through Wednesday from 10:30am to 6:30pm. Station: Asakusa (then a few minutes' walk).

FLOWER-ARRANGING & TEA-CEREMONY ACCESSORIES

Department stores sometimes carry vases and tea-ceremony accessories. In addition, the **Japan Traditional Craft Center** (described earlier in this section) often carries beautiful bamboo vases and other accessories used to enhance flower arranging.

TSUTAYA, 5-10-5 Minami Aoyama, Minato-ku. Tel. 3400-3815.

This shop has everything you might need for ikebana (flower arranging) or the Japanese tea ceremony, including vases of unusual shapes and sizes, scissors, and tea whisks. Open daily from 9am to 6:30pm; closed the first and fourth Sunday and the second and third Friday of every month. Station: Omotesando (then a two-minute walk).

KIMONOS

Elaborate silk kimonos, such as those used in wedding ceremonies, are so expensive that most Westerners who purchase one display it much as they would a piece of art. Much cheaper are cotton yukata, used for lounging around at home, as well as used silk kimonos. In addition to these shops, the **Oriental Bazaar** (described above) has a good selection of new and used kimonos, including wedding kimonos. Also, department stores sell kimonos, notably **Takashimaya** and **Mitsukoshi** in Nihombashi and **Isetan** in Shinjuku. They have sales on rental wedding kimonos at least twice a year (check the *Tokyo Journal* for sales). Flea markets are also good for used kimonos and yukata.

CHICAGO, 6-31-21 Jingumae. Tel. 3409-5017.

Despite its improbable name, this shop specializing in used clothing stocks hundreds of kimonos and cotton yukata in the very back of the shop, past the 1950s clothing. Many kimonos are in the ¥2,000 to ¥5,000 ($18.20 to $45.45) range. The shop is located on Omotesando Dori in Harajuku. Open daily from 11am to 8:30pm. Station: Harajuku or Meiji-Jingumae.

HAYASHI KIMONO, in the International Arcade, 1-7-23 Uchisaiwaicho. Tel. 3501-4014 or 3591-9825.

With two locations in the International Arcade, Hayashi deals in kimonos, including wedding kimonos, cotton yukata, happicoats, obi (the sash used in securing kimonos), and polyester versions. With men's, women's, and children's selections, it's a good place to start if you're buying gifts for people back home. Open Monday through Saturday from 9:30am to 7pm and on Sunday from 9:30am to 6pm. Station: Hibiya or Yurakucho.

NOREN

BENGARA, 2-35-11 Asakusa, Taito-ku. Tel. 3841-6613.

Noren are the doorway curtains hanging in front of Japanese restaurants, public bathhouses, and shops signaling that the establishment is open. A rather new shop, Bengara sells both traditional and modern noren, including those bearing kanji (Chinese characters) or scenes from famous woodblock prints. You can even have one custom-made with your own name. Open Friday through Wednesday from 10am to 7pm. Station: Asakusa.

JAPANESE PAPER PRODUCTS

Folkcraft shops such as **Takumi** in Ginza and the **Oriental Bazaar** in Harajuku have items made of Japanese paper.

KURODAYA, 1-2-5 Asakusa, Taito-ku. Tel. 3844-7511.

Opened in 1856, this small shop sells traditional Japanese papers, kites, papier-mâché masks, boxes, and other products made of paper. Open Tuesday through Sunday from 11am to 7pm. Station: Asakusa (located next to Kaminarimon Gate).

WASHIKOBO, 1-8-10 Nishi Azabu, Minato-ku. Tel. 3405-1841.

This shop sells paper and cardboard boxes, paper wallets, notebooks, paper lamps, toys, and sheets of beautifully crafted paper from around Japan. Open Monday through Saturday from 10am to 6pm; closed holidays. Station: Roppongi (then a seven-minute walk; it's on the right side of Roppongi Dori as you walk toward Shibuya).

SAKE

NIHONSHU CENTER, 5-9-1 Ginza. Tel. 3575-0656.

This shop in the heart of Ginza on Harumi Dori specializes in sake from around Japan, with a different selection available every month. For ¥300 ($2.75), visitors can try five different kinds of sake and keep the cup. Open Friday through Wednesday from 10:30am to 6:30pm; closed holidays. Station: Ginza (then 30 seconds' walk away in the direction of Kabukiza; look for a sign that says SAKESPO 101).

STONE LANTERNS

ISHIKATSU, 3-4-7 Minami Aoyama, Minato-ku. Tel. 3401-1677.

If you're so enamored of the huge stone lanterns you see at shrines and landscaped gardens that you want to take one home, this shop has been in operation since 1706 and has a catalog of various stone lanterns available. And, of course, they ship. Open Monday through Saturday from 9am to 5pm; closed holidays. Station: Roppongi or Omotesando (then take a taxi).

SWORDS

In addition to this shop, other places to look for swords include the **Oriental Bazaar,** the **Tokyo Antique Hall** in Ikebukuro, and the **Antique Market** in the basement of the Hanae Mori Building on Omotesando.

JAPAN SWORD, 3-8-1 Toranomon. Tel. 3434-4321.

This is Tokyo's best-known sword shop, which also stocks sword accessories, sword guards, and kitchen cutlery. Displays are so extensive, it's like visiting a museum. Open Monday through Saturday from 9:30am to 6pm; closed holidays. Station: Toranomon or Kamiyacho.

WOODBLOCK PRINTS

In addition to this store, other good places for woodblock prints, including original antiques and reproductions, are the **Oriental Bazaar** and the **Antique Market** in the basement of the Hanae Mori Building, both on Omotesando Dori in Harajuku.

SAKAI KOKODO GALLERY, 1-2-14 Yurakucho. Tel. 3591-4678.

Located across from the Imperial Hotel, this gallery claims to be the oldest woodblock-print shop in Japan. First opened in 1870 in Kanda by the present owner's great-grandfather, it is now tended by the fourth generation of the Sakai family and is a great place for original prints, as well as reproductions of such great masters of Hiroshige. Open daily from 11am to 6pm. Station: Hibiya (then a few minutes' walk).

DEPARTMENT STORES

Japanese department stores are institutions in themselves. Usually enormous, well designed, and chock-full of merchandise, they have about everything you can imagine, including art galleries, pet stores, rooftop playgrounds or greenhouses, travel agencies, restaurants, food markets, and flower shops.

One of the most wonderful aspects of the Japanese department store is its service. If you arrive as a store opens at 10am, you will be on hand to witness a daily rite—the staff lined up at the front door, bowing to welcome the day's first customers. Sales clerks are everywhere to help you, so that in many instances you don't even have to go to the cash register once you've made your choice. Simply hand over the product along with your money to the sales clerk, who will return with your change, your purchase neatly wrapped, and an "*arigato gozaimashita*" (thank you very much). And if you don't want to be burdened with packages, most department stores will deliver them to your hotel free of charge.

Department stores are good and convenient places to shop for traditional Japanese items. To find out what's where, stop by the store's information counter located close to the front entrance. Gallery exhibitions and bargain sales are listed in the *Tokyo Journal*, the monthly guide to what's going on in Tokyo.

Hours are generally 10am to 7pm, and since department stores close on a different day of the week, you can always find several that are open, even on Sunday and holidays.

GINZA & NIHOMBASHI

HANKYU, 2-5-1 Yurakucho. Tel. 3575-2233.

A relative newcomer to the Ginza department-store scene, this large store has the usual food, clothing, and household goods departments. Open 10am to 7pm; closed Thursday. Station: Yurakucho or Hibiya.

MATSUYA, 3-6-1 Ginza. Tel. 3567-1211.

Located on Chuo Dori Avenue, this is one of my favorite department stores. It has a good selection of Japanese folkcraft items, kitchenware, and beautifully designed contemporary household goods in addition to the usual clothes and accessories. If I were buying a wedding gift, this is one of the first places I'd look. Open 10am to 7pm; closed Tuesday. Station: Ginza.

MITSUKOSHI, 1-4-1 Nihombashi Muromachi. Tel. 3241-3311.
One of Japan's oldest department stores, it first opened as a kimono shop back in the 1600s and today has many name-brand boutiques, including Givenchy, Dunhill, Lanvin, Chanel, Hanae Mori, Oscar de la Renta, Christian Dior, and Tiffany. Its kimonos, by the way, are still hot items. The building itself is old, stately, and attractive, making shopping here a pleasure. Open 10am to 7pm; closed Monday. Station: Mitsukoshimae (which means, appropriately enough, "In Front of Mitsukoshi").

MITSUKOSHI, 4-6-16 Ginza. Tel. 3562-1111.
Located right on Ginza 4-chome Crossing, this is a branch of the famous Mitsukoshi in Nihombashi and is popular with young shoppers. Open 10am to 7pm; closed Monday. Station: Ginza.

PRINTEMPS, 3-2-1 Ginza. Tel. 3567-0077.
A relative newcomer on the Ginza scene, this is a branch of Paris's fashionable Au Printemps but with a selection more suited to the Japanese. A fun, young store with announcements in both French and Japanese, it is very popular with Tokyo's young generation. Boutiques sell the fashions of Hiroko Koshino (one of Japan's up-and-coming young designers), Jurgen Lehl, Sonia Rykiel, Kenzo, and Kansai. Open 10am to 7pm; closed Wednesday. Station: Yurakucho or Hibiya.

SEIBU, 2-5-1 Yurakucho. Tel. 3286-0111.
A branch of Ikebukuro's Seibu, this department store consists of two buildings, one selling clothing and accessories (including designs of Giorgio Armani, Kenzo, Jasper Conran, Katharine Hamnett, Jean-Paul Gaultier), the other specializing in interior design and kitchenware. Open 10am to 7pm; closed Wednesday. Station: Yurakucho or Hibiya.

TAKASHIMAYA, 2-4-1 Nihombashi. Tel. 3211-4111.
This store provides stiff competition for Mitsukoshi, with a history just as long. It features boutiques by such famous designers as Chanel, Laroche, Dunhill, Celine, Lanvin, Louis Vuitton, Gucci, Christian Dior, Issey Miyake, and Kenzo, and it also has a good tableware department with beautiful selections of china and lacquerware. Open 10am to 7pm; closed Wednesday. Station: Nihombashi.

WAKO, 4-5-11 Ginza. Tel. 3562-2111.
This sophisticated department store, located on the corner of Ginza 4-chome Crossing, is one of the few buildings in the area to have survived World War II. Its distinctive clock tower and innovative window displays are Ginza landmarks. It specializes in imported fashions, luxury items, and Seiko timepieces, with prices to match. One of the classiest stores around. Open Monday through Friday from 10am to 5:30pm and on Saturday from 10am to 6pm; closed Sunday and holidays. Station: Ginza.

IKEBUKURO

SEIBU, 1-28-1 Minami Ikebukuro. Tel. 3981-0111.
Seibu once claimed to be the largest department store in the

world, but these days it has lost rank to its updated neighbor Tobu, and to Yokohama's Sogo. Still it is impressive, with 47 entrances, 12 floors, and dozens of restaurants. On an average weekday 170,000 shoppers pass through the store. Located practically on top of Ikebukuro Station, it devotes two basement floors to foodstuffs alone, with dishes set out so you can nibble and sample food as you move along. The other floors are devoted to clothing, furniture, art galleries, kitchenware, and a thousand other things, and many of the best Japanese and Western designers have boutiques here. The eighth floor has more than a dozen restaurants offering everything from teppanyaki and sushi to Indian and French cuisine. There are also four floors devoted to interior design, in a section of the store called the Loft. Open 10am to 7pm; closed Tuesday. Station: Ikebukuro.

TOBU/METROPOLITAN PLAZA, 1-1-25 Nishi-Ikebukuro. Tel. 3981-2211.

Reopened and expanded to 83,000 square meters in 1993, Tobu's Ikebukuro store is now Japan's largest. As many as 180,000 customers pass through its doors daily, and they are served by nearly 3,000 clerks. Tobu has tripled its basement food floor to 254 shops, since food sales make up 15% to 20% of total department store sales. Yearly sales come to a whopping ¥180 billion ($1.6 billion). Adjoining Metropolitan Plaza houses the Tobu Museum of Art, 130 specialized boutiques, 25 restaurants, a sports club, and parking. Open 10am to 7pm; closed Tuesday. Station: Ikebukuro.

SHIBUYA

KIDS FARM PAO, 1-22-14 Jinnan. Tel. 5458-0111.

Just imagine a department store for children—nine floors of toys, fashion (including the latest from Ralph Lauren, Kenzo, and Moschino, in case your pockets are lined with gold), and things to do. There's even a café for mom only. A family-event information desk and ticket center, a photo salon, baking supplies, a beauty salon, party supplies, a toy hospital, a rooftop play area, and even a shrine are all here. In short, everything your youngsters could want. Free rental strollers, areas for nappy changing, and cots for naps are among the user-friendly services. Only one catch: How to get them back home after they've seen Kids Farm Pao? Open 10am to 7pm; closed Wednesday.

ONE OH NINE, 28-6 Udagawacho. Tel. 3477-6711.

The three One Oh Nine department stores cater to shoppers in their 20s and 30s with jewelry and accessories, women's clothing (with an emphasis on work clothes and casual wear), men's clothing, housewares, and recordings of the latest music. There's even a Body Shop. It belongs to the Tokyu group of stores. Open daily from 10am to 9pm. Station: Shibuya.

TOKYU, 2-24-1 Dogenzaka. Tel. 3477-3111.

A more conservative department store, Tokyu appeals to a 30s and up group. Tokyu's adjacent, ultramodern Bunkamura complex—a museum, theaters (the Tokyo Film Festival is held here), bookstore, and cafés—is worth a visit if you're in the neighborhood. A branch of Tokyu is located above Shibuya Station. Both branches open 10am to 7pm; main store closed Tuesday, branch store closed Thursday. Station: Shibuya.

SEIBU, 21-1 Udagawacho. Tel. 3462-0111.

Similar to its main store in Ikebukuro, this branch carries everything from accessories and art to stationery and wine. Designers here include boutiques for Rei Kawakubo's Comme des Garçons, Giorgio Armani, Issey Miyake, Jun Ashida, Kenzo, and Yohji Yamamoto. Open 10am to 7pm; closed Wednesday. Station: Shibuya.

SHINJUKU

ISETAN, 3-14-1 Shinjuku. Tel. 3352-1111.
A favorite among foreigners living in Tokyo, Isetan has a good line of conservative clothing appropriate for working situations as well as contemporary and fashionable styles, including designer clothes. Norma Kamali, Issey Miyake, Kenzo, Kansai, Yohji Yamamoto, Hanae Mori, Gucci, Fendi, Chanel, and Rei Kawakubo all have boutiques here. It also has a great kimono department. Open 10am to 7pm; closed Wednesday. Station: Shinjuku (then a five-minute walk east on Shinjuku Dori Avenue).

KEIO, 1-1-4 Nishi Shinjuku. Tel. 3342-2111.
Located atop sprawling Shinjuku Station, Keio sells everyday products to the hordes of commuters passing through. Open 10am to 7pm; closed Thursday. Station: Shinjuku.

MITSUKOSHI, 3-29-1 Shinjuku. Tel. 3354-1111.
This is the Shinjuku branch of one of Japan's oldest department stores. Open 10am to 7pm; closed Monday. Station: Shinjuku (then a few minutes' walk east).

ODAKYU, 1-1-3 Nishi Shinjuku. Tel. 3342-1111.
It's hard to miss this place, since it sits practically on top of the station. Its merchandise is fairly middle-of-the-road. Open 10am to 7pm; closed Tuesday. Station: Shinjuku.

ELECTRONICS

Akihabara is the name of an area of Tokyo with the largest concentration of electronic and electrical shops in Japan. With more than 600 stores, shops, and stalls, it accounts for one-tenth of the nation's electronic and electrical appliance sales, and it may surprise you to learn that 80% of Japan's consumer electronics market is domestic.

If you do decide to purchase anything, make sure that it was made for export—that is, that there are instructions in English, an international warranty, and the correct electrical connectors. All the larger shops in Akihabara have tax-free floors where the products are especially designed for export. And be sure to bargain. One woman I know who was looking for a portable cassette player bought it at the third shop she went to for ¥4,000 ($36.35) less than what was quoted to her at the first shop. Most shops in Akihabara are open daily from 10am to 7pm. Some of the largest shops here are **Yamagiwa,** 3-13-12 Soto-Kanda (tel. 3253-2111); **Laox,** 1-2-9 Soto-Kanda (tel. 3253-7111); and **Hirose Musen,** 1-10-5 Soto-Kanda (tel. 3255-2211).

The easiest way to get to Akihabara is via the Yamanote Line or Keihin Tohoku Line to the JR Akihabara Station. You can also take the Hibiya Line to Akihabara, but it's a longer walk.

Another place to look for electrical and electronic equipment is the **Nishi Ginza Electric Center,** 2-1-1 Yurakucho (tel. 3503-4481), located right next to the International Arcade, under the train tracks. Shops here sell radios, cassette players, calculators, compact disk players, and other gadgets. It's open Tuesday through Saturday from 10am to 7pm and on Sunday and holidays from 10am to 6pm. The nearest stations are Yurakucho and Hibiya.

FASHIONS

FASHION DEPARTMENT STORES

In Harajuku

LA FORET, 1-11-6 Jingumae. Tel. 3475-0411.

Located on Harajuku's main intersection of Omotesando Dori and Meiji Dori Avenues, this is one of the most fashionable clothing stores in the area, with designer clothing by Jurgen Lehl, Issey Miyake, and Kansai, among others. Although some of the boutiques are expensive, there are some great deals to be found here, particularly in the shops in the basement. This shop also has children's clothing boutiques. Open daily from 11am to 8pm. Station: Harajuku or Meiji-Jingumae.

VIVRE 21, 5-10-1 Jingumae. Tel. 3498-2221.

A sleek, white building on Omotesando Dori filled with fashionable boutiques selling designer clothing and jewelry, it includes Nicole, Kenzo, Montana, Thierry Mugler, Jean-Paul Gaultier, and Junko Shimada among its concessions. In the basement is an interesting shop selling kitchenware and a café. Open daily from 11am to 8pm. Station: Meiji-Jingumae or Omotesando.

In Shibuya

109, 2-29-1 Dogenzaka. Tel. 3477-5111.

Owned by the Tokyu conglomerate, 109 (called "one-oh-nine") is geared toward high-school and college-age consumers. There are two other branches of this store nearby. The one called 109-2, at 1-23-10 Jinnan (tel. 3477-8111), appeals to more affluent workers in their 20s. Both are filled with boutiques carrying lines that are largely unknown outside Japan, but there are some bargains, particularly on the lower floors. Open daily from 10am to 9pm for both. Station: Shibuya.

MARUI HONKAN, 1-21-3 Jinnan. Tel. 3464-0101.

This fashion store is geared to young people, especially those who have just joined the work force and are in the market for new clothes and items for their apartments. Many young Japanese get their first charge cards here. The main store, Marui Honkan, has clothing and accessories as well as furniture and kitchenware, while Marui Young, 1-22-6 Jinnan (tel. 3464-0101), has inexpensive fashion. These two stores are located across from each other, on Koen Dori Avenue. Look for their 0101 logo. Open Thursday through Tuesday from 10:30am to 8pm. Station: Shibuya.

PARCO, 15-1 Udagawacho. Tel. 3464-5111.

A division of Seibu, Parco is divided into four buildings called Parco 1, 2, and 3, and Quattro. Parco 1 and 2 are filled with designer boutiques for men and women, including such well-known Japanese designers and designs as Kansai, Yohji Yamamoto, Nicole (designer Mitsuhiro Matsuda, known in the United States as Matsuda for Nicole in Japan), Comme des Garçons (designer Rei Kawakubo), and Issey Miyake, as well as some boutiques selling kimonos. Parco 1 has some good restaurants on its seventh floor. Parco 3 has more fashions, but its emphasis is on household goods and interiors.

Quattro is for music and videos, and has a music venue on the top floor. Open daily from 10am to 8:30pm. Station: Shibuya.

SEED, 21-1 Udagawacho. Tel. 3462-0111.
Seed is one of Seibu's newest ventures in the store war of Shibuya and offers eight floors devoted to the newest of the new. Because each story is actually quite small, it won't take as long as you might think to work your way through the various boutiques, where you'll find a lot of names you may or may not be familiar with, along with such well-knowns as Paul Smith, Missoni, Katharine Hamnett, Takeo Kikuchi, Jean-Paul Gaultier, Kensho Abe, and Junko Shimada. Open Thursday through Tuesday from 10am to 7pm. Station: Shibuya.

DESIGNER BOUTIQUES

COMME DES GARÇONS, 5-2-1 Minami Aoyama. Tel. 3406-3951.
Located on the right side as you walk from Omotesando east of Aoyama Dori toward Nezu, this showcase store of Rei Kawakubo's designs for both men and women is large and wonderful. Kawakubo is one of my favorite Japanese designers and is one of the few females in the business. Her line of Comme des Garçons consists mainly of loose-fitting, unusually cut clothing that is black, off-white, or plain neutral. Open daily from 11am to 8pm. Station: Omotesando.

HANAE MORI, 3-6-1 Kita-Aoyama. Tel. 3406-1021.
Hanae Mori is the grande dame of Japanese design, one of the first to become known abroad and famous for her evening wear. Her entire collection is shown in this main shop on Omotesando Dori, the building of which was designed by architect Kenzo Tange (who also designed the controversial Akasaka Prince Hotel). Open daily from 10:30am to 7pm. Station: Omotesando.

KANSAI, 3-28-7 Jingumae. Tel. 3478-1958.
It's hard to go unnoticed if you're wearing Yamamoto Kansai's colorful, theatrical creations. His clothing is casual, usually knits and cottons, with bright and bold designs and splashes of color. Open daily from 11am to 8pm. Station: Meiji-Jingumae (then about a 10-minute walk).

PLANTATION, on the fifth floor of La Florêt, 1-11-6 Jingumae. Tel. 3423-7690.
Plantation, Issey Miyake's line for women, is just one of several Issey Miyake shops on this street (others include Permanente, located in the same building as Plantation, and Issey Miyake Men, practically next door at 3-18-11 Minami Aoyama). Now well known both at home and abroad, Miyake was one of many Japanese who first had to go abroad to make a name for himself before the Japanese took notice. His clothes are rich in texture and fabrics. Open daily from 11am to 8pm. Station: Omotesando.

YOHJI YAMAMOTO, 5-3-6 Minami Aoyama. Tel. 3409-6006.
This shop has an interesting, avant-garde interior, as do all Yohji Yamamoto shops. It reminds me of the inside of a mine, or perhaps the underbelly of a railroad trestle, or . . . who knows. At any rate, clothes are sparingly hung, flaunting the luxury of space. The shop is on the same street as Comme des Garçons and Plantation. Open daily from 11am to 8pm. Station: Omotesando.

INTERIOR DESIGN

The department stores listed above have furniture and design sections. My favorite is Ginza's **Matsuya** department store's Design Collection on the seventh floor, which displays items from around the world selected by the Japan Design Committee as examples of fine design. Included have been the Alessi teapot from Italy, Braun razors and clocks, and Porsche sunglasses.

AXIS BUILDING, 5-17-1 Roppongi. Tel. 3587-2781.

Axis is a building with more than two dozen shops, most devoted to the latest in contemporary, high-tech interior design. The majority of products are Japanese, but there are also selected goods from the United States and Europe. There are shops selling sleek and unusual lighting fixtures, clocks, kitchenware, office accessories, lacquered furniture, textiles, and linen—and don't neglect the shops in the basement. Hours vary for each shop, but most are open Monday through Saturday from 11am to 7pm; closed holidays. Station: Roppongi (then about a four-minute walk on Gaien-Higashi Dori in the direction of Tokyo Tower).

IN THE ROOM, 1-21-3 Jinnan, Shibuya-ku. Tel. 3464-0101.

One of the big department store chains, Marui has opened In the Room, a nine-floor building of interior goods. Part of the surge in department stores in Shibuya and the wave of interest in home furnishings as fashion sales fall off, In the Room is filled with interesting goods from the cute (teddy bears) to serious functional furniture. On the second floor, have a cup of tea at a branch of the Parisian purveyors Marriage Frères. Open on Thursday and Friday from 11am to 8pm. Station: Shibuya.

LOFT, 21-1 Udagawacho, Shibuya-ku. Tel. 3462-0111.

Seibu's answer to Tokyu Hands (see below), Loft also sells items for the homeowner and hobbyist, with an eye more toward the trendy. It's crowded with young shoppers in search of simple furniture, games, telephones, stationery, office supplies, cookware, glassware, and more, and on the sixth floor is a "designer's corner," with well-designed products from various countries. There's a branch of Loft in Ikebukuro's Seibu department store. Open Thursday through Tuesday from 10am to 7pm. Station: Shibuya.

TOKYU HANDS, 12-18 Udagawacho, Shibuya-ku. Tel. 5489-5111.

Billing itself as the "Creative Life Store," Tokyu Hands is a huge department store for the homeowner and hobbyist, with departments devoted to camping and picnic equipment, games, gadgets, party supplies, sewing machines, cookware, Japanese knives, plastic lunchboxes, Japanese papers, office supplies, and all the equipment and materials for do-it-yourselfers. If you're setting up an apartment in Tokyo, this is the place to come. There's a branch in Ikebukuro beside the Sunshine Building. Open daily from 10am to 8pm; closed the second and third Wednesday of every month. Station: Shibuya.

KITCHENWARE & TABLEWARE

The department stores listed above and the buildings devoted to interior design and the home offer kitchenware and tableware. In particular, be sure to check out **Savoir Vivre,** located in the Axis Building, for its contemporary Japanese pottery and cookware.

In addition, there are two areas in Tokyo with a number of shops filled with items related to cooking and serving. In **Tsukiji** along the streets stretching between Tsukiji Station and the Tsukiji Fish Market are shops selling pottery, serving trays, bamboo products, knives, bowls, dishes, and lunchboxes. The second place to look is on **Kappabashi Dori Street** near the Tawaramachi subway station, Japan's largest wholesale area for cookware with approximately 150 specialty stores. Stores here sell sukiyaki pots, woks, lunchboxes, pots and pans, aprons, knives, china, and bulk packages of disposable chopsticks. This is also the place to come to buy plastic models of food.

MARKETS

Flea markets are good for the occasional antique, but mainly they're rich in delightful junk. Held once or twice every month, they begin early in the morning and last until 4pm or later. *Bargaining is expected.* Check the *Tokyo Journal* for a list of the month's flea markets.

ARAI YAKUSHIJI TEMPLE, Arai, Nakano-ku. Tel. 3386-1355.

Open the first Sunday of every month (canceled in case of rain), dawn to dusk. Station: Arai Yakushi-mae, on the Seibu Shinjuku Line.

HANAZONO SHRINE, Yasukuni Dori Ave., 5-17-3 Shinjuku, Shinjuku-ku. Tel. 3200-3093.

Open the second and third Sunday of every month from 4am to 5pm (canceled in case of rain). Station: Shinjuku-Sanchome.

NOGI SHRINE, 8-11-27 Akasaka, Minato-ku. Tel. 3402-2181.

Open the second Sunday of every month from dawn to dusk (canceled in case of rain). Station: Nogizaka, on the Chiyoda Line.

ROPPONGI FLEA MARKET, on the steps of the Roi Bldg., Gaien-Higashi Dori, 5-chome Roppongi, Minato-ku. Tel. 3583-2081.

Open the fourth Thursday and Friday of every month from 7am to 8pm. Station: Roppongi.

TOGO SHRINE, 1-5-3 Jingumae, Shibuya-ku. Tel. 3403-3591.

Open the first and fourth Sunday of every month, from 4am to 4pm. Station: Meiji-Jingumae or Harajuku.

YOYOGI PARK, Shibuya-Koen Dori (near NHK Hall), Harajuku. Tel. 3226-6800.

A flea market dealing exclusively in secondhand goods, including clothing, housewares, and odds and ends. It's held irregularly once or twice a month, usually on a Sunday (check the *Tokyo Journal*). Station: Harajuku.

AMEYA YOKOCHO

This is the closest thing Tokyo has to a permanent marketplace. Located under and along the west side of the elevated tracks of the Yamanote Line between Ueno and Okachimachi Stations, Ameya Yokocho (often shortened to Ameyoko or Ameyacho) is an area of stalls and tiny shops selling produce, clothing, and accessories. Housewives shop here for fresh cuts of tuna, squid, crab, fish eggs, eel, fruits, and vegetables, while Tokyo's youth come here for costume jewelry, cosmetics, socks, jackets, hosiery, watches, handbags, and clothing. Some shops are closed the second or third Wednesday of every month, but otherwise it's open daily from 10am to 7pm.

PEARLS

IMPERIAL HOTEL ARCADE, in the Imperial Hotel, 1-1-1 Uchisaiwaicho.

There are several pearl shops here, including a branch of Mikimoto (tel. 3591-5001); K. Uyeda (tel. 3503-2587), in business since 1884; and Asahi Shoten (tel. 3503-2528). Hours vary, but shops are generally open from 10am to 7pm; some shops are closed Sunday. Station: Hibiya.

MIKIMOTO, 4-5-5 Ginza. Tel. 3535-4611.

Koichi Mikimoto was the first to produce a really good cultured pearl, back in 1913. Today the name Mikimoto is one of the most famous names in cultured pearls, and this is the main shop. Open Thursday through Tuesday from 10:30am to 7pm. Station: Ginza (near Ginza 4-chome crossing on Chuo Dori).

SECONDHAND SHOPS

While you might not shop in secondhand shops at home, with Japanese designer prices being what they are, you may want to consider doing so in Tokyo. Harajuku has the oldest used-clothing shops, including **Chicago's** on Omotesando Dori and **Santa Monica** in the La Forêt basement, but they offer mostly U.S. nostalgia at 10 times U.S. thrift-store prices. Trendy Daikanyama, one stop beyond Shibuya on the Toyoko Line and a good place for a stroll, has lots of secondhand shops. **Circus** (across the lane from the Red Thunder Café) offers designer fashions (Romeo Gigli, Katharine Hamnett) for a fraction of the original costs, and **Screaming Mimi's,** a branch of the New York shop, displays corsets in acid colors as well as 1940s watches. One of the few consignment shops is **Garret,** in Ebisu (a one-minute walk from the small exit of the JR Ebisu Station), where I've found Issey Miyake Plantation and Rei Kawakubo's Comme des Garçon. Consider, however, that a deeply discounted Comme des Garçons jacket still runs ¥35,000 ($318). Next door to Garret is **Norma Jean,** which carries new factory overstock with prices from ¥2,500 to ¥25,000 ($22.70 to $227).

SOUVENIRS

Shops listed under "Crafts and Traditional Japanese Products" carry a wide range of souvenir items, especially the **Oriental Bazaar.** In addition, **Nakamise Dori,** a lane in Asakusa, is lined with stalls selling everything from cotton yukata to traditional hairpins.

INTERNATIONAL ARCADE, 1-7-23 Uchisaiwaicho. Tel. 3501-5775.

This arcade, located underneath the train tracks in Hibiya not far from the Imperial Hotel, is full of shops selling kimonos, china, woodblock prints, pearls, and other Japanese products. Open daily from 10am to 6pm. Station: Hibiya or Yurakucho.

STATIONERY & BUSINESS CARDS

ITOYA, 2-7-15 Ginza. Tel. 3561-8311.

This is one of Tokyo's best-known office-supply shops, stocked with stationery, Japanese paper, pens, staplers, and whatever else you might need for your business. If you like desk-top gadgets, you'll enjoy walking through the several floors here, especially the fourth floor. You can also have business cards made here (orders take about one week). Open Monday through Saturday from 9:30am to 7pm, and on Sunday and holidays from 10am to 6pm. Station: Ginza or Ginza-Itchome, on Chuo Dori.

PRINTBOY, on the second floor of the Tomo Bldg., 3-8-23 Roppongi. Tel. 3402-5581.

Printboy, located just down the street toward the ANA Hotel from Roppongi crossroads, is where I have had my visiting cards printed for years now. The staff, headed by Shinichi Tomioka, who speaks English, are used to foreigners and very helpful. It takes only one week to have English/Japanese cards printed and the cost for 100 visiting cards starts at ¥3,500 ($31.80). Open Monday through Friday from 9am to 6pm. Station: Roppongi (then a one-minute walk).

TOYS

HAKUHINKAN TOY PARK, 8-8-11 Ginza. Tel. 3571-8008.

Four floors of games, gifts, and toys make this one of Tokyo's largest and best toy stores. In addition to the usual dolls, puzzles, games, and other items, there's also a large assortment of gag gifts. Open daily from 11am to 8pm. Station: Shimbashi or Ginza.

KIDDY LAND, 6-1-9 Jingumae. Tel. 3409-3431.

Toys, games, puzzles, and much more are packed into this immensely popular shop on Omotesando in Harajuku, usually so crowded with teenagers that it's impossible to get in the front door. It has a large selection of gag gifts, including temporary tattoos, fake breasts made of rubber, and who knows what else. Open daily from 10am to 8pm; closed the third Tuesday of every month. Station: Meiji-Jingumae, Harajuku, or Omotesando.

CHAPTER 9

TOKYO NIGHTS

Come dusk, Tokyo blossoms into a profusion of giant neon lights and paper lanterns, as millions of overworked Japanese become hell-bent on having a good time. If you ask me, Tokyo at night is one of the craziest cities in the world, a city that never gives up and never seems to sleep. Entertainment districts can be as crowded at 3am as they are at 10pm, and many establishments remain open until the first subways start humming at 5am. Whether it's jazz, reggae, gay bars, sex shows, dance clubs, hostess bars, mania, or madness you're searching for, Tokyo has it all.

In case you're wondering, a hostess bar is simply a bar in which women will sit at your table, talk to you, pour your drinks, listen to your problems, and boost your ego. Usually small, tiny places managed and owned by a reigning Mama-san, they cater primarily to regular male customers, who are used to the high prices for drinks in exchange for the opportunity to escape the world of both work and family. And as for those famous geisha clubs, they are located mainly in Kyoto, where the only way to get your foot in the door is by introduction.

To make your explorations of Tokyo's nightlife easier, I have arranged this chapter according to the various entertainment districts. Most of Tokyo's nighttime revelers head for one district and remain there the whole evening.

By far the most common way to spend an evening in Tokyo is at a drinking establishment, which is where Tokyo's army of office workers, college students, and expatriates hang out. These places include Western-style bars, most commonly found in Roppongi, as well as Japanese-style watering holes, called *nomi-ya.* Yakitori-ya (restaurant/bars that serve yakitori and other snacks) are included in this group.

One thing you should be aware of is the "table charge" that some bars and cocktail lounges levy on customers. Included in the table charge is usually a small appetizer, maybe nuts, chips, or a pickled vegetable, and the charge is usually ¥300 to ¥500 ($2.75 to $4.55) per person. Some establishments levy a table charge only after a certain time in the evening; others may add it only if you don't order food from their menu. If you're not sure and it matters to you, be sure to ask. Some places call it an *otsumami,* or snack charge. Remember, too, that a 3% consumption tax will be added to your bill; hostess bars and some of the more exclusive clubs will also add a 20% service charge.

For a rundown of concerts and entertainment in the city, consult the *Tokyo Journal* or *Tokyo Time Out,* both published monthly. The *Tokyo Journal* also carries movie reviews, along with a long list of what's playing where. However, movies are expensive in Tokyo, with admission averaging ¥1,700 ($15.45), theaters are usually plagued by long lines and huge crowds, and Hollywood releases usually take several months to reach Japan.

To secure concert tickets, you can always go to the theater or hall itself to buy tickets. However, if you're staying in one of the upper-class hotels, the concierge or guest-relations manager will usually obtain tickets for you. Otherwise, a much easier way to secure tickets is through one of the several **ticket services** available, though you should have someone who speaks Japanese make the call for you. Ticket services include Ticket PIA (tel. 5237-9990), Ticket Saison (tel. 3286-5482), and Playguide (tel. 5802-9999).

And finally, keep in mind that taxis become scarce after midnight. If it's a weekend night and you've missed the last subway home, you may have to resign yourself to staying out until 2 or 3am when it becomes easier to catch a taxi. And, of course, you can also simply stay out all night until the first subways start running again at 5am. I've seen dawn hit Roppongi more times than I care to remember.

1. GINZA & HIBIYA

THE CLUB & MUSIC SCENE

A MUSICAL REVUE

TAKARAZUKA KAGEKIDAN, Tokyo Takarazuka Gekijo, 1-1-3 Yuraku-cho. Tel. 3591-1711, or 3201-7777 for reservations.

Takarazuka Kagekidan is a world-famous all-female troupe that stages elaborate revues with dancing, singing, and gorgeous costumes. The first Takarazuka troupe formed back in 1912 in a resort near Osaka and gained instant notoriety because it was all women, just as Kabuki is all men. Its audience is made up almost entirely of women, mainly middle-aged housewives. To find out what's being staged, check with Tour Companion's *Tokyo City Guide* or contact the Tourist Information Center. Performances are held six or seven months a year, generally March, April, July, August, November, and December, and sometimes June. Performances are also occasionally held in the Kabukiza theater. Station: Yurakucho or Hibiya (then a few minutes' walk).

Admission: Tickets, ¥1,200–¥5,000 ($10.90–$45.45).

OLDIES ROCK

KENTO'S, on the top floor of the Takiyamacho Bldg., 6-7-12 Ginza. Tel. 3572-9161.

Kento's is a chain of highly successful entertainment houses that is in large part responsible for Japan's current infatuation with oldies nostalgia, particularly music of the 1950s and '60s. It features a live band dressed in clothing and hairstyles of the '50s, and even the microphones are authentically old-looking. There's room to twist and shout and dance to your favorite tunes. Open Monday through Saturday from 6pm to 3am and on Sunday and holidays from 6pm to midnight. Beer starts at ¥600 ($5.45). Station: Ginza (then about a five-minute walk).

Admission: ¥1,400 ($12.70).

IMPRESSIONS

Then I saw for the first time the true beauty of Tokyo, and of all Japanese cities. They are only beautiful at night, when they become fairylands of gorgeous neon: towers and sheets and globes and rivers of neon, in stunning profusion, a wild razzle-dazzle of colors and shapes and movements, fierce and delicate, restrained and violent against the final afterglow of sunset.

—JAMES KIRKUP, *THESE HORNED ISLANDS*, 1962

THE BAR SCENE

A HOSTESS CLUB

CLUB MAIKO, Suzuran Dori St., on the fourth floor of the Aster Plaza Bldg., 7-7-6 Ginza. Tel. 3574-7745.

If you're interested in visiting a hostess bar, this one is receptive to foreigners and is not prohibitively expensive. Its hostesses, dressed in traditional geisha kimonos with painted faces and elaborate hairdos, perform four dancing shows nightly, talking and sitting with customers between performances. With this small locale's traditional music and atmosphere, this may be the closest you'll get to Japan's geisha bars. Open Monday through Saturday from 6pm to midnight; closed holidays. Station: Ginza (then a three-minute walk).

Admission: Special package deal for foreigners ¥8,800 ($80), including entrance, show charge, snacks, and drinks; hostess drinks ¥1,000 ($9.10).

THE MAJOR CONCERT & PERFORMANCE HALLS

Bunkamura (including Orchard Hall and Theatre Cocoon), 2-24-1 Dogenzaka, Shibuya-ku (Shibuya Station). Tel. 3477-3244.

Kabukiza, 4-12-15 Ginza (Higashi-Ginza Station). Tel. 3541-3131 or 5565-6000.

National Theatre of Japan (Kokuritsu Gekijo), 4-1 Hayabusacho, Chiyoda-ku (Hanzomon, Kojimachi or Nagatacho Station). Tel. 3265-7411.

NHK Hall, 2-2-1 Jinnan, Shibuya-ku (Harajuku or Shibuya Station). Tel. 3465-1751.

Nakano Sun Plaza, 4-1-1 Nakano, Nakano-ku (Nakano Station). Tel. 3388-1151.

Sunshine Gekijo Theater, Sunshine city Bunka Kaikan, 4th Floor, 3-1-4 Higashi-Ikebukuro (Higashi-Ikebukuro Station). Tel. 3987-5281.

Suntory Hall, Ark Hills, 1-13-1 Akasaka (Akasaka or Roppongi Station). Tel. 3505-1001.

Tokyo Bunka Kaikan, 5-45 Ueno Park (Ueno Station, Koen exit). Tel. 3828-2111.

Tokyo Geijutsu Gekijo, 1-8-1 Nishi Ikebukuro, Toshima-ku (Ikebukuro Station). Tel. 5391-2111.

A COCKTAIL LOUNGE

RAINBOW LOUNGE, on the 17th floor of the Imperial Hotel, 1-1-1 Uchisaiwaicho. Tel. 3504-1111.

This sophisticated lounge is a good place for a quiet drink and a great view of the city lights stretched below. Stop by for before-dinner cocktails or an after-dinner drink. Cocktails start at ¥1,200 ($10.90). Open daily from noon to midnight. Station: Hibiya (then a one-minute walk).

PUBS & BARS

HENRY AFRICA, 7-2-17 Ginza. Tel. 3573-4563.

This is one of several Henry Africa pubs in Tokyo, and like the others, it's decorated in the spirit of the African hut with potted plants, Tiffany-style lampshades, and a wood-plank floor. A comfortable place for a drink, visitors should feel right at home here. Beer prices start at ¥700 ($6.35). Open Monday through Saturday from 10am to 11:30pm, and on Sunday and holidays from 3:30 to 10:30pm. Station: Hibiya or Yurakucho (then a few minutes' walk; it's located across from the Yamanote elevated tracks, with the entrance around the corner, past the tobacco shop).

KIRIN CITY, 8-8 Ginza. Tel. 3571-9694.

Featuring Kirin beer, this pleasant and modern bar is located on Hanatsubaki Dori, just off Chuo Dori near the Shiseido boutique. Snacks include assorted sausages, chili beans and crackers, and salads. Beer starts at ¥470 ($4.25). Open daily from 11:30am to 11pm. Station: Ginza (then about a three-minute walk).

LUPIN (53), 5-5-11 Ginza. Tel. 3571-0750.

If you're looking for a quiet place for a drink, you can't find a more subdued bar than this. Located in an alley behind the German restaurant Ketel, this tiny basement bar opened back in 1928 and has changed little over the decades. Featuring a long wooden bar and wooden booths and cabinets, it's so quiet you can hear yourself think, and as though the world of jukeboxes and stereos has passed it by, no music is ever played here—a very civilized place. A large bottle of beer starts at ¥800 ($7.25); mixed drinks start at ¥1,000 ($9.10). Open Monday through Saturday from 5 to 11pm; closed holidays. Station: Ginza (then a few minutes' walk).

SAPPORO LION, 7-9-20 Ginza. Tel. 3571-2590.

Sapporo beer is the lure of this beer hall, decorated in imitation Gothic and located on Chuo Dori Avenue not far from the Matsuzakaya department store. A plastic display case shows such snacks as pizza, sausage, beef stew, and spaghetti, and there's an English menu. Beer starts at ¥500 ($4.55). Open daily from 11:30am to 11pm. Station: Ginza (then about a three-minute walk).

SKYAIR PRONTO, 8-6-25 Ginza. Tel. 3571-7864.

Easy to find on Namiki Dori, this is one of the cheapest so-called café/bars in Ginza. A coffee shop by day with coffee a mere ¥160 ($1.45) a cup, from 5:30pm it's a bar, with beer starting at ¥430 ($3.90). Shots are its specialty, costing only ¥380 ($3.45). There's an English menu. Open Monday through Saturday from 8am to 11pm and on Sunday from 8am to 9:30pm. Station: Ginza (then a few minutes' walk).

YAKITORI-YA

ATARIYA (11), 3-5-17 Ginza. Tel. 3564-0045.

Located on the small side street that runs behind the Wako department store on Ginza 4-chome Crossing, this is a convivial place to come for an evening of yakitori and beer, made easy with an English menu. Beer from ¥500 ($4.55). Open Monday through Saturday from 4:30 to 10:30pm. Station: Ginza (then a three-minute walk).

NANBANTEI, 5-6-6 Ginza. Tel. 3571-5700.

Another lively watering hole, Nanbantei combines the modern with the traditional in its decor and is located in a basement on Suzuran Street. Its à la carte menu lists skewers of pork with asparagus, Japanese mushrooms, large shrimp, quail eggs, gingko nuts, and chicken meatballs, among many other dishes. Beer starts at ¥600 ($5.45). Open daily from 5 to 10pm. Station: Ginza (then a few minutes' walk).

YAGURA CHAYA (54), 6-2-1 Ginza. Tel. 3571-3494.

Popular with couples and groups of office workers from the area, this lively Japanese-style yakitori-ya decorated with antiques and traditional crafts is in the basement of the Riccar Building not far from the Imperial Hotel. Look for a traditional-looking restaurant with lockers just inside the door where you're supposed to deposit your shoes. Its menu, in Japanese only, includes sashimi, yakitori, fish, oden, and pizza. Beer starts at ¥550 ($5); sake, at ¥320 ($2.90). Open daily from 5pm to midnight. Station: Hibiya or Ginza (then less than a five-minute walk).

2. AKASAKA

THE CLUB & MUSIC SCENE

CORDON BLEU, 6-6-4 Akasaka. Tel. 3582-7800 or 3585-6980.

Small and intimate, this well-known nightclub is actually a 150-seat dinner theater featuring topless Japanese and foreign dancers. Former guests have included boxer Muhammad Ali and the late John Lennon. There are three different admission prices, depending on whether you choose to have one of the dinners or only snacks. Open daily from 6pm, with shows at 7:30, 9:30, and 11pm. Station: Akasaka (then about a five-minute walk).

Admission (including tax and service charge): ¥16,500 and ¥20,000 ($150 and $181.80) for dinner and drinks, ¥13,500 ($122.70) for hors d'oeuvres and drinks.

THE BAR SCENE

COCKTAIL LOUNGES

GARDEN LOUNGE, in the Hotel New Otani, 4-1 Kioi-cho. Tel. 3265-1111.

Start the evening here before it turns dark and you'll be treated to a view of a beautiful 400-year-old garden, complete with waterfall, pond, bridges, and manicured bushes. There's soft, live music Monday through Saturday starting at 7pm, for which there's a cover charge of ¥300 ($2.75) Monday through Friday and ¥600 ($5.45) on Saturday. Cocktails, which begin at ¥1,400 ($12.70), are served every evening from 6 to 10pm. Station: Akasaka-mitsuke (then a three-minute walk).

TOP OF AKASAKA, on the 40th floor of the Akasaka Prince Hotel, 1-2 Kioi-cho. Tel. 3234-1111.

Fancy and romantic, this is a great perch from which to watch the day fade into darkness, as millions of lights and neon signs twinkle on in the distance. By the way, young people under drinking age are unwelcome here. Cocktails average ¥1,300 ($11.80). Open daily from 5pm to 2am. Station: Akasaka-mitsuke (then a three-minute walk).

PUBS & BARS

HENRY AFRICA, on the second floor of the Akasaka Ishida Bldg., 3-13-14 Akasaka. Tel. 3585-0149.

Yet another one of this chain of pubs in Tokyo. Decorated in the theme of the African hunt, with elephant tusks, potted palms, and Tiffany-style lampshades, this place is very popular with young Japanese office workers—maybe because of the free popcorn available in the evenings. Beer starts at ¥480 ($4.35); cocktails, at ¥800 ($7.25). Open Monday through Friday from 11:30am to 11:30pm and on Saturday, Sunday, and holidays from 5:30 to 11:30pm. Station: Akasaka (then a 30-second walk; it's located across from the TBS Kaikan television building on Hitotsugi Street).

PRONTO, 3-12-1 Akasaka. Tel. 3582-3717.

Similar to Skyair Pronto in Ginza, this café/bar serves as an inexpensive coffee shop by day and a bar by night. Its decor is plain and unexciting, but prices are low, with beer starting at ¥430 ($3.90) and cocktails at ¥600 ($5.45). Open Monday through Saturday from 7:30am to 5pm as a coffee shop, from 5 to 11pm as a bar; closed holidays. Station: Between Akasaka and Akasaka-mitsuke, on Tamachi Dori.

3. ROPPONGI

THE CLUB & MUSIC SCENE

JAZZ

BIRDLAND, in the basement of the Square Bldg., 3-10-3 Roppongi. Tel. 3478-3456.

Located in a building famous for its eight discos, Birdland is a welcome refuge from Roppongi's madding crowd, featuring straightforward jazz by Japanese musicians. It's small and cozy with candles and soft lighting. Drinks start at ¥850 ($7.70). Doors open at 5:30pm; music is played Sunday through Thursday from 7 to 11:30pm and on Friday and Saturday from 8:30pm to 1am. Station: Roppongi (then a two-minute walk).

Admission: ¥2,700 ($24.55).

BODY AND SOUL, 7-14-12 Roppongi. Tel. 5466-3348.

This is a no-nonsense and very casual jazz club featuring mostly Japanese musicians playing both traditional and modern jazz. Respected for the quality of its shows, it is small, with room for only 50 people, and musicians who have finished gigs elsewhere have been known to show up for impromptu jam sessions with the band. Beer is ¥750 ($6.80). Open Monday through Saturday from 6:30pm to 2am, with shows usually at 8, 9:30, and 11pm. Station: Roppongi (then a one-minute walk on Roppongi Dori in the direction of Shibuya).

Admission: ¥3,000 ($22.70).

ROPPONGI PIT INN, 3-17-7 Roppongi. Tel. 3585-1063.

This is one of Tokyo's best-known live houses. A no-frills basement establishment catering to a younger crowd, it boasts some of the finest in native and imported jazz, jazz rock, fusion, and blues. Beer costs ¥600 ($5.45). Doors open daily at 6:30pm; shows start at 7:30 and 9pm. Station: Roppongi (then about a seven-minute walk; it's located on the left side of Gaien-Higashi Dori in the direction of Tokyo Tower).

Admission: ¥3,000 ($22.70).

NOSTALGIA, REGGAE & MORE

BAU HAUS, on the sixth floor of the Wada Bldg., 7-15-9 Roppongi. Tel. 3403-0092.

This small club reminds me of somebody's '60s garage with the addition of low velveteen sofas. It's owned and operated by the house band, who serve the regular clientele, mostly foreigners, between sets! The band plays rock 'n' roll, led by singer Kay-chan, a kind of Japanese David Bowie, who puts on quite a show—a bit raunchy in places. Kind of like a weird hostess club, he'll come and sit at your table between sets if you ask him. Beer costs ¥750 ($6.80), cocktails run ¥750 to ¥1,050 ($6.80 to $9.55), and snacks like pizza, cheese, and veggie sticks go for ¥850 to ¥1,200 ($7.70 to $10.90). It's located on the second street on your right as you walk toward Nishi-Azabu from Roppongi Crossing. Open: Monday through Saturday from 8pm to 1am. Station: Roppongi (then a three-minute walk).

Admission: ¥1,800 ($16.35).

CAVERN CLUB, 5-3-2 Roppongi. Tel. 3405-5207.

If you know your Beatles history, you'll know that the Cavern Club is the name of the Liverpool club where the Beatles got their start. The Tokyo club features house bands that perform Beatles music exclusively, and they're so convincing that if you close your eyes, you might believe you've been transported back in time to the real thing. Extremely popular with both Japanese and foreigners, it's packed on weekends with long waiting lines, and unfortunately reservations are taken only for one show. Beer starts at ¥650 ($5.90); cocktails, at ¥850 ($6.80). Open Monday through Saturday from 6pm to 2:30am and on Sunday and holidays from 6pm to midnight. Station: Roppongi (then about a four-minute walk).

Admission: ¥1,400 ($12.70), plus a 20% service charge.

HOT CO-ROCKET, 5-18-2 Roppongi. Tel. 3583-9409.

Live reggae bands, and occasional salsa, regale the crowds here as they compete for space on a tiny dance floor. The atmosphere is slightly tropical, with tropical drinks to match. Sunday features disco music instead of the live thing. In any case, the music here is loud.

Open Monday through Saturday from 7pm to 3am and on Sunday from 7pm to midnight. Station: Roppongi (then a seven-minute walk; it's located on the right side of Gaien-Higashi Dori, across from the Porsche dealership, in the direction of Tokyo Tower).

Admission: ¥3,000 ($22.70) for women, ¥4,000 ($36.35) for men, including two drinks.

KARAOKE THEATRE, 4-10-3 Roppongi. Tel. 3402-7772.

The Kento's group does it again, this time cashing in on the karaoke craze with this classy karaoke bar in the heart of Roppongi. Anyone in the audience can get up on the stage and sing to the background music of their choice—they'll even be projected onto a large screen. Everyone's chance to be the star of the minute. There are more than 50 English songs to choose from, including Beatles' songs, "Johnny B. Good," and "Blue Suede Shoes." Beer starts at ¥500 ($4.55); cocktails, at ¥600 ($5.45). Open Monday through Saturday from 7pm to 3am. Station: Roppongi (then a one-minute walk; it's located on the street behind Victoria Station).

KENTO'S, 5-3-1 Roppongi. Tel. 3401-5755.

Under the same ownership as the Cavern Club and the Karaoke Theatre, Kento's was one of the first establishments to open when the wave of 1950s nostalgia hit Japan earlier this decade and has since opened in locales all over Japan. Decorated with posters of such stars as Elvis and Connie Francis, this is where enthusiasts of yesterday come to hear bands play music of the 1950s and 1960s. Although there's hardly room to dance, that doesn't stop the largely over-30 Japanese audience from doing a kind of rock 'n' roll–twist in the aisles. Snacks include pizza, spaghetti, sausage, salads, and a rather peculiar treat consisting of raisins in butter. Beer starts at ¥650 ($5.90); cocktails, at ¥850 ($7.70). Open Monday through Saturday from 6pm to 2:30am and on Sunday and holidays from 6pm to midnight. Station: Roppongi (then about a four-minute walk).

Admission: ¥1,400 ($12.70).

SALSA CORONA, 7-7-4 Roppongi. Tel. 3746-0244.

Part of the Latin American music fad in Tokyo, this faux Spanish tile and adobe-walled basement bar is adorned with Latin music album covers and posters. Everyone's dancing, although there's no real dance floor. Corona beers and various cocktails cost ¥1,000 ($9.10) and food, like feijoada or empanada or nachos, run about the same. Exotic bartenders include a Chilean/Australian the night I was there. Open daily from 7pm to 6am. Station: Roppongi (then a five-minute walk; it's located on the first alleyway to the right off the diagonal street, second left, as you walk on Gaien-Higashi Dori toward Nogizaka).

DANCE CLUBS/DISCOS

Several live entertainment places listed above offer dancing, as does the 1960s-oriented club **Lollipop,** on the second floor of the Nittaku Building, 3-8-15 Roppongi (tel. 3478-0028). Otherwise, discos are usually the cheapest way to spend an evening, since the cover charge often includes at least a few drinks. Note that cover charges are usually higher on weekends.

AREA, in the basement of the Nittaku Bldg., 3-8-15 Roppongi. Tel. 3479-3721.

An appropriate name for a disco with the highest ceiling in town,

Area has a spaciousness that belies the fact that it's actually in a basement. This is one of the best discos for dancing and observing; there are small stages for those who like to show what they can do. The lighting is good, curtains lower and rise on the dance floor, and the ceiling is mirrored. All in all, this place somehow seems a bit wilder than most, and it's popular mainly with young Japanese women. Beer costs ¥500 ($4.55). Open Sunday through Thursday from 6pm to 2am and on Friday and Saturday from 6pm to 4am. Station: Roppongi (then a three-minute walk).

Admission (including drinks, except beer): ¥4,000 ($36.35) women, ¥4,500 ($40.90) men; ¥500 ($4.55) extra charge for men Fri–Sat and the eve before hols.

BUZZ, on the fifth floor of the Square Bldg., 3-10-3 Roppongi. Tel. 3470-6391.

The Square Building is filled with discos on almost every floor. This one is decorated like a "New York rooftop," whatever that means, complete with clouds painted on the walls, and—get this—giant flies hanging from the ceiling. There are rock videos everywhere so you can watch your favorite performer as you dance. Although the "official" closing time is midnight, in actuality it's open daily from 6pm to 5am. Station: Roppongi (then about a three-minute walk).

Admission (including tickets good for about two or three drinks, excluding beer): ¥3,000 ($27.25) women, ¥4,000 ($36.35) men.

JAVA JIVE, in the basement of the Square Bldg., 3-10-3 Roppongi. Tel. 3478-0088.

The disco of the moment is the immensely popular Java Jive, decorated in a Caribbean-beach theme, with loose-limbed Jamaican cut-out silhouettes on the wall, tropical palms, and the flicker of electric candles. The dance floor was sand for a while, though it was covered up when it proved difficult to writhe upon. This place is huge, with a bar and tables upstairs and a live band downstairs playing reggae and salsa every night except Sunday, when it's disco night instead. This place is so cavernous, however, that the band seems nonexistent. Wild partying takes place here until the light of dawn. Open daily from 6pm to midnight officially, but unofficially to 4am or later. Station: Roppongi (then a three-minute walk).

Admission (including 10 tickets good for food and drinks; most drinks take 2 or 3 tickets, beer excluded—you must purchase it from vending machines): ¥3,000 ($27.25) women, ¥4,000 ($36.35) men.

LEXINGTON QUEEN, in the basement of the Daisan Goto Bldg., 3-13-14 Roppongi. Tel. 3401-1661.

This is an old-timer in the crazy world of discos—it opened in 1980 and has been swinging ever since. The list of its guests reads like a *Who's Who* of foreign movie and rock stars who have visited Tokyo—Stevie Wonder, Rod Stewart, Liza Minelli, Sheena Easton, Joe Cocker, Dustin Hoffman, John Denver, Jacqueline Bisset, Spandau Ballet, and Jennifer Beals, to name only a few. One night when I was there Duran Duran walked in. Much of the disco's popularity is due to manager Bill Hersey, a well-known personality in Tokyo who, appropriately enough, writes a gossip column for the *Weekender* and somehow manages to get every visiting star to drop by his disco. Note that men unaccompanied by women are not allowed entrance. Open daily from 6pm to midnight officially, unofficially to 2 or 3am. Station: Roppongi (then about a three-minute walk).

Admission (including unlimited drinks—excluding beer, which costs extra—and ¥1,000/$9.10 worth of sushi): ¥3,000 ($27.25) women, ¥4,000 ($36.35) men.

THE BAR SCENE

PUBS & BARS

ACARAJÉ, 1-8-19 Nishi-Azabu. Tel. 3401-0973.

This tiny Brazilian bar is a friendly place, filled with regulars. In fact, the atmosphere is more like that of a private party, since it's out of the mainstream of Roppongi revelers and is frequented only by people in-the-know. Highly recommended. Beer and cocktails start at ¥800 ($7.25). Open Monday through Saturday from 7pm to 1am. Station: Roppongi (then about a seven-minute walk; it's located off Roppongi Dori in the direction of Shibuya, behind Sunset Strip).

CHARLESTON, 3-8-11 Roppongi. Tel. 3402-0372.

This used to be the place to hang out in Roppongi back in the early 1980s, but in ensuing years has had its ups and downs. Filled mainly with foreigners, it has a different clientele and correspondingly different atmosphere every time I come here. Sometimes it's filled with U.S. military men on leave, sometimes with foreign businessmen dressed in suits, and sometimes with characters that must have dragged themselves up from the deep. Other times it's completely empty. You never know with Charleston; but it's always at its most crowded at around 3am. Beer is ¥780 ($7.10); cocktails start at ¥880 ($8). Open daily from 6pm to 6am. Station: Roppongi (then less than a five-minute walk; it's beside a graveyard).

DEJAVU, 3-15-24 Roppongi. Tel. 3403-8777.

If there's any one bar responsible for Charleston's demise, this is it. Although popular nightspots in Tokyo seem to come and go with both the brilliancy and durability of a shooting star, Dejavu has been the hottest spot for several years now. Some people find the chaotic and colorful walls gaudy, others find them interesting, but everyone seems to be trying to get into this tiny place—they'll even line up outside and wait. The clientele is mainly foreign, many of whom seem absorbed in their own importance. Cocktails start at ¥800 ($7.25). Open daily from 7pm to 5am. Station: Roppongi (then about a four-minute walk).

DRUGSTORE, in the Wall Bldg., 4-2-4 Nishi-Azabu. Tel. 3409-8222.

A contemporary bar on the first and second floors of the Wall (an entertainment building with the Wanna Dance Disco downstairs and the romantic Italian restaurant Cibrero upstairs), DrugStore's attractions are contemporary sounds, a sculpture by designer Nigel Coates behind the bar, outdoor seating, and wide-open doors—a blessing for nonsmokers. Managed by and popular with the gaijin (foreigners), it's packed out to the sidewalks late at night, where some sit on Harleys and talk over beer (¥750/$6.80). The Wall is a great building for a one-stop evening. Open daily from 7pm to 5am. Station: Roppongi (then a 15-minute walk; it's on Gaien-Nishi Dori—walking from Roppongi, turn left at the Nishi-Azabu crossroads).

EX, 7-7-6 Roppongi. Tel. 3408-5487.

For a bit of old Germany in the heart of Tokyo, pay a visit to Ex, which means "bottoms up" in German. Although it's primarily a beer-drinking establishment, owner Horst serves hearty German food as well. There's no menu so you just have to ask Horst what's cooking, but common dishes are Schnitzel, various kinds of wurst, boiled ribs of pork, Sauerkraut, and fried potatoes. A tiny place consisting of a half-circular bar with seating for only 15 people, it's packed with German businessmen and expatriates who don't mind standing to imbibe their favorite German beer. Eating is usually done good-naturedly in shifts. Beer starts at ¥700 ($6.35). Open Monday through Saturday from 5pm to 2am; closed holidays. Station: Roppongi (then less than a five-minute walk; it's located on the diagonal street across from the Defense Agency as you walk on Gaien-Higashi Dori toward Nogizaka).

HARD ROCK CAFE, 5-4-20 Roppongi. Tel. 3408-7018.

Buy your Tokyo Hard Rock Café T-shirts here. Easily recognizable by King Kong scaling an outside wall, the inside looks like the modern Yuppie version of the local hamburger joint and is decorated with rock 'n' roll memorabilia. The menu contains more than just hamburgers, including steaks, chili, sandwiches, salads, and daily specials. The music, by the way, is loud. A beer here starts at ¥850 ($7.70). Open Monday through Saturday from 11:30am to 2am and on Sunday from 11:30am to 11:30pm. Station: Roppongi (then a three-minute walk, in the direction of Tokyo Tower, then a right at McDonald's).

INTER-NATIONAL STATION, 6-1-5 Roppongi. Tel. 3423-4667.

A very civilized yet casual meeting place, it's owned by Hiro, who speaks English and serves as the amiable bartender. There are little gadgets and toys to play with, and the music is at a level that allows for conversation. Single women can feel comfortable coming here alone. Beer costs ¥800 ($7.25); cocktails start at ¥1,000 ($9.10). Open Saturday through Thursday from 7pm to 2am and on Friday from 7pm to 5am. Station: Roppongi (then a one-minute walk; it's located on the right side of the diagonal street that leads downhill beside the Almond Coffee Shop).

Admission ¥300 ($2.75) cover charge.

MAGGIE'S REVENGE, 3-8-12 Roppongi. Tel. 3479-1096.

Popular with Japanese and expatriates, it's run by an Australian woman and features live music every night, usually provided by a guitar or piano soloist. Sometimes the music is good, sometimes not—you take your chances, but the cover charge is low, so what the heck. It's decorated with the severed neckties of former customers (presumably with their permission) and has a good selection of liqueurs, brandy, and champagne. Beers start at ¥660 ($6); cocktails, at ¥880 ($8). Open Monday through Thursday from 6:30pm to 2:30am and on Friday and Saturday from 6:30pm to 3am. Station: Roppongi (then less than a four-minute walk).

Admission: ¥700 ($6.35) cover charge.

PARADISO, 3-13-12 Roppongi. Tel. 3478-4211.

Located in the basement of a building next to the Lexington Queen disco, this place is popular, chic, and avant garde, and stretches on and on like some underground cavern. The clientele is mainly Japanese. This is one of the few bars that levies a counter charge. Good for people-watching, but expensive. Cocktails start at

¥1,000 ($9.10). Open Monday through Saturday from 7pm to 4am and on Sunday from 7pm to 11pm. Station: Roppongi (then about a three-minute walk).

Admission: ¥1,000 ($9.10) cover charge at a counter.

RED SHOES, 2-25-18 Nishi-Azabu. Tel. 3499-4319.
This basement bar is pleasant, with a decor that's one of my favorites—sleek, with modern lamps, red walls, stark-black pillars, and tabletops streaked with white paint to imitate marble. The music, provided by a jukebox, is at low enough decibels that you can actually carry on a conversation. The action doesn't start here until after midnight. Beer and wine from ¥800 ($7.25). Open daily from 7pm to 7am. Station: Roppongi (then about a 10-minute walk; it's located on the right side of Roppongi Dori in the direction of Shibuya, just past Gaien-Nishi Dori).

Admission: ¥700 ($6.35) table charge.

ZEST, 2-13-15 Nishi-Azabu. Tel. 3400-3985.
This is a chain of breezy, California-style bar/restaurants, which serves tacos, burgers, and light cuisine in addition to its extensive cocktail list, with most cocktails averaging ¥900 ($8.20). Beer starts at ¥700 ($6.35). Open daily from 11:30am to 5am. Station: Roppongi (then about a 10-minute walk on Roppongi Dori in the direction of Shibuya, and then a right on Gaien-Higashi Dori).

Admission: ¥800 ($7.25) minimum charge after 6pm.

YAKITORI-YA

GANCHAN, 6-8-23 Roppongi. Tel. 3478-0092.
This tiny yakitori-ya has room for only a dozen or so diners, who sit elbow-to-elbow along a counter in true nomi-ya fashion. The staff is young, and the atmosphere fun. Yakitori skewers start at ¥200 ($1.80); beer starts at ¥600 ($5.45). Open Monday through Saturday from 6pm to 3am and on Sunday and holidays from 6pm to midnight. Station: Roppongi (then about a five-minute walk, on the right side of the small street running downhill beside the Almond Coffee Shop, at the bottom of the hill).

KAMAKURA, 4-10-11 Roppongi. Tel. 3405-4377.
A refined yakitori-ya in the heart of Roppongi, this basement establishment features black walls, paper lanterns, and sprigs of fake but cheerful spring blossoms. Skewers of yakitori start at ¥160 ($1.45); beer starts at ¥550 ($5). Open Monday through Saturday from 6 to 11pm. Station: Roppongi (then about a one-minute walk, on a small side street opposite the Ibis Hotel).

4. SHINJUKU

THE CLUB & MUSIC SCENE

JAZZ

SHINJUKU PIT INN, 3-16-4 Shinjuku. Tel. 3354-2024.

An institution for more than 20 years, this is one of Tokyo's most famous jazz, fusion, and blues clubs. A basement locale with exposed pipes and bare concrete walls, it obviously places more emphasis on good music than on atmosphere and features both Japanese and foreign talents. It's one of few places in town where you can listen to jazz in the middle of the day. There are three shows daily, at 2:30, 7:30, and 9:30pm. Station: Shinjuku-Sanchome (then a few minutes' walk; it's located near the Isetan department store).

Admission (including one drink): From ¥1,300 ($11.80) for the 2:30pm show; from ¥3,000 ($27.25) for the 7:30 and 9:30pm shows.

DANCE CLUBS/DISCOS

MILOS GARAGE, 5-17-6 Shinjuku. Tel. 3207-6953.

I'm not sure how this disco's name accounts for its decor, which is a mixture of early Greek ruin and cave interior. Anyway, it occupies a basement where predecessors have come and gone, so there's no telling how long this one will survive. Catering primarily to a Japanese crowd in their early 20s, it features different themes different nights of the week. Sunday and Monday are reggae nights, Tuesday night features rap and reggae, Wednesday it's the blues, Thursday it's rock 'n' roll, and Friday is regular disco music. Saturday has traditionally been the night for gays, but the management said that would probably change. Come to think of it, the whole schedule of themes could change, since management tends to go with what will sell. Drinks cost ¥600 ($5.45). Open daily from 8pm to 5am. Station: Shinjuku (then about a 10-minute walk) or Shinjuku-Sanchome (then a 5-minute walk). It's located off Yasukuni Dori on the pathway leading to Hanazono Shrine.

Admission (including one drink): ¥2,000 ($18.20), more for special entertainment.

THE BAR SCENE

PUBS & BARS

IROHANIHOHETO (26), 3-15-15 Shinjuku. Tel. 3359-1682.

This is one of the most popular hangouts for the younger generation, primarily because of its low prices and large selection of Japanese and Western snacks and food (see Chapter 5 for a description of its menu). It's located on Yasukuni Dori Avenue, on the sixth floor of a building next to Isetan Kaikan. Beer starts at ¥440 ($4). Open Sunday through Thursday from 5 to 11:30pm and on Friday and Saturday from 5pm to 4am. Station: Shinjuku (then about a 10-minute walk) or Shinjuku-Sanchome (then a 5-minute walk).

VAGABOND, 1-4-20 Nishi Shinjuku. Tel. 3348-9109.

Although most of the night action in Shinjuku is east of the station, the west side also has an area of inexpensive restaurants and bars. This second-floor establishment is small and cozy, popular with foreigners living near or commuting through Shinjuku Station and with Japanese who want to rub elbows with foreigners. Its Guinness on tap draws in people from the U.K. It's owned by the effervescent Mr. Matsuoka, who treats foreigners like visiting royalty and is either orchestrating seating arrangements or is down the street imbibing at Volga (see below). There's a jazz pianist nightly, for which there's no music charge per se, though there is an obligatory snack charge of ¥500 ($4.55) for the bowl of chips automatically brought to your table. Draft beer starts at ¥600 ($5.45); bottled beer, at ¥500 ($4.55). Open Monday through Saturday from 5:30 to 11:30pm and on Sunday 4:30 to 10:30pm. Station: Shinjuku, west side (then a few minutes' walk; it's located on the second alley behind Odakyu Halc).

VOLGA (55), 1-4 Nishi Shinjuku. Tel. 3342-4996.

Located right down the street from Vagabond, Volga is a yakitori-ya, with an open grill facing the street and an ivy-covered, two-story brick facade. It has been here more than 40 years and is owned by a famous haiku poet. Typical of older establishments across the country, it's smoky, simply decorated with wooden tables and chairs, and packed with middle-aged Japanese, most of them obviously regulars and ranging from businessmen to artistic types. The place has a slightly bohemian air, and is one of my favorite bars in Shinjuku. Skewers of yakitori start at ¥100 (90¢), a large bottle of beer (big enough for two to share) is ¥700 ($6.35), and sake is ¥400 ($3.65). Open Monday through Saturday from 5:30 to 10:30pm; closed holidays. Station: Shinjuku, west side (then a few minutes' walk; it's located on the second alley behind Odakyu Halc).

THE WINE BAR, on the 30th floor of the N.S. Bldg., 2-4-1 Nishi-Shinjuku. Tel. 3348-8993.

The Wine Bar is a chain of middle-of-the-road wine bars, this one classier than most and a good place for visitors who don't want to venture into the madness of Kabuki-cho. Located high above the west side of Shinjuku in one of its best-known skyscrapers, it offers more than 60 different kinds of wine, as well as food ranging from seafood and salad to fish and chips and spaghetti. A glass of wine starts at ¥800 ($7.25); bottles of wine start at ¥2,000 ($18.20). Open daily from 11am to 10:30pm. Station: Shinjuku, west exit (then an eight-minute walk).

Admission: ¥500 ($4.55) per person table charge.

BARS IN GORUDEN GAI

East of Kabuki-cho is a small area called Goruden Gai ("Golden Guy"). It's a neighborhood of tiny alleyways leading past even tinier bars, each consisting of just a counter and a few chairs. Usually closed to outsiders, these bars cater to regular customers. On hot summer evenings the "mama-san" of these bars sit outside on stools and fan themselves, bathed in soft red lights melting out the open doorways. Things aren't as they appear, however. These aren't brothels, they are simply bars, and the mama-san—well, they're as likely to be men as they are women.

ANYO (56), 1-1-8 Kabuki-cho. Tel. 3209-7253.

Typical of the dozens of miniature establishments of Goruden Gai, this bar is tiny, with room for only a dozen or so customers. Atypical, however, is the fact that it welcomes foreigners and is run by a very friendly woman who speaks some English and French. In business for more than 20 years, it attracts a regular clientele that ranges from businessmen to those in the advertising industry. This place is a true find for the opportunity it affords of a different view of Japanese life, but prices can add up. Beer ranges from ¥500 to ¥800 ($4.55 to $7.25). Open Monday through Saturday from 7pm to 2am; closed holidays and for a few weeks in mid-August. Station: Shinjuku-Sanchome (then about a 10-minute walk).

Admission: ¥500 ($4.55) table charge, plus a ¥500 ($4.55) snack charge, per person.

BON'S, 1-1-10 Kabuki-cho. Tel. 3209-6334.

Located on the very eastern edge of Goruden Gai opposite Hanazono Shrine, this place is small but not as small as most locales here. It caters to a 30-ish Japanese clientele and boasts a Mickey Mouse collection behind a glass case. Beer starts at ¥600 ($5.45). Open Monday through Saturday from 7pm to 5am and on Sunday and holidays from 7pm to 3am. Station: Shinjuku-Sanchome (then about a 10-minute walk).

Admission: ¥600 ($5.45) table charge.

HUNGRY HUMPHREY, 1-1-10 Kabuki-cho. Tel. 3200-6165.

Located upstairs from Bon's, this place also tolerates foreigners and has a rustic, European feel to it. It specializes in various shots of vodka, the most popular of which is Lubrovka Polish vodka. If you wish, you can keep a bottle here with your name on it (a common custom in Japan for regulars who frequent a favorite bar), properly frozen until your next visit. A shot of vodka, a beer, or a sake costs ¥600 ($5.45). Open Monday through Saturday from 6:30pm to 1:30am; closed holidays. Station: Shinjuku-Sanchome (then about a 10-minute walk).

OUI OUI, 5-17-6 Shinjuku. Tel. 3200-5958.

Although not in Goruden Gai, this very popular and inexpensive student bar is only a few minutes away, on the other side of Hanazono Shrine. Located in a basement next to the Milos Garage disco described earlier, it's usually packed by 11pm. Snacks include such Japanese favorites as potato fry (french fries), potato salad, tuna salad, potato chips, pizza, and pilaff. Beer ranges from ¥500 to ¥700 ($4.55 to $6.35), and mixed drinks start at ¥550 ($5). Open Monday through Thursday from 6pm to 2am, on Friday and Saturday from 6pm to 5am, and on holidays from 6pm to midnight. Station: Shinjuku (then about a 10-minute walk) or Shinjuku-Sanchome (then a 5-minute walk); it's located off Yasukuni Dori on the pathway leading to Hanazono Shrine.

GAY BARS

Shinjuku 2-chome (pronounced "Ni-chome") is Shinjuku's gay district, with a wide range of both straight and gay bars. It's here that I was once taken to a host bar featuring young men in crotchless pants. Strangely enough, the clientele included both gay men and groups of giggling young women. The place has since closed down, but Shinjuku is riddled with places bordering on the absurd. To reach 2-chome, walk east on Yasukuni Dori until you come to a large intersection where you can see a large building called Bygs. These establishments are located on a small street behind Bygs.

69, in the basement of the Daini Seiko Bldg., 2-18-5 Shinjuku. Tel. 3341-6358.

This is one of the undisputed old-timers here, beginning first as a gay bar but now mainly heterosexual. It used to be the most popular place to be in 2-chome after midnight, but now that it closes early customers come here for a drink and then migrate to the other bars listed below. Playing primarily reggae music, this dive is tiny, and often so packed it reminds me of the Yamanote Line during rush hour. It usually has a healthy mix of both foreigners and Japanese, with an atmosphere unlike any other place in town. The first drink costs ¥1,000 ($9.10); thereafter drinks cost ¥600 ($5.45). Open Friday through Wednesday from 8:30pm to midnight. Station: Shinjuku-Sanchome (then about a five-minute walk).

KINSMEN, 2-18-5 Shinjuku. Tel. 3354-4949.
This gay bar, located in the building next to 69 up on the second floor, is a very civilized place, welcoming customers of both persuasions and with music low enough to encourage conversation. A pleasant oasis in 2-chome, it's small and comfortable, with a huge flower arrangement dominating the center of the room. Beer prices start at ¥600 ($5.45). Open daily from 9pm to 5am. Station: Shinjuku-Sanchome.

NEW SAZAE, on the second floor of the Ishikawa Bldg., 2-18-5 Shinjuku. Tel. 3354-1745.
Located around the corner from the above establishments, this is a dive of a place, rowdy and not for the weak-hearted. Customers, who usually migrate here after other bars in the area have closed down for the night, are a weird mix, and if you get this far you're probably where you belong. The first drink costs ¥1,000 ($9.10); thereafter drinks cost ¥700 ($6.35). Open daily from 10pm to 6am. Station: Shinjuku-Sanchome.

5. HARAJUKU & AOYAMA

THE CLUB & MUSIC SCENE

JAZZ

BLUE NOTE, 5-13-3 Minami Aoyama. Tel. 3407-5781.
Cousin to the famous Blue Note in New York and almost an exact replica with its interior of blue, this expensive and sophisticated jazz club draws top-notch American musicians. Oscar Peterson, Sarah Vaughan, Tony Bennett, Betty Carter, Lou Rawls, Sergio Mendes, and the Milt Jackson Quartet have all performed here. Open Monday through Saturday from 6pm to 1am; shows start at 7:30 and 10pm. Station: Omotosando (then about a five-minute walk).

Admission (including one drink): ¥7,000–¥13,000 ($63.65–$118.20).

ROCK, FUSION & EXPERIMENTAL

CROCODILE, 6-18-8 Jingumae. Tel. 3499-5205.
About as far from the Blue Note as you can get in the way of music and customers, Crocodile is a showcase for energetic bands ranging from rock and reggae to blues, jazz-fusion, rock 'n' roll, experimental, and even country. It's popular with a young crowd, which can range from Japanese with bleached-blond hair and earrings to foreign English teachers, depending on the music. Casual, with an interesting interior, it even has a pool table. Prices for a beer start at ¥600 ($5.45). Open daily from 6pm to 2am; shows are usually presented from 8 to 9:30pm. Station: Meiji-Jingumae (then about a 10-minute walk; it's located on the left side of Meiji Dori in the direction of Shibuya).

Admission: ¥2,000–¥3,000 ($18.20–$27.25).

THE BAR SCENE

OH GOD, 6-7-18 Jingumae. Tel. 3406-3206.

One of the best places to go if you find yourself in Harajuku after nightfall, this bar shows a foreign film every night, for which there's no cover charge. I've seen everything from James Bond and Fassbinder to B-grade horror movies here. Mellow and dimly lit, it's located off Omotesando Dori, at the end of the alleyway that runs beside the Café de Rope. A plus is its two pool tables. Beer starts at ¥650 ($5.90); cocktails, at ¥750 ($6.80). Open daily from 6pm to 6am; films are shown Monday through Thursday beginning at 9pm, and Friday through Sunday and holidays beginning at 6pm. Station: Meiji-Jingumae (then a few minutes' walk).

6. AROUND TOWN

THE CLUB & MUSIC SCENE

BODEGUITA, 1-7-3 Ebisu Minami, Shibuya-ku. Tel. 3715-7721.

Where once every other place was a jazz club, there are now Latin music clubs. Bodeguita is a Cuban club—very small, crowded and friendly. Despite the space, regulars are dancing while others are enjoying arroz saltado (rice, fried potatoes, and meat) or arroz con frijoles (the classic rice and beans). The food, which costs ¥900 to ¥1,200 ($8.20 to $10.90), is delicious and portions are generous. Wash it down with beer (Tecate) at ¥700 ($6.35) or cocktails for ¥700 to ¥1,000 ($6.35 to $9.10). Since it's run by a family, single women will feel welcome. Open Monday through Saturday from 6pm to midnight. Station: Ebisu (then a two-minute walk; it's located one block left on the second street away from and parallel to the tracks, near Piga Piga, below).

JULIANA'S, 1-13-10 Shibaura. Tel. 3452-9990.

This eclectic, colorful modern disco with hand-painted murals draws the trendy 21- to 30-year-olds in smart dress. The DJs, at this writing, are into "techno" sounds. They're all British, for that's the theme of the club, a tie-up with a Japanese firm and Britain's Wembly Co. The club boasts a 120-square-meter dance floor, a wall of video monitors, and a "body sonic" sound system. There are lots of young O.L.s (office ladies). If you're cool, you may get into the VIP room. Beer is about three tickets and a cocktail is two; extra tickets are on sale inside at ¥2,000 ($18.20) for eight. Open daily from 6:30pm to midnight. Station: JR Tomachi (then a five-minute walk).

Admission (including eight tickets worth about four drinks): ¥4,500 ($40.90) for women Mon–Thurs, ¥5,000 ($45.45) Fri–Sat, free Sun (but no tickets); ¥5,000 ($45.45) men Mon–Thurs, ¥5,500 ($50) Fri–Sun.

PIGA PIGA, in the second basement of the Nanshin Bldg., 1-8-16 Ebisu Minami. Tel. 3715-3431.

Although the place is pricey, the music is great, with live African bands from Tanzania, Zaire, and Kenya—the real thing. You have to buy 10 (*piga*) tickets at the door for ¥2,500 ($22.70), which you spend on food and drink. When you leave you get a refund for tickets you don't use, but there's a minimum charge of ¥4,000 ($36.35). The decor is African, as are the beer and cocktails or African pilaf, each about three piga (¥750/$6.80). There are five sets a night, but you sometimes have to stand in line to get in. Open Monday through Saturday from 6pm to 1am. Station: JR Ebisu (then a two-minute walk from the station; turn left down the second street away from and parallel to the tracks).

Admission: ¥2,500 ($22.70) music charge Mon–Thurs, ¥3,000 ($27.25) Sat–Sun.

A SPORTS BAR

NFL EXPERIENCE, in the second basement of the Beam Bldg., 31-2 Udagawacho. Tel. 5458-4486.

In Shibuya's razzy new Beam Building, you'll find American clubhouse decor and NFL merchandise. Live or freshly recorded sports on giant screens and many of the latest video and sports games, plus live bands on Friday and Saturday (no music charge, but a 10% service charge after 5pm) mean that you won't be bored. Beer starts at ¥550 ($5) and cocktails begin at ¥800 ($7.25), while snacks—from garlic toast to fried chicken and American steak—go for ¥800 to ¥1,500 ($7.25 to $13.65). Open daily from 11am to 4am. Station: Shibuya (then a five-minute walk; it's located on the street that runs between Seibu A and B department stores, across from Quattro by Parco).

7. BEER GARDENS

If you're in Tokyo during the summer months, you should take advantage of the very popular beer gardens. These sprout up all over Japan when the weather turns warm, often atop office buildings. In addition to the places below, another good place for an outdoor beer is **Hibiya Park,** located across from the Imperial Hotel, where there are various beer gardens and bars, open from about April to October, daily from 11am to 8pm.

GARDEN RESTAURANT, in the Tokyo Price Hotel, 3-3-1 Shibakoen. Tel. 3432-1111.

In this lovely garden setting, you can hardly believe you're in the middle of Tokyo. Purchase the tickets for the meal you want and the waiters will serve you. You can choose three different meals for ¥6,500, ¥7,500, and ¥10,000 ($59, $68.70, and $90.90); all include steak and vegetables, snacks, noodles, salad, and dessert. Beer starts at ¥750 ($6.80) and cocktails at ¥700 ($6.35). Open May through mid-September, daily from 5:30 to 9:30pm; closed mid-September to April. Station: Kamiyacho or Onarimon (then a five-minute walk).

HANEZAWA BEER GARDEN, 3-12-15 Hiroo, Shibuya-ku. Tel. 3400-6500.

This is a lovely place to go for a meal or drinks. An outdoor garden spread under trees and paper lanterns, it looks traditionally Japanese and serves sukiyaki, shabu-shabu, Mongolian barbecue that can be cooked at your table, and a variety of snacks and other dishes. Note, however, that if you want sukiyaki or shabu-shabu, you must notify the restaurant the day before. A mug of foaming beer costs ¥500 to ¥900 ($4.55 to $8.20). Open April through September, daily from 5 to 9:30pm. Station: Ebisu, Omotesando or Shibuya (then take a taxi).

SUNTORY BEER GARDEN, on the roof of the Suntory Bldg., 1-2-3 Moto-Akasaka. Tel. 3401-4367.

With a great view of surrounding Akasaka, this rooftop beer garden is better and more sophisticated than most, with real palms and bushes circling the dining area instead of the usual plastic that seems to plague most beer gardens. In addition to its draft Suntory beer, it also offers a barbecue meal of sirloin you can grill at your own table, as well as the usual beer snacks listed on an English menu. Purchase what you want from the ticket booth, sit down, and then hand the waiter your ticket. A mug of Suntory beer is ¥630 ($5.70). Open May through August, Monday through Saturday from 5 to 9pm (last order); closed holidays. Station: Akasaka-mitsuke (then a one-minute walk).

CHAPTER 10

EASY EXCURSIONS FROM TOKYO

1. KAMAKURA
2. NIKKO
3. YOKOHAMA
4. HAKONE
5. MT. FUJI

If your stay in Tokyo is three days or more, you should consider excursions in the vicinity. Kamakura and Nikko rank as two of the most important sights in Japan, each representing a completely different but equally exciting period of Japanese history. Yokohama has a few worthwhile museums and a beautiful garden, while the Fuji-Hakone-Izu National Park serves as a huge recreational playground for the residents of Tokyo. For more information, drop by the Tourist Information Center for its color brochure called "Side Trips from Tokyo" with information on Kamakura, Nikko, Hakone, and the Mt. Fuji area, as well as other pamphlets on individual destinations.

1. KAMAKURA

30 miles S of Tokyo

GETTING THERE **By Train** Take the Yokosuka Line train, which departs about every 10 or 20 minutes from the Yokohama, Shinagawa, Shimbashi, and Tokyo JR stations. The trip from Tokyo Station takes one hour and costs ¥880 ($8) one-way, while the trip from Shinagawa (on the southern loop of the Yamanote Line) takes 49 minutes and costs ¥680 ($6.20).

If you have a full day for sightseeing, I suggest getting off the train at Kita-Kamakura Station, which is the stop just before Kamakura Station. But if you have only a few hours, head straight for Kamakura Station and begin your sightseeing there.

ESSENTIALS **Information** Before leaving Tokyo, pick up a free pamphlet called "Hakone and Kamakura" from the Tourist Information Center. It has a map of Kamakura and tells how to get around to the town's most important sights by bus.

There's a **tourist information window** (tel. 0467/22-3350) at Kamakura Station, immediately to the right after you exit from the station's east exit in the direction of Tsurugaoka Hachimangu Shrine. Open from 9am to 6pm daily (until 5pm in winter), it sells a color brochure with a map of Kamakura for ¥200 ($1.80), but also has a free map in both English and Japanese that it seems reluctant to give out unless you insist. Ask here for directions on how to get to the village's most important sights.

Getting Around Transportation in Kamakura is by bus, as well as a quaint two-car train that travels from Kamakura Station to Hase Station, where you can then walk to the Great Buddha and Hase Kannon Temple. Kamakura's other major attraction, Tsurugaoka Hachimangu Shrine, is an easy walk from Kamakura Station.

If you take only one excursion from Tokyo, Kamakura should be your destination. Only an hour south of Tokyo by train, Kamakura is a seaside town with no fewer than 65 Buddhist temples and 19 Shinto shrines spread throughout the village and in the surrounding wooded hills. Most of the religious structures were first built centuries ago, when a warrior named Minamoto Yoritomo seized political power and established his shogunate government in Kamakura in 1192. He chose Kamakura because it was far from the corrupt imperial court in Kyoto, and because it was easy to defend, enclosed on three sides by wooded hills and on the fourth by the sea.

After Yoritomo's death, both of his sons were assassinated. The first son, Yoriie, was murdered by order of his own mother (Yoritomo's widow), and the second son was killed by Yoriie's son. Power then passed to the family of Yoritomo's widow, the Hojo family. They ruled until 1333, when the emperor in Kyoto dispatched troops to crush the shogunate government. Unable to halt the imperial troops, 800 soldiers retired to the Hojo family temple at Toshoji, where they all disemboweled themselves in ritualistic suicide known as seppuku.

Although Kamakura remained the military and political center of the nation for only 150 years, the Kamakura Period (1192–1333) remains significant in Japanese history for the ascendancy of the samurai warrior class and the spread of Zen Buddhism. Today Kamakura is a thriving seaside resort with a population of 175,000.

WHAT TO SEE & DO

In terms of historical and architectural importance, the most significant attractions of Kamakura are considered to be the Great Buddha, Hase Kannon Temple, and Tsurugaoka Hachimangu Shrine. Visitors with more time on their hands should also take in Engakuji Temple, Kenchoji Temple, and other temples as well. Keep in mind that most temples and shrines open about 8 or 9am and close between 4 and 5pm.

AROUND KITA-KAMAKURA STATION

Within a few minutes' walk from Kita-Kamakura Station is **Engakuji Temple** (tel. 22-0478). Founded in 1282, this Zen temple was once one of the most important and imposing in Kamakura, and although it has been reduced in grandeur by fires and earthquakes through the centuries, it's still considered by many to be the best remaining piece of architecture from the Kamakura Period. Most noteworthy is the **Shariden,** built in 1282. It enshrines a sacred tooth of Buddha and is the oldest Chinese-style structure in Japan.

Tokeiji Temple (tel. 22-1663), a five-minute walk from Kita-Kamakura Station, is a Zen temple founded in 1285. Today it is visited for its apricot blossoms (mid-February), magnolias and peach blossoms (late March/April), peonies (late April/May), and irises (May/June). Back in feudal times visitors came to Tokeiji for quite another reason. Known as the Divorce Temple, it was a place of refuge for women fleeing cruel husbands and disagreeable mothers-in-law. In those days only men could obtain a divorce. Women had no legal recourse, but if they could make it to Tokeiji, they were given protection and allowed to live among the nuns. Summer hours are 9am to 4pm daily, with shorter hours in winter.

Kenchoji Temple (tel. 22-0981), about a 20-minute walk from Kita-Kamakura Station, along with Engakuji is considered to be among the five great Zen temples of Kamakura. It, too, however, has suffered the ravages of fire and civil war. Note the magnificent cedars surrounding the temple as well as the ceremonial gate held together with wooden wedges. From Kenchoji it's just a 15-minute walk onward to Tsurugaoka Hachimangu Shrine.

AROUND KAMAKURA STATION

If you're arriving in Kamakura at Kamakura Station, take the east exit and then continue walking straight ahead. You will soon come to **Wakamiya Oji,** a pedestrian lane lined with cherry trees and marked by a huge vermilion-colored torii gate. Wakamiya Oji extends from the sea all the way to Tsurugaoka Hachimangu Shrine and was constructed by Yoritomo back in the 1180s so that his eldest son Yoriie's first visit to the family shrine could be accomplished in style with an elaborate procession. Along the pathway are souvenir and antiques shops selling Kamakura bori (reliefs chiseled in hardwood and then lacquered in black and vermilion), paper products, folk art, and Japanese sweets and cakes.

The ✪ **Tsurugaoka Hachimangu Shrine** (tel. 22-0315), a 10-minute walk from Kamakura Station, is the spiritual heart of Kamakura and is the second-biggest tourist attraction after the Great Buddha. It was first built by Yoritomo in 1191 and is named after Hachiman, the Shinto god of war who served as the clan deity of the Minamoto family. To the left of the stone steps leading up to the shrine is a gigantic gingko tree, which marks the spot where Yoritomo's second son was assassinated. The present shrine dates from 1828 and is a bright vermilion, a colorful contrast to the green of the surrounding woods. On the shrine grounds are two museums, described below, both worth a visit.

Zeniarai-Benten Shrine is a bit out of the way, about a 20-minute walk west of Kamakura Station, but it might pay to make a visit. This shrine is dedicated to the goddess of good fortune, and since the Kamakura Period worshippers have believed that if you take your money and wash it in the spring water of a small cave on the shrine grounds, it will double or triple itself later on. Of course, this being modern Japan, don't be surprised by a little ingenuity. My Japanese landlady told me that when she visited the shrine she didn't have much cash on her so she used the next best thing—her plastic credit card. Admission to the shrine is free. From Zeniarai-Benten Shrine there's a hiking path that leads over a hill to the Great Buddha in about 20 minutes.

KOKUHOKAN [Kamakura Municipal Museum], Hachimangu Shrine. Tel. 22-0753.

This small museum houses Kamakura's important art and cultural treasures from its many Buddhist temples and Shinto shrines, and from private individuals, including scrolls, urns, carvings, sculpture, bronzes, swords, calligraphy, and lacquerware.

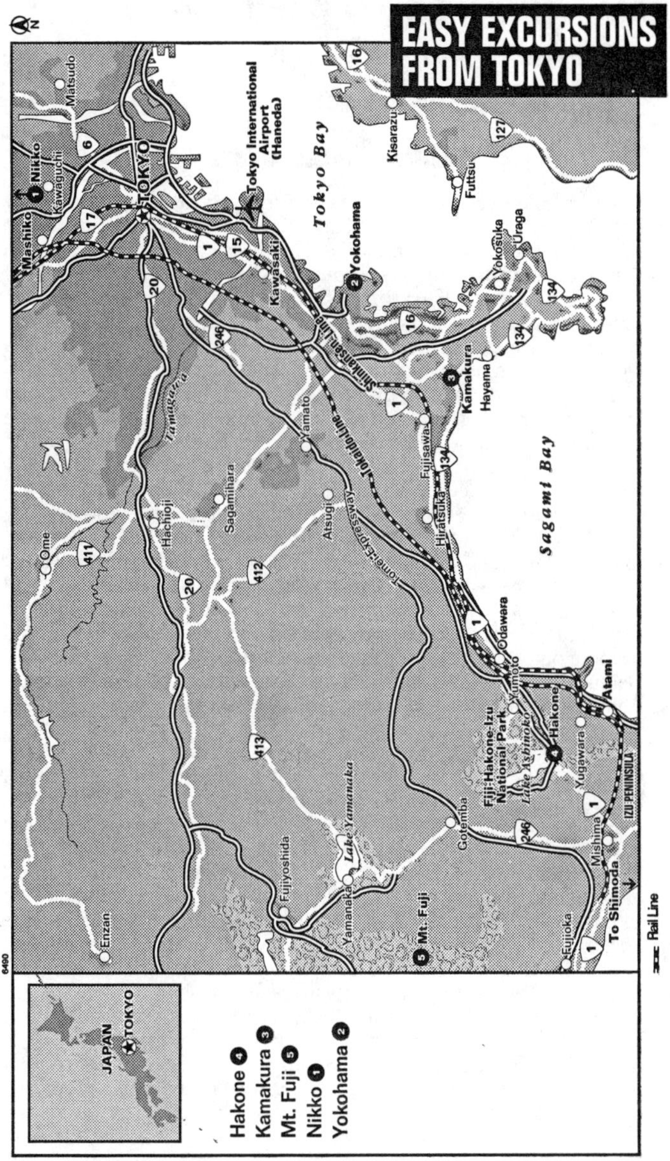

Admission: ¥300 ($2.75).
Open: Tues–Sat 9am–4pm.

KANAGAWA-KEN RITSU-KINDAI BIJUTSUKAN (Kanagawa Prefectural Modern Art Museum), Hachimangu Shrine. Tel. 22-5000.

Changing exhibitions of contemporary art are displayed here, including paintings, sculptures, and woodblock prints.

Admission: ¥700–¥1,000 ($6.35–$9.10), depending on the exhibition.

Open: Tues–Sat 10am–4pm.

AROUND HASE STATION

From Kamakura Station you can get directly to the Great Buddha by bus. You could then walk to Hase Kannon Temple and return to Kamakura Station via the Enoden train line, a charming two-car train that putts its way seemingly through backyards.

The ✪ **Great Buddha** shrine (tel. 22-0703), called the Daibutsu in Japanese, is Kamakura's most famous attraction. Weighing 93 tons and measuring 37 feet high, it was made according to the wishes of Yoritomo and is the second-largest bronze image in Japan. The largest Buddha is in Nara, but in my opinion the Kamakura Daibutsu is much more impressive. For one thing, while the Nara Buddha sits enclosed in a wooden hall, which reduces the impact of its size, the Kamakura Daibutsu sits outside, against a dramatic backdrop of wooded hills. Cast in 1252, the Kamakura Buddha was once housed in a succession of wooden halls, each destroyed by storms or tidal waves. Since 1495 it has remained under the sun, snow, and stars. Its face is calm and serene, as though it is above the worries of the world of wars, natural disasters, calamities, and sorrow. It's as though it represents the plane above human suffering, the point at which birth and death, joy and sadness, merge and become one and the same. You can go inside the hollow statue. The Daibutsu is open daily from 9am to 6pm, closing at 5pm in winter. Admission is ¥150 ($1.35), and your entry ticket is also a bookmark, a nice souvenir.

Hase Kannon Temple (Hasedera) (tel. 22-6300), a 10-minute walk from the Great Buddha or a 5-minute walk from Hase Station, is constructed on a hill with a sweeping view of the sea. Its main hall, the Kannon-do, houses an 11-headed gilt statue of Kannon, the goddess of mercy. More than 30 feet in height, it's the tallest wooden image in Japan and was made from a single piece of camphor wood back in the 8th century. According to popular lore, there were actually two images made from a single camphor tree. One of the images was kept in a temple near Nara, while the second image, after a short ceremony, was tossed into the sea to find a home of its own. The image drifted 300 miles eastward before washing ashore, but was thrown in again when all who touched it became ill or incurred bad luck. Finally, the image reached Kamakura, where it gave the people no trouble. This was interpreted as a sign that the image was content with its surroundings and Hase Temple was erected at its present site sometime during the Kamakura Period. On the temple grounds is a treasury hall with religious objects, as well as a snack pavilion with indoor and outdoor seating. If the weather is fine, its outdoor tables overlooking the village are a great place for a snack or a drink.

By the way, as you climb up the steps to Hase Temple and its Kannon, you'll encounter statues of a different sort. All around you will be statues of Jizo, the guardian deity of children. Although originally parents came to Hase Temple to set up statues to represent their children in hopes that the deity would protect and watch over them, since World War II the purpose of the Jizo has changed. Today they represent miscarried, stillborn, or, most frequently, aborted children. More than 50,000 Jizo statues have been offered here since the war, but the thousand or so you now see remain only a year

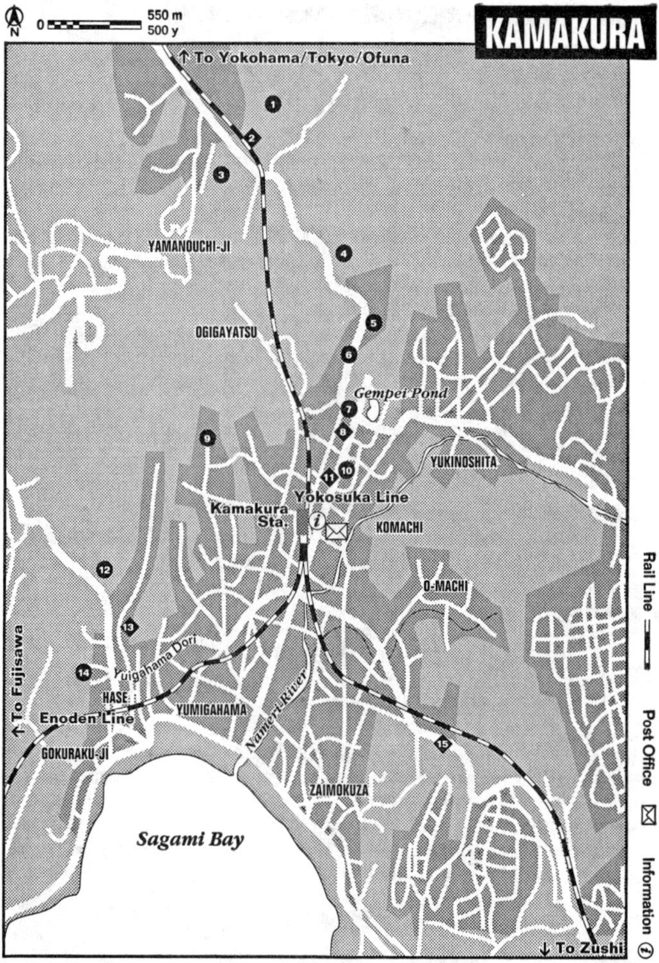

ATTRACTIONS

Engakuji 1
Great Buddha (Daibutsu) 12
Hase Kannon Temple 14
Kamakura-bori (lacquered woodcarvings) 10
Kamakura Municipal Museum 6
Kanagawa Prefectural Modern Art Museum 7
Kenchoji 4
Tokeiji 3
Tsurugaoka Hachimangu Shrine 5
Zeniarai-Benten Shrine 9

DINING

Kayagi-ya 8
Miyokawa 13
Monzen 2
Nakamura-an 11
Raitei 15

before being burned or buried to make way for others. The statues can be purchased on the temple grounds and range in price from ¥2,000 to ¥50,000 ($18.20 to $455). Some of them wear hand-knitted caps and sweaters provided by the would-be mothers. The effect is quite chilling.

Admission to Hase Kannon Temple is ¥200 ($1.80) for adults and ¥100 (90¢) for children 6 to 11. If you wish to visit its treasure hall, it's an extra ¥100 (90¢) for adults and ¥50 (45¢) for children. It's open daily from 9am to 6pm in summer and from 9am to 5pm in winter.

WHERE TO DINE

MODERATE

MIYOKAWA (57), 1-16-17 Hase. Tel. 25-5556.

Cuisine: MINI-KAISEKI/OBENTO. **Reservations:** Recommended Sat–Sun. **Station:** Hase Station (then about a five-minute walk).

$ Prices: Obento ¥2,300–¥5,000 ($20.90–$45.45); mini-kaiseki ¥5,500–¥7,000 ($50–$63.65); Japanese steak set meal ¥3,500 ($31.20). No credit cards.

Open: Daily 11am–9:30pm.

This modern restaurant, located on the main road that leads from Hase Station to the Great Buddha, specializes in kaiseki, including beautifully prepared mini-kaiseki set meals that change with the seasons. Much cheaper, however, are its wonderful obento lunchboxes, the least expensive of which is served in a container shaped like a gourd, as well as a set meal featuring steak prepared Japanese style.

MONZEN (58), Yamanouchi 407. Tel. 25-1121.

Cuisine: KAISEKI/OBENTO/VEGETARIAN. **Reservations:** Recommended. **Station:** Kita-Kamakura Station (then a one-minute walk).

$ Prices: Obento teishoku ¥3,000–¥5,000 ($27.25–$45.45); shojin-ryori vegetarian meals from ¥4,400 ($40); kaiseki from ¥6,000 ($54.54). AE, DC, JCB, MC, V.

Open: Lunch Mon–Fri 11am–3pm; dinner Mon–Fri 5–9pm, Sat–Sun 11am–9pm (7:30pm last order).

This modern-looking kaiseki restaurant is located just across the tracks from Engakuji Temple in Kita-Kamakura. The main dining hall is on the second floor, which consists of tatami mats at low tables. This is a good place to try shojin-ryori, a vegetarian set meal commonly served at Buddhist temples. Although there's no English menu, there are photographs of the various meals available, which also include kaiseki and obento lunchboxes.

BUDGET

KAYAGI-YA (59), 2-11-16 Komachi. Tel. 22-1460.

Cuisine: EEL. **Station:** Kamakura Station (then a five-minute walk).

$ Prices: Dishes ¥1,200–¥2,000 ($10.90–$18.20); teishoku ¥2,000–¥2,500 ($18.20–$22.70). No credit cards.

Open: Sat–Thurs noon–6pm.

This modest, older-looking establishment is on Wakamiya Oji, next to a lumberyard (on the right side if you're walking *away* from Hachimangu Shrine). It serves several different kinds of inexpensive eel dishes, my favorite of which is the unagi donburi (eel served on top of rice).

NAKAMURA-AN (60), 1-7-6 Komachi. Tel. 25-3500.

Cuisine: NOODLES. **Station:** Kamakura Station (then about a three-minute walk).

$ Prices: Noodle dishes ¥550–¥1,650 ($5–$15). No credit cards.

Open: Fri–Wed noon–6pm.

This small noodle shop is located on a side street off Wakamiya Oji between Kamakura Station and Hachimangu Shrine. If you're coming from the station, walk under the red torii (visible from the station) and then take the first right; the restaurant is easy to spot because of its front window where you can watch noodles being made. There's also an outdoor display case of plastic food.

RAITEI (61), Takasago. Tel. 32-5656.
Cuisine: NOODLES/OBENTO. **Bus:** From Platform 3 in front of the Kamakura Station to the Takasago bus stop (make sure the bus is going to Takasago, as not all buses from Platform 3 go there).
$ Prices: Noodles ¥700–¥2,500 ($6.35–$22.70) obento lunchboxes ¥3,500–¥4,500 ($31.20–$40.90). AE, DC.
Open: Daily 11am–sundown (about 6:30pm in summer).

This place wins hands down as the loveliest spot in Kamakura for lunch. It's situated on the edge of Kamakura, surrounded by verdant countryside, and the wonder is that it serves inexpensive soba (Japanese noodles), as well as princely feasts of kaiseki (which you must reserve in advance, with prices beginning at ¥6,000/$54.55). Upon entering at the front gate, you must pay an entry fee of ¥500 ($4.55), which counts toward the price of your meal at the restaurant. If you're here for soba or one of the obento lunchboxes, go down the stone steps to the back of the restaurant where, in rustic surroundings, you'll be given an English menu with such offerings as noodles with chicken, mountain vegetables, tempura, and more. The pottery is made especially for Raitei and comes from the restaurant's own kiln. When you've finished your meal, be sure to walk the path circling through the garden past a bamboo grove, stone images, and a miniature shrine. The stroll takes about 20 minutes.

2. NIKKO

90 miles N of Tokyo

GETTING THERE By Train Before leaving Tokyo, pick up a leaflet called "Nikko" from the Tourist Information Center. It gives the train schedule for both the Tobu Line, which departs from Akasaka Station, and JR trains that depart from Ueno Station. The easiest, fastest, and most luxurious way to get to Nikko is on the Tobu Line's limited express, which costs ¥2,530 ($23) one-way and takes almost 2 hours. There are also so-called rapid trains on the Tobu Line that cost half as much and travel to Nikko in about 2¼ hours. Trains depart every hour or less, but note that some trains are not direct but require a change at Shimo-Imaichi Station. If you have a Japan Rail Pass, you'll want to take the JR train departing from Ueno, in which case you'll have to change trains in Utsunomiya. At any rate, the Tobu and JR stations in Nikko are located almost side by side in the village's downtown area.

ESSENTIALS Information Tobu Station has a **tourist information counter,** but unfortunately no one here speaks English. However, they do have an English map of Nikko and vicinity and can point you in the right direction. You can also make hotel and ryokan reservations here for a processing fee of ¥200 to ¥500 ($1.80 to $4.55), as well as buy bus tickets onward to Lake Chuzenju.

More useful to foreigners is the **Nikko Information Center** (tel. 0288/54-2496), located about a 15-minute walk from the station on the main road leading to Toshogu Shrine. You're more likely to find someone who speaks English there and can pick up more information about Nikko. It's open daily from 8:30pm to 5pm.

Getting Around As for getting around Nikko, you can walk to Toshogu Shrine from the train station in less than half an hour. From Tobu Station, simply walk straight out the main exit, pass the bus stands, and then turn right. Keep walking on this main road (you'll pass the Nikko Information Center about halfway down, on the left side) until you come to a T-intersection with a vermilion-colored bridge spanning a river (about a 15-minute walk from the train stations). The stone steps opposite lead up the hill into the woods and to the mausoleum.

You can also get to the T-intersection by bus from Tobu Station, getting off at the Shinkyo bus stop. If you're heading to Chuzenji Lake, buses depart from in front of Tobu Station, with a stop at the Shinkyo bus stop near Toshogu Shrine. You can therefore visit the historical sights in Nikko before reboarding the bus and continuing on to Chuzenji.

Along with Kamakura, Nikko ranks as one of the most significant historical sites in all of Japan. This is where Tokugawa Ieyasu was laid to rest, that powerful shogun of the 1600s who unified Japan and served as the model for James Clavell's fictional leader in his popular novel *Shogun*. One of the best-known figures in Japanese history, Ieyasu was so shrewd a statesman, eliminating all his enemies and quashing all rebellion, that his heirs continued to rule Japan for the next 250 years without serious challenge.

A mausoleum in Nikko was constructed in the 17th century to contain Ieyasu Tokugawa's remains. *Nikko* means "sunlight," an apt description of the way the sun's rays play upon this sumptuous mausoleum of wood and gold leaf, the most ornate mausoleum in all of Japan. Surrounding the mausoleum, which is officially known as Toshogu Shrine, are thousands of cedar trees in a 200,000-acre national park. A trip to Nikko can be combined with a visit to Lake Chuzenji, about an hour's bus ride from the mausoleum.

WHAT TO SEE & DO

The first indication that you're nearing Tokugawa's mausoleum, or Toshogu Shrine, is a vermilion-lacquered bridge arching 92 feet over the rushing Daiyagawa River. Called the **Shinkyo,** or Sacred Bridge, it was built in 1636 and for more than three centuries only shoguns and their emissaries were allowed to cross it. Even today mortal souls like us are prevented from completely crossing it because of a barrier on one end, removed only during the Grand Festival of Toshogu Shrine in May.

IMPRESSIONS

The Japanese proverb says
Nikko wo minai uchi wa kekko to iu na:
Until you have seen Nikko,
do not say kekko, *i.e., grand or splendid.*
—Douglas Sladen, *Queer Things About Japan*, 1903

Across the road from the bridge are some steps leading into a forest of cedar, where after a five-minute walk you'll see a statue of a priest named Shodo, who founded Nikko 1,200 years ago, and the first major temple, **Rinnoji Temple.** Founded in 766, its Sanbutsudo Hall contains three images of Buddha. If you'd like to see it, you can purchase a combination ticket here for ¥900 ($8.20), which allows entry to Rinnoji, Toshogu Shrine, neighboring Futarasan Shrine, and another Tokugawa mausoleum. It does not, however, include the ¥500 ($4.55) extra charge to see Ieyasu's actual tomb, but you can pay for that once you reach Toshogu Shrine. Otherwise, combination tickets are also sold at the entrance to Toshogu Shrine for ¥1,250 ($11.35), which include admission to the tomb; admission for children 6 to 11 is ¥400 ($3.65), free for children under 6.

At any rate, one of the best things to see at Rinnoji Temple is its **Shoyo-en Garden,** which requires a separate admission of ¥250 ($2.25) for adults and ¥80 (70¢) for children 6 to 11 (free for children under 6) and is located opposite the Sanbutsudo Hall. Completed in 1815 and typical of Japanese landscaped gardens of the Edo Period, this strolling garden provides a different vista with each turn of the path, making it seem much larger than it actually is. The garden's English pamphlet says that Ulysses S. Grant visited here in 1879.

Climbing higher up the hill, you'll pass under a massive stone torii, one of the largest in Japan, that marks the beginning of ✪ **Toshogu Shrine.** To your left is a five-story, 115-foot-high pagoda. Although pagodas are usually found only at Buddhist temples, Toshogu Shrine is eclectic in that it combines principles of both Buddhist and Shinto architecture. It is also rather eccentric in its colors and richness, especially when compared to the somber simplicity of most of Japan's religious structures.

But, then, Toshogu Shrine, which contains the tomb of Ieyasu Tokugawa, is no ordinary Japanese structure and is by far the most important and famous site in Nikko. Although Ieyasu died in 1616, construction of his mausoleum did not begin until 1634, when his grandson, Tokugawa Iemitsu, undertook the project as an act of devotion. It seems that no expense was too great. Some 15,000 artists and craftsmen were brought to Nikko from all over Japan, and after two years' work they had succeeded in erecting a group of buildings more elaborate and gorgeous than any other Japanese temple or shrine. Rich in colors and carvings, Toshogu Shrine is bedecked with an incredible amount of gilding: Altogether 2.4 million sheets of gold leaf were used (enough to cover an area of almost six acres). The mausoleum was completed in 1636, almost 20 years after Ieyasu's death.

Passing by the ticket windows (where you can purchase your combination ticket if you haven't already done so) and climbing another flight of stairs, you'll turn left and will soon see the **Sacred Stable.** Look for the three monkeys carved above the stable door, fixed eternally in the poses of "hear no evil, speak no evil, see no evil."

At the next flight of stairs is **Yomeimon Gate,** considered the showpiece and crowning jewel of Nikko. It's popularly known as the Twilight Gate, implying that you could gaze upon it all day until twilight to see everything carved onto it. Painted in red, blue, and green and decorated with gilding and lacquerwork, this gate has about 400 carvings of flowers, dragons, birds, and other animals. It's almost too much to take in at once.

To the left of the gate is the hall where the portable shrines are kept when they're not being used for festivals, as well as **Honchido Hall,** famous for its dragon painting on the ceiling. If you clap your hands under this painting, the echo supposedly resembles a dragon's roar.

Take off your shoes to enter the main building of the shrine, where guides explain its history and point out its main features—alas, only in Japanese. You can sit on the floor along with the other visitors, however, and study the elaborate interior. Afterward, put on your shoes and head toward the tomb itself (to the right if you face the main shrine). Admission costs an additional ¥500 ($4.55) if you bought only the ¥900 combination ticket. Note the main gate with the carving of the sleeping cat. Beyond that are 200 stone steps leading past a forest of cedars to Ieyasu's tomb, which is surprisingly simple compared to the fanfare of the shrine.

Toshogu Shrine is open daily from 8am to 5pm (to 4pm November through March). You must enter the shrine grounds at least 30 minutes prior to closing time.

Directly to the west of Toshogu Shrine is **Futarasan Shrine,** the oldest extant building in the area, dating from 1617. It has a pleasant garden, as well as the so-called ghost lantern, enclosed in a wooden structure on the shrine grounds. According to legend, it used to come alive at night and sweep around Nikko in the form of a ghost. It apparently scared one of the guards so much that he struck it with his sword; the marks are still visible on the lamp's rim.

Past Futarasan Shrine to the west is the second mausoleum, **Daiyuin Mausoleum** (a seven-minute walk from Toshogu Shrine). It's the final resting place of Iemitsu, grandson of Ieyasu and the third Tokugawa shogun. Completed in 1653, it's not nearly so ornate as the Toshogu Shrine. It's also not as crowded, making it a pleasant last stop on your tour of Nikko.

CHUZENJI

After touring Nikko's shrines, you can board a bus not far away, at either the Shinkyo bus stop or the nearby Nishi-sando bus stop, for Lake Chuzenji. The ride costs ¥1,050 ($9.55) and takes 50 minutes, the road winding higher and higher along hairpin turns. The view is breathtaking—I've even seen bands of monkeys along the side of the road.

On Lake Chuzenji are many ryokan with hot-spring baths, souvenir stores, and coffee shops, making it a popular holiday resort. Things to do here include visiting Tachiki Kannon Temple beside the lake, going on an hour-long boat cruise, and visiting nearby Kegon Falls, a 300-foot waterfall considered to be one of the most beautiful falls in Japan (I find its beauty marred by the elevator that whisks visitors to an observation platform). If you want to do some hiking, an aerial cable car near the falls deposits passengers at an observatory atop a hill laced with pathways through the woods. There are more trails along the lake. Even more vigorous exercise is offered by Mt. Nantai, more than 8,000 feet high and open to climbers from the beginning of May to mid-October. A path from Chuzenji leading straight to the top takes about five hours to ascend and three hours to descend.

Past Lake Chuzenji, and another 25 minutes by bus, is a smaller lake called Yunoko with a small resort town called **Yumoto Spa.** There are more ryokan with hot-springs baths here, as well as several

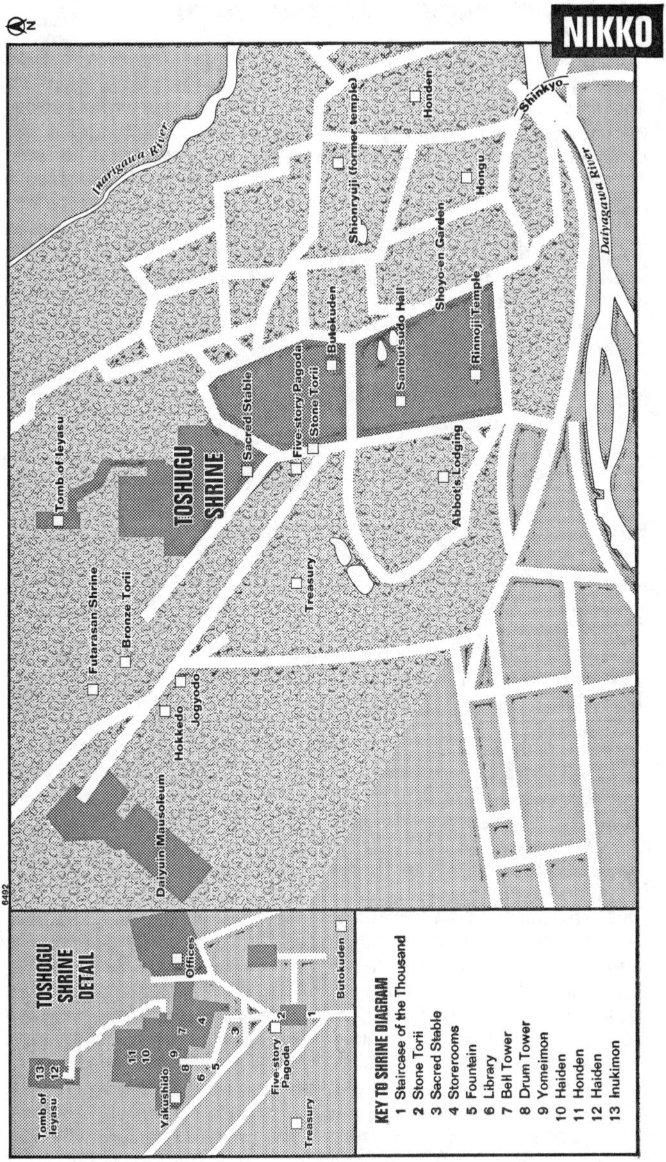

hiking trails. It takes approximately an hour to hike around Lake Yunoko.

WHERE TO STAY

JAPANESE-STYLE ACCOMMODATIONS

Most ryokan in the area of Nikko are strung along the shores of Lake Chuzenji at **Chuzenji Spa** (Chuzenji Onsen) and at **Yumoto Spa**

(Yumoto Onsen) on Lake Yunoko. Keep in mind, however, that the majority of them are open only from mid-April to mid-November. You should reserve a room to stay in one of these ryokan, since owners in this area do not speak English and aren't likely to take you in if you simply show up at their door. If it's peak season, you should reserve a room in advance before leaving Tokyo at a travel agency such as the Japan Travel Bureau. In other seasons you can reserve a room upon arrival in Nikko at the tourist information counter at Tobu Station. Most ryokan start at ¥10,000 ($91) per person including two meals, rising to as much as ¥20,000 ($182) on holidays. This being a typical Japanese resort, the ryokan here are more functional than they are aesthetic, and are generally concrete structures. There's little difference in what they offer: basically a tatami room; coin-operated TV; hot tea, breakfast, and dinner served in your room; and cotton kimono. Be sure to specify if you want a lakeside view; you may have to pay a bit more.

WESTERN-STYLE ACCOMMODATIONS

Most Western-style accommodations are open throughout the year.

NIKKO KANAYA HOTEL, 1300 Kami-Hatsuishi, Nikko, Tochigi Prefecture 321-14. Tel. 0288/54-0111. Fax 0288/53-2487. 81 rms (65 with bath). MINIBAR TV TEL **Directions:** 5-minute bus ride from the Nikko stations (get off at the Shinkyo stop); or it's about a 15-minute walk.

$ **Rates:** ¥8,800 ($80) single with toilet only, ¥11,000 ($100) single with shower and toilet, ¥11,000–¥35,000 ($100–$318) single with bath; ¥11,000 ($100) twin with toilet only, ¥12,000 ($109) twin with toilet and shower, ¥13,000–¥40,000 ($118–$363) twin with bath. ¥3,000 ($27) extra on Sat and the evening before national hols; ¥5,000–¥10,000 ($45–$91) extra during peak season. AE, DC, JCB, MC, V.

Established back in 1873, this is Nikko's oldest and grandest hotel, and through the decades has played host to a number of visiting VIPs—Charles Lindbergh, Indira Gandhi, Helen Keller, Eleanor Roosevelt, David Rockefeller, Shirley MacLaine, and Albert Einstein, to name only a few. A distinguished-looking, old-fashioned hotel secluded on a hill above the sacred Shinkyo bridge, about a 15-minute walk or 5-minute bus ride from the Nikko stations, it combines the rustic heartiness of a European country lodge with elements of old Japan. Rooms, all Western-style twins or doubles, are rather old-fashioned but cozy, giving you a feeling that things haven't changed all that much around here in the past 50 years. The cheapest rooms have toilets only. Facilities include souvenir shops, a small outdoor heated swimming pool, outdoor skating rink, a Japanese garden, and a public bath. Its dining hall is quaint but grand and is the best place for a Western meal in Nikko. There's also a coffee shop and a small Japanese restaurant open only evenings serving shabu-shabu.

PENSION TURTLE, 2-16 Takumi-cho, Nikko, Tochigi Prefecture 321-14. Tel. 0288/53-3168. Fax 0288/53-3883. 12 rms (3 with bath). TV **Bus:** A seven-minute ride from Nikko stations to Sogo Kaikan-mae bus stop (then a five-minute walk).

$ **Rates:** ¥3,900–¥5,000 ($35–$45) single without bath, ¥5,500

($50) single with bath; ¥7,800–¥9,000 ($71–$82) twin without bath, ¥10,000 ($91) twin with bath; ¥11,000–¥13,000 ($100–$118) triple without bath. AE, MC, V.

I highly recommend this pension run by the very friendly Fukuda family. Mr. Fukuda speaks English very well and can help you plan a sightseeing itinerary for the area. The dining room is cheerful; in fact the whole place is cheerful and spotless. Three of its rooms are Japanese style (all without bath), making it a good bet if you're on a budget but want to try tatami and futon. There's even a combination room that has a tatami area as well as twin beds. Both Japanese and continental breakfasts are available, as well as Japanese and Western dinners. A member of the Japanese Inn Group, Pension Turtle is located on a quiet side street beside the Daiyagawa River, not far from the sacred Shinkyo bridge and Toshogu Shrine.

ST. BOIS, 1560 Tokorono, Nikko, Tochigi Prefecture 321-14. Tel. 0288/53-3399. Fax 0288/53-0082. 11 rms (4 with bath). TV **Directions:** Walk 15 minutes north of the Nikko stations, across the river.

$ **Rates:** ¥5,500 ($50) single without bath, ¥6,000 ($55) single with bath; ¥10,000 ($91) twin without bath, ¥11,000 ($100) twin with bath; ¥14,400 ($131) triple without bath, ¥15,900 ($145) triple with bath. AE, MC, V.

Another member of the Japanese Inn Group, this country-style lodge sits atop a hill nestled among pine trees on the edge of Nikko. It's very pleasant and peaceful here, making it an inexpensive getaway from Tokyo. Two of the rooms are Japanese style, and five rooms facing the front have their own balconies. A Western-style breakfast is available for ¥800 ($7.25) if you let the manager know the night before, and dinner if you order it by 3pm.

YOUTH HOSTELS

NIKKO YOUTH HOSTEL, 2854 Tokorono, Nikko, Tochigi Prefecture 321-14. Tel. 0288/54-1013. 48 beds. **Directions:** Walk 25 minutes north of the stations, across the river.

$ **Rates:** ¥2,450 ($22.25) for members and nonmembers. Breakfast ¥460 ($4.20) extra; dinner ¥720 ($6.55) extra. No credit cards.

Located north across the river in quiet surroundings, a 25-minute walk from the stations, this hostel accepts both members and nonmembers. Guests sleep on bunk beds, four to eight to a room, and there's a coin-operated laundry facility.

DAIYAGAWA YOUTH HOSTEL, 1075 Nakahatsuishi, Nikko, Tochigi Prefecture 321-14. Tel. 0288/54-1974. 26 beds. **Directions:** Bus from the stations (to the Shiyakusho-mae stop); or a 20-minute walk from the stations.

$ **Rates:** ¥2,300 ($20.90) for members, ¥3,000 ($27.25) for nonmembers. Breakfast ¥400 ($3.65) extra; dinner ¥800 ($7.25) extra. No credit cards.

This hostel is located right beside the Daiyagawa River, a 20-minute walk from the stations. Guests sleep on bunk beds, with four to eight to a room. It's run by a woman who doesn't speak any English, and the front doors are locked at 9:30pm.

WHERE TO DINE

MODERATE

MAIN DINING HALL, in the Nikko Kanaya Hotel, 1300 Kami-Hatsuishi. Tel. 54-0001.

Cuisine: WESTERN. **Reservations:** Recommended during peak season. **Directions:** Walk 15 minutes from the stations or 10 minutes from Toshogu Shrine, near the Shinkyo bridge spanning the Daiyagawa River.

$ Prices: Appetizers and soups ¥700–¥3,500 ($6.35–$31.20); main dishes ¥2,500–¥8,000 ($22.70–$72.70); set lunch ¥3,500 ($31.20). AE, DC, JCB, MC, V.

Open: Lunch daily noon–3pm; dinner daily 6–7:30pm.

This is the best place in town for lunch. Not only is the Nikko Kanaya Hotel the area's oldest and most famous hotel, but it's also conveniently located near Toshogu Shrine. Its dining hall is quaint and old-fashioned, with elaborately decorated pillars. I recommend Nikko's specialty, locally caught rainbow trout, prepared here in three different styles. I had mine cooked Kanaya style, covered with soy sauce, sugar, and sake, grilled and served whole. Other items on the menu include steak, veal cutlet Cordon Bleu, lobster, chicken, and beef Stroganoff. The best bargain is the set lunch, available to 3pm, which comes with soup, salad, and main dish.

MASUDAYA, 439 Ichiyamachi. Tel. 54-2151.

Cuisine: LOCAL JAPANESE SPECIALTIES. **Reservations:** Recommended for private rooms. **Directions:** Walk five minutes from the stations, on the left side of the main street leading to Toshogu Shrine.

$ Prices: Set meals ¥3,980 and ¥5,300 ($36.20 and $48.20). No credit cards.

Open: Fri–Wed Lunch only, 11:30am–2pm.

If you enjoy trying local Japanese dishes, you'll want to stop for lunch at this Japanese-style traditional restaurant. Only two fixed-price meals are served, both featuring a local specialty called *yuba*. Made from soybeans, yuba could be eaten only by priests and members of the imperial family until about 100 years ago. Now you can enjoy it too, along with a variety of side dishes that may include rice, sashimi, soup, fried fish, and vegetables. Dining is either in a common dining hall with chairs, or, for the more expensive course, in private tatami rooms, for which you should make a reservation.

BUDGET

GYOZA HOUSE, 257 Matsubara-cho. Tel. 53-0494.

Cuisine: GYOZA. **Directions:** Walk two minutes from the Tobu train station, on the left side of the main street leading to Toshogu Shrine.

$ Prices: ¥400–¥800 ($3.65–$7.25). No credit cards.

Open: Summer, daily 11am–8pm; winter, daily 11am–7pm.

Red banners and a red facade mark the spot of this simple restaurant, which offers gyoza (Chinese dumplings) and ramen (noodle-and-vegetable soup). It has an English menu and pictures, listing such unique dishes as curry gyoza, shoyu gyoza (in a soup broth), and spicy ramen. It also offers an obento, but only for take-out—which you could eat on the grounds of Toshogu Shrine.

3. YOKOHAMA

20 miles S of Tokyo

GETTING THERE **By Train** Yokohama is easily reached by train from a number of Tokyo's stations, including Tokyo, Yurakucho, Shimbashi, and Shinagawa Stations via the JR Keihin-Tohoku Line and Shibuya Station via the Tokyu-Toyoko Line. It takes about 40 minutes to reach Yokohama Station from Tokyo Station and about 30 minutes from Shinagawa.

If you want to go to Kannai Station in the old part of Yokohama where most of its attractions are centered, it is also reached via the Keihin-Tohoku Line. Kannai Station is the second stop after Yokohama Station. Kannai Station is also connected to Yokohama Station by subway, bus, and even boat.

In addition to the two train lines above, you can also take the Yokosuka Line that departs from Tokyo, Shinagawa, and Shimbashi Stations. Note, however, that it stops only at Yokohama Station, not at Kannai Station.

ESSENTIALS **Information** The **Yokohama Municipal Tourist Association** is in the Sangyo Boeki Center, 2 Yamashita-cho, Naka-ku (tel. 045/641-5824), located near the harbor and a short walk from Kannai Station. Pick up the city's excellent English map, as well as its wealth of brochures. Yokohama also has the Home-Visit System (described in Chapter 1) which arranges a visit with a Japanese family. Call the Yokohama Tourist Association to set up the appointment at least a day in advance of your visit. The tourist office is open daily from 10am to 6pm.

Next door to the city tourist office in the Silk Center is the **Kanagawa Prefectural Office** (tel. 045/681-0007), where you can also obtain information on Hakone and Kamakura since they're both in Kanagawa Prefecture. This office is open Monday through Friday from 9am to 5pm and on Saturday from 9am to noon.

Getting Around As for transportation within Yokohama, both JR Keihin-Tohoku Line and Tokyu-Toyoko Line **trains** pass through Yokohama Station and continue on to Sakuragicho and Kannai Stations, convenient to most of Yokohama's attractions.

Another way to get to Kannai from Yokohama Station is by **shuttle boat.** It departs from a pier beside the Sogo department store (take the east exit from Yokohama Station) about three times an hour and deposits passengers at Yamashita Park 15 minutes later. The fare for the shuttle boat, called *Sea Bass,* is ¥500 ($4.55), which is considerably cheaper than taking a harbor cruise. Hours of operation are daily from 10am to 7pm.

There are also **buses** that serve the city. The most important one for visitors is bus no. 8, which departs from Yokohama Station and winds its way through Kannai (bus stop: Kencho-mae) and past Chinatown before reaching Sankei-en Garden.

Only 20 miles from Tokyo, Yokohama is Japan's second-largest city, with a population of more than three million. Despite its size, the city is relatively young. When Commodore Perry arrived in the mid-1800s and demanded that Japan open its doors to trade, Yokohama was nothing more than a tiny fishing village with only 100 houses.

In 1859 the first foreign settlers arrived here and sparked the curiosity of the Japanese who were emerging from centuries of isolation. The Japanese were intensely curious about these strange newcomers and came from as far away as Tokyo for a glimpse of them and to marvel at the Western goods that were being imported and unloaded at Yokohama's port. Serving as the capital city's port, Yokohama grew by such leaps and bounds that the first railroad in Japan was laid in 1872 to link Tokyo with Yokohama, reducing the 10-hour journey by foot to less than an hour.

Today Yokohama is still an important international port and supports a large international community that commutes to Tokyo but prefers to live in Yokohama.

WHAT TO SEE & DO

AROUND YOKOHAMA STATION

Just across the street from Yokohama Station's east exit is Japan's second-largest department store, Sogo.

SOGO, 2-18-1 Takashima, Nishi-ku. Tel. 465-2111.

This huge store's 92,665 square yards of retail space and restaurants could easily occupy your entire day. It employs 5,000 sales clerks who serve as many as 150,000 customers a day, a number that swells to 200,000 on a weekend. Designers with boutiques here include Hanae Mori, Kansai, Kenzo, Yohji Yamamoto, Issey Miyake, Rei Kawakubo, Christian Dior, and Ralph Lauren, to name only a few. For bargains and special promotions, head for the eighth floor. Its many restaurants are up on the 10th floor. Incidentally, next to Sogo are shuttle boats departing for Yamashita Park.

Also in Sogo is the **Hiraki Ukiyoe Museum (Hiraki Ukiyoe Bijitsukan),** a delightful museum devoted exclusively to woodblock prints. They have an impressive collection of some 6,000 prints and exhibitions change every month. The museum is open the same days and hours as the store, and entrance fees are ¥500 ($4.55) for adults, ¥400 ($3.65) for junior high to college students, and ¥300 ($2.75) for children 6 to 11 (free for children under 6).

Open: Wed–Mon 10am–7pm (restaurants open until 10pm). **Station:** Yokohama.

AROUND KANNAI STATION

SILK HAKUBUTSUKAN [Silk Museum], 1 Yamashita-cho, Naka-ku. Tel. 641-0841.

For many years after Japan first opened its doors to trade, silk was its chief export item. Almost all raw silk left Japan from Yokohama, which quickly grew into the nation's largest silk market. The museum is in tribute to the role silk played in Yokohama's history, with displays showing the metamorphosis of the silkworm and how silk is obtained from cocoons. Did you know, for example, that as many as 10,000 cocoons are needed to make just one kimono? There are some gorgeous kimonos and silk fabrics on display here, and by the way, even though Japan today produces about 33% of the world's silk, it's still not enough to satisfy the demands of its people, who use 50% of the world's total output of silk.

Admission: ¥300 ($2.75) adults, ¥200 ($1.80) students, ¥100 (90¢) children 6–11, free for children under 6.

Open: Tues–Sun 9am–4:30pm. **Closed:** The day after hols. **Station:** Kannai (then less than a 15-minute walk).

YAMASHITA KOEN [Yamashita Park], Naka-ku.

This broad expanse of greenery just a couple of minutes' walk east of the Silk Center was Japan's first seaside park, laid out after the huge 1923 earthquake destroyed much of Tokyo and Yokohama. It's a pleasant place for a stroll along the waterfront, where you have a view of the city's harbor. This is also where you'll arrive if you've come to Kannai by the *Sea Bass* shuttle boat.

At one end of the park is a 348-foot-high **Marine Tower,** with an observation platform providing views of the city, port, and sometimes even Mt. Fuji. It's open daily from 10am to 9pm (to 7pm in winter) and charges ¥700 ($6.35) for adults, ¥350 ($3.20) for children 6 to 11, free for children under 6.

Moored at a pier off the park is the ***Hikawa Maru,*** a transpacific liner built in 1930. Its maiden voyage was to Seattle, after which it crossed the Pacific 238 times until it was retired in 1960. Today it houses a restaurant and beer garden, but the ¥800 ($7.25) admission fee (half price for children 6 to 11, free for children under 6) may deter you from wishing to dine here. From Yamashita Park there are also **harbor cruises,** but they're only in Japanese. There's one 40-minute cruise daily at 3:40pm which costs ¥800 ($7.25) for those over 11 and ¥400 ($3.65) for children 6 to 11 (free for children under 6). There's also a 60-minute cruise at 10:30am daily which costs ¥1,200 ($10.90), and four daily 90-minute cruises which cost ¥2,000 ($18.20); reductions available for children.

YOKOHAMA KAIKO SHIRYOKAN [Yokohama Archives of History], 3 Nippon O-dori, Naka-ku. Tel. 201-2100.

Just a minute's walk from the Silk Center, this museum focuses on exhibits and pictures relating to the opening of Japan and the establishment of Yokohama as an international port. It's a very small museum and can be toured quickly to get an idea of Yokohama's history.

Admission: ¥200 ($1.80) adults, ¥100 (90¢) children.

Open: Tues–Sun 9:30am–5pm. **Closed:** The day after hols. **Station:** Kannai (then less than a 15-minute walk).

AROUND SAKURAGICHO STATION

KANAGAWA KENRITSU HAKUBUTSUKAN [Kanagawa Prefectural Museum], 5-60 Minaminaka-dori, Naka-ku. Tel. 201-0926.

Yokohama serves as the seat of government for Kanagawa Prefecture, which also includes Hakone and Kamakura. This museum exhibits items related to the prefecture, including its history, natural science, archeology, and folklore. On display are a traditional Japanese farmhouse, tools for farming and silk production, and models of both Perry's ships and of Japan's first train which ran between Yokohama and Tokyo. The building housing the museum is also of interest, constructed in 1904 to house the nation's first foreign-exchange bank.

Admission: ¥200 ($1.80) adults, ¥50 (45¢) children.

Open: Mon–Fri 9am–4pm. **Station:** Sakuragicho (then about a seven-minute walk).

YOKOHAMA BIJUTSUKAN [Yokohama Museum of Art], 3-4-1 Minatomirai, Nishi-ku. Tel. 221-0300.

With an emphasis on works by Western and Japanese artists since the 1850s, this museum has an ambitious goal: to collect art that reflects the mutual influence between modern art of the West and Japan since the opening of Yokohama's port in 1859. The museum, designed by Kenzo Tange and Urtec, Inc., houses exhibits from its permanent collections that are changed several times a year, as well as special exhibits on loan from other museums. Thus, no matter how often you visit the museum, there's always something new to see. Works in the museum's collections include those by Cézanne, Picasso, Braque, Klee, Kandinsky, Kishida, and Taikan Yokoyama.

Admission: ¥500 ($4.55) adults, ¥300 ($2.75) students, ¥100 (90¢) children 6 to 11, free for children under 6. More for special events.

Open: Fri–Wed 10am–6pm. **Station:** Sakuragicho (then a 10-minute walk).

ELSEWHERE IN YOKOHAMA

SANKEI-EN GARDEN, 293 Honmoku-Sannotani, Naka-ku. Tel. 621-0634.

In my opinion, this is the best reason for visiting Yokohama. Once the private gardens of a millionaire named Tomitaro Hara, Sankei-en Garden dates only from 1906 but is a lovely park with a number of old historical buildings that were brought here from other parts of Japan and reconstructed around streams and ponds. Hara made his fortune exporting silk, and, in addition to his home here, there's a villa built in 1649 by the Tokugawa Shogunate clan, tea arbors, a 500-year-old pagoda, and a farmhouse built in 1650 without the use of nails. There are gently winding pathways through both an inner and outer garden, and no matter what the season the views are always beautiful. The park is divided into an Inner Garden and an Outer Garden.

Admission: ¥300 ($2.75) for the Outer Garden, another ¥300 ($2.75) for the Inner Garden.

Open: Daily 9am–4:30pm (last entry at 4pm). **Bus:** 8 from Yokohama Station, Sakuragicho Station, or the Kencho-mae bus stop in Kannai to the Sankei-en-mae bus stop.

YOKOHAMA BAY BRIDGE, Yokohama Bay. Tel. 506-0500.

From Yamashita Park as you gaze out over the harbor, you can see one of Yokohama's newest sights, the Yokohama Bay Bridge. Designed to ease congestion, it also features a 1,000-foot pedestrian walkway (called the Sky Walk) on the underbelly of the bridge that

---

IMPRESSIONS

Yokohama does not improve on further acquaintance. It has a dead-alive look. It has irregularity without picturesqueness, and the gray sky, gray sea, gray houses, and gray roofs look harmoniously dull.

—ISABELLA BIRD, *UNBEATEN TRACKS IN JAPAN*, 1880

extends to an observation deck, offering a bird's-eye-view of the harbor.

Admission: ¥600 ($5.45) adults, ¥300 ($2.75) children 6 to 11, free for children under 6.

Open: Summer, daily 9am–9pm; winter, daily 10am–6pm. **Bus:** 109 from Sakuragicho Station's Platform 6, getting off at the Daikoku bus stop on the other side of the harbor.

WHERE TO DINE

Occupying a central part of town, ✪ **Chinatown** (Chukagai), Yamashita-cho, Naka-ku, consists of one main street and numerous side streets, with restaurant after restaurant serving Chinese food. Almost every Japanese who visits Yokohama makes a point of eating here—they'll even come from Tokyo for the sole purpose of a Chinese meal. Altogether there are about 100 restaurants and shops selling Chinese foodstuffs and souvenirs here, so your best policy is to walk around and choose a place that suits your fancy. Most of the restaurants have plastic-food displays or pictures of their menus, so ordering is easy. Most dishes are in the ¥800 to ¥3,000 ($7.25 to $27.25) price range, and set lunches are also available. Restaurants that accept credit and charge cards display them on the front door or window. Most Chinatown restaurants are open from 11am to 8:30 or 9pm. Some are closed on Tuesday, others on Wednesday, but there are always restaurants open. For information on Chinatown or Chinese restaurants, call the Chinatown Information Office (tel. 045/662-1252), open Monday through Friday from 9am to 5pm and on Saturday from 1:30 to 5pm. Station: Kannai (then about a 15-minute walk) or Ishikawacho (then a 10-minute walk).

If you'd rather have Japanese or Western food, try one of the restaurants in the Sogo department store:

SOGO DEPARTMENT STORE, 2-18-1 Takashima, 10th floor, Nishi-ku. Tel. 465-2111.

Cuisine: JAPANESE/WESTERN. **Station:** Yokohama Station, across the street from the east exit.

$ Prices: Dishes ¥650–¥1,500 ($5.90–$13.65); set meals ¥1,700–¥7,500 ($15.45–$68.20). Some accept credit cards; those that do display them on the door.

Open: Wed–Mon 10am–10pm.

There are 39 restaurants and coffee shops here in Japan's second-largest department store. The best of these, known as the Gourmet Ten, are on the 10th floor and are branches of many famous restaurants. Included are Tenichi, which serves tempura; the Shisen Chinese restaurant; Chikuyotei, a famous eel restaurant; and Sabatini, an Italian restaurant from Rome with a branch also in Tokyo. Other restaurants serve udon noodles, Kyoto specialties, kaiseki, shabu-shabu, sukiyaki, sushi, and Kobe beef. Since all restaurants have plastic-food display cases outside their doors, ordering is easy.

4. HAKONE

60 miles SW of Tokyo

GETTING THERE Before leaving Tokyo, pick up the "Hakone and Kamakura" leaflet available from the Tourist Information Center.

It lists the schedules for the extensive network of trains, buses, cable cars, and pleasure boats throughout the Hakone area. In fact, Hakone's transportation system is part of what makes a trip here so much fun. Starting out by train from Tokyo, you can switch to a small two-car train that zigzags up the mountain, change to a cable car and then a smaller ropeway, and end your trip with a boat ride across Lake Ashi, stopping off to see major attractions along the way. From Lake Ashi (from either Togendai or Hakone-machi), you can then board a bus bound for Odawara Station (an hour's ride), where you can then take the train back to Tokyo. From Togendai there are also buses that go directly to Shinjuku Station.

The most economical way to see Hakone is to purchase the **Hakone Free Pass,** which despite its name isn't free but does give you a round-trip ticket from Tokyo's Shinjuku Station to Odawara or Hakone Yumoto in Hakone and includes almost all other modes of transportation in Hakone, including the two-car train, cable car and ropeway, boat ride, and buses belonging to the Hakone Tozan bus company. The pass avoids the hassle of having to buy individual tickets and also provides discounts to several of Hakone's attractions, including a ¥100 (90¢) discount to the Hakone Open-Air Museum. Valid for four days, the pass costs ¥6,450 ($58.65) if you take the nonstop Odakyu Romance Car and ¥4,850 ($44.10) if you take the slower, ordinary Odakyu express train. The Romance Car travels from Shinjuku all the way to Hakone Yumoto Station in about 1½ hours; the slower train travels from Shinjuku only to Odawara in the same amount of time.

If you have a Japan Rail Pass, you should take the Shinkansen bullet train from Tokyo Station to Odawara (not all bullet trains stop there, so make sure yours does). From Odawara you can purchase a cheaper Hakone Free Pass for ¥3,500 ($31.20) which doesn't include the round-trip ticket from Tokyo but does include travel within Hakone. In any case, Hakone Free Passes can be purchased at any station of the Odakyu Railway, including Shinjuku Station.

ESSENTIALS As for transportation in Hakone, your sightseeing route should be from Odawara or Yumoto Hakone by two-car train to Gora; by cable car from Gora to Sounzan; by ropeway from Sounzan to Togendai; and by boat from Togendai to Hakone-machi. From Lake Ashi (from either Togendai or Hakone-machi), you can board a bus bound for Odawara Station (an hour's ride), where you can take the train back to Tokyo. Incidentally, the bus from Hakone-machi to Odawara passes through Miyanoshita and Tonosawa, two mountain villages with a number of accommodations.

In the days of the shogun, Hakone was one of several checkpoints on the old Tokaido Highway that linked Edo (present-day Tokyo) with Kyoto. Today it serves as one of the closest and most popular resort areas for residents of the capital city. It receives 17 million visitors a year, including many foreign visitors, who come for the beautiful scenery, hot-spring resorts, mountains, lakes, and diversions in the form of interesting historical sites, natural wonders, and museums. As part of the Fuji-Hakone-Izu National Park, Hakone is also considered one of the best places for breathtaking views of Mt. Fuji. Located about 60 miles southwest of Tokyo, Hakone can be toured in a day if you're pressed for time. However, an overnight stay in the mountains where you can soak in the water of hot springs is much more pleasant. I suggest leaving your luggage in storage at your Tokyo hotel and traveling to Hakone with only a very light overnight bag.

WHAT TO SEE & DO

If you plan on spending only one day in Hakone, you should leave Tokyo very early in the morning. Otherwise, you can arrange your itinerary in a more leisurely fashion. You may wish to travel only as far as your hotel the first day, stopping at sights along the way and in the vicinity. The next day you could continue with the rest of the circuit through Hakone.

THE TRAIN TRIP

If you leave Tokyo via the Shinkansen or the ordinary Odakyu express, you will arrive at Odawara Station, the gateway to Hakone. If you've never seen a Japanese castle, you may wish to visit **Odawara Castle** (tel. 33-1133), located about a five-minute walk south of the train station. Built in 1416, it's the closest castle to Tokyo, but actually only the four-story donjon remains. Inside the donjon are various historical relics associated with the town, and from the top of the keep visitors have a view of the surrounding town. It's open daily from 9am to 4pm, and admission is ¥300 ($2.75).

If you leave Tokyo by Odakyu Romance Car, you'll pass through Odawara before arriving in Hakone at Hakone Yumoto Station (if you wish to see the castle, get off at Odawara).

At any rate, from either Odawara or Hakone Yumoto Station you should transfer to the Hakone Tozan Railway, a two-car train that winds through forests and over streams as it travels upward to Gora, making several switchbacks along the way. The entire trip from Yumoto Station to Gora takes only 45 minutes, but it's a beautiful ride, on a narrow track through the mountains. It makes about a dozen stops before reaching Gora, including Tonosawa and Miyanoshita, two hot-springs resorts with a number of old ryokan and hotels (see "Where to Stay," below). Miyanoshita is also the best place for lunch. **Chokoku-no-Mori** is the most important stop to remember, however, for it's here you'll find Hakone's famous open-air sculpture museum. Here are things to do along the way:

KAPPA TENGOKU (52), **Hakone Yumoto. Tel. 0460/5-6121.**

These are the closest open-air public baths to Tokyo and are located on a hill behind the Hakone Yumoto train station. From the station, take a right and go under the train tracks, and then an immediate right again. Walk uphill and follow the sign (in kanji only) up the steps to what looks like a house. The baths are in the woods behind the house.

Admission: ¥500 ($4.55) adults, ¥200 ($1.80) children 6–11, free for children under 6.

Open: Daily 10am–10pm. **Station:** Hakone Yumoto (then a three-minute walk).

HAKONE OPEN-AIR MUSEUM, Chokoku-no-Mori. Tel. 0460/2-1161.

This is Hakone's most famous museum, containing more than 100 sculptures on landscaped grounds. Using nature itself as a dramatic backdrop, this museum spreads through glens and gardens and over ponds, displaying works by Rodin, Henry Moore,

Imoto Atusushi, and Yodoi Toshio, among others. There's also an excellent exhibit of Picasso's works, including his ceramics, lithographs, and tapestries. The Picasso collection is so extensive that the exhibit changes annually. There's also a picture gallery of 20th-century European and Japanese artists, with works by Renoir, Utrillo, Chagall, Ryuzaburo Umehara, Takashi Hayashi, and others. You'll want to spend at least two hours here.

Admission: ¥1,500 ($13.65) adults, ¥800 ($7.25) children 6 to 11, free for children under 6.

Open: Mar–Oct, daily 8:30am–5pm; Nov–Feb, daily 9am–4pm. **Station:** Chokoku-no-Mori (a few minutes' walk).

BY CABLE CAR

From Gora you travel by cable car, which departs every 15 minutes and arrives 9 minutes later at the end station of Sounzan, located on top of a mountain. The stop to look for on this cable car ride is Koen-Kami:

HAKONE BIJUTSUKAN [Hakone Art Museum], Koen-Kami. Tel. 0460/2-2623.

This museum displays Japanese pottery and ceramics dating from the Jomon Period around 4,000 B.C. to the Edo Period. Included are water jars, terra-cotta taken from burial grounds dating from before the 7th century, Bizen ware from Okayama, and Imari ware of the 17th century. On the museum grounds is a lovely landscape garden of moss and bamboo.

Admission: ¥800 ($7.25) adults, ¥300 ($2.75) children 6–11, free for children under 6.

Open: Fri–Wed 9am–4pm (last entry at 3:30pm). **Station:** Next to Koen-Kami.

BY ROPEWAY

From Sounzan you board a small ropeway for a long haul over a mountain up to Owakudani (the first intermediary station) and then downward to Togendai, which lies beside Lake Ashi (also called Lake Hakone in some brochures). Be sure, however, to get off at Owakudani, because it's the highest point around and offers a great view. If Mt. Fuji is visible, you'll be astounded by its size—it looms up as nothing short of gigantic. The best view is probably from atop the science museum. If you want a snack or drink, on the second floor of the ropeway station is a restaurant with great panoramic views.

The other thing to do here is to hike 30 minutes along a nature path through Owakudani, which means "Great Boiling Valley." Sulfurous steam escapes from fissures in the rock, testimony to the volcanic activity still taking place here. If you're interested in this sort of thing, you'll also want to visit the Natural Science Museum. Note that the cable car stops running at 5 or 5:30pm, depending on the season.

NATURAL SCIENCE MUSEUM, Owakudani. Tel. 0460/4-9149.

Displays of the fauna, flora, geology, and volcanic origins of Hakone are the focus of this museum. Included is a huge model of the Hakone area, as well as a georama complete with sound and lighting effects of a volcanic eruption. Be sure to pick up the English pamphlet.

Admission: ¥400 ($3.65) adults, ¥250 ($2.25) children 6–11, free for children under 6.

Open: Daily 9am–5pm. **Station:** Owakudani.

CROSSING LAKE ASHI

From Togendai you can take a pleasure boat across Lake Ashi (called Ashinoko in Japanese), a crater lake formed by volcanic activity some thousands of years ago and considered one of Hakone's principal attractions. The boat takes about half an hour to cross the lake to **Hakone-Machi** (also called simply Hakone; *machi* means city) and **Moto-Hakone,** two resort towns right next to each other. This end of the lake affords what many consider to be the best view of Fuji, reflected on the waters of the lake, if it's not obscured by clouds.

Before heading back to Odawara by bus from Hakone-Machi or Moto-Hakone, there are a couple of things near these two towns worth visiting. After all, this is the route of the famous **Tokaido Highway,** which connected Edo (present-day Tokyo) and Kyoto. In feudal days, local lords, the daimyo, were required to spend time every other year in Edo, where their families were kept permanently as hostages to ensure their good behavior. A five-minute walk from Hakone-Machi stands the old **Hakone Checkpoint** (Hakone Sekisho), a reconstructed guardhouse originally built in 1618 for the defense of Edo. Its purpose was to strictly control travel and it was one of several points along the highway where travelers were checked. Although it was possible to sneak around it, violators who were caught were promptly executed. The checkpoint is open daily from 8:30am to 5pm (to 4:30pm in winter) and admission is ¥150 ($1.35) for adults and ¥80 (70¢) for children 6 to 11 (free for children under 6).

Not far from the checkpoint is the **Hakone Detached Palace Garden,** which lies on a small promontory on Lake Ashi. Originally part of an imperial villa built in 1887, the garden is open free to the public and offers a fine view of the lake and also displays historical materials relating to the old Tokaido Highway, including weapons, armor, palanquins, and items from life during the Edo Period. For more information on either the checkpoint or the Detached Palace Garden, call the Hakone Town Office (tel. 0460/5-7111).

Between Hakone-Machi and Moto-Hakone is part of the Tokaido Highway itself. Lined with ancient and mighty cedars, the 1¼ miles of the old highway follows the curve of Lake Ashi and makes a pleasant stroll (unfortunately, a modern road has been built right beside it). The cryptomerias were planted back in 1618 to shade travelers in summer and to protect them from snow in winter.

And finally, a 15-minute walk past Moto-Hakone is **Hakone Shrine,** revered by samurai until the Meiji Restoration in 1868. Founded in the 8th century, the present shrine dates from 1667. Especially picturesque is its red torii gate standing in the water, often pictured on brochures of Hakone.

WHERE TO STAY

JAPANESE-STYLE ACCOMMODATIONS

NARAYA, 162 Miyanoshita, Hakone, Ashigarashimo-gun 250-04. Tel. 0460/2-2411. Fax 0460/7-6231. 20 rms (19 with bath). MINIBAR TV TEL **Station:** Miyanoshita, on the Hakone Tozan Railway (then a five-minute walk).

$ **Rates** (including two meals and service charge): ¥30,000–¥40,000 ($272–$363) per person. AE, DC, V.

This elegant ryokan is situated in a 12-acre garden with a main building and eight separate cottages (which accommodate groups of 4 to 20 people). Founded in the 16th century, it was an officially appointed inn for passing daimyo, and after the Meiji Restoration, both the emperor and the empress stayed here. Its present buildings are about a century old, with tile roofs, wooden walls, shoji screens, and hot-springs baths. The tatami rooms have inspiring views of the large landscape garden and mountains beyond, and dinner is an extravaganza. This is a great place to relax and revel in nature's beauty. It's located across the street from the Fujiya Hotel.

ICHINOYU (62), 90 Tonosawa, Hakone, Ashigarashimo-gun 250-03. Tel. 0460/5-5331. Fax 0460/5-5335. 22 rms (12 with bath). A/C MINIBAR TV TEL **Station:** Tonosawa, on the two-car Hakone Tozan Railway (then a six-minute walk).

$ **Rates** (including two meals and service charge): ¥16,000–¥20,000 ($145–$182) per person without bath, ¥18,000–¥22,000 ($164–$200) per person with bath. AE, DC, JCB, MC, V.

Opened more than 350 years ago and now in its 14th generation of owners, Ichinoyu is a delightful, rambling wooden inn on a tree-shaded winding road, beside a roaring river. It claims to be Hakone's oldest ryokan and was once honored by the visit of a shogun. Rebuilt several times, its oldest rooms date from the Meiji Period more than 100 years ago. The two rooms I like best are called Seseragi and Matsu (rooms are usually named rather than numbered in a ryokan). Old-fashioned, they face the river and consist mainly of seasoned and weathered wood. Old artwork, wall hangings, and paintings decorate the ryokan, and some of the rooms have old wooden bathtubs. Both the communal tubs and the tubs in the rooms have hot water supplied from a natural spring.

MOTO-HAKONE GUEST HOUSE, 103 Moto-Hakone, Hakone, Kanagawa 250-05. Tel. 0460/3-7880. Fax 0460/4-6578. 5 rms (none with bath). **Bus:** Hakone Tozan Bus (included in the Hakone Free Pass) from Odawara Station (one hour) to the Ashinoko-en stop; then less than a minute's walk.

$ **Rates:** ¥5,500 ($50) single; ¥11,000 ($100) double; ¥15,000 ($136) triple. AE, MC, V.

Conveniently located in Moto-Hakone less than a 15-minute walk from Lake Ashi, this simple guesthouse offers five Japanese-style tatami rooms, a shared communal bath, and a coin-operated laundry. Western breakfast is available for ¥800 ($7.25) in this cozy inn, which is a member of the Japanese Inn Group.

FUJI-HAKONE GUEST HOUSE, 912 Sengoku, Kanagawa 250-06. Tel. 0460/4-6577. Fax 0460/4-6578. 12 rms (none with bath). **Bus:** Hakone Tozan Bus (included in the Hakone Free Pass) from Togendai (10 minutes) or from Odawara Station (45 minutes), to the Senkyoro-mae bus stop; the stop is announced in English and the guesthouse is then only a minute's walk away.

$ **Rates:** ¥5,000–¥6,000 ($45–$55) single; ¥10,000–¥12,000

($91–$109) twin; ¥14,000–¥16,000 ($127–$145) triple. AE, MC, V.

This is the place to come if you want to experience a Japanese-style inn at affordable prices. A member of the Japanese Inn Group, it offers spotless tatami rooms in a modern house. Although a bit isolated, it's in tranquil surroundings set back from a tree-shaded road and is run by a man who speaks very good English. Some of the rooms face the Hakone mountain range. Facilities include a hot-springs bath, coin-operated washer and dryer, a large lounge area, bilingual TV, and a communal refrigerator. The family running the guesthouse prefers that guests stay at least two nights.

WESTERN-STYLE ACCOMMODATIONS

FUJIYA HOTEL, 359 Miyanoshita, Hakone, Ashigara-shimo-gun 250-04. Tel. 0460/2-2211. Fax 0460/2-2210. 146 rms (all with bath). A/C MINIBAR TV TEL **Station:** Miyanoshita, on the Hakone Tozan Railway (then a five-minute walk).

$ Rates: Single or double, ¥20,000–¥25,000 ($182–$227) Sun–Fri; ¥25,000–¥40,000 ($227–$363) Sat, day before a national hol, and during Golden Week (Apr 28–May 4); ¥30,000–¥45,000 ($272–$409) during New Year's and July–Aug. AE, DC, JCB, MC, V.

The Fujiya was established in 1878 as one of Japan's first Western-style hotels for visiting foreigners. Today it's the grandest and most majestic old hotel in Hakone, a lovely establishment with a Japanese-style roof, lots of windows, turrets, and wooden corridors. In fact, despite the fact that it's a Western-style hotel, its air is distinctly Asian, but from the grand age of yesterday. Famous guests have included Albert Einstein, Douglas Fairbanks and Mary Pickford, Helen Keller, and Charlie Chaplin, and so little has changed here that you half expect to still see these guests any second.

The hotel consists of five separate buildings, each different and added on at various times in its 112-year history. The main building with its front desk dates from 1891, while the most expensive rooms are in the Flower Palace, which was built in 1936 and resembles a Japanese palace. As expected, rooms throughout are old-fashioned with high ceilings and wooden furniture. All said, this is one of my favorite hotels in Japan.

Dining/Entertainment: The Fujiya's main dining hall, dating from 1930, is one of the best places for a meal in Hakone. It offers a variety of Western dishes, from spaghetti and sandwiches for lunch to steaks for dinner.

Services: Free newspaper.

Facilities: Shops, hot-springs baths, outdoor swimming pool, small indoor swimming pool (fed with thermal-spring water), pleasant garden, golf course.

WHERE TO DINE

MAIN DINING ROOM, in the Fujiya Hotel, 359 Miyanoshita. Tel. 2-2211.

Cuisine: WESTERN. **Reservations:** Not required, except during peak season. **Station:** Miyanoshita, on the Hakone Tozan Railway (then a five-minute walk).

$ Prices: Main dishes ¥4,000–¥6,000 ($36.35–$54.55) at lunch

¥4,000–¥15,000 ($36.35–$136.35) at dinner. AE, DC, JCB, MC, V.

Open: Lunch Mon–Fri noon–2pm, Sat–Sun noon–3pm; dinner daily 6–8:30pm.

The Fujiya Hotel, Hakone's grandest hotel, is conveniently located near a stop on the two-car Hakone Tozan Railway. It's the most memorable place for a meal. Its main dining hall, dating from 1930, is very bright and cheerful, with a high ceiling, large windows with Japanese screens, a wooden floor, and an intricately detailed ceiling. The views are nice and the service is attentive. For lunch you can opt for pilaf, sandwiches, spaghetti, chicken, rainbow trout, and hamburger steak. The dinner menu is more extensive and includes steaks, fish, grilled chicken, stews, and more.

5. MT. FUJI

62 miles SW of Tokyo

GETTING THERE **By Bus** Most climbs to the top of Mt. Fuji start at Go-go-me, or the Fifth Stage on either the Kawaguchiko Trail or the Gotemba Trail, though there are others. The Kawaguchiko Trail winds from Kawaguchiko Station to the summit; the Gotemba Trail, from Gotemba Station to Fuji's top. Direct bus service is available to the Fifth Stage from Hammatsucho or Shinjuku in Tokyo. There are some 15 buses a day from mid-July to the end of August, with less frequent service April through mid-July and September through October. The one-way fare from Hamatsucho to Go-go-me (Fifth Stage) is ¥2,340 ($21.25) and it takes about 3 hours. From Shinjuku to the Fifth Stage, the one-way fare is ¥2,160 ($19.65) and the trip takes 2½ hours. Reservations are necessary through a travel agent. If you want to use your Japan Rail Pass, you can take a JR train from Tokyo Station to Gotemba on the JR Tokaido and Gotemba Lines. The train takes 2½ hours. Note, however, that there's only one train a day. From Gotemba Station you can take a bus for ¥950 ($8.65) to the Fifth Stage, but it only runs July through August.

At this writing, the Fuji Subaru Line road between the fourth and fifth stages was closed, as was the Kawaguchiko Trail Fifth Stage, because of construction. So you should definitely check for more information before you set out.

ESSENTIALS Mt. Fuji is part of a larger national park called Fuji-Hakone-Izu National Park. Of the five climbing trails, the most popular ones for Tokyoites are Kawaguchiko Trail for the ascent and Subashiri Trail for the descent. Although each trail is divided into 10 stations, almost all climbers begin and end their climbs from the fifth stage. It takes about 5 hours to reach the summit from the Kawaguchiko Fifth Stage; the descent to the Subashiri New Fifth Stage takes about 2½ hours.

More information regarding train and bus schedules to Mt. Fuji and its surrounding area is available from the Tourist Information Center in two very good leaflets called "Mt. Fuji and Fiji Five Lakes" and "Climbing Mt. Fuji."

Mount Fuji, soaring in perfect symmetry, is Japan's most photographed subject. Japan's tallest peak, it has been revered since ancient times, and throughout the centuries Japanese poets have written about it, painters have painted it, pilgrims have flocked to it, and more than a few people have died on it. The Japanese refer to it affectionately as "Fuji-san." Since *-san* is the form of address also used for people, the implication is that the mountain is a living spirit, dear to the Japanese heart. To see it for the first time is almost a religious experience.

Visible on a clear day from as far as 100 miles away, Mt. Fuji is stunningly impressive. At 12,388 feet, it towers far above everything else around it, a symmetrical cone of almost perfect proportions. It's majestic. It's grand. It's awe-inspiring. Unfortunately, even though Mt. Fuji is something every visitor to Japan should see, few ever do—it is almost always cloaked in clouds. If you do catch a glimpse of this mighty mountain, consider yourself extremely lucky.

On a clear day you can see Mt. Fuji from any tall building in Tokyo, even though the mountain is 62 miles away. The best views are considered to be from Hakone (see above). But the most popular pastime regarding the mountain is to climb it. Some climbers spend the night in a mountain hut; others climb through the night.

Altogether there are five well-marked trails leading to the summit. They are open throughout the year, but because of snow and inclement weather from fall through late spring, the "official" climbing season is from July 1 to August 31, considered the best time to make an ascent. It's also the most crowded time of the year. Ask any Japanese where he would go if he could travel to only one place in his lifetime, and most likely he will answer "Fuji-san." Consider that there are approximately 120 million Japanese, most of whom wouldn't dream of climbing the mountain outside the "official" two months, and you begin to get the picture. More specifically, according to the latest statistics issued by the Japan National Tourist Organization, two million people climb Fuji-san every year during July and August, mostly on weekends.

In other words, unless you climb Mt. Fuji outside the summer months, it will not be a solitary venture, and the experience must be viewed as something you can undertake with a determined group of Japanese climbers who are following in their fathers' footsteps by making pilgrimages to the top. Women, incidentally, weren't allowed to climb Mt. Fuji until 1868. Climbing Mt. Fuji is not technically difficult, but it is extremely strenuous, rather like climbing stairs all day long. You'll be amazed at the number of children and old people doggedly making their way to the top.

But there is a saying in Japan: "Everyone should climb Mt. Fuji once; only a fool would climb it twice."

CLIMBING MT. FUJI

Don't be disappointed when your bus deposits you at Kawaguchiko Fifth Stage, where you'll be bombarded with an overflow of souvenir shops, restaurants, and busloads of tourists. Most of these tourists aren't climbing to the top (evident from the overwhelming number of women in skirts, hose, and high heels), and as soon as you get past them and the blaring loudspeakers you'll find yourself on a steep rocky path surrounded only by scrub brush and hikers on the path below and above you. After a couple of hours you'll probably find yourself above the roily clouds which stretch in all directions. It will be as if you're on an island, barren and rocky, in the middle of an ocean. Like most mountains, Mt. Fuji is more impressive when viewed from afar than when standing on top of it.

You needn't have climbing experience to ascend Mt. Fuji, but you do need stamina. It goes without saying that you also need good walking shoes. It's possible to do it in tennis shoes, but if rocks are wet they can get awfully slippery and dangerous. You're much better off with hiking boots. You should also bring a light plastic raincoat (which you can buy at souvenir shops at the fifth stage), a sun hat, and a sweater for evening. It gets very chilly on Mt. Fuji at night. Even during the day in August temperatures hover around 44°F on the summit. Although there are huts along the way selling food and water, you'd be wise to bring your own water canteen.

The usual procedure for climbing Mt. Fuji is to start out in early afternoon, spend the night near the summit, get up while it's still dark to watch the sunrise, climb the rest of the way to the top, circle the crater at the top, and then make the descent, reaching the Subashiri New Fifth Stage before noon.

In recent years, however, a new trend has started: Climbers arrive at the Fifth Stage late in the evening and then climb through the night to the top with the aid of flashlights. After sunrise they make their descent. That way they don't have to spend the night in one of the huts and they save time.

WHERE TO STAY

As for sleeping, there are about 25 mountain huts along the Kawaguchiko Trail between the fifth and ninth stages. They're very primitive, providing only a futon and toilet facilities. Most are open only in July and August and cost ¥4,000 ($36.35) per person without meals and ¥6,000 ($54.55) with two meals. When I stayed at one of these huts (admittedly only once, a few years ago—I'm no fool), dinner consisted of dried fish, rice, bean-paste soup, and pickled vegetables; breakfast was exactly the same. However, unless you want to pack your own food, it's the only food around. It's best to make a reservation; contact the TIC for information on agencies that handle such arrangements.

APPENDIX

A. JAPANESE VOCABULARY

Needless to say, it takes years to become fluent in the Japanese language, particularly written Japanese with its thousands of *kanji*, or Chinese characters, and its many *hiragana* and *katakana* characters. Knowing just a few words of Japanese, however, is not only useful but will also delight the Japanese you meet during your trip.

In pronouncing the following vocabulary, keep in mind that there's very little stress on individual syllables. Here is an approximation of some of the sounds of Japanese:

a	as in father
e	as in pen
i	as in see
o	as in oh
oo	long *o* as in oooh
u	as in book
g	as in *g*ift at the beginning of words; like *ng* in si*ng* in the middle or at the end of a word

Vowel sounds are always short unless they are double, in which case you hold the vowel a bit longer. Similarly, double consonants are given more emphasis. *Okashi,* for example, means "a sweet," whereas *okashii* means "strange." As you can see, even slight mispronunciation of a word can result in confusion or hilarity. Incidentally, jokes in Japanese are nearly always plays on words.

GENERAL WORDS & PHRASES

Good morning **Ohayo gozaimasu**
Good afternoon **Kon-nichi-wa**
Good evening **Kon-ban-wa**
Good night **Oyasumi-nasai**
Hello **Haro (*or* Kon-nichi-wa)**
Good-bye **Sayonara (*or* bye-bye!)**
Excuse me, I'm sorry **Sumimasen**
Thank you **Domo arigatoo**
You're welcome **Doo-itashi-mashite**
Please (go ahead) **Doozo**
Yes **Hai**
No **I-ie**
Foreigner **Gaijin**
Japanese person **Nihonjin**
Japanese language **Nihongo**
American person **Amerikajin**
English language **Eigo**
Do you understand? **Wakarimasu ka?**
I understand **Wakarimasu**
I don't understand **Wakarimasen**
How much? **Ikura desu ka?**
Where? **Doko desu ka?**
When? **Itsu desu ka?**
Expensive **Takai**
Cheap **Yasui**
I like it **Suki desu (pronounced "ski")**

TRAVELING

Train station **Eki**
Airport **Kuukoo**
Subway **Chika-tetsu**
Bus **Bus-u**

Taxi **Takushi**
Airplane **Hikooki**
Ferry **Ferri**
Train **Densha**
Bullet train **Shinkansen**
Limited express train **Tokkyu**
Ordinary express train **Kyuko**
Local train **Futsu**
Ticket **Kippu**
Exit **Deguchi**
Extrance **Iriguchi**
North **Kita**
South **Minami**
East **Higashi**
West **Nishi**
Left **Hidari**
Right **Migi**
Straight ahead **Massugu (*or* zutto)**
Far **Toi**
Near **Chikai**
Can I walk there? **Aruite ikemasu ka?**
Street **Dori (or michi)**
Tourist Information office **Kanko annaijo**
Map **Chizu**
Post office **Yubin-kyoku**
Stamp **Kitte**
Bank **Ginko**
Hospital **Byooin**
Toilet **Toire, Ben joh, Goh fu joh, O teh ahmai**
Spa **Onsen**
Bath **Ofuro**
Public Bath **Sento**

FOOD & LODGING

Restaurant **Resutoran**
I wish to make a reservation **Yoyaku onegai shimasu**
For one person **Hitori**
For two people **Futari**
Menu **Menyu**
Tea **Ocha**
Coffee **Koohi**
Water **Mizu**
Lunch or daily special **Teishoku**
Delicious **Oishii**
Thank you for the meal **Gochisoo-sama deshita**
Hotel **Hoteru**
Youth hostel **Yusu hosuteru**
Room **Heya**
Does that include meals? **Shokuji wa tsuite imasu ka?**
Key **Kagi**
Balcony **Baranda**

TIME

Now **Ima**
Later **Ato de**
Today **Kyoo**
Tomorrow **Ashita**
Day after tomorrow **Asatte**
Which day? **Nan-nichi desu ka?**
Daytime **Hiruma**
Morning **Asa**
Night **Yoru**
Afternoon **Gogo**
Sunday **Nichiyoobi**
Monday **Getsuyoobi**
Tuesday **Kayoobi**
Wednesday **Suiyoobi**
Thursday **Mokuyoobi**
Friday **Kinyoobi**
Saturday **Doyoobi**
January **Ichi-gatsu**
February **Ni-gatsu**
March **San-gatsu**
April **Shi-gatsu**
May **Go-gatsu**
June **Roku-gatsu**
July **Shichi-gatsu**
August **Hachi-gatsu**
September **Kyuu-gatsu**
October **Juu-gatsu**
November **Juuichi-gatsu**
December **Juuni-gatsu**

NUMBERS

1 **Ichi**
2 **Ni**
3 **San**
4 **Shi**
5 **Go**
6 **Roku**
7 **Shichi (nana)**
8 **Hachi**
9 **Kyuu**
10 **Juu**
11 **Juuichi**
12 **Juuni**
20 **Nijuu**
30 **Sanjuu**

40	**Shijuu (yonjuu)**	60	**Rokujuu**	90	**Kyuuju**
50	**Gojuu**	70	**Nanajuu**	100	**Hyaku**
		80	**Hachijuu**	1,000	**Sen**

B. JAPANESE SYMBOLS

In Japan many hotels, restaurants, and other establishments do not have signs displaying their names in English letters. This section lists the name in Japanese symbols for all such places in this guide.

Each such establishment has a number in an oval following its boldfaced name. For example: **Suehiro** ⑦ means that the restaurant's name is number 7 in the Japanese symbol list that follows.

TOKYO

1. Shimizu Bekkan
しみず別館

2. Tokyo YWCA Sadowara Hostel
東京ＹＷＣＡ砂土原ホステル

3. Kinsen
金扇

4. Sushiko
寿司幸

5. Ohmatsuya
大松屋

6. Shabusen
しゃぶせん

7. Suehiro
スエヒロ

8. Ginza Daimasu
銀座大増

9. Kushi Colza
串コルザ

10. Sushi Sei
寿司清

11. Atariya
当りや

12. Donto
どんと

13. Otako
おた幸

14. Tamura
田村

15. Tentake
天竹

16. Edogin
江戸銀

17. Sushi Dai
寿司大

18. Inakaya
田舎家

19. Zakuro
ざくろ

20. Hayashi
はやし

21. Kushinobo
串の坊

22. Sharaku
写楽

23. Kakiden
柿伝

24. Tsunahachi
つな八

25. Daikokuya
大黒家

26. Irohanihoheto
いろはにほへと

27. Negishi
ねぎし

28. Takamura
篁

29. Fukuzushi
福鮨

30. Gonin Byakusho
五人百姓

31. Hassan
八山

32. Shabu Zen
しゃぶ禅

33. Ganchan
がんちゃん

34. Ichioku
一億

35. O Edo Hana Yatai
お江戸華屋台

36. Torigin
鳥ぎん

37. Kuremutsu
暮六つ

38. Mugitoro
むぎとろ

39. Ichimon
一文

40. Komagata Dojo
駒形どじょう

41. Chinya
ちんや

42. Keyaki
けやき
欅

43. Namiki
並木藪

44. Izu'ei
伊豆栄

45. Genrokusushi
元禄寿司

46. JuJu
寿寿

47. Seiyo Hiroba
せいよう広場

48. Tenmi
天味

49. Kandagawa
神田川

50. Yabu-Soba
やぶそば

51. Tonki
とんき

52. Kappa Tengoku
かっぱ天国

53. Lupin
ルパン

54. Yagura Chaya
櫓茶屋

55. Volga
ボルガ

56. Anyo
あんよ

KAMAKURA

57. Miyokawa
御代川

58. Monzen
門前

59. Kayagi-ya
茅木屋

60. Nakamura-an
なかむら庵

61. Raitei
檑亭

HAKONE

62. Ichinoyu
一の湯

INDEX

Please Send Me the Books Checked Below:

FROMMER'S COMPREHENSIVE GUIDES

(Guides listing facilities from budget to deluxe, with emphasis on the medium-priced)

	Retail Price	Code
☐ Acapulco/Ixtapa/Taxco 1993–94	$15.00	C120
☐ Alaska 1994–95	$17.00	C131
☐ Arizona 1993–94	$18.00	C101
☐ Australia 1992–93	$18.00	C002
☐ Austria 1993–94	$19.00	C119
☐ Bahamas 1994–95	$17.00	C121
☐ Belgium/Holland/Luxembourg 1993–94	$18.00	C106
☐ Bermuda 1994–95	$15.00	C122
☐ Brazil 1993–94	$20.00	C111
☐ California 1994	$15.00	C134
☐ Canada 1994–95 (Avail. 4/94)	$19.00	C145
☐ Caribbean 1994	$18.00	C123
☐ Carolinas/Georgia 1994–95	$17.00	C128
☐ Colorado 1994–95 (Avail. 3/94)	$16.00	C143
☐ Cruises 1993–94	$19.00	C107
☐ Delaware/Maryland 1994–95 (Avail. 1/94)	$15.00	C136
☐ England 1994	$18.00	C129
☐ Florida 1994	$18.00	C124
☐ France 1994–95	$20.00	C132
☐ Germany 1994	$19.00	C125
☐ Italy 1994	$19.00	C130
☐ Jamaica/Barbados 1993–94	$15.00	C105
☐ Japan 1994–95 (Avail. 3/94)	$19.00	C144
☐ Morocco 1992–93	$18.00	C021
☐ Nepal 1994–95	$18.00	C126
☐ New England 1994 (Avail. 1/94)	$16.00	C137
☐ New Mexico 1993–94	$15.00	C117
☐ New York State 1994–95	$19.00	C133
☐ Northwest 1994–95 (Avail. 2/94)	$17.00	C140
☐ Portugal 1994–95 (Avail. 2/94)	$17.00	C141
☐ Puerto Rico 1993–94	$15.00	C103
☐ Puerto Vallarta/Manzanillo/Guadalajara 1994–95 (Avail. 1/94)	$14.00	C028
☐ Scandinavia 1993–94	$19.00	C135
☐ Scotland 1994–95 (Avail. 4/94)	$17.00	C146
☐ South Pacific 1994–95 (Avail. 1/94)	$20.00	C138
☐ Spain 1993–94	$19.00	C115
☐ Switzerland/Liechtenstein 1994–95 (Avail. 1/94)	$19.00	C139
☐ Thailand 1992–93	$20.00	C033
☐ U.S.A. 1993–94	$19.00	C116
☐ Virgin Islands 1994–95	$13.00	C127
☐ Virginia 1994–95 (Avail. 2/94)	$14.00	C142
☐ Yucatán 1993–94	$18.00	C110

FROMMER'S $-A-DAY GUIDES

(Guides to low-cost tourist accommodations and facilities)

	Retail Price	Code
☐ Australia on $45 1993–94	$18.00	D102
☐ Costa Rica/Guatemala/Belize on $35 1993–94	$17.00	D108
☐ Eastern Europe on $30 1993–94	$18.00	D110
☐ England on $60 1994	$18.00	D112
☐ Europe on $50 1994	$19.00	D115
☐ Greece on $45 1993–94	$19.00	D100
☐ Hawaii on $75 1994	$19.00	D113
☐ India on $40 1992–93	$20.00	D010
☐ Ireland on $45 1994–95 (Avail. 1/94)	$17.00	D117
☐ Israel on $45 1993–94	$18.00	D101
☐ Mexico on $45 1994	$19.00	D116
☐ New York on $70 1994–95	$16.00	D120
☐ New Zealand on $45 1993–94	$18.00	D103
☐ Scotland/Wales on $50 1992–93	$18.00	D019
☐ South America on $40 1993–94	$19.00	D109
☐ Turkey on $40 1992–93	$22.00	D023
☐ Washington, D.C. on $40 1994–95 (Avail. 2/94)	$17.00	D119

FROMMER'S CITY $-A-DAY GUIDES

(Pocket-size guides to low-cost tourist accommodations and facilities)

	Retail Price	Code
☐ Berlin on $40 1994–95	$12.00	D111
☐ Copenhagen on $50 1992–93	$12.00	D003
☐ London on $45 1994–95	$12.00	D114
☐ Madrid on $50 1994–95 (Avail. 1/94)	$13.00	D118
☐ Paris on $50 1994–95	$12.00	D117
☐ Stockholm on $50 1992–93	$13.00	D022

FROMMER'S WALKING TOURS

(With routes and detailed maps, these companion guides point out the places and pleasures that make a city unique)

	Retail Price	Code		Retail Price	Code
☐ Berlin	$12.00	W100	☐ Paris	$12.00	W103
☐ London	$12.00	W101	☐ San Francisco	$12.00	W104
☐ New York	$12.00	W102	☐ Washington, D.C.	$12.00	W105

FROMMER'S TOURING GUIDES

(Color-illustrated guides that include walking tours, cultural and historic sights, and practical information)

	Retail Price	Code		Retail Price	Code
☐ Amsterdam	$11.00	T001	☐ New York	$11.00	T008
☐ Barcelona	$14.00	T015	☐ Rome	$11.00	T010
☐ Brazil	$11.00	T003	☐ Scotland	$10.00	T011
☐ Florence	$ 9.00	T005	☐ Sicily	$15.00	T017
☐ Hong Kong/Singapore/ Macau	$11.00	T006	☐ Tokyo	$15.00	T016
☐ Kenya	$14.00	T018	☐ Turkey	$11.00	T013
☐ London	$13.00	T007	☐ Venice	$ 9.00	T014

FROMMER'S FAMILY GUIDES

	Retail Price	Code		Retail Price	Code
☐ California with Kids	$18.00	F100	☐ San Francisco with Kids (Avail. 4/94)	$17.00	F104
☐ Los Angeles with Kids (Avail. 4/94)	$17.00	F103	☐ Washington, D.C. with Kids (Avail. 2/94)	$17.00	F102
☐ New York City with Kids (Avail. 2/94)	$18.00	F101			

FROMMER'S CITY GUIDES

(Pocket-size guides to sightseeing and tourist accommodations and facilities in all price ranges)

	Retail Price	Code		Retail Price	Code
☐ Amsterdam 1993–94	$13.00	S110	☐ Montréal/Québec City 1993–94	$13.00	S125
☐ Athens 1993–94	$13.00	S114	☐ Nashville/Memphis 1994–95 (Avail. 4/94)	$13.00	S141
☐ Atlanta 1993–94	$13.00	S112	☐ New Orleans 1993–94	$13.00	S103
☐ Atlantic City/Cape May 1993–94	$13.00	S130	☐ New York 1994 (Avail. 1/94)	$13.00	S138
☐ Bangkok 1992–93	$13.00	S005	☐ Orlando 1994	$13.00	S135
☐ Barcelona/Majorca/ Minorca/Ibiza 1993–94	$13.00	S115	☐ Paris 1993–94	$13.00	S109
☐ Berlin 1993–94	$13.00	S116	☐ Philadelphia 1993–94	$13.00	S113
☐ Boston 1993–94	$13.00	S117	☐ San Diego 1993–94	$13.00	S107
☐ Budapest 1994–95 (Avail. 2/94)	$13.00	S139	☐ San Francisco 1994	$13.00	S133
☐ Chicago 1993–94	$13.00	S122	☐ Santa Fe/Taos/ Albuquerque 1993–94	$13.00	S108
☐ Denver/Boulder/ Colorado Springs 1993–94	$13.00	S131	☐ Seattle/Portland 1994–95	$13.00	S137
☐ Dublin 1993–94	$13.00	S128	☐ St. Louis/Kansas City 1993–94	$13.00	S127
☐ Hong Kong 1994–95 (Avail. 4/94)	$13.00	S140	☐ Sydney 1993–94	$13.00	S129
☐ Honolulu/Oahu 1994	$13.00	S134	☐ Tampa/St. Petersburg 1993–94	$13.00	S105
☐ Las Vegas 1993–94	$13.00	S121	☐ Tokyo 1992–93	$13.00	S039
☐ London 1994	$13.00	S132	☐ Toronto 1993–94	$13.00	S126
☐ Los Angeles 1993–94	$13.00	S123	☐ Vancouver/Victoria 1994–95 (Avail. 1/94)	$13.00	S142
☐ Madrid/Costa del Sol 1993–94	$13.00	S124	☐ Washington, D.C. 1994 (Avail. 1/94)	$13.00	S136
☐ Miami 1993–94	$13.00	S118			
☐ Minneapolis/St. Paul 1993–94	$13.00	S119			

SPECIAL EDITIONS

	Retail Price	Code
☐ Bed & Breakfast Southwest	$16.00	P100
☐ Bed & Breakfast Great American Cities (Avail. 1/94	$16.00	P104
☐ Caribbean Hideaways	$16.00	P103
☐ National Park Guide 1994 (Avail. 3/94)	$16.00	P105
☐ Where to Stay U.S.A.	$15.00	P102

Please note: if the availability of a book is several months away, we may have back issues of guides to that particular destination. Call customer service at (815) 734-1104.